New Perspectives on

CREATING WEB PAGES WITH HTML

3rd Edition

Introductory

PATRICK CAREY
Carey Associates, Inc.

MARY KEMPER
Contributing Author

THOMSON
COURSE TECHNOLOGY

Australia • Canada • Mexico • Singapore • Spain • United Kingdom • United States

New Perspectives on Creating Web Pages with HTML, 3rd Edition Introductory
is published by Course Technology.

Managing Editor:
Rachel Crapser

Technology Product Manager:
Amanda Young

Production Editor:
Danielle Power

Senior Editor:
Donna Gridley

Associate Product Manager:
Brianna Germain

Composition:
GEX Publishing Services

Senior Product Manager:
Kathy Finnegan

Marketing Manager:
Sean Teare

Text Designer:
Meral Dabcovich

Product Manager:
Melissa Hathaway

Developmental Editor:
Paul Griffin

Cover Designer:
Efrat Reis

New Perspectives

Preface

Course Technology is the world leader in information technology education. The New Perspectives Series is an integral part of Course Technology's success. Visit our Web site to see a whole new perspective on teaching and learning solutions.

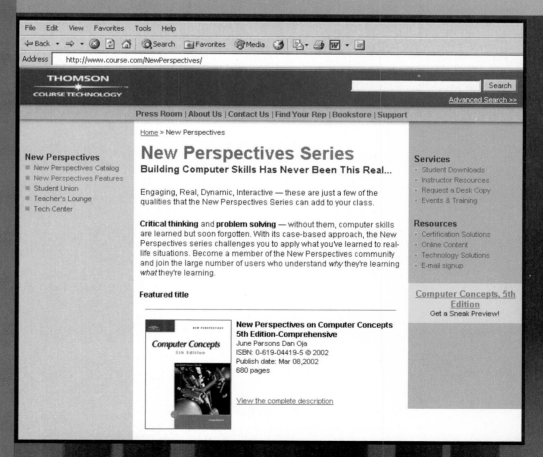

New Perspectives—Building Computer Skills Has Never Been This Real

Why New Perspectives will work for you.

Critical thinking and **problem solving**—without them, computer skills are learned but soon forgotten. With its **case-based** approach, the New Perspectives Series challenges students to apply what they've learned to real-life situations. Become a member of the New Perspectives community and watch your students not only **master** computer skills, but also **retain** and carry this **knowledge** into the world.

New Perspectives catalog

Our online catalog is never out of date! Go to the Catalog link on our Web site to check out our available titles, request a desk copy, download a book preview, or locate online files.

Complete system of offerings

Whether you're looking for a Brief book, an Advanced book, or something in between, we've got you covered. Go to the Catalog link on our Web site to find the level of coverage that's right for you.

Instructor materials

We have all the tools you need—data files, solution files, figure files, a sample syllabus, and ExamView, our powerful testing software package.

How well do your students know Microsoft Office?

Experience the power, ease, and flexibility of SAM XP and TOM. These innovative software tools provide the first truly integrated technology-based training and assessment solution for your applications course. Click the Tech Center link to learn more.

Get certified

If you want to get certified, we have the titles for you. Find out more by clicking the Teacher's Lounge link.

Interested in online learning?

Enhance your course with rich online content for use through MyCourse 2.0, WebCT, and Blackboard. Go to the Teacher's Lounge to find the platform that's right for you.

Your link to the future is at
www.course.com/NewPerspectives

What you need to know about this book.

- Student Online Companion takes students to the Web for additional work where they will be able to access a clip art gallery, sound and video library, and a wide selection of Web page authoring software.

- ExamView testing software gives you the option of generating a printed test, LAN-based test, or test over the Internet.

- New tutorial cases and case problems have been added for this edition!

- Students will enjoy learning how to work with colors and graphics, and create tables in their Web pages.

- Our coverage of code has been updated to reflect HTML 4.01 standards, and be compatible with Internet Explorer 6.0 and Netscape Navigator 6.0.

- Students will appreciate the new coverage of XHTML in the tutorials, and also in the appendix on XHTML.

CASE	TROUBLE?	SESSION 1.1	QUICK CHECK	RW
Tutorial Case Each tutorial begins with a problem presented in a case that is meaningful to students. The case sets the scene to help students understand what they will do in the tutorial.	**TROUBLE? Paragraphs** These paragraphs anticipate the mistakes or problems that students may have and help them continue with the tutorial.	**Sessions** Each tutorial is divided into sessions designed to be completed in about 45 minutes each. Students should take as much time as they need and take a break between sessions.	**Quick Check Questions** Each session concludes with conceptual Quick Check questions that test students' understanding of what they learned in the session.	**Reference Windows** Reference Windows are succinct summaries of the most important tasks covered in a tutorial. They preview actions students will perform in the steps to follow.

Creating Web Pages with HTML—Level I Tutorials   HTML 1.01

Tutorial 1 *Developing a Basic Web Page*   HTML 1.03
Create a Web Page for Stephen Dubé's Chemistry Classes

Tutorial 2 *Adding Hypertext Links to a Web Page*   HTML 2.01
Developing a Chemistry Web Site with Hypertext Links

Creating Web Pages with HTML—Level II Tutorials   HTML 3.01

Tutorial 3 *Designing a Web Page*   HTML 3.03
Working with Fonts, Colors, and Graphics

Tutorial 4 *Designing a Web Page with Tables*   HTML 4.01
Creating a News Page

Tutorial 5 *Using Frames in a Web Site*   HTML 5.01
Using Frames to Display Multiple Web Pages

Appendix A *HTML Color Names*   HTML A.01

Appendix B *HTML Character Entities*   HTML B.01

Appendix C *Putting a Document on the World Wide Web*   HTML C.01

Appendix D *HTML Tags and Attributes*   HTML D.01

Appendix E *Working with XHTML*   HTML E.01

Index   1

File Finder   12

TABLE OF CONTENTS

Preface **v**

Creating Web Pages with HTML

Level I Tutorials | **HTML 1.01**

Read This Before You Begin | **HTML 1.02**

Tutorial 1   HTML 1.03

Developing a Basic Web Page

Create a Web Page for Stephen Dubé's Chemistry Classes

SESSION 1.1 | **HTML 1.04**

Introducing the World Wide Web | HTML 1.04

    The Development of the World Wide Web | HTML 1.05

    Web Servers and Web Browsers | HTML 1.06

HTML: The Language of the Web | HTML 1.07

    Versions of HTML | HTML 1.08

    Extensions, XML, and the Future | HTML 1.08

    Tools for Creating HTML Documents | HTML 1.09

Quick Check | HTML 1.09

SESSION 1.2 | **HTML 1.10**

Creating an HTML Document | HTML 1.10

    HTML Syntax | HTML 1.11

    Creating Basic Tags | HTML 1.12

    Displaying Your HTML Files | HTML 1.13

Creating Headings, Paragraphs, and Lists | HTML 1.14

    Creating Heading Tags | HTML 1.15

    Entering Paragraph Text | HTML 1.17

    Creating Lists | HTML 1.22

Creating Character Tags | HTML 1.26

Quick Check | HTML 1.29

SESSION 1.3 | **HTML 1.29**

Inserting a Graphic | HTML 1.29

Adding Special Characters | HTML 1.31

Inserting Horizontal Lines | HTML 1.32

Quick Check | HTML 1.36

Review Assignments | HTML 1.36

Case Problems | HTML 1.39

Quick Check Answers | HTML 1.45

Tutorial 2   HTML 2.01

Adding Hypertext Links to a Web Page

Developing a Chemistry Web Site with Hypertext Links

SESSION 2.1 | **HTML 2.02**

Creating a Hypertext Document | HTML 2.02

Creating Anchors | HTML 2.04

Creating Links | HTML 2.07

Quick Check | HTML 2.10

SESSION 2.2 | **HTML 2.10**

Web Page Structures | HTML 2.11

    Linear Structures | HTML 2.12

    Hierarchical Structures | HTML 2.12

    Mixed Structures | HTML 2.14

Creating Links Among Documents | HTML 2.15

    Linking to a Document | HTML 2.15

    Linking to a Section of a Document | HTML 2.20

Quick Check | HTML 2.22

SESSION 2.3 | **HTML 2.22**

Linking to Documents in Other Folders | HTML 2.22

    Absolute Pathnames | HTML 2.23

    Relative Pathnames | HTML 2.24

Linking to Documents on the Internet | HTML 2.24

Displaying Linked Documents in a New Window | HTML 2.25

Linking to Other Internet Objects | HTML 2.27

    Linking to FTP Servers | HTML 2.28

    Linking to Usenet News | HTML 2.28

    Linking to E-mail | HTML 2.29

    Adding an E-mail Link to Stephen's Chemistry Page | HTML 2.30

Quick Check | HTML 2.32

Review Assignments | HTML 2.32

Case Problems | HTML 2.34

Quick Check Answers | HTML 2.41

Creating Web Pages with HTML

Level II Tutorials	**HTML 3.01**
Read This Before You Begin	**HTML 3.02**

Tutorial 3   HTML 3.03

Designing a Web Page

Working with Fonts, Colors, and Graphics

SESSION 3.1	**HTML 3.04**
Working with Color in HTML	HTML 3.04
Using Color Names	HTML 3.05
Using Color Values	HTML 3.06
Specifying a Color Scheme for Your Page	HTML 3.08
Modifying Text with the <font> Tag	HTML 3.10
Changing the Font Size	HTML 3.11
Changing the Font Color	HTML 3.12
Changing the Font Face	HTML 3.12
Using the <font> Tag to Specify Color	HTML 3.14
Inserting a Background Image	HTML 3.15
Extensions to the <font> and <body> Tags	HTML 3.19
Deprecated Tags	HTML 3.19
Quick Check	HTML 3.20
SESSION 3.2	**HTML 3.20**
Working with GIF Files	HTML 3.20
Interlaced and Noninterlaced GIFs	HTML 3.20
Transparent GIFs	HTML 3.22
Animated GIFs	HTML 3.23
The GIF Controversy	HTML 3.24
Working with JPEG Files	HTML 3.25
Controlling Image Placement and Size	HTML 3.27
Controlling Image Alignment	HTML 3.28
Controlling Vertical and Horizontal Space	HTML 3.29
Controlling Image Size	HTML 3.31
Using the alt Attribute	HTML 3.32
General Tips for Working with Color and Images	HTML 3.33
Reduce the Size of Your Pages	HTML 3.33
Manage Your Colors	HTML 3.34
Quick Check	HTML 3.35
SESSION 3.3	**HTML 3.35**
Understanding Image Maps	HTML 3.35
Server-Side Image Maps	HTML 3.36
Client-Side Image Maps	HTML 3.37
Defining Image Map Hotspots	HTML 3.39
Creating a Rectangular Hotspot	HTML 3.41
Creating a Circular Hotspot	HTML 3.41
Creating a Polygonal Hotspot	HTML 3.42
Using an Image Map	HTML 3.43
Using the border Attribute	HTML 3.45
Quick Check	HTML 3.47
Review Assignments	HTML 3.47
Case Problems	HTML 3.48
Quick Check Answers	HTML 3.55

Tutorial 4   HTML 4.01

Designing a Web Page with Tables

Creating a News Page

SESSION 4.1	**HTML 4.02**
Tables on the World Wide Web	HTML 4.02
Creating a Text Table	HTML 4.03
Using Fixed-Width Fonts	HTML 4.04
Using the <pre> Tag	HTML 4.05
Defining a Table Structure	HTML 4.07
Using the <table>, <tr>, and <td> Tags	HTML 4.07
Creating Headings with the <th> Tag	HTML 4.10
Identifying the Table Heading, Body, and Footer	HTML 4.11
Creating a Table Caption	HTML 4.12
Quick Check	HTML 4.13

SESSION 4.2   **HTML 4.14**

Modifying the Appearance of a Table   HTML 4.14

Adding a Table Border   HTML 4.14

Controlling Cell Spacing   HTML 4.16

Defining Cell Padding   HTML 4.17

Creating Frames and Rules   HTML 4.18

Working with Table and Cell Size   HTML 4.20

Defining the Table Size   HTML 4.20

Defining Cell and Column Sizes   HTML 4.22

Aligning a Table and Its Contents   HTML 4.22

Aligning a Table on the Web Page   HTML 4.23

Aligning the Contents of a Table   HTML 4.24

Spanning Rows and Columns   HTML 4.26

Applying a Color Scheme to a Table   HTML 4.29

Applying a Background Color   HTML 4.29

Applying a Table Background   HTML 4.32

Working with Column Groups   HTML 4.33

Quick Check   HTML 4.35

SESSION 4.3   **HTML 4.35**

Designing a Page Layout with Tables   HTML 4.35

Creating the Outer Table   HTML 4.37

Creating the Nested Table   HTML 4.43

Combining the Outer and Inner Tables   HTML 4.51

Quick Check   HTML 4.54

Review Assignments   HTML 4.54

Case Problems   HTML 4.57

Quick Check Answers   HTML 4.63

Tutorial 5   **HTML 5.01**

Using Frames in a Web Site

Using Frames to Display Multiple Web Pages

SESSION 5.1   **HTML 5.02**

Introducing Frames   HTML 5.02

Planning Your Frames   HTML 5.05

Creating a Frame Layout   HTML 5.06

Specifying Frame Size and Orientation   HTML 5.07

Specifying a Frame Source   HTML 5.09

Nesting <frameset> Tags   HTML 5.11

Controlling the Appearance of Your Frames   HTML 5.13

Controlling the Appearance of Scroll Bars   HTML 5.14

Controlling Frame Margins   HTML 5.15

Controlling Frame Resizing   HTML 5.17

Quick Check   HTML 5.17

SESSION 5.2   **HTML 5.18**

Working with Frames and Hypertext Links   HTML 5.18

Assigning a Name to a Frame   HTML 5.19

Specifying a Link Target   HTML 5.20

Using the <base> Tag   HTML 5.21

Using Reserved Target Names   HTML 5.22

Using the <noframes> Tag   HTML 5.28

Working with Frame Borders   HTML 5.31

Setting the Border Color   HTML 5.32

Setting the Border Width   HTML 5.33

Creating Floating Frames   HTML 5.34

Quick Check   HTML 5.37

Review Assignments   HTML 5.37

Case Problems   HTML 5.39

Quick Check Answers   HTML 5.46

Appendix A   **HTML A.01**

HTML Color Names

Appendix B   **HTML B.01**

HTML Character Entities

Appendix C   **HTML C.01**

Putting a Document on the World Wide Web

Appendix D   HTML D.01

HTML Tags and Attributes

Appendix E   HTML E.01

Working with XHTML

Introducing XHTML	HTML E.01
SGML	HTML E.01
HTML	HTML E.01
XML	HTML E.02
XHTML	HTML E.03

Working with the Syntax of XHTML	HTML E.03
XHTML Syntax	HTML E.03
Using the Name and ID Attributes	HTML E.05
Working with Embedded Style Sheets and Scripts	HTML E.05
The Structure of an XHTML Document	HTML E.06
Converting From HTML To XHTML	HTML E.08

Index   1

File Finder   12

Acknowledgments

I would like to thank the people who worked so hard to make this book possible. Special thanks to Mary Kemper for her work in revising Tutorials 1 and 2; Anne Nelson for her work in updating Appendix D; Paul Griffin, our Developmental Editor, for his excellent ideas and suggestions that improved the manuscript; and to Amanda Young, our Technology Product Manager, who kept the book on task and on target. Other people at Course Technology who deserve credit are Rachel Crapser, Managing Editor; Donna Gridley, Senior Editor; Brianna Germain, Associate Product Manager; Danielle Power, Production Editor; John Bosco, Quality Assurance Project Leader; and John Freitas, Jeff Schwartz, and Vitaly Davidovich, Quality Assurance Testers.

Feedback is an important part of writing any book, and thanks go to the following reviewers for their ideas and comments: Robert Cormia of Foothill College, Candace Garrods of Red Rocks Community College, Anne Nelson of High Point University, WJ Patterson of Sullivan University, and John Whitney of Fox Valley Technical College.

I want to thank my wife Joan for her love and encouragement, and my six children: John Paul, Thomas, Peter, Michael, Stephen, and Catherine, to whom this book is dedicated.

New Perspectives on

CREATING WEB PAGES
WITH HTML

3rd Edition

TUTORIAL 1   HTML 1.03

Developing a Basic Web Page
Create a Web Page for Stephen Dubé's Chemistry Classes

TUTORIAL 2   HTML 2.01

Adding Hypertext Links to a Web Page
Developing a Chemistry Web Site with Hypertext Links

Read This Before You Begin

To the Student

Data Disks

To complete the Level I tutorials, Review Assignments, and Case Problems, you need one Data Disk. Your instructor will either provide you with this Data Disk or ask you to make your own.

If you are making your own Data Disk, you will need **one** blank, formatted high-density disk. You will need to copy a set of files and/or folders from a file server, standalone computer, or the Web onto your disk. Your instructor will tell you which computer, drive letter, and folders contain the files you need. You could also download the files by going to **www.course.com** and following the instructions on the screen.

The information below shows you the Data Disk you need so that you will have enough disk space to complete all the tutorials, Review Assignments, and Case Problems:

Data Disk 1

Write this on the disk label:
Data Disk 1: HTML Tutorials 1 and 2

When you begin each tutorial, Review Assignment, or Case Problem, be sure you are using the correct Data Disk. Refer to the "File Finder" chart at the back of this text for more detailed information on which files are used in which tutorials.

See the inside front cover of this book for more information on Data Disk files, or ask your instructor or technical support person for assistance.

Using Your Own Computer

If you are going to work through this book using your own computer, you need:

- **Computer System** A text editor and a Web browser (preferably Netscape Navigator or Internet Explorer, versions 4.0 or higher) must be installed on your computer. If you are using a non-standard browser, it must support frames and HTML 4.0 or higher.

- **Data Disk** You will not be able to complete the tutorials or exercises in this book using your own computer until you have your Data Disk.

Visit Our World Wide Web Site

Additional materials designed especially for you are available on the World Wide Web. Go to http://www.course.com/NewPerspectives.

To the Instructor

The Data Disk Files are available on the Instructor's Resource Kit for this title. Follow the instructions in the Help file on the CD-ROM to install the programs to your network or standalone computer. For information on creating Data Disks, see the "To the Student" section above.

You are granted a license to copy the Data Files to any computer or computer network used by students who have purchased this book.

OBJECTIVES

In this tutorial you will:

- Explore the structure of the World Wide Web

- Learn the basic principles of Web documents

- Create an HTML document

- View an HTML file using a Web browser

- Use HTML tags for text, headings, paragraphs, and lists

- Insert character tags into an HTML document

- Insert an inline graphic image into an HTML document

- Add special characters to an HTML document

- Insert horizontal lines into an HTML document

DEVELOPING A BASIC WEB PAGE

Create a Web Page for Stephen Dubé's Chemistry Classes

CASE

Stephen Dubé's Chemistry Classes

Stephen Dubé teaches chemistry at Robert Service High School in Edmonton, Alberta (Canada). In previous years, he has provided course information to students and parents with handouts. This year, he wants to put that information on the World Wide Web, where it will be easily accessible by everyone. Eventually, he hopes to post homework assignments, practice tests, and even grades on the Web site. Stephen is new to this technology and has never created a Web page. He has asked you to create a Web page for his class.

In this session you will learn the basics of how the World Wide Web is structured and how it operates. You will then begin to explore the HTML language that is used to create Web sites.

Introducing the World Wide Web

Before you start creating a Web page for Stephen, it's a good idea to first look at how and why the World Wide Web was developed in the first place.

In order for computers to share resources efficiently, they can be linked together in a structure called a **network**. If the computers are close together, as they would be in the computer lab at Mr. Dubé's school, the network is called a **local area network** or **LAN**. A network that covers a wider area, perhaps several buildings or cities, is called a **wide area network** or **WAN**. Because networks are so useful, it is not surprising that their use led to a "network of networks" called the **Internet**.

The Internet consists of millions of interconnected computers that enable users to communicate and share information. The physical structure of the Internet uses fiber-optic cables, satellites, phone lines, and other telecommunications media to send data back and forth (see Figure 1-1).

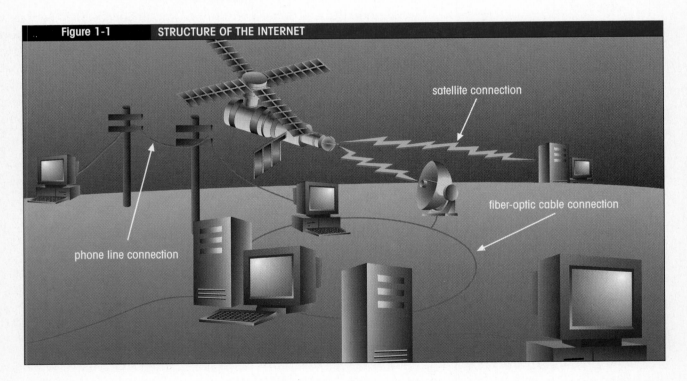

Figure 1-1   STRUCTURE OF THE INTERNET

satellite connection

fiber-optic cable connection

phone line connection

Before 1989, using the Internet was not without its problems and challenges. Many Internet tools required users to master a bewildering array of terms, acronyms, and commands before they could navigate the Internet. What users needed was a tool that would be easy to use and would allow quick access to any resource on the Internet, regardless of its location. This tool would prove to be the World Wide Web.

The Development of the World Wide Web

In 1989, Timothy Berners-Lee and other researchers at the CERN nuclear research facility near Geneva, Switzerland, laid the foundation of the World Wide Web, or the Web. They wanted to create an information system that made it easy for researchers to locate and share data and that required minimal training and support. They developed a system of **hypertext documents**, electronic files that contain elements that you can select, usually by clicking a mouse, to open other documents, and so on.

Hypertext offered a better way of locating information. When you read a book, you follow a linear progression, reading one page after another. With hypertext, you progress through pages in whatever way is best suited to you and your objectives. Hypertext lets you skip from one topic to another, following a path of information that interests you. Figure 1-2 shows how topics can be related in a hypertext fashion, as opposed to a linear fashion.

Figure 1-2	LINEAR VERSUS HYPERTEXT DOCUMENTS

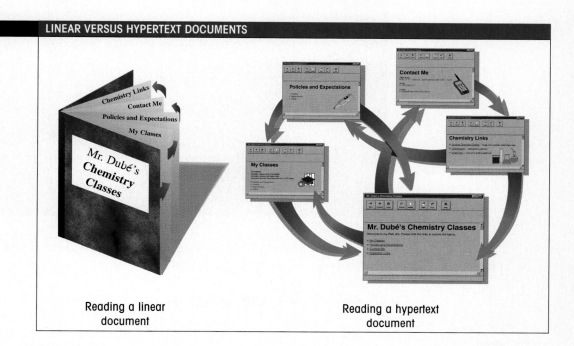

Reading a linear
document

Reading a hypertext
document

The key to hypertext is the use of **links**, which you activate (usually with a mouse click) to move from one topic to another. Activating a link takes you to another section of the document, or it might take you to another document entirely. A link can open a document on your computer or a document on a computer anywhere in the world.

The hypertext approach proved to be so useful that within a few years it became the dominant method of sharing and retrieving information on the Internet, becoming known as the **World Wide Web**, or more simply the **Web**.

Documents on the Web are known as **Web pages**, but they're not limited to text. Web pages can contain images, video and sound clips, and even programs that run directly from a Web page. The Web designer has a great deal of control over the format of the page. As Figure 1-3 shows, a Web page is not only a source of information, it can also be a work of art.

Figure 1-3	WEB PAGE WITH INTERESTING FONTS, GRAPHICS, AND LAYOUT

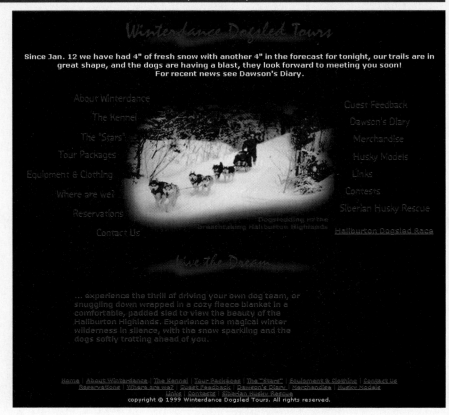

As you will see in this book, another feature that continues to contribute to the Web's popularity is the ease with which Web pages can be created.

Web Servers and Web Browsers

A Web page is stored on a **Web server**, which makes the page available to users of the Web. To view the page, the user runs a **Web browser**, a software program that retrieves the page and displays it (see Figure 1-4).

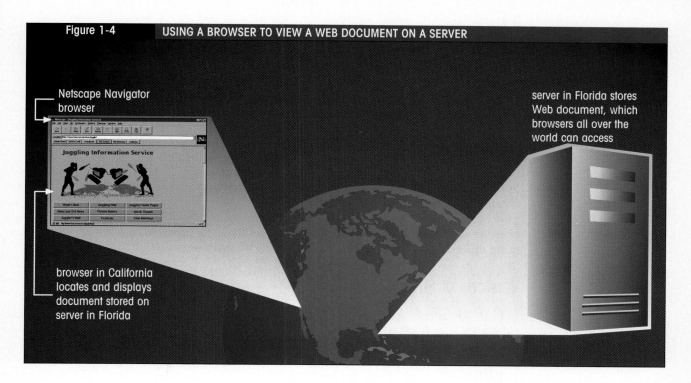

Figure 1-4   USING A BROWSER TO VIEW A WEB DOCUMENT ON A SERVER

Netscape Navigator
browser

server in Florida stores
Web document, which
browsers all over the
world can access

browser in California
locates and displays
document stored on
server in Florida

Browsers can either be text-based, like the Lynx browser found on UNIX machines, or graphical, like the popular Internet Explorer and Netscape browsers. With a **text-based browser**, you navigate the Web by typing commands; with a **graphical browser**, you use the mouse to move from page to page. Browsers are typically installed on personal computers, but increasingly, devices such as cell phones and PDAs (personal data assistants) are providing Web capability.

HTML: The Language of the Web

Web pages are text files, written in a language called **Hypertext Markup Language** or **HTML**. A **markup language** is a language used to describe the content and format of documents. HTML was developed from the **Standard Generalized Markup Language (SGML)**, a language used for large-scale documents. SGML proved to be too cumbersome and difficult for use on the Internet, and thus HTML was created based on the principles of SGML.

The success of the World Wide Web is due in no small part to HTML. HTML allows Web authors to create documents that can be displayed across different operating systems, and the HTML code is easy enough to use that even nonprogrammers can learn to use it. Millions of Web sites are based on HTML, and there is every indication that HTML will continue to be the dominant language of the Web for a long time to come.

HTML describes the format of Web pages through the use of **tags**. Text appearing in the document's heading is marked with a heading tag. Text appearing in a bulleted list is marked with a list tag, and so on. It's the job of the Web browser to interpret these tags and render the text accordingly.

There are a few good reasons to put the formatting in the control of the Web browser rather than the Web server. Web pages must be able to work well with a wide variety of operating systems and browsers. Because different operating systems and browsers differ in how they display information, it would be a daunting task to create a page for all users. Portability frees Web page authors from this concern.

For the most part, Web designers don't have to worry about what devices users are using to display a Web page because HTML works with everything from clunky teletypes to highly sophisticated PDAs. HTML is also supported by nonvisual media such as speech recognition software. Web pages can even be rendered in Braille.

Of course, portability does limit a Web designer's ability to precisely define the appearance of a Web page. For this reason, HTML uses **style sheets**, with which a Web designer can explicitly define the fonts and formatting the Web browser applies to the document. The use of style sheets is an advanced topic that should be mastered only after becoming familiar with basic HTML.

Another reason to put the formatting choices in the browser's control is speed. Specifying the exact appearance of a page can dramatically increase both the size of the document file and the time required to retrieve it. It is more efficient to allow the Web browser to do the work. The disadvantage of this approach is that you cannot be sure how each browser will display your document. For this reason, it's a good idea to view your Web page using different browsers, and if possible, different operating systems.

Versions of HTML

HTML has a set of rules, called **syntax**, that specify how document code is written. These rules appear as a set of **standards** or **specifications** developed by a consortium of Web developers, programmers, and authors called the **World Wide Web Consortium**, more commonly known as the **W3C**. Figure 1-5 presents a history of the various versions of HTML that have been released by the W3C. For more information on the W3C, see their Web site at **http://www.w3c.org**.

Figure 1-5	VERSIONS OF HTML	
VERSION	**DATE**	**DESCRIPTION**
HTML 1.0	1989–1994	The first public version of HTML which included browser support for inline images and text controls.
HTML 2.0	1995	The first version supported by all graphical browsers. It introduced interactive form elements such as option buttons and text boxes. A document written to HTML 2.0 should be compatible with all browsers on the World Wide Web.
HTML 3.0	1997	This version included additional support for creating and formatting tables and expanded the options for interactive form elements.
HTML 4.01	1999	This version added support for style sheets to give Web designers greater control over page layout. It added new features to tables and forms and provided support for international features. This version also expanded HTML's scripting capability and added increased support for multimedia elements.
XHTML 1.0	2001	This version is a reformulation of HTML 4.01 in XML and combines the strength of HTML 4.0 with the power of XML. XHTML brings the rigor of XML to Web pages and provides standards for more robust Web content on a wide range of browser platforms.

Extensions, XML, and the Future

The world of Web browsers is a competitive one, and over the years each browser has added **extensions** to HTML that support new features. Netscape and Internet Explorer have added the most extensions to HTML, and often these extensions have been adopted in subsequent sets of standards released by the W3C. These extensions have provided Web page authors with more options, but at the expense of fragmenting Web page development and decreasing compatibility across browsers.

Before using an extension, the Web designer needs to determine which browsers and browser versions support it and, if necessary, create a workaround for browsers that do not support the extension. All of this extra work complicates Web page development and betrays the simplicity of HTML that made it so integral to the success of the Web in the first place.

Primarily for this reason, future Web development is focusing more on XML and XHTML. **XML (Extensible Markup Language)** is used for developing document content. With XML, Web designers can create their own tags and attributes for their documents. XML combined with style sheets provides the same functionality as HTML, but with greater flexibility. **XHTML (Extensible HyperText Markup Language)** is a stricter version of HTML, designed to overcome some of the problems that competing HTML standards have introduced, and to better integrate HTML with XML.

Don't worry about HTML becoming obsolete anytime soon. There is a significant amount of overlap between HTML and XML coding. HTML is an excellent stepping stone to the various languages of the future.

Tools for Creating HTML Documents

Because HTML documents are text files, the only software you need to create them is a basic text editor such as Windows Notepad. If you want a software program to do some of the work of creating an HTML document, you can use an HTML converter or an HTML editor.

An **HTML converter** takes text in one format and converts it to HTML code. For example, you can create the source document with a word processor such as Microsoft Word, and then have the converter save the document as an HTML file. Converters have several advantages. They free you from the laborious task of typing HTML code, and, because the conversion is automated, you do not have to worry about typographical errors in your code.

Converters have the disadvantage of creating HTML code that may be longer and more complicated than it needs to be, resulting in larger-than-necessary files. Also, if you need to edit the HTML code directly, it is more difficult to do so with a file created by a converter.

An **HTML editor** helps you create an HTML file by inserting HTML codes for you as you work. HTML editors can save you a lot of time and help you work more efficiently. They have many of the same advantages and limitations as converters. They do let you set up your Web page quickly, but to create the finished document, you often still have to work directly with the HTML code.

Session 1.1 QUICK CHECK

1. What is hypertext?

2. What is a Web server? A Web browser? Describe how they work together.

3. What is HTML?

4. How do HTML documents differ from documents created with a word processor such as Word or WordPerfect?

5. What are the advantages of letting Web browsers determine the appearance of Web pages?

6. What are HTML extensions? What are some advantages and disadvantages of using extensions?

7. What software program do you need to create an HTML document?

In the next session, you'll begin writing your first HTML document, using a text editor.

SESSION 1.2

In this session you begin entering the HTML code for Stephen's Web page. You'll learn how to create and apply HTML tags to format page headings, paragraphs, lists, and individual characters.

Creating an HTML Document

It's always a good idea to plan the appearance of your Web page before you start writing code. Each semester, Stephen distributes a handout listing his classes and describing his class policies. He thinks this handout is a good place to start for his Web site (see Figure 1-6).

| Figure 1-6 | STEPHEN'S PAPER HANDOUT |

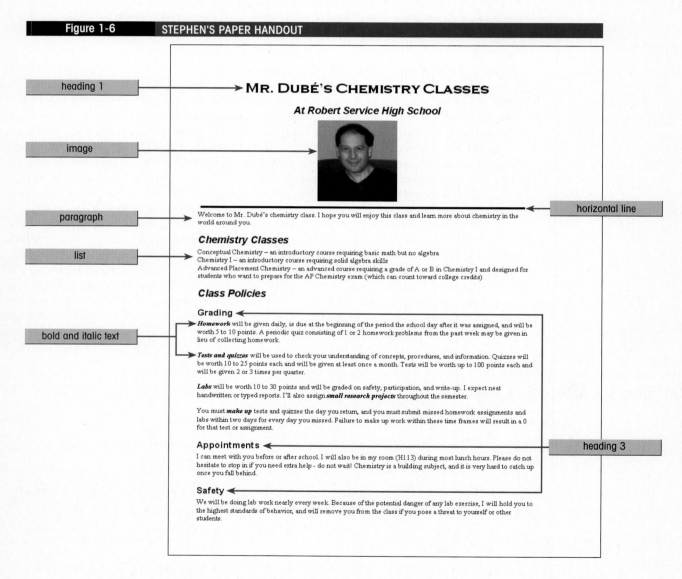

Stephen's handout includes several features that he would like to include on his Web page. A heading prominently displays his name, and beneath the heading is his photo and a horizontal line. The handout has a brief introductory paragraph and is divided into two sections: Chemistry Classes and Class Policies. In the Chemistry Classes section there is a list of the three classes he teaches. In the Class Policies section, three smaller headings list and describe his policies on Grading, Appointments, and Safety.

As you can see, Stephen's handout has three heading levels, a list, formatted characters such as bold and italic text, a horizontal line, and an image. When he creates the Web page with HTML, he wants to include these features. As you help Stephen create this document for the Web, you should periodically refer to Figure 1-6.

HTML Syntax

An HTML file contains both formatting tags and content. **Document content** is what the users see on the page, such as headings and images. **Tags** are the HTML codes that control the appearance of the document content.

The HTML syntax for creating the features that Stephen wants in his page follows a very basic structure. HTML tags are applied to document content using the following syntax:

```
<tag attributes>document content</tag>
```

where *tag* is the name of the HTML tag, *attributes* are properties of the tag, and *document content* is the actual content that appears in the Web page. This type of tag is known as a **two-sided tag** because it contains an **opening tag** that tells the browser to turn on a feature and apply it to the content that follows, and a **closing tag** that turns off the feature. Note that closing tags are identified by the slash (/) that precedes the tag name.

Not every tag is two-sided. Some tags are **one-sided tags** or **empty tags**, because they require only a single tag without content. The syntax for a one-sided tag is simply:

```
<tag attributes>
```

A one-sided tag is used to insert noncharacter data into the Web page, such as a graphic image or a video clip. You'll see examples of one-sided tags later in the tutorial.

Let's look at the first line of the course handout, "Mr. Dubé's Chemistry Classes," from Figure 1-6. You can format this line with the HTML tag as follows:

```
<h1 align="center">Mr. Dube's Chemistry Classes</h1>
```

Here the <h1 align="center"> opening tag instructs the browser to display the text that follows the tag in an h1 (heading level 1) format. ("h1" stands for Heading 1; you'll learn what this means later.) The HTML code also includes the **align attribute**, which instructs the browser how to align the text (in this case, centered). Following the opening tag is the content: "Mr. Dubé's Chemistry Classes". Finally, the </h1> tag signals the browser to turn off the h1 format.

Remember that each browser determines the exact effect of the h1 tag. One browser might apply a 14-point Times Roman bold font to Heading 1 text, whereas another browser might use 18-point italic Arial. In each case, the font is appropriately larger than the lower-level headings such as h2, h3, etc. Figure 1-7 shows how three different browsers might interpret this line of HTML code.

Figure 1-7	INTERPRETATION OF THE <H1> TAG BY DIFFERENT BROWSERS
BROWSER INTERPRETING THE <H1> TAG	**APPEARANCE OF THE DOCUMENT CONTENT**
Browser A	Mr. Dubé's Chemistry Classes
Browser B	**Mr. Dubé's Chemistry Classes**
Browser C	*Mr. Dubé's Chemistry Classes*

Tags are not case sensitive. Both the Internet Explorer and Netscape browser will treat the <h1> tag as they do the <H1> tag. However, in the interest of consistency, the current standard is to display all tags in lowercase letters. We'll follow this lowercase convention throughout this book.

Creating Basic Tags

When you create a Web page, the first step is to identify the markup language being used, identify the document's key sections, and assign a title to the page.

In the steps that follow, type the text exactly as it is displayed. To create an HTML file, you need a text editor such as Notepad or WordPad.

To create an HTML file:

1. Place your Data Disk in drive A.

TROUBLE? If you don't have a Data Disk, you need to get one. Your instructor will either give you one or ask you to make your own. See the Read This Before You Begin page at the beginning of the tutorials for instructions.

2. Create a new document with a text editor.

TROUBLE? If you don't know how to locate, start, or use the text editor on your system, ask your instructor or technical support person for help.

3. Type the following lines of code into your document. Press the **Enter** key after each line. Press the **Enter** key twice for a blank line between lines of code.

```
<html>
<head>
<title>Mr. Dube's Chemistry Classes</title>
</head>

<body>
</body>

</html>
```

Note that the name Dube should contain an accent mark over the "e". You'll learn how to add special characters such as accent marks later in the tutorial.

4. Using your text editor, save the file as **chem.htm** in the tutorial folder of the tutorial.01 folder on your Data Disk, but do not close your text editor. The text you typed should look similar to the text displayed in Figure 1-8.

Figure 1-8	INITIAL HTML TAGS IN NOTEPAD

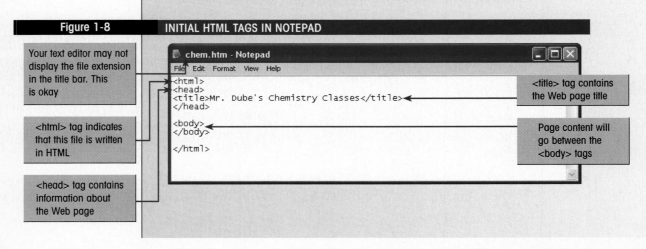

Your text editor may not display the file extension in the title bar. This is okay

<html> tag indicates that this file is written in HTML

<head> tag contains information about the Web page

<title> tag contains the Web page title

Page content will go between the <body> tags

```
chem.htm - Notepad
File  Edit  Format  View  Help
<html>
<head>
<title>Mr. Dube's Chemistry Classes</title>
</head>

<body>
</body>

</html>
```

TROUBLE? If you don't know how to save a file on your Data Disk, ask your instructor or technical support person for assistance.

TROUBLE? Don't worry if your screen doesn't look exactly like Figure 1-8. The text editor shown in the figures is the Windows Notepad editor. Your text may look different. Take the time to ensure that you entered the text correctly.

TROUBLE? If you are using the Windows Notepad text editor to create your HTML file, make sure you don't save the file with the extension .txt, which is the default for Notepad. Using an invalid file extension renders the file unreadable to Web browsers, which require .htm or .html as file extensions. So make sure you save the file with an .htm or .html file extension.

TROUBLE? If you are using Microsoft Word for your text editor, be sure to save your files as Web page files and not as Word documents.

The opening and closing <html> tags bracket the remaining code you'll enter in the document. This indicates to a browser that the page is written in the HTML language. While you don't have to include this tag, it is necessary if the file is to be read by another SGML application. Moreover, it is considered good form to include it.

The <head> tag identifies the area where you enter information about the Web page itself. One such piece of information is the title of the page, which is displayed in the title bar of the Web browser. This information is entered using the <title> tag. The title in this example is "Mr. Dube's Chemistry Classes".

Finally, the portion of the document that Web users will see is contained between the <body> tags. At this point, the page is blank, with no text or graphics. You'll add those later. The <head> and <body> tags are not strictly required, but you should include them to better organize your document and make the code more readable to others. The extra space before and after the <body> tags is also not required, but it makes your code easier to understand, especially as you add more code and it becomes more complex.

Displaying Your HTML Files

As you continue adding to Stephen's HTML file, you should occasionally view the formatted page with your Web browser to verify that there are no syntax errors or other problems. You may even want to view the results using different browsers to check for compatibility. In the steps and figures that follow, the Internet Explorer browser is used to display Stephen's page as it is developed. If you are using a different browser, ask your instructor how to view local files (those stored on your own computer rather than on the Web).

To view Stephen's Web page:

1. Start your browser. You do not need to be connected to the Internet to view local files stored on your computer.

TROUBLE? If you try to start your browser and are not connected to the Internet, you might get a warning message. Netscape Navigator, for example, gives a warning message telling you that it was unable to create a network socket connection. Click OK to ignore the message and continue.

2. After your browser loads its home page open the **chem.htm** file that you saved in the tutorial folder of the tutorial.01 folder on your Data Disk.

Your browser displays Stephen's file, as shown in Figure 1-9. Note that the page title, which you typed earlier between the <title> tags, appears in the browser's title bar.

TROUBLE? To open a file in most browsers, click File on the menu bar, click Open, and click the Browse button to locate the file.

TROUBLE? Depending on the browser you're using, you may have to use a different command to open the file from your Data Disk. Talk to your instructor or technical support person to find out how to open the file.

Figure 1-9	THE INITIAL HTML FILE IN INTERNET EXPLORER

the title you entered between the <title> tags

address box indicates the name and location of the HTML file

page content will appear here

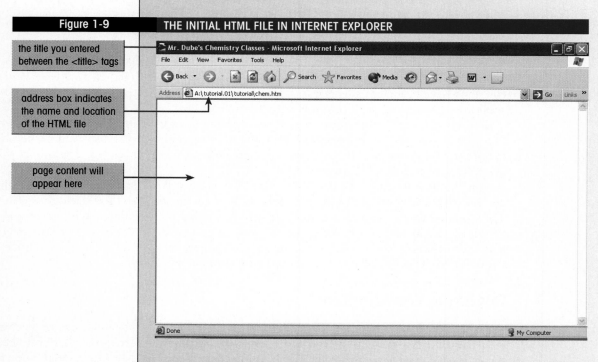

TROUBLE? If your browser displays something different, compare the code in your file to the code shown in Figure 1-8, and correct any errors. So far you have only entered a title for the Web page, which is why the main content area of the Web page is blank.

Creating Headings, Paragraphs, and Lists

Now that the basic structure of Stephen's page is set, you can start filling in the page content. A good place to start is with the headings for the various sections of the document. You need a heading for the entire page and headings for each of two sections: Chemistry Classes and Class Policies. The Class Policies section has three additional headings for Grading, Appointments, and Safety. You can create all these headings using HTML heading tags.

Creating Heading Tags

HTML supports six levels of headings, numbered <h1> through <h6>, with <h1> being the largest and most prominent. Headings are always displayed in a bold font. The syntax for a heading tag is:

```
<hy>heading text</hy>
```

where *y* is a heading numbered 1 through 6 and *heading text* is the text that is displayed in the heading.

Figure 1-10 illustrates the general appearance of the six heading styles. Your browser might use slightly different fonts and sizes.

Figure 1-10	SIX HEADING LEVELS

This is an h1 heading

This is an h2 heading

This is an h3 heading

This is an h4 heading

This is an h5 heading

This is an h6 heading

REFERENCE WINDOW   **RW**

Creating a Heading Tag
- Open the HTML file with your text editor.
- Type <h*y*> where *y* is the heading number you want to use.
- If you want to use a special alignment, specify the alignment attribute setting after *y* and before the closing symbol, >.
- Type the text that you want to appear in the heading.
- Type </h*y*> to turn off the heading tag.

As of HTML 3.2, the heading tag can contain additional attributes, one of which is the alignment attribute. Stephen wants some headings to be centered, so you'll be using align attribute tags as shown in the code that follows.

To add headings to the chemistry file:

1. Using your text editor, open **chem.htm** if it is not currently open.

2. Place the insertion point after the <body> tag, press the **Enter** key to move to the next line, and then type the following code. Be sure to press the **Enter** key at the end of each line of code.

```
<h1 align="center">Mr. Dube's Chemistry Classes</h1>
<h2 align="center">at Robert Service High School</h2>
<h2>Chemistry Classes</h2>
<h2>Class Policies</h2>
<h3>Grading</h3>
<h3>Appointments</h3>
<h3>Safety</h3>
```

The revised code is displayed in Figure 1-11. To make it easier for you to follow the changes to the HTML file, new and modified text in the figures is highlighted in red. This will not be the case in your own text files.

| Figure 1-11 | ENTERING HEADING TAGS AND TEXT |

```
<html>
<head>
<title>Mr. Dube's Chemistry Classes</title>
</head>

<body>
<h1 align="center">Mr. Dube's Chemistry Classes</h1>
<h2 align="center">at Robert Service High School</h2>
<h2>Chemistry Classes</h2>
<h2>Class Policies</h2>
<h3>Grading</h3>
<h3>Appointments</h3>
<h3>Safety</h3>
</body>

</html>
```

3. Save chem.htm in the Tutorial folder of the Tutorial.01 folder on your Data Disk. You can leave your text editor open.

The first two headings use the align="center" attribute to center the text on the page. The two <h2> headings Chemistry Classes and Class Policies and the three <h3> headings in the Policies section, however, are aligned left, which is the default setting.

To display the revised version of the chemistry page:

1. Return to your Web browser. Note that the previous version of chem.htm probably appears in the browser window.

2. To view the revised file, click **View** on the menu bar, and then click **Refresh**. If you are using Netscape, you will need to click **View** and then click **Reload**.

TROUBLE? If you closed the browser or the file in the last set of steps, reopen your browser and the chem.htm file.

The updated file looks like Figure 1-12.

Figure 1-12	HEADINGS AS THEY APPEAR IN THE BROWSER

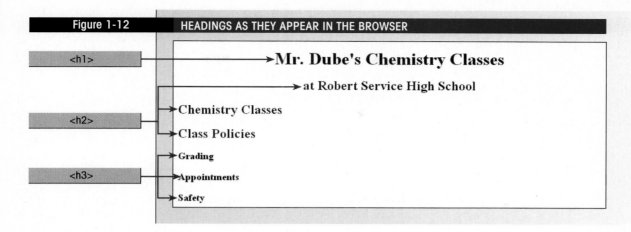

Entering Paragraph Text

The next step is to enter text information for each section. If your paragraph does not require any formatting, you can enter the text without tags.

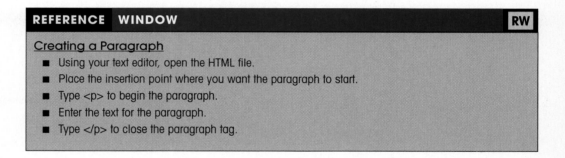

REFERENCE WINDOW   **RW**

<u>Creating a Paragraph</u>
- Using your text editor, open the HTML file.
- Place the insertion point where you want the paragraph to start.
- Type <p> to begin the paragraph.
- Enter the text for the paragraph.
- Type </p> to close the paragraph tag.

Stephen's introductory paragraph, which appears just below the horizontal line in his handout, does not require formatting, so you can enter the text without any HTML formatting tags. He would like to revise the paragraph that appears in Figure 1-6 slightly so that it applies to his Web page.

To enter paragraph text:

1. Using your text editor, open **chem.htm** if it is not currently open.

2. Place the insertion point at the end of the line that specifies the <h2> heading "at Robert Service High School", and press the **Enter** key to create a blank line.

3. Type the following text. As you type, let the text wrap to the next line; don't press Enter.

   ```
   Welcome to Mr. Dube's Web site. I hope you will use
   this site to learn more about your class, my
   expectations, and chemistry in the world around you.
   ```

   Your text should be placed after the first <h2> head and before the <h2> Chemistry Classes head, as shown in Figure 1-13. Check your work for mistakes, and edit your file if necessary.

Figure 1-13   ENTERING PARAGRAPH TEXT

```
<html>
<head>
<title>Mr. Dube's Chemistry Classes</title>
</head>

<body>
<h1 align="center">Mr. Dube's Chemistry Classes</h1>
<h2 align="center">at Robert Service High School</h2>
Welcome to Mr. Dube's Web site. I hope you will use this site to learn more about your class, my
expectations, and chemistry in the world around you.
<h2>Chemistry Classes</h2>
<h2>Class Policies</h2>
<h3>Grading</h3>
<h3>Appointments</h3>
<h3>Safety</h3>
</body>

</html>
```

TROUBLE? If you are using a text editor like Notepad, the text might not wrap to the next line automatically. Do not press the Enter key. Instead, you might need to select the Word Wrap command from the Format menu, or a similar command, so you can see all the text on your screen.

3. Save your changes to chem.htm.

4. Using your Web browser, refresh or reload chem.htm to view the text you've added. See Figure 1-14.

Figure 1-14   PARAGRAPH TEXT IN THE BROWSER

Mr. Dube's Chemistry Classes

at Robert Service High School

Welcome to Mr. Dube's Web site. I hope you will use this site to learn more about your class, my expectations, and chemistry in the world around you.

Chemistry Classes

Class Policies

Grading

Appointments

Safety

Now you need to add the four paragraphs under the Grading heading and a single paragraph under both Appointments and Safety. Be sure to press the Enter key only where indicated. It is important to allow your text editor to wrap the text to the next line.

To enter remaining paragraphs:

1. Using your text editor, open **chem.htm** if it is not currently open.

2. Place the insertion point at the end of the <h3> Grading heading and then press the **Enter** key to create a blank line.

3. Type the following text:

```
Homework will be given daily, is due at the beginning
of the period the school day after it was assigned, and
will be worth 5 to 10 points. A periodic quiz
consisting of 1 or 2 homework problems from the past
week may be given in lieu of collecting homework.
```

4. Press the **Enter** key two times and then type:

```
Tests and quizzes will be used to check your
understanding of concepts, procedures, and information.
Quizzes will be worth 10 to 25 points and will be
given at least once a month. Tests will be worth up to
100 points and will be given 2 or 3 times a quarter.
```

5. Press the **Enter** key two times and then type:

```
Labs will be worth 10 to 30 points and will be graded
on safety, participation, and write-up. I expect neat
handwritten or typed reports. I'll also assign small
research projects throughout the semester.
```

6. Press the **Enter** key two times and then type:

```
You must make up missed tests and quizzes the day you
return, and you must submit missed homework assignments
and labs within two days for every one day you missed.
Failure to make up work within these time frames will
result in a 0 for that test or assignment.
```

TROUBLE? Note that in Stephen's handout, a keyword or phrase is bold in each paragraph. You'll learn how to format text, such as bold, later in the tutorial.

7. Move to the end of the <h3> Appointments heading, press the **Enter** key once, and then type:

```
I can meet with you before or after school. I will also
be in my room (H113) during most lunch hours. Please do
not hesitate to stop in if you need extra help -- do not
wait! Chemistry is a building subject, and it is very
hard to catch up once you fall behind.
```

8. Move to the end of the <h3> Safety heading, press the **Enter** key once, and then type:

```
We will be doing lab work nearly every week. Because of
the potential danger of any lab exercise, I will hold
you to the highest standards of behavior, and will
remove you from the class if you pose a threat to
yourself or other students.
```

Figure 1-15 shows the new code in Stephen's file.

| Figure 1-15 | ADDING THE SIX REMAINING PARAGRAPHS |

```
<body>
<h1 align="center">Mr. Dube's Chemistry Classes</h1>
<h2 align="center">at Robert Service High School</h2>
Welcome to Mr. Dube's Web site. I hope you will use this site to learn more about your class,
my expectations, and chemistry in the world around you.
<h2>Chemistry Classes</h2>
<h2>Class Policies</h2>
<h3>Grading</h3>
Homework will be given daily, is due at the beginning of the period the school day after it was
assigned, and will be worth 5 to 10 points. A periodic quiz consisting of 1 or 2 homework
problems from the past week may be given in lieu of collecting homework.

Tests and quizzes will be used to check your understanding of concepts, procedures, and
information. Quizzes will be worth 10 to 25 points and will be given at least once a month.
Tests will be worth up to 100 points and will be given 2 or 3 times a quarter.

Labs will be worth 10 to 30 points and will be graded on safety, participation, and write-up. I
expect neat handwritten or typed reports. I'll also assign small research projects throughout
the semester.

You must make up missed tests and quizzes the day you return, and you must submit missed
homework assignments and labs within two days for every one day you missed. Failure to make up
work within these time frames will result in a 0 for that test or assignment.
<h3>Appointments</h3>
I can meet with you before or after school. I will also be in my room (H113) during most lunch
hours. Please do not hesitate to stop in if you need extra help -- do not wait! Chemistry is a
building subject, and it is very hard to catch up once you fall behind.
<h3>Safety</h3>
We will be doing lab work nearly every week. Because of the potential danger of any lab
exercise, I will hold you to the highest standards of behavior, and will remove you from the
class if you pose a threat to yourself or other students.
</body>
```

9. Save your changes to chem.htm.

10. Using your Web browser, refresh or reload chem.htm and view the changes. Figure 1-16 displays the revised version.

| Figure 1-16 | THE PARAGRAPHS DISPLAYED BY THE BROWSER |

Mr. Dube's Chemistry Classes

at Robert Service High School

Welcome to Mr. Dube's Web site. I hope you will use this site to learn more about your class, my expectations, and chemistry in the world around you.

Chemistry Classes

Class Policies

Grading

four grading paragraphs are not separated →

Homework will be given daily, is due at the beginning of the period the school day after it was assigned, and will be worth 5 to 10 points. A periodic quiz consisting of 1 or 2 homework problems from the past week may be given in lieu of collecting homework. Tests and quizzes will be used to check your understanding of concepts, procedures, and information. Quizzes will be worth 10 to 25 points and will be given at least once a month. Tests will be worth up to 100 points and will be given 2 or 3 times a quarter. Labs will be worth 10 to 30 points and will be graded on safety, participation, and write-up. I expect neat handwritten or typed reports. I'll also assign small research projects throughout the semester. You must make up missed tests and quizzes the day you return, and you must submit missed homework assignments and labs within two days for every one day you missed. Failure to make up work within these time frames will result in a 0 for that test or assignment.

As you can see from Figure 1-16, the text you typed into chem.htm looks nothing like what is displayed in the browser. Instead of being separated by blank lines, the four Grading paragraphs are running together. What went wrong?

Remember that HTML formats text only through the use of tags and ignores such things as extra blank spaces, blank lines, or tabs. To demonstrate this, study the following three examples of code that look different:

```
<h1>To be or not to be. That is the question.</h1>
<h1>To be or not to be.    That is the question.</h1>
<h1>To be or not to be.
              That is the question.</h1>
```

Though the spacing in these three examples is different, the three examples would look identical in a browser.

At first glance, the Grading section did not appear to need any formatting other than bolding some words. However, we now know that each new paragraph needs to be set off by a blank line. To add this space between paragraphs, you use the **paragraph tag, <p>**, which adds a blank paragraph (the extra line you need) to separate a block of text from text that precedes it.

To add paragraph tags for blank lines:

1. Using your text editor, open **chem.htm**.

2. Modify the Grading text, bracketing each paragraph between a **<p>** and **</p>** tags, so that the text reads as follows:

```
<p> Homework will be given daily, is due at the
beginning of the period the school day after it was
assigned, and will be worth 5 to 10 points. A periodic
quiz consisting of 1 or 2 homework problems from the
past week may be given in lieu of collecting
homework.</p>
<p>Tests and quizzes will be used to check your
understanding of concepts, procedures, and information.
Quizzes will be worth 10 to 25 points and will be
given at least once a month. Tests will be worth up to
100 pointsand will be given 2 or 3 times a quarter.</p>
<p> Labs will be worth 10 to 30 points and will be
graded on safety, participation, and write-up. I expect
neat handwritten or typed reports. I'll also assign
small research projects throughout the semester.</p>
<p>You must make up missed tests and quizzes the day
you return, and you must submit missed homework
assignments and labs within two days for every one
day you missed. Failure to make up work within these
time frames will result in a 0 for that test or
assignment.</p>
```

TROUBLE? If adding the new tags results in awkward word wrapping, adjust the formatting as necessary to keep your file clear and easy to read.

3. Save your changes to chem.htm.

4. Using your Web browser, refresh or reload chem.htm. The text in the Grading section is now properly separated into distinct paragraphs, as shown in Figure 1-17.

Figure 1-17   **THE GRADING TEXT SEPARATED INTO PARAGRAPHS**

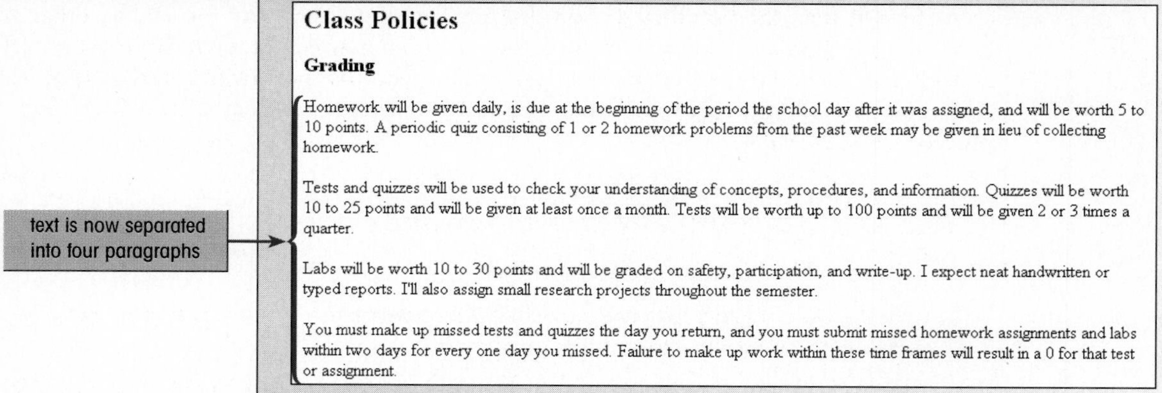

Class Policies

Grading

Homework will be given daily, is due at the beginning of the period the school day after it was assigned, and will be worth 5 to 10 points. A periodic quiz consisting of 1 or 2 homework problems from the past week may be given in lieu of collecting homework.

Tests and quizzes will be used to check your understanding of concepts, procedures, and information. Quizzes will be worth 10 to 25 points and will be given at least once a month. Tests will be worth up to 100 points and will be given 2 or 3 times a quarter.

Labs will be worth 10 to 30 points and will be graded on safety, participation, and write-up. I expect neat handwritten or typed reports. I'll also assign small research projects throughout the semester.

You must make up missed tests and quizzes the day you return, and you must submit missed homework assignments and labs within two days for every one day you missed. Failure to make up work within these time frames will result in a 0 for that test or assignment.

text is now separated into four paragraphs

If you begin to explore the HTML code for pages that you encounter on the Web, you may notice that the <p> tag is sometimes used in varying ways. This is because in early versions of HTML, <p> was a one-sided tag. However, both the latest HTML specifications and XHTML require a two-sided tag, so you should follow that convention in your documents.

Creating Lists

You still need to enter the list describing Stephen's three chemistry courses. HTML supports three kinds of lists: ordered, unordered, and definition.

An **ordered list** is used to display information in a numeric order. The syntax for creating an ordered list is:

```
<ol type="option">
    <li>Item1
    <li>Item2
    ...
</ol>
```

where *option* specifies the type of character to number the list and *Item1*, *Item2*, etc, are items in the list. The type attribute must have one of the following values: "1", "a", "A", "i", or "I".

■ A value of "1" displays a list with numbers.

■ The values "a" and "A" create a list with either lowercase or uppercase letters.

■ The values "i" and "I" create a list with Roman numerals.

If you omit the type attribute, browsers assume that you want to create an ordered list using numbers.

For example, Stephen might want to list the three classes from the least difficult to the most difficult. To do so, the following code can be used to list the courses from easiest to hardest in an ordered list:

```
<ol type="1">
    <li>Conceptual Chemistry
    <li>Chemistry
    <li>Advanced Placement Chemistry
</ol>
```

and the browser displays the text as:

1. Conceptual Chemistry

2. Chemistry

3. Advanced Placement Chemistry

If you change the value of the type attribute to "a", the browser displays the text as:

a. Conceptual Chemistry

b. Chemistry

c. Advanced Placement Chemistry

If you remove an item from the list, HTML updates the numbers to accurately reflect the new order.

You can also create an **unordered list**, in which list items are not listed in a particular order. The syntax for an unordered list is:

```
<ul type="option">
      <li>Item1
      <li>Item2
      ...
</ul>
```

where the type attribute can have one of the following values: "disc", "circle", or "square". A value of "disc" inserts a bullet before each list item, "circle" instructs the browser to use an open circle, and "square" creates a filled-in square.

If Stephen wanted to display his classes without regard to their importance, you could create the following unordered list:

```
<ul type="circle">
      <li>Conceptual Chemistry
      <li>Chemistry
      <li>Advanced Placement Chemistry
</ul>
```

and the browser would display the list as:

° Conceptual Chemistry
° Chemistry
° Advanced Placement Chemistry

Ordered and unordered lists can also be nested inside one another. For example, to create the following list of numbered and bulleted items:

1. Homework

- Given daily
- Worth 5 to 10 points

2. Quizzes

- Given at least once a month
- Worth 10 to 25 points

you would use the following HTML tags:

```
<ol>
     <li>Homework
          <ul type="disc">
               <li>Given daily
               <li>Worth 5 to 10 points
          </ul>
     <li>Quizzes
          <ul type="disc">
               <li>Given at least once a month
               <li>Worth 10 to 25 points
          </ul>
</ol>
```

A third list type you can create with HTML is a definition list. A **definition list** is a list of terms, each followed by a definition line that is typically indented slightly to the right. The syntax for creating a definition list is:

```
<dl>
     <dt>term1 <dd>definition1
     <dt>term2 <dd>definition2
...
</dl>
```

where *term1*, *term2*, etc. are the terms in the list, and *definition1*, *definition2*, etc. are the term definitions.

If Stephen wanted to create a list of his classes and briefly describe each one, he could use a definition list. To create a definition list for his classes, you would enter the following code:

```
<dl>
<dt>Conceptual Chemistry<dd>An introductory course
requiring basic mathematics but no algebra
<dt>Chemistry I<dd>An introductory course requiring solid
algebra skills
<dt>Advanced Placement Chemistry<dd>An advanced course for
students who passed Chemistry I with an A or B and who want
to prepare for the AP Chemistry exam (which can count toward
college credits)
</dl>
```

A Web browser displays this code as:

Conceptual Chemistry

   An introductory course requiring basic mathematics but no algebra

Chemistry I

   An introductory course requiring solid algebra skills

Advanced Placement Chemistry

   An advanced course for students who passed Chemistry I with an A or B and who want to prepare for the AP Chemistry exam (which can count toward college credits)

REFERENCE WINDOW   **RW**

Creating Lists

- Using your text editor, open the HTML file.
- Place the insertion point in the document where you want the list to appear.
- Type <ol> to start an ordered list, <ul> to start an unordered list, or <dl> to start a definition list.
- For each item in an ordered or unordered list, type <li> followed by the text for the list item. For each item in a definition list, type <dt> before the term and <dd> before the definition. Note that both <li> and <dt> are one-sided tags, so there is no closing tag.
- To turn off the list, type </ol> for an ordered list, </ul> for an unordered list, and </dl> for a definition list.

In his handout (Figure 1-6), you notice that Stephen's classes are not displayed in a bulleted or numbered list. You decide that the list will look fine as an unordered list, using the default bullet.

To add an unordered list to the chemistry file:

1. Using your text editor, open **chem.htm** if it is not currently open.

2. Place the insertion point at the end of the line specifying the "Chemistry Classes" heading and press the **Enter** key to create a blank line.

3. Type the following code:

```
<ul>
<li>Conceptual Chemistry: An introductory course
requiring basic math but no algebra
<li>Chemistry I: An introductory course requiring solid
algebra skills
<li>Advanced Placement Chemistry: An advanced course
requiring a grade of A or B in Chemistry I and designed
for students who want to prepare for the AP Chemistry
exam (which can count toward college credits)
</ul>
```

The new lines in the file should look like Figure 1-18.

| Figure 1-18 | ENTERING AN UNORDERED LIST |

```
<html>
<head>
<title>Mr. Dube's Chemistry Classes</title>
</head>

<body>
<h1 align="center">Mr. Dube's Chemistry Classes</h1>
<h2 align="center">at Robert Service High School</h2>
Welcome to Mr. Dube's Web site. I hope you will use this site to learn more about your class,
my expectations, and chemistry in the world around you.
<h2>Chemistry Classes</h2>
<ul>
<li>Conceptual Chemistry: An introductory course requiring basic math but no algebra
<li>Chemistry I: An introductory course requiring solid algebra skills
<li>Advanced Placement Chemistry: An advanced course requiring a grade of A or B in Chemistry I
and designed for students who want to prepare for the AP Chemistry exam (which can count toward
college credits)
</ul>
<h2>Class Policies</h2>
<h3>Grading</h3>
<p>Homework will be given daily, is due at the beginning of the period the school day after it
was assigned, and will be worth 5 to 10 points. A periodic quiz consisting of 1 or 2 homework
problems from the past week may be given in lieu of collecting homework.</p>
```

4. Save the file when you are sure that it matches the code in Figure 1-18.

5. Using your Web browser, refresh or reload chem.htm. The latest version of the file is displayed in Figure 1-19.

Figure 1-19	THE UNORDERED LIST IN THE BROWSER

Mr. Dube's Chemistry Classes

at Robert Service High School

Welcome to Mr. Dube's Web site. I hope you will use this site to learn more about your class, my expectations, and chemistry in the world around you.

Chemistry Classes

- Conceptual Chemistry: An introductory course requiring basic math but no algebra
- Chemistry I: An introductory course requiring solid algebra skills
- Advanced Placement Chemistry: An advanced course requiring a grade of A or B in Chemistry I and designed for students who want to prepare for the AP Chemistry exam (which can count toward college credits)

Stephen's page now includes a list formatted to closely resemble his course handout. If your browser does not display a page that looks like Figure 1-19, return to the HTML file and check for errors in the code that you entered.

Creating **Character Tags**

So far in this tutorial, you've worked with HTML tags that format either the entire document or individual lines of text. HTML also lets you format individual characters. A tag that you apply to an individual character is called a **character tag.** There are two types of character tags: logical and physical. **Logical character tags** specify how you want to use text, not necessarily how you want it displayed. Figure 1-20 lists some common logical character tags.

Figure 1-20	COMMON LOGICAL CHARACTER TAGS

TAG	DESCRIPTION
<em>	Indicates that characters should be emphasized in some way. Usually displayed with italics.
<strong>	Emphasizes characters more strongly than <em>. Usually displayed in a bold font.
<code>	Indicates a sample of code. Usually displayed in a Courier font or a similar monospace font.
<kbd>	Used to offset text that the user should enter. Often displayed in a Courier font or a similar monospace font.
<var>	Indicates a variable. Often displayed in italics or underlined.
<cite>	Indicates short quotes or citations. Often italicized by browsers.

For example, if you want some text to stand out from the rest of the page, you could use the <em> tag; one browser might render the text in bold, while another might use italics.

Figure 1-21 shows examples of how these tags can be displayed in a browser. Note that you can combine tags, allowing you to create bold and italic text by using the <em> and <strong> tags, for example.

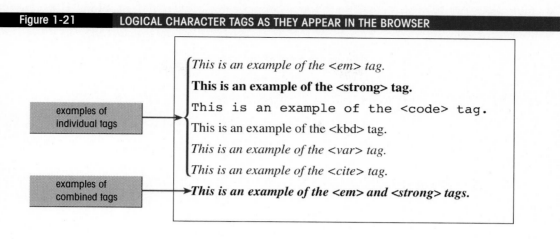

Figure 1-21 LOGICAL CHARACTER TAGS AS THEY APPEAR IN THE BROWSER

examples of individual tags

This is an example of the <em> tag.

This is an example of the <strong> tag.

`This is an example of the <code> tag.`

This is an example of the <kbd> tag.

This is an example of the <var> tag.

This is an example of the <cite> tag.

examples of combined tags

This is an example of the <em> and <strong> tags.

When you combine tags, it is a good idea for one tag to completely contain the other. For example, you can combine the <em> and <strong> tags like this:

```
<em><strong>strong emphasized text</strong></em>
```

But you should *not* overlap the opening and closing tags, as shown in the following code:

```
<em><strong>strong emphasized text</em></strong>
```

Some browsers cannot interpret combined tags. Combining tags also makes code more difficult to follow.

Web designers can also use **physical character tags** to format text. Figure 1-22 shows common examples of physical character tags.

Figure 1-22 COMMON PHYSICAL CHARACTER TAGS

TAG	DESCRIPTION
<b>	Enclosed text is bold.
<i>	Enclosed text is italic.
<u>	Enclosed text is underlined.
<tt>	Enclosed text is typewriter text, which is a monospace font such as Courier.
<big>	Enclosed text is displayed bigger than surrounding text.
<small>	Enclosed text is displayed smaller than surrounding text.
<sub>	Enclosed text is displayed as a subscript, in a smaller font if possible.
<sup>	Enclosed text is displayed as a superscript, in a smaller font if possible.

Figure 1-23 shows examples of how these tags can be displayed in a browser. Note that underlined text can sometimes be confused with hyperlinked text (which is usually underlined), and for that reason, use of the <u> tag is discouraged.

Figure 1-23	PHYSICAL CHARACTER TAGS AS THEY APPEAR IN THE BROWSER

This is an example of the <b> tag.

This is an example of the <i> tag.

<u>This is an example of the <u> tag.</u>

`This is an example of the <tt> tag.`

This is an example of the <big> tag.

This is an example of the <small> tag.

This is an example of the $_{<sub>\,tag}$.

This is an example of the $^{<sup>\,tag}$.

Given the overlapping functions of logical and physical character tags, which should you use to display text in an italicized font, <em> or <i>? Some older versions of browsers are text-based and cannot display italics, so these browsers ignore the <i> tag. If you suspect that many of your users are using older browsers, you should use a logical tag. Otherwise, use physical tags, which are more common and easier to interpret.

Only the Grading section in Stephen's handout requires the use of character tags, where he wants to highlight certain key words of each grading topic. He decides to use a combination of the <b> and <i> tags to display the key words in bold and italics.

To add character tags to the chemistry file:

1. Using your text editor, open **chem.htm** if it is not currently open.

2. Type the <i> and <b> tags around the keywords in the Grading section of the handout as follows:

   ```
   <i><b>Homework</b></i> will be given daily…
   <i><b>Tests and quizzes</b></i> will be used…
   <i><b>Labs</b></i> will be worth…
   <i><b>small research projects</b></i> throughout the
   semester…
   <i><b>make up</b></i> missed tests and quizzes…
   ```

   See Figure 1-24.

Figure 1-24	APPLYING CHARACTER TAGS

```
<h2>Class Policies</h2>
<h3>Grading</h3>
<p><i><b>Homework</b></i> will be given daily, is due at the beginning of the period the school
day after it was assigned, and will be worth 5 to 10 points. A periodic quiz consisting of 1 or
2 homework problems from the past week may be given in lieu of collecting homework.</p>

<p><i><b>Tests and quizzes</b></i> will be used to check your understanding of concepts,
procedures, and information. Quizzes will be worth 10 to 25 points and will be given at least
once a month. Tests will be worth up to 100 points and will be given 2 or 3 times a quarter.
</p>

<p><i><b>Labs</b></i> will be worth 10 to 30 points and will be graded on safety,
participation, and write-up. I expect neat handwritten or typed reports.  I'll also assign
<i><b>small research projects</b></i> throughout the semester.</p>

<p>You must <i><b>make up</b></i> missed tests and quizzes the day you return, and you must
submit missed homework assignments and labs within two days for every one day you missed.
Failure to make up work within these time frames will result in a 0 for that test or
assignment.</p>
```

3. Save your changes to chem.htm.

4. Using your Web browser, refresh or reload chem.htm. The updated Grading section of your page should look like Figure 1-25.

Figure 1-25	THE EFFECT OF THE CHARACTER TAGS IN THE BROWSER

Class Policies

Grading

Homework will be given daily, is due at the beginning of the period the school day after it was assigned, and will be worth 5 to 10 points. A periodic quiz consisting of 1 or 2 homework problems from the past week may be given in lieu of collecting homework.

Tests and quizzes will be used to check your understanding of concepts, procedures, and information. Quizzes will be worth 10 to 25 points and will be given at least once a month. Tests will be worth up to 100 points and will be given 2 or 3 times a quarter.

Labs will be worth 10 to 30 points and will be graded on safety, participation, and write-up. I expect neat handwritten or typed reports. I'll also assign *small research projects* throughout the semester.

You must *make up* missed tests and quizzes the day you return, and you must submit missed homework assignments and labs within two days for every one day you missed. Failure to make up work within these time frames will result in a 0 for that test or assignment.

text formatted with bold and italics

5. If you are continuing to Session 1.3, leave your text editor and browser open. Otherwise you can close them at this time.

You have finished adding text to Stephen's online handout. In Session 1.3, you will add special formatting elements such as horizontal lines and images to the Web page.

Session 1.2 QUICK CHECK

1. Why should you include the <html> tag in your Web document?

2. What is the syntax for creating a centered Heading 1?

3. What is the syntax for creating a paragraph?

4. If you want to create an extra blank line between paragraphs, why can't you simply add a blank line in the HTML file?

5. Show the syntax for creating an ordered list, an unordered list, and a definition list.

6. List two ways of italicizing text in your Web document. What are the advantages and disadvantages of each method?

SESSION 1.3

In this session you'll insert three special elements into Stephen's Web page: an image, a special character for the "e" in his last name, and a horizontal line separating his picture and page title from the rest of the Web page.

Inserting a Graphic

One feature of Web pages that has made the Web so popular is the ease with which images can be displayed. Images can be displayed in two ways: as inline images or as external images.

An **inline image** is displayed directly on the Web page and is displayed when the page is accessed by a user. An inline image can be placed on a separate line in your HTML code, or it can be placed directly within a line of text—hence the term inline. Inline images should be in one of two file formats: GIF (Graphics Interchange Format) or JPEG (Joint Photographic Experts Group). Image editing applications such as Adobe Photoshop can be used to convert images to either the GIF or JPEG file format.

An **external image** is not displayed with the Web page. Instead, the browser must have a file viewer, which is a separate program that the browser launches when it encounters an external image file. Most browsers make it easy to set up viewers for use with the Web. External images have one major disadvantage: you can't actually display them on the Web page. Instead they are represented by an icon that a user clicks to view the image. The advantage is that external images are not limited to the GIF or JPEG formats.

REFERENCE   WINDOW   **RW**

Inserting an Inline Image
- Using your text editor, open the HTML file.
- Place the insertion point where you want the inline image to appear.
- Type <img src="*file*"> where *file* is the name of the GIF or JPEG image file.

Stephen has decided to use an inline image rather than an external image. The syntax for creating an inline image is:

```
<img src="file">
```

where *file* is the name of the image file. If the image file is located in the same folder as the HTML file, you do not need to include any file location path information. However, if the image file is located in another folder or on another computer, you need to include the full location path and use the src attribute. Tutorial 2 discusses directory paths and filenames in more detail. For now, assume that Stephen's image file is located in the folder that contains the HTML file.

The image file that Stephen wants you to use is a photograph of himself that has been saved as a JPEG file. The image is displayed in Figure 1.26. The image file **dube.jpg** is located in the Tutorial folder in the Tutorial.01 folder on your data disk.

Figure 1-26   **IMAGE FOR THE TOP OF STEPHEN'S PAGE**

Because this file includes the title of the page, you no longer need the text "Mr. Dube's Chemistry Classes at Robert Service High School" that you entered earlier.

Stephen wants to center the image on the page. There is no attribute in the <img> tag that allows you to center it on a page, but you can nest the <img> tag within a paragraph tag, <p>, and then center the paragraph on the page using the align="center" attribute for the <p> tag. This has the effect of centering all of the text in the paragraph, including any inline images.

To add Stephen's image to the Web page:

1. Using your text editor, open **chem.htm**.

2. Near the top of the file, select the two lines of code just below the `<body>` tag (from the `<h1>` opening tag to the `</h2>` closing tag), and then press the **Delete** key.

3. Press the **Enter** key to insert a blank line if necessary, and then type:

   ```
   <p align="center"><img src="dube.jpg"></p>
   ```

4. Save your changes to chem.htm. See Figure 1-27.

Figure 1-27	ADDING THE IMAGE FILE

use the `<p>` tag so you can center the image →

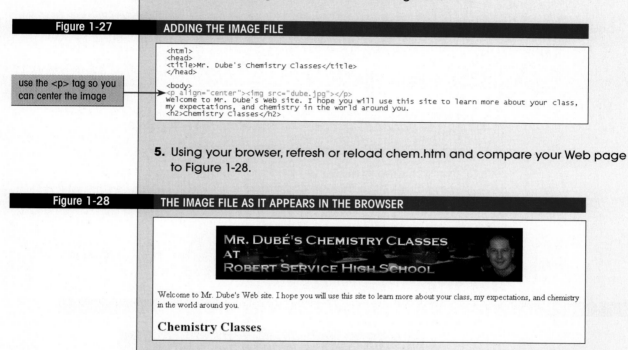

```
<html>
<head>
<title>Mr. Dube's Chemistry Classes</title>
</head>

<body>
<p align="center"><img src="dube.jpg"></p>
Welcome to Mr. Dube's web site. I hope you will use this site to learn more about your class,
my expectations, and chemistry in the world around you.
<h2>Chemistry Classes</h2>
```

5. Using your browser, refresh or reload chem.htm and compare your Web page to Figure 1-28.

Figure 1-28	THE IMAGE FILE AS IT APPEARS IN THE BROWSER

MR. DUBÉ'S CHEMISTRY CLASSES
AT
ROBERT SERVICE HIGH SCHOOL

Welcome to Mr. Dube's Web site. I hope you will use this site to learn more about your class, my expectations, and chemistry in the world around you.

Chemistry Classes

Stephen is pleased with the way the image looks. Your next task is to format the e at the end of "Dubé" to include the accent. You do this using special character symbols.

Adding Special Characters

Occasionally you will want to include special characters in your Web page that do not appear on your keyboard. For example, a page might require mathematical symbols such as β or μ, or you might need to place the copyright symbol © to show that an image or text is copyrighted.

Stephen needs to use a special symbol, the accented "é," in his last name, which appears twice in his Web page: once in the title at the top of the page, and again in the short introductory paragraph. You've just inserted a graphic that includes the é at the top, so you need to add the symbol only once.

HTML supports the use of character symbols that are identified by a code number or name. To create a special character, type an ampersand (&) followed either by the code name or the code number, and then a semicolon. Code numbers are preceded by a pound symbol (#). Figure 1-29 shows some HTML symbols and the corresponding code numbers or names. A more complete list of special characters is included in Appendix B.

Figure 1-29		SPECIAL CHARACTERS AND CODES	
SYMBOL	**CODE**	**CODE NAME**	**DESCRIPTION**
©	&#169;	&copy;	Copyright symbol
®	&#174;	&reg;	Registered trademark
•	&#183;	&middot;	Middle dot
°	&#186;	&ordm;	Masculine ordinal
TM	&#153;	&trade;	Trademark symbol
			Nonbreaking space, useful when you want to insert several blank spaces, one after another
<	&#60;	&lt;	Less than symbol
>	&#62;	&gt;	Greater than symbol
&	&#38;	&amp;	Ampersand

To add a character code to the chemistry page:

1. Using your text editor, open **chem.htm** if it is not currently open.

2. In the "Welcome to Mr. Dube's Web site" paragraph, select the **e** in "Dube" and then type **&#233** so that the code reads as follows:

```
Welcome to Mr. Dub&#233's Web site
```

3. Save your changes to chem.htm.

4. Using your Web browser, refresh or reload chem.htm. Figure 1-30 shows Stephen's page with the accented é in his last name.

Figure 1-30	SPECIAL CHARACTER IN THE BROWSER

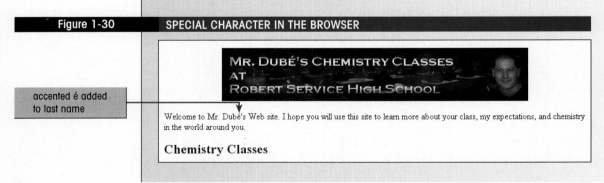

accented é added
to last name

The final thing Stephen wants to include in his page is a horizontal line separating his picture and the large title at the top from the rest of the page.

Inserting Horizontal Lines

The horizontal line after Stephen's photo and title in Figure 1-6 improves the appearance of his paper handout, and he'd like to duplicate that look on the Web page. The syntax for creating a horizontal line is:

```
<hr align="align" size="size" width="width" color="color"
noshade>
```

where *align* specifies the horizontal alignment of the line on the page (center, left, or right), *size* specifies the height of the line, *width* indicates the width of the line, *color* indicates the color of the line, and *noshade* specifies that the browser display a solid line. Note that the color attribute is supported by Internet Explorer but not Netscape.

The size and width attributes are measured in either **pixels** (a square dot on your computer screen about 1/72 inch wide) or as a percentage of the screen width. For example, <hr width="50%"> instructs the browser to place the line so that its length covers half of the width of the page. Figure 1-31 shows how a browser would interpret the following lines of HTML code:

```
<hr align="center" size="12" width="100%">
<hr align="center" size="6" width="50%">
<hr align="center" size="3" width="25%">
<hr align="center" size="1" width="10%">
```

Figure 1-31   DIFFERENT LINE STYLES

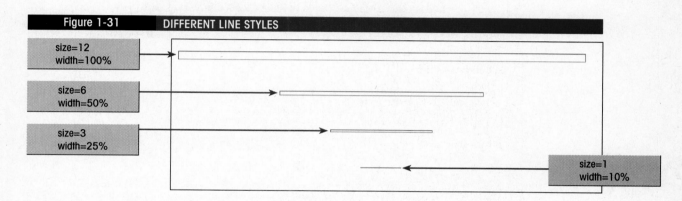

To add a horizontal line to the chemistry file:

1. Using your text editor, open **chem.htm** if it is not currently open.

2. At the end of the line specifying the dube.jpg image (just above the "Welcome" paragraph), press the **Enter** key to insert a new blank line.

3. In the new line, type **<hr>**.

4. Save your changes to chem.htm.

5. Using your Web browser, refresh or reload the chem.htm file. The new horizontal line is displayed in Figure 1-32.

Figure 1-32   HORIZONTAL LINE ADDED TO THE PAGE

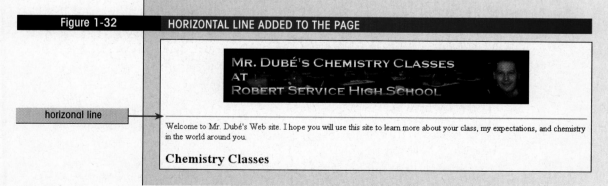

Now that you've completed the Web page for Stephen, you decide to print both the text file and the Web page as it appears in the browser for his review.

To print the text file and Web page:

1. Using your browser, carefully compare your Web page to Figure 1-33, which shows the entire page. If you see any errors, return to your text editor to fix them. When the page is error-free, use your browser to print the page.

Figure 1-33	STEPHEN'S COMPLETED CHEMISTRY PAGE

Welcome to Mr. Dubé's Web site. I hope you will use this site to learn more about your class, my expectations, and chemistry in the world around you.

Chemistry Classes

- Conceptual Chemistry: An introductory course requiring basic math but no algebra
- Chemistry I: An introductory course requiring solid algebra skills
- Advanced Placement Chemistry: An advanced course requiring a grade of A or B in Chemistry I and designed for students who want to prepare for the AP Chemistry exam (which can count toward college credits)

Class Policies

Grading

Homework will be given daily, is due at the beginning of the period the school day after it was assigned, and will be worth 5 to 10 points. A periodic quiz consisting of 1 or 2 homework problems from the past week may be given in lieu of collecting homework.

Tests and quizzes will be used to check your understanding of concepts, procedures, and information. Quizzes will be worth 10 to 25 points and will be given at least once a month. Tests will be worth up to 100 points and will be given 2 or 3 times a quarter.

Labs will be worth 10 to 30 points and will be graded on safety, participation, and write-up. I expect neat handwritten or typed reports. I'll also assign *small research projects* throughout the semester.

You must *make up* missed tests and quizzes the day you return, and you must submit missed homework assignments and labs within two days for every one day you missed. Failure to make up work within these time frames will result in a 0 for that test or assignment.

Appointments

I can meet with you before or after school. I will also be in my room (H113) during most lunch hours. Please do not hesitate to stop in if you need extra help -- do not wait! Chemistry is a building subject, and it is very hard to catch up once you fall behind.

Safety

We will be doing lab work nearly every week. Because of the potential danger of any lab exercise, I will hold you to the highest standards of behavior, and will remove you from the class if you pose a threat to yourself or other students.

2. Using your text editor, print chem.htm, and compare it to the following code. When you are finished, you can close your text editor and browser unless you are continuing on to the Review Assignments.

```
<html>
<head>
<title>Mr. Dube's Chemistry Classes</title>
</head>
<body>
<p align="center"><img src="dube.jpg"></p>
<hr>
Welcome to Mr. Dub&#233's Web site. I hope you will
use this site to learn more about your class, my
expectations, and chemistry in the world around you.
<h2>Chemistry Classes</h2>
<ul>
<li>Conceptual Chemistry: An introductory course
requiring basic math but no algebra
<li>Chemistry I: An introductory course requiring solid
algebra skills
<li>Advanced Placement Chemistry: An advanced course
requiring a grade of A or B in Chemistry I and designed
for students who want to prepare for the AP Chemistry
exam (which can count toward college credits)
</ul>
<h2>Class Policies</h2>
<h3>Grading</h3>
<p><i><b>Homework</b></i> will be given daily, is due at
the beginning of the period the school day after it was
assigned, and will be worth 5 to 10 points. A periodic
homework quiz consisting of 1 or 2 homework problems
from the past week may be given in lieu of collecting
homework.</p>
<p><i><b>Tests and quizzes</b></i> will be used to check
your understanding of concepts, procedures, and
information. Quizzes will be worth 10 to 25 points and
will be given at least once a month. Tests will be worth
up to 100 points and will be given 2 or 3 times a
quarter.</p>
<p><i><b>Labs</b></i> will be worth 10 to 30 points and
will be graded on safety, participation, and write-up.
I expect neat handwritten or typed reports. I'll also
assign <i><b>small research projects</b></i> throughout
the semester.</p>
<p>You must <i><b>make up</b></i> missed tests and quizzes
the day you return, and you must submit missed homework
assignments and labs within two days for every one day
you missed.
Failure to make up work within these time frames will
result in a 0 for that test or assignment.</p>
<h3>Appointments</h3>
I can meet with you before or after school. I will also
be in my room (H113) during most lunch hours. Please do
not hesitate to stop in if you need extra help -- do not
wait! Chemistry is a building subject, and it is very
hard to catch up once you fall behind.
<h3>Safety</h3>
We will be doing lab work nearly every week. Because of
```

Note:
Continued on
next page

```
the potential danger of any lab exercise, I will hold you
to the highest standards of behavior, and will remove you
from the class if you pose a threat to yourself or other
students.
</body>
</html>
```

Stephen is pleased with your work on his Web site and feels that it effectively captures the look and feel of the original handout. You explain to him that the next step is adding hypertext links to his Web page so that you can add contact information and create links to the interesting chemistry Web sites you've discovered. You'll do this in Tutorial 2.

Session 1.3 QUICK CHECK

1. How would you insert a copyright symbol, ©, into your Web page?

2. What is the syntax for inserting a horizontal line into a page?

3. What is the syntax for creating a horizontal line that is 70% of the display width of the screen and 4 pixels high?

4. What is an inline image?

5. What is an external image?

6. What is the syntax for inserting a graphic named mouse.jpg into a Web document as an inline image?

7. What are two graphic file formats you can use for inline images?

REVIEW ASSIGNMENTS

After further review, Stephen decides that he wants you to add a few more items to the Web page. In the Chemistry Classes section, he wants you to add a new class that he'll be offering next semester. He would like a numbered list in the Safety section listing his five main safety rules. He would also like to add a whimsical sentence at the bottom of the site to let his students know that though he is serious about learning and safety, he wants his classes to be fun. He'd like the line to read: "Chemistry with Dubé is like medicine with a spoonful of $C_{12}H_{22}O_{11}$!". $C_{12}H_{22}O_{11}$ is the formula for sugar. You'll use the <sub> tag to format the subscript numbers in the formula. You suggest to him that adding a horizontal line to separate this line from the rest of the page would be a nice touch, and he agrees.

The file you'll create is shown in Figure 1-34.

Figure 1-34

Welcome to Mr. Dubé's Web site. I hope you will use this site to learn more about your class, my expectations, and chemistry in the world around you.

Chemistry Classes

- Conceptual Chemistry: An introductory course requiring basic math but no algebra
- Chemistry I: An introductory course requiring solid algebra skills
- Applied Chemistry: An introductory course requiring solid algebra skills and an interest in using critical thinking to solve real-world, chemistry-related problems
- Advanced Placement Chemistry: An advanced course requiring a grade of A or B in Chemistry I and designed for students who want to prepare for the AP Chemistry exam (which can count toward college credits)

Class Policies

Grading

Homework will be given daily, is due at the beginning of the period the school day after it was assigned, and will be worth 5 to 10 points. A periodic quiz consisting of 1 or 2 homework problems from the past week may be given in lieu of collecting homework.

Tests and quizzes will be used to check your understanding of concepts, procedures, and information. Quizzes will be worth 10 to 25 points and will be given at least once a month. Tests will be worth up to 100 points and will be given 2 or 3 times a quarter.

Labs will be worth 10 to 30 points and will be graded on safety, participation, and write-up. I expect neat handwritten or typed reports. I'll also assign *small research projects* throughout the semester.

You must *make up* missed tests and quizzes the day you return, and you must submit missed homework assignments and labs within two days for every one day you missed. Failure to make up work within these time frames will result in a 0 for that test or assignment.

Appointments

I can meet with you before or after school. I will also be in my room (H113) during most lunch hours. Please do not hesitate to stop in if you need extra help -- do not wait! Chemistry is a building subject, and it is very hard to catch up once you fall behind.

Safety

We will be doing lab work nearly every week. Because of the potential danger of any lab exercise, I will hold you to the highest standards of behavior, and will remove you from the class if you pose a threat to yourself or other students.

1. Follow my written and oral directions carefully and immediately.
2. Never perform any procedure not specifically directed by me or assigned in the lab.
3. No playful behavior is permitted in the lab.
4. Safety equipment must be worn as directed at all times, even if you find it uncomfortable or unbecoming.
5. No food, drinks, or loose clothing are permitted in the lab.

Chemistry with Dubé is like medicine with a spoonful of $C_{12}H_{22}O_{11}$!

To complete this task:

1. Using your text editor, open **chem.htm** located in the tutorial folder of the tutorial.01 folder on your Data Disk. This is the file you created over the course of this tutorial.

2. Save the file on your Data Disk in the tutorial.01/review folder with a new name, **chem2.htm**, so that you leave your work from the tutorial intact.

3. In the unordered list section, after the line specifying the Chemistry I class, add a new item to the list using the <li> tag to specify the following:

   "Applied Chemistry: An introductory course requiring solid algebra skills and an interest in using critical thinking to solve real-world, chemistry-related problems"

4. Move to the Safety section of chem2.htm.

5. After the paragraph describing Stephen's safety standards, use the <ol> and <li> tags to create a numbered list with the following five list items:

   1. Follow my written and oral directions carefully and immediately.
   2. Never perform any procedure not specifically directed by me or assigned in the lab.
   3. No playful behavior is permitted in the lab.
   4. Safety equipment must be worn as directed at all times, even if you find it uncomfortable or unbecoming.
   5. No food, drinks, or loose clothing are permitted in the lab.

Explore

6. Go to the end of the file, and just before the closing </body> tag, insert a blank line and enter the code for the following text:

   "Chemistry with Dube is like medicine with a spoonful of $C_{12}H_{22}O_{11}$!"

   You'll need to enter the symbol **&#233** for the accented é at the end of his name, and the <sub> tag for each of the three numbers that need to be formatted as subscript characters. Your code should look like the following:

   <p>Chemistry with Dub&#233 is like medicine with a spoonful of C₁₂H₂₂O₁₁!</p>

Explore

7. Insert a blank line before the code you just entered, and then type the code for a horizontal line using the <hr> tag. Set the thickness of the line to 6 pixels.

8. Save your changes to chem2.htm.

9. View the file with your Web browser and compare it with Figure 1-34.

10. Correct any errors that you see, and then print a copy of the page as viewed by your browser and a copy of the code in your text editor.

11. Close your browser and text editor.

CASE PROBLEMS

Case 1. ChildLink, Inc. You are on the board of directors for ChildLink, Inc., a small, nonprofit agency in Las Cruces, New Mexico that provides financial and emotional support for families with children who have newly discovered physical or mental disabilities. The agency received significantly more donations in the last year than expected, and it has decided to offer qualifying clients temporary help with housing and medical costs. The board has asked you to post the eligibility requirements and application process on the Web. The page should appear as displayed in Figure 1-35.

Figure 1-35

ChildLink of Las Cruces

A Loving Connection between Children with Disabilities and the Resources They Need

Temporary Financial Assistance Available

To be eligible for this program, you must meet the following criteria:

- Have a child with a physical or mental disability diagnosed within the last 6 months (the diagnosis can be prenatal or at any age)
- Be at or below the State of New Mexico's poverty line

To apply, please do the following:

1. Pick up an application from ChildLink (address below)
2. Assemble the following papers:
    a. Your completed application
    b. Doctor's record of your child's diagnosis
    c. Tax records or New Mexico Social Services certificate of your income level
    d. Your lease, mortgage, or medical bills, depending on which you need help with
3. Make an appointment with a ChildLink volunteer, available these times:
    a. Ida: MW 10:30 a.m. to 3:30 p.m.
    b. Juan: TR 9:00 a.m. to noon
    c. Chris: F 10:30 a.m. to 3:30 p.m.

ChildLink

1443 Cortnic Drive

Las Cruces, NM 88001

505-555-2371

The page needs an inline image, three headings, a list of eligibility requirements, and application instructions. Two of the items in the list also have nested lists.

To create this page:

1. Start your text editor program.

2. Type the <html>, <head>, and <body> tags to identify different sections of the page.

3. Save the file as **child.htm** in the case1 folder of the tutorial.01 folder on your Data Disk.

4. Within the head section, insert a <title> tag with the text, "ChildLink Temporary Financial Assistance". This text appears in the title bar of the browser.

5. Within the body section, create an <h1> heading with the text "ChildLink of Las Cruces", and center the heading on the page using the align attribute.

6. Below the <h1> heading, create an <h3> heading with the text "A Loving Connection between Children with Disabilities and the Resources They Need", and center the heading on the page.

7. Below the <h3> heading, create an <h2> heading with the text "Temporary Financial Assistance Available", and center the heading.

8. Below the <h2> heading, create an <h4> heading with the text "To be eligible for this program, you must meet the following criteria:". Leave this heading left-aligned.

Explore   9. Below the <h4> heading, create a bulleted list using the <ul> tag and the type attribute to make the bullet a square. Include the two list items shown in Figure 1-35. Make sure you include a closing </ul> tag.

10. Below the closing </ul> tag for the bulleted list, create an <h4> heading with the text "To apply, please do the following:". Leave this heading left-aligned.

11. Below the second <h4> heading, create an ordered list with the three items shown in Figure 1-35. Make sure you include a closing </ol> tag.

Explore   12. Within the "Assemble the following papers:" item, create an ordered list with the four items shown in Figure 1-35. Use the type attribute to have this nested list numbered with a, b, c, and d.

Explore   13. Within the "Make an appointment" list, create another ordered list with the three volunteer names and times as shown in Figure 1-35, again using the type attribute to number the list with a, b, and c.

14. Below the numbered list, type the address shown in Figure 1-35 using the <p> tag to keep each line separate. Remember to right-align the paragraphs and to use the <b> and <i> tags for the ChildLink name.

15. After the <h3> heading ("A Loving Connection…") near the top, insert the inline image **newborn.jpg** (located in the case1 folder of the tutorial.01 folder on your Data Disk), centered on the page.

16. After the image, insert a horizontal line that extends the width of the page and is 1 pixel in height.

17. Save the file, view it in your browser, compare it to Figure 1-35, and then make any corrections necessary in your text editor.

18. Add <p> tags where necessary to insert blank lines to space the text, image, and horizontal lines attractively.

19. Save the file again, view it with your Web browser, print it from the browser and the text editor, and then close your browser and text editor.

Case 2. Mathematics Department, Coastal University Professor Laureen Coe of the Mathematics Department at Coastal University in Beachside, Connecticut is preparing material for her course on the history of mathematics. As part of the course, she has written short profiles of famous mathematicians. Laureen would like you to use content she's already written to create several Web pages to be placed on the Coastal University's Web server. You'll create the first one in this exercise. A preview of one of the pages about the mathematician Leonhard Euler is shown in Figure 1-36.

Figure 1-36

Euler, Leonhard

(1707-1783)

The greatest mathematician of the eighteenth century, **Leonhard Euler** was born in Basel, Switzerland. There, he studied under another giant of mathematics, **Jean Bernoulli**. In 1731 Euler became a professor of physics and mathematics at St. Petersburg Academy of Sciences. Euler was the most prolific mathematician of all time, publishing over *800 different books and papers*. His influence was felt in physics and astronomy as well. Euler's work on mathematical analysis, Introductio in analysin infinitorum (1748) remained a standard textbook for well over a century. For the princess of Anhalt-Dessau he wrote *Lettres à une princesse d'Allemagne* (1768-1772), giving a clear non-technical outline of the main physical theories of the time.

One can hardly write mathematical equations without copying Euler. Notations still in use today, such as e and π, were developed by Euler. He is perhaps best known for his research into mathematical analysis. Euler's formula:

$$\cos(x) + i\sin(x) = e^{(ix)}$$

demonstrates the relationship between analysis, trignometry and imaginary numbers, in one beautiful and elegant equation.

Leonhard Euler died in 1783, leaving behind a legacy perhaps unmatched, and certainly unsurpassed, in the annals of mathematics.

Math 895: The History of Mathematics

To complete this task:

1. Using your text editor, open **eulertxt.htm** located in the case2 folder of the tutorial.01 folder on your Data Disk, and save it as **euler.htm**.

2. Add the opening and closing <html>, <head>, and <body> tags to the file in the appropriate locations.

3. Insert "Leonhard Euler" as a page title in the head section of the document.

4. Insert the inline image **euler.jpg** (located in the case2 folder of the tutorial.01 folder on your Data Disk) at the top of the body of the document.

5. Format the first line of the page's body, "Euler, Leonhard", with the <h1> tag, and format the second line of the page's body, "(1707-1783)", with the <h3> tag.

6. Add the appropriate paragraph tags, <p>, to the document to separate the paragraphs.

7. Within the first paragraph, display the names "Leonhard Euler" and "Jean Bernoulli" in boldface. Italicize the phrase "800 different books and papers", and underline the publication "Introductio in analysin infinitorum".

8. Replace the one-letter word "a" in "Lettres a une princesse d'Allemagne" with an *à*, using the character code &agrave, and then italicize the entire name of the publication.

9. In the second paragraph, italicize the notation "e" and replace the word "pi" with the inline image **pi.jpg**, located in the case2 folder on your Data Disk.

10. Center the equation and italicize the letters "x", "i", and "e" in the equation. Display the term "*(ix)*" as a superscript, using the <sup> tag.

11. Format the name of the course at the bottom of the page using the <cite> tag.

12. Add horizontal lines before and after the biographical information.

13. Save euler.htm, and then print it from your text editor.

14. View the file in your Web browser, and then print a copy of the page as displayed by the browser.

Case 3. Frostbite Freeze You are on the organizing committee for the Frostbite Freeze, Montana's craziest running race. The Frostbite Freeze is a fun but competitive event held each January in Butte, Montana, and you've volunteered to publish the race results on the Web. You'd like to have a snowflake background behind the text, which you can do using a graphic image. Such backgrounds are called tile-image backgrounds because the image is repeated throughout the entire page. To create a tile-image background, you must have an image in either GIF or JPEG file format. You insert the file in the background by adding the background attribute to the <body> tag with the syntax:

```
<body background="filename">
```

You have a JPEG file named **flakes.jpg**, which contains a pattern of repeating snowflakes. You also have a JPEG file named **runner.jpg**, a picture of a Frostbite Freeze racer. A preview of the page you'll create is shown in Figure 1-37.

Figure 1-37

Frostbite Freeze

Montana's Craziest Footrace

The results are in...

257 runners braved the -10° weather on January 19 and ran, in one fashion or another, the icy 5-kilometer course through downtown Butte. About half the runners sported costumes rather than serious running gear, and many runners posted good times (costumed or not). For many, this was the season's first run (not race – *run*), a motivational warm-up for the fun and work that lies ahead.

Awards were given for best time in four age categories for both sexes.

Girls 14-19

Jamie Harrington 19:33 · Sorcia Besay 20:06 · Rachel Stores 25:44

Boys 14-19

Bruce Bevin 18:55 · Endre Witthoeft 19:46 · Joe Wesevich 21:19

Women 20-39

Marie Sillers 17:45 · Denise Wortenhau 18:33 · Lorel Dwiers 18:56

Women 39-49

Jannie Gilbert 17:48 · Mia Saphi 19:23 · Dawn Severson 21:31

Women 50+

Julia Gent 21:09 · Mandy Reming 34:24 · Sung Bon 41:02

Men 20-39

Gary Cruz 17:11 · Lanny Sorla 18:40 · Kip Oestin 18:55

Men 40-49

Steve Jackson 18:50 · Jim Kostenberger 24:33 · Lee Whisten 27:18

Men 50+

Billy Tisa 18:22 · Alois Anderson 28:48 · Lyle Tolbor 35:46

To create this page:

1. Using your text editor, open **frosttxt.htm** from the case3 folder of the tutorial.01 folder on your Data Disk, and then save it as frostrun.htm.

2. Insert the <html>, <head>, and <body> tags in the appropriate locations.

3. Insert a <title> tag in the head section, giving the Web page the title "Frostbite Freeze Results".

4. Insert the **flakes.jpg** file (in the case3 folder) as the background for the page. To do this, modify the <body> tag to read:

   `<body background="flakes.jpg">`

5. Format the text "Frostbite Freeze" with the <h1> tag and center it on the Web page.

6. Format the text "Montana's Craziest Footrace" with the <h2> tag and center it on the page.

Explore ▷ 7. Insert a horizontal line below the <h2> heading that is 50% of the width of the screen, is 10 pixels tall, and is purple. (*Hint*: use the color attribute and the word "purple.")

8. Format the text "The results are in" with the <h3> heading tag, leaving the text left aligned.

Explore ▷ 9. Add ellipses (…) after the text "The results are in" so it reads, "The results are in…" You'll need to use the character for the ellipses symbol, which you can find in Appendix B of this book.

10. Add a degree symbol after "-10" in the first line of the first paragraph. (The degree symbol is also located in Appendix B.)

11. Insert <p> tags around the two main paragraphs (one starts with "257 runners" and the other starts with "Awards were given").

12. Near the end of the first text paragraph, format the word "run" that appears in parentheses in Figure 1-37 with italics using the <i> tag.

13. Add <p> tags around each of the eight age-sex categories (for example, "Girls 14-19"). (*Hint*: For Steps 13, 14, and 15, use your text editor's copy and paste functions to reduce the amount of typing you have to do.)

14. Format the eight age-sex categories with bold using the <b> tag.

15. Insert a middle dot symbol, with a nonbreaking space on each side of the dot, between each of the three names in each of the eight age-sex categories, as shown in Figure 1-37. To do this, type &#183 after the time for the first two names in each category. Because you are inserting nonbreaking spaces, make sure there is no space after the time or before the next name. For example, in the Girls 14-19 category, the names appear as

   Jamie Harrington 19:33 &#183 Sorcia Besay
   20:06 &#183 Rachel Stores 25:44

16. Insert the inline image **runner.jpg** (located in the case3 folder of the tutorial.01 folder on your Data Disk) between the top two headings, as shown in Figure 1-37. Center it on the page.

17. Save frostrun.htm and print it from your text editor.

18. View the file in your Web browser and print it from your browser.

Case 4. Create Your Own Resume   Using the techniques from this tutorial, design and create a resume for yourself. Be sure to include these features: section headings, bulleted or numbered lists, bold and/or italic fonts, paragraphs, inline graphic images, and horizontal lines.

1. Start your text editor, and then create a file called **myresume.htm** in the case4 folder of the tutorial.01 folder on your Data Disk. Type the appropriate HTML code and content.

2. Add any other tags you think will improve the appearance of your document.

3. You could take a picture of yourself to your lab or a local office services business and have it scanned. If you do, save it as a GIF or JPEG file. Then place the graphic file in the case4 folder of the tutorial.01 folder on your Data Disk. Add the appropriate code in your myresume.htm file. If you don't have your own image file, use the file **kirk.jpg** located in the case4 folder of the tutorial.01 folder on your Data Disk.

4. Test your code as you develop your resume by viewing myresume.htm in your browser.

5. When you finish entering the code, save and print the myresume.htm file from your text editor.

6. View the final version in your browser, print the Web page, and then close your browser and text editor.

QUICK CHECK ANSWERS

Session 1.1

1. Hypertext refers to text that contains points called links that allow the user to move to other places within the document, or to open other documents, by activating the link.

2. A Web server stores the files used in creating World Wide Web documents. The Web browser retrieves the files from the Web server and displays them. The files stored on the Web server are described in a very general way; it is the Web browser that determines how the files will eventually appear to the user.

3. HTML, which stands for Hypertext Markup Language, is used to create Web documents.

4. HTML documents do not exactly specify the appearance of a document; rather they describe the purpose of different elements in the document and leave it to the Web browser to determine the final appearance. A word processor like Word exactly specifies the appearance of each document element.

5. Documents are transferred more quickly over the Internet and are available to a wider range of machines.

6. Extensions are special formats supported by a particular browser, but not generally accepted by all browsers. The advantage is that people who use that browser have a wider range of document elements to work with. The disadvantage is that the document will not work for users who do not have that particular browser.

7. All you need is a simple text editor.

Session 1.2

1. The <html> tag identifies the language of the file as HTML to packages that support more than one kind of generalized markup language.

2. <h1 align="center"> Heading text </h1>

3. <p> Paragraph text </p>

4. HTML does not recognize the blank lines as format elements. A Web browser ignores blank lines and runs the paragraphs together on the page.

5. Ordered list:

```
<ol>
    <li> List item
    <li> List item
</ol>
```

Unordered list:

```
<ul>
    <li> List item
    <li> List item
</ul>
```

Definition list:

```
<dl>
    <dt> List term <dd> Term definition
    <dt> List term <dd> Term definition
</dl>
```

6. <em> Italicized text </em>

   and

```
<i> Italicized text </i>
```

   The advantage of using the <em> tag is that it will be recognized even by older browsers that do not support italics (such as a terminal connected to a UNIX machine), and those browsers will still emphasize the text in some way. The <i> tag, on the other hand, will be ignored by those machines. Using the <i> tag has the advantage of explicitly describing how you want the text to appear.

Session 1.3

1. ©

2. <hr>

3. <hr width="70%" size="4">

4. An inline image is a GIF or JPEG file that appears in a Web document. A browser can display it without a file viewer.

5. An external image is a graphic that requires the use of a software program, called a viewer, to display it.

6. <img align="left" src="**mouse.jpg**">

7. GIF and JPEG

OBJECTIVES

In this tutorial you will:

- Create hypertext links between elements within a Web page

- Create hypertext links between Web pages

- Review basic Web page structures

- Create hypertext links to Web pages on the Internet

- Distinguish between and be able to use absolute and relative pathnames

- Create hypertext links to various Internet resources, including FTP servers and newsgroups

ADDING
HYPERTEXT LINKS TO A WEB PAGE

Developing a Chemistry Web Site with Hypertext Links

CASE

Creating a Chemistry Web Site, continued

In Tutorial 1 you created the basic structure and content of a Web page for Stephen Dubé, a chemistry teacher in Edmonton, Alberta. Stephen has made a few changes to the Web page, and he has ideas for additional content. Stephen notes that although the appearance of the Web page reflects the course handout on which he originally based his Web page, there are some limitations that he would like to see removed. For example, students and their parents must scroll through the document window to find information about his classes. Stephen wants to make it as easy to navigate from topic to topic on his Web page as it is to scan the single-page handout.

Stephen also wants to add more information to his Web site, but he is concerned about making the original page too large and difficult to navigate. He'd like to have a separate page that lists the ways students and parents can contact him (office hours, e-mail, phone numbers, and so forth). He also has found several helpful chemistry Web sites that he'd like to share with his students.

SESSION 2.1

In this session, you'll create anchors on a Web page that let users navigate to specific points within a document. After creating anchors, you'll create and test your first hypertext link.

Creating a Hypertext Document

In Tutorial 1 you learned that a hypertext document contains **hypertext links**, items that you can select, usually by clicking a mouse, to view another topic or document, often called the **destination** of the link. These links can point to another section in the same document, to a different document, to a different Web page, or to a variety of other Web objects, which you'll learn about later in this tutorial.

Stephen's Web page has two main sections: Chemistry Classes and Class Policies. You and Stephen have made some modifications, including removing the <h2> heading "Class Policies" and upgrading the three <h3> headings to <h2> headings. You have also added the new Applied Chemistry course to the Classes list, the numbered list to his Safety section, the spoonful of sugar sentence, and some horizontal lines. However, because of the document window's small size, the opening screen shows only the first heading in the document. The browser in Figure 2-1 displays Stephen's photo, his introductory paragraph, and the beginning of his Classes list, but nothing about Grading, Appointments, or Safety; users must scroll through the document to locate this information.

Figure 2-1	OPENING SCREEN OF STEPHEN'S CHEMISTRY PAGE

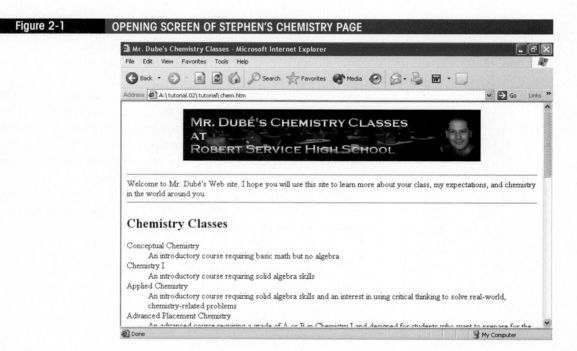

Without hypertext links, you can do little to show more of Stephen's page in the browser except remove the image file or move it to the end of the page, which he doesn't want you to do. One solution is to place text for the four headings (Classes, Grading, Appointments, and Safety) at the top of the document and make these headings hypertext links. When users open Stephen's page, they'll not only see his name and photo, but they will also see links to the main parts of his page. They can then click a link and navigate to that section of the document. The hypertext links that you create here point to sections within the same document. You'll create these hypertext links in Stephen's page using the following steps:

1. Type the headings into the HTML file.

2. Mark each section in the HTML file using an anchor. You'll learn about anchors shortly.

3. Link the text you added in Step 1 to the anchors you added in Step 2.

You can accomplish the first step using techniques you learned in Tutorial 1. You need to open the Chemistry text file in your text editor and then enter the text. You want the text to appear just above his introductory paragraph, as shown in Figure 2-2.

Figure 2-2	TEXT LINKS STEPHEN WANTS TO ADD

Classes · Grading · Appointments · Safety

Welcome to Mr. Dubé's Web site. I hope you will use this site to learn more about your class, my expectations, and chemistry in the world around you.

To achieve this, you place the text within paragraph tags that you'll center, and then you'll add the middle dot symbol (•) with a space on each side. You could type all the text into the HTML file on the same line, but to keep the HTML file as legible as possible, you'll add the text in two lines instead. This way, when you add more tags to the text later, it will still be easy to read. Remember, with HTML, placing text on different lines in the text file does not affect its appearance when viewed with a browser.

To add text that will become links in the Web page:

1. Start your text editor.

2. Open **chemtxt.htm** from the tutorial folder in the tutorial.02 folder on your Data Disk, and then save it as **chem.htm** in the tutorial folder so that the original remains intact.

TROUBLE? If you can't locate **chemtxt.htm** in the Tutorial folder in your text editor's Open dialog box, you may need to set the file type to All Files.

3. Before "Welcome to Mr. ...," type the following, pressing the **Enter** key at the end of each line:

```
<p align="center">
Classes &#183; 
Grading &#183; 
Appointments &#183; 
Safety</p>
```

See Figure 2-3. The new code uses the <p> tag with the center attribute to center the text. It includes the special character codes   and ·, which insert a middle dot surrounded by nonbreaking spaces, to separate the section headings.

Figure 2-3 | ADDING TEXT FOR THE LINKS

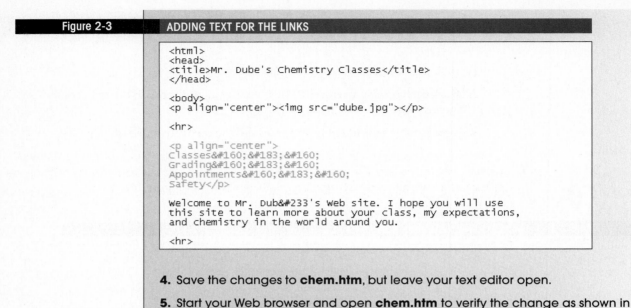

```
<html>
<head>
<title>Mr. Dube's Chemistry Classes</title>
</head>

<body>
<p align="center"><img src="dube.jpg"></p>

<hr>

<p align="center">
Classes &#183; 
Grading &#183; 
Appointments &#183; 
Safety</p>

Welcome to Mr. Dub&#233's web site. I hope you will use
this site to learn more about your class, my expectations,
and chemistry in the world around you.

<hr>
```

4. Save the changes to **chem.htm**, but leave your text editor open.

5. Start your Web browser and open **chem.htm** to verify the change as shown in Figure 2-4. You do not need to be connected to the Internet.

Figure 2-4 | TEXT ADDED FOR FUTURE LINKS

these four words will become links

Classes · Grading · Appointments · Safety

Welcome to Mr. Dubé's Web site. I hope you will use this site to learn more about your class, my expectations, and chemistry in the world around you.

Creating **Anchors**

Now that you've created the text describing the different sections of the Web page, you need to locate each heading in the document and mark it using the <a> tag. The <a> tag creates an **anchor**, text that is specially marked so that you can link to it from other points in the document. Text that is anchored is the destination of a link; it is not the text you click on. You assign each anchor its own anchor name, using the "name" attribute. For example, if you want the text "Chemistry Classes" to be an anchor, you could assign it the anchor name "cc":

```
<a name="cc">Classes</a>
```

Later, when you create a link to this anchor from the headings you just inserted at the beginning of Stephen's page, the link will point to this place in the document, identified by the anchor name, cc. Figure 2-5 illustrates how the anchor you create works as a reference point to a link.

Figure 2-5 **HOW AN ANCHOR WORKS**

MR. DUBÉ'S CHEMISTRY CLASSES
AT
ROBERT SERVICE HIGH SCHOOL

Classes · Grading · Appointments · Safety

Welcome to Mr. Dubé's Web site. I hope you will use this site to _____ out your class, my expectations, and chemistry in the world around you.

Chemistry Classes

Conceptual Chemistry
    An introductory course requiring basic math but no algebra
Chemistry I
    An introductory course requiring solid algebra skills
Applied Chemistry
    An introductory course requiring solid algebra skills and a_____ using critical thinking to solve real-world, chemistry-related problems
Advanced Placement Chemistry
    An advanced course requiring a grade of A or B in Che_____ designed for students who want to prepare for the AP Chemistry exam (which can count toward college _____

Grading

Homework will be given daily, is due at the beginning o_____ od the school day after it was assigned, and will be worth 5 to 10 points. A periodic quiz consisting of 1 or 2 homewo_____ blems from the past week may be given in lieu of collecting homework.

Tests and quizzes will be used to check your unde_____ ng of concepts, procedures, and information. Quizzes will be worth 10 to 25 points and will be given at least once a m_____ ests will be worth up to 100 points and will be given 2 or 3 times a quarter.

Labs will be worth 10 to 30 points and will be _____ d on safety, participation, and write-up. I expect neat handwritten or typed reports. I'll also assign _small research_ _ects_ throughout the semester.

You must _make up_ missed tests and quizz_____ e day you return, and you must submit missed homework assignments and labs within two days for every one day you m_____. Failure to make up work within these time frames will result in a 0 for that test or assignment.

Appointments

I can meet with you before or after school. I will also be in my room (H113) during most lunch hours. Please do not hesitate to stop in if you need extra help -- do not wait! Chemistry is a building subject, and it is very hard to catch up once you fall behind.

Safety

We will be doing lab work nearly every week. Because of the potential danger of any lab exercise, I will hold you to the highest standards of behavior, and will remove you from the class if you pose a threat to yourself or other students.

  1. Follow my written and oral directions carefully and immediately.
  2. Never perform any procedure not specifically directed by me or assigned in the lab.
  3. No playful behavior is permitted in the lab.
  4. Safety equipment must be worn as directed at all times, even if you find it uncomfortable or unbecoming.
  5. No food, drinks, or loose clothing are permitted in the lab.

Chemistry with Dubé is like medicine with a spoonful of $C_{12}H_{22}O_{11}$!

An anchor doesn't have to be text. You can also mark an inline image as an anchor using the same syntax:

```
<a name="photo"><img src="dube.jpg"></a>
```

In the above example, you anchor an image. You can create a link to this photo from other points in the document by using the anchor name "photo." As you'll see, adding an anchor does not change your document's appearance in any way. It merely creates locations in your Web page that become destinations of links.

REFERENCE WINDOW   RW

Creating Anchors
- Using your text editor, locate the text or graphic you want to anchor.
- Before the text or graphic, place the tag
  <a name="anchor_name"> where anchor_name is the name you assign to your anchor.
- Immediately after the text or image, place a closing </a> tag to turn off the anchor.

For Stephen's Chemistry file, you decide to create four anchors named cc, gra, app, and safe that correspond to Chemistry Classes, Grading, Appointments, and Safety sections.

To add anchors to the section headings:

1. Using your text editor, open **chem.htm** if it is not currently open.

2. Locate the <h2> heading for the Chemistry Classes section. This line currently reads:

   `<h2>Chemistry Classes</h2>`

3. Add an anchor tag around the Chemistry Classes heading so that it reads:

   `<h2><a name="cc">Chemistry Classes</a></h2>`

4. Locate the <h2> heading for the Grading section. This line currently reads:

   `<h2>Grading</h2>`

5. Add an anchor tag around the Grading heading so that it reads:

   `<h2><a name="gra">Grading</a></h2>`

6. Locate the <h2> heading for the Appointments section, which reads:

   `<h2>Appointments</h2>`

   and add an anchor tag so that it reads:

   `<h2><a name="app">Appointments</a></h2>`

7. Locate the <h2> heading for the Safety section, which reads:

   `<h2>Safety</h2>`

   and add an anchor tag so that it reads:

   `<h2><a name="safe">Safety</a></h2>`

8. Save your changes to **chem.htm**.

9. Using your Web browser, refresh or reload chem.htm, and scroll through the file to confirm that it appears unchanged. Remember that the anchors you placed in the document are reference points and do not change the appearance of the Web page.

   TROUBLE? If you see a change in the document, check to make sure that you correctly typed the code for adding anchors.

You created four anchors in the Web page. The next step is to create links to those anchors.

Creating **Links**

After you create the anchors that serve as destinations for your links, you need to create the links themselves. For Stephen's page, you want to link the headings that you centered above the introductory paragraph to the four sections in the document. Figure 2-6 shows the four links you want to create.

Figure 2-6   LINKS YOU'LL CREATE

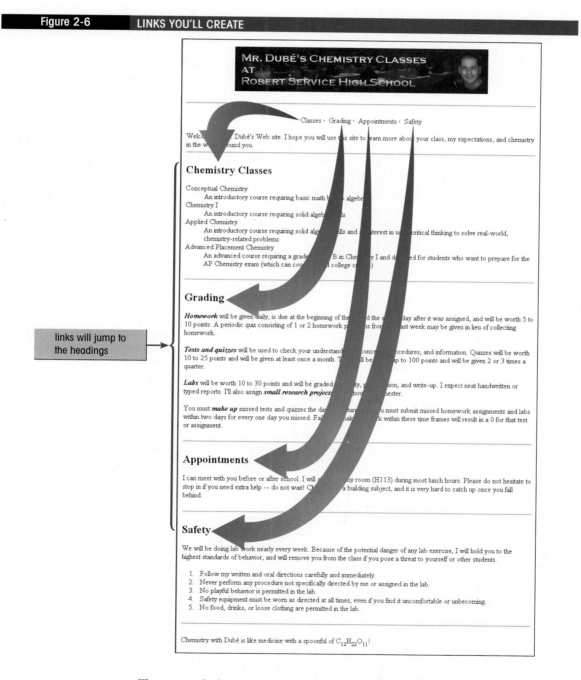

To create a link to an anchor, you use the same <a> tag you used to create the anchor. The difference is that instead of using the name attribute to define the anchor, you use the **href**

attribute, which is short for **Hypertext Reference**, to indicate the location to jump to. "href" can refer to an anchor that you place in the document or, as you'll see later, to a different Web page or a resource anywhere on the Internet. The <a> tags used to create links are sometimes called **link tags**.

You link to an anchor using the anchor name preceded by a pound (#) symbol. For example, to create a link to Stephen's Grading heading, you use the anchor name "gra" and the following HTML code:

```
<a href="#gra">Grading</a>
```

In this example, the entire word "Grading" is defined as a hypertext link. Clicking on any part of the word Grading (in a browser) navigates you to the location of the gra anchor.

You can also designate an inline image as a hypertext link. To turn an inline image into a hypertext link, place it within link tags, as follows:

```
<a href="#app"><img src="dube.jpg"></a>
```

REFERENCE WINDOW | **RW**

Linking to Text Within a Document

- Using your text editor, mark the destination text with an anchor, if you haven't already done so.
- Locate the text or image you want to designate as the link.
- Before the text or graphic, place the tag
  <a href="#anchor_name"> where anchor_name is the name of the anchor.
- Close the link tag with the </a> closing tag after the text or graphic you designated as the link.

It is important to note that the href attribute is case sensitive. Because of this, the anchor name "EMP" is not the same as "emp". Therefore, you should be careful to make each anchor name unique within a document. Using the same anchor name more than once creates confusion, and your links won't go where you expect them to.

In the current HTML document, you've created four anchors to which you can create links. You're ready to place the link tags around the appropriate text in the HTML file.

To add link tags to the Chemistry file:

1. Using your text editor, open **chem.htm** if it is not already open.

2. Locate the following lines of code:

```
<p align="center">
Classes &#183; 
Grading &#183; 
Appointments &#183; 
Safety</p>
```

and add the <a href> tags so the code reads:

```
<p align="center">
<a href="#cc">Classes</a> &#183; 
<a href="#gra">Grading</a> &#183; 
<a href="#app">Appointments</a> &#183; 
<a href="#safe">Safety</a></p>
```

3. Compare your **chem.htm** file to Figure 2-7.

Figure 2-7	ADDING LINK TAGS

```
<body>
<p align="center"><img src="dube.jpg"></p>

<hr>

<p align="center">
<a href="#cc">Classes</a> &#183; 
<a href="#gra">Grading</a> &#183; 
<a href="#app">Appointments</a> &#183; 
<a href="#safe">Safety</a></p>

Welcome to Mr. Dub&#233;'s web site. I hope you will use
this site to learn more about your class, my expectations,
and chemistry in the world around you.
```

4. Save your changes to **chem.htm**.

5. Using your Web browser, refresh or reload **chem.htm**. The headings should now be a different color and be underlined. This is the standard formatting for links. See Figure 2-8.

Figure 2-8	TEXT LINKS IN THE BROWSER

text formatted as links

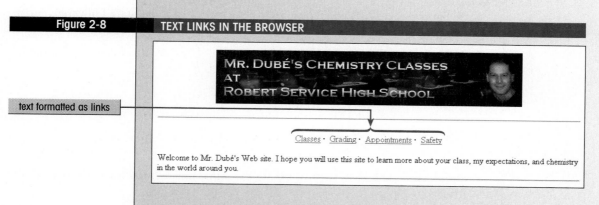

TROUBLE? If the headings do not appear as text links, check your code to make sure that you are using the <a> and </a> tags around the appropriate text, the href attribute within the tag, and the quotes and # symbols, as shown previously.

Before continuing, you should verify that the links work as you expect them to. To test a link, simply click it and see where it takes you.

To test your links:

1. Click one of the links. Your browser should display the section of the document indicated by the link. If it does not, check your code for errors by comparing it to Figure 2-7.

2. Click each of the other links, scrolling back to the top of the page after each test.

3. If you are continuing to Session 2.2, leave your browser and text editor open. If you are not, you can close them at this time.

TROUBLE? If your links still don't work, make sure you used the correct case and that you coded the anchor and link tags correctly.

When you add an anchor to a large section of text, such as a section heading, make sure to place the anchor within the heading tags. For example, write your tag as:

```
<h2><a name="gra">Grading</a></h2>
```

not as:

```
<a name="gra"><h2>Grading</h2></a>
```

The latter example can confuse some browsers. The general rule is to always place anchors within other tag elements. Do not insert any tag elements within an anchor, except for tags that create document objects such as inline graphics.

You show the new links to Stephen and he's confident that they will help his students and their parents to quickly find the information they want. In the next session, you'll learn how to create links that allow users to navigate to other HTML documents.

Session 2.1 QUICK CHECK

1. What is the HTML code for marking the text "Colorado State University" with the anchor name "csu"?

2. What is the HTML code for linking the text "Universities" to an anchor that is named "csu"?

3. What is wrong with the following statement?

   <a name="info"><h3>For more information</h3></a>

4. What is the HTML code for marking an inline image, **photo.jpg**, with the anchor name "photo"?

5. What is the HTML code for linking the inline image **button.jpg** to an anchor with the name "links"?

6. True or False: Anchor names are case-sensitive.

SESSION 2.2

In Session 2.1 you created hypertext links to locations within the same Web page. In this session you'll create links to other Web pages.

Stephen wants to add two more pages to his Chemistry site: a page showing his contact information and a page listing his favorite chemistry links. Both of these pages, in turn, require links of their own, making it easy to go from each of the three pages to the others. Figure 2-9 shows what he has in mind.

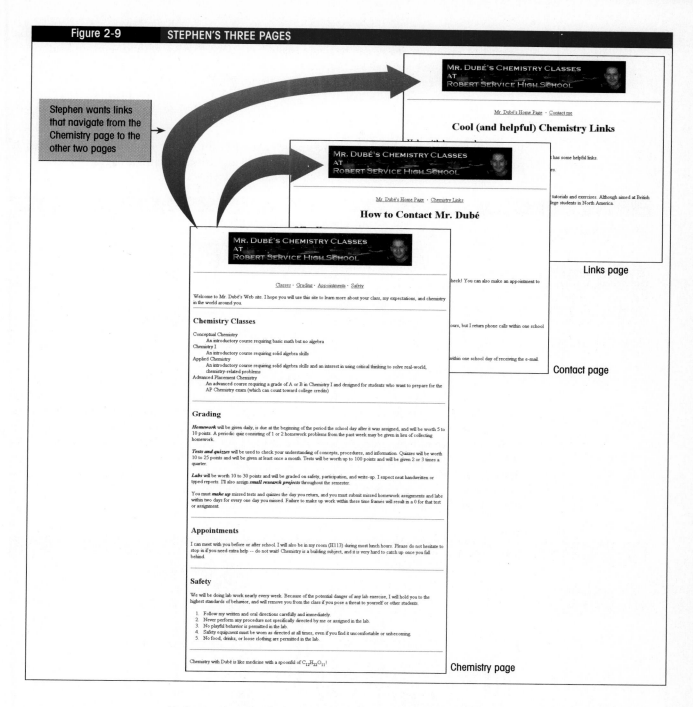

Figure 2-9   STEPHEN'S THREE PAGES

Stephen wants links that navigate from the Chemistry page to the other two pages

Links page

Contact page

Chemistry page

Before you start linking documents together as Stephen has instructed you to do, it would be a good idea to take a look at the basics of Web page structures.

Web Page Structures

The three pages that will make up Stephen's chemistry site, Chemistry, Contacts, and Links, are part of a system of Web pages. Before you set up links for navigating a group of Web pages, it's worthwhile to map out exactly how you want the pages to relate, using a technique known as storyboarding. **Storyboarding** your Web pages before you create links helps you determine which structure works best for the type of information you're presenting. You want to ensure that readers can navigate easily from page to page without getting lost.

You'll encounter several Web structures as you navigate the Web. Examining some of these structures can help you decide how to design your own system of Web pages.

Linear Structures

Figure 2-10 shows one common Web page structure, the **linear structure**, in which each page is linked to the next and to previous pages, in an ordered chain of pages.

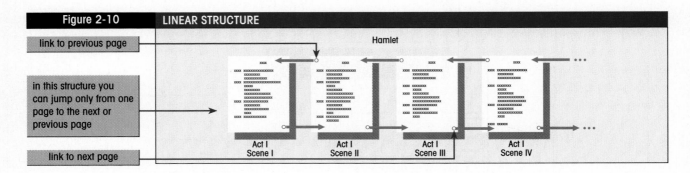

Figure 2-10   LINEAR STRUCTURE

link to previous page

in this structure you can jump only from one page to the next or previous page

link to next page

You could use this type of structure in Web pages that have a defined order. Suppose that a Web site of Shakespeare's *Hamlet* has a single page for each scene. If you use a linear structure for these pages, you assume that users want to progress through the scenes in a particular order.

You might, however, want to make it easier for users to return immediately to the opening scene, rather than backtrack through several scenes to get to their destination. Figure 2-11 shows an **augmented linear structure**, in which you include a link in each page that jumps directly back to the first page, while keeping the links that allow you to move to the next and previous pages. This kind of storyboarding can reveal approaches to organizing a Web site that otherwise you may have overlooked.

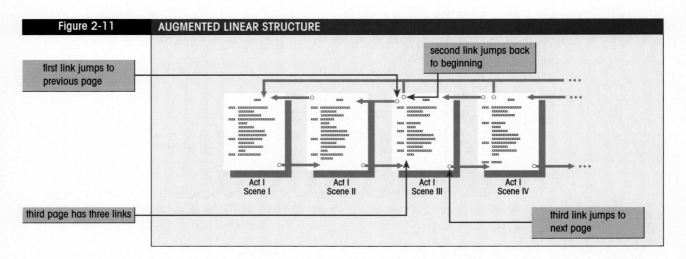

Figure 2-11   AUGMENTED LINEAR STRUCTURE

second link jumps back to beginning

first link jumps to previous page

third page has three links

third link jumps to next page

Hierarchical Structures

Another popular structure is the hierarchical structure of Web pages, shown in Figure 2-12. A **hierarchical structure** starts with a general topic that includes links to more specific topics. Each specific topic includes links to yet more specialized topics, and so on. In a hierarchical structure, users can move easily from general to specific and back, but not from specific to specific.

| Figure 2-12 | HIERARCHICAL STRUCTURE |

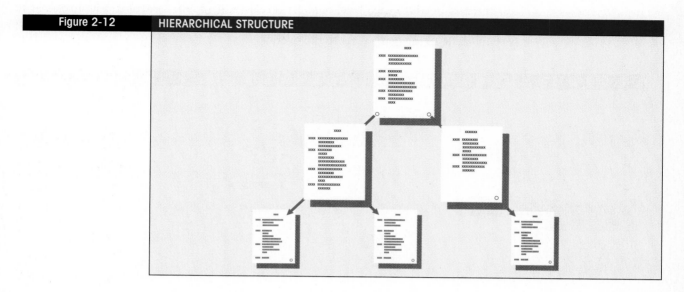

As with the linear structure, including a link to the top of the structure on each page gives users an easy path back to the beginning. Subject catalogs such as the AltaVista directory of Web pages often use this structure. Figure 2-13 shows this site, located at *http://www.altavista.com*.

| Figure 2-13 | HIERARCHICAL STRUCTURE ON ALTAVISTA WEB PAGE |

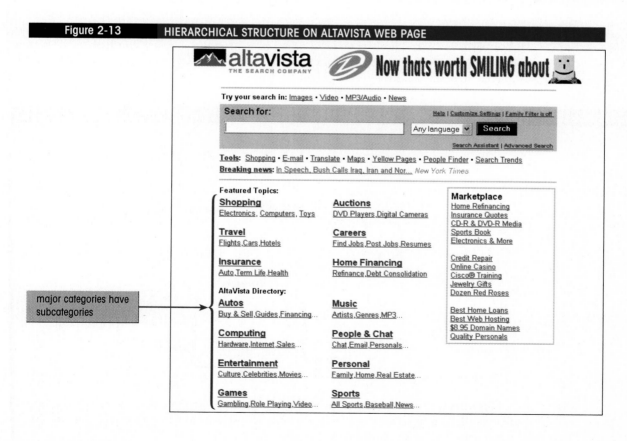

major categories have subcategories

Mixed Structures

As you may have guessed, you can also combine structures. Figure 2-14 shows a hierarchical structure in which each level of pages is related in a linear structure. You might use this system for the *Hamlet* Web site to let the user move from scene to scene linearly, or from a specific scene to the general act to the overall play.

| Figure 2-14 | COMBINATION OF LINEAR AND HIERARCHICAL STRUCTURES |

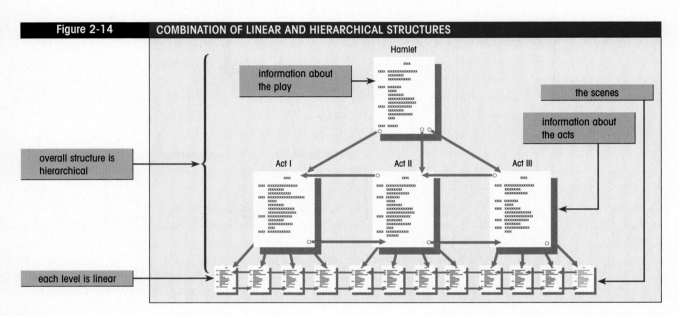

As these examples show, a little foresight can go a long way toward making your Web pages easier to use. The best time to organize a structure is when you first start creating pages, when those pages are small in number and more easily managed. If you're not careful, your structure might look like Figure 2-15.

| Figure 2-15 | MULTIPAGE DOCUMENT WITH NO COHERENT STRUCTURE |

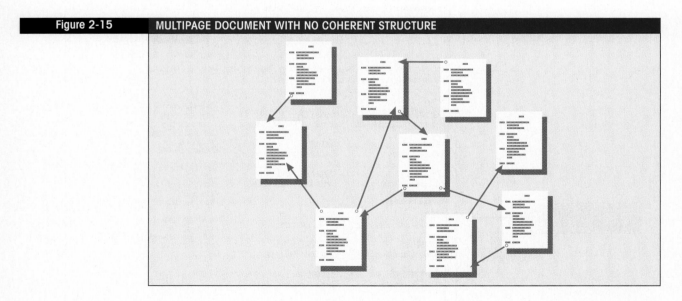

This structure is confusing, and it makes it difficult for readers to grasp the contents of the overall Web site. Moreover, a user who enters this structure at a certain page might not be aware of the presence of the other pages.

Creating **Links Among Documents**

You and Stephen discuss the type of structure that will work best for his chemistry pages. He wants students to be able to move effortlessly between the three documents. Because there are only three Web pages in this site and all focus on the same topic, you decide to include links within each document to the other two. For this relatively simple, three-page Web site, the structure shown in Figure 2-16 works just fine.

Figure 2-16	STRUCTURE OF MARY'S WEB PAGES

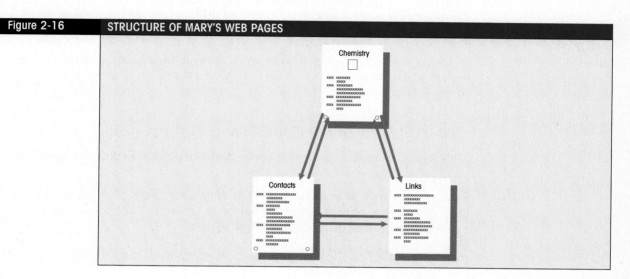

Stephen has given you the information to create two additional HTML files: **conttxt.htm**, a page containing his contact information; and **linktxt.htm**, a page containing links to various chemistry Web sites that he has found particularly helpful to his students. These files are located in the tutorial folder in the tutorial.02 folder on your Data Disk. You should save the text files with new names, **contact.htm** and **links.htm**, to keep the originals intact.

> *To rename the conttxt.htm and linktxt.htm files:*
>
> **1.** Using your text editor, open **conttxt.htm** from the tutorial folder in the tutorial.02 folder on your Data Disk, and save it as **contact.htm**.
>
> **2.** Using your text editor, open **linktxt.htm** from the tutorial folder in the tutorial.02 folder, and save it as **links.htm**.

Linking to a Document

You begin by linking Stephen's Chemistry page to the Contact and Links pages. Use the same <a> tag with the href attribute that you used earlier. For example, if you want a user to be able to click the phrase "Contact me" to navigate to the contact.htm file, you enter the following HTML code in your current document:

```
<a href="contact.htm">Contact me</a>
```

In this example, the phrase "Contact me" is linked to the HTML file contact.htm. In order for the browser to be able to locate and open contact.htm, it must be in the same folder as the chem.htm file, the document containing the link.

REFERENCE WINDOW   RW

Linking to a Document on Your Computer
■ Using your text editor, locate the text or image you want to act as a link.
■ Before the text or image, insert the following code:
   `<a href="filename">`
   where filename is the name of the destination document.
■ After the text or image link, place the tag `</a>`.

Unlike creating hypertext links between elements on the same page, this process does not require you to set an anchor in a file to link to it; the filename serves as the anchor or destination point.

To add links to the Contact and Links pages:

1. Using your text editor, open **chem.htm** that you worked on in Session 2.1 of this tutorial. You can close **links.htm**.

2. Locate the links you created in the last session, just above the introductory "Welcome" paragraph, and if necessary, insert a blank line below the links and above the introductory paragraph.

3. In the blank line, type:

   ```
   <p align="center">
   <a href="contact.htm">Contact me</a>
   ```

   Do not include a closing `</p>` tag; you'll do that in a moment.

4. Press the **Enter** key to move to the next line, and then type:

   ```
    &#183; 
   <a href="links.htm">Chemistry Links</a></p>
   ```

   See Figure 2-17.

| Figure 2-17 | LINKING TO OTHER FILES |

```
<body>
<p align="center"><img src="dube.jpg"></p>

<hr>

<p align="center">
<a href="#cc">Classes</a> &#183; 
<a href="#gra">Grading</a> &#183; 
<a href="#app">Appointments</a> &#183; 
<a href="#safe">Safety</a></p>

<p align="center">
<a href="contact.htm">Contact me</a>
 &#183; 
<a href="links.htm">Chemistry Links</a></p>

Welcome to Mr. Dub&#233;'s web site. I hope you will use
this site to learn more about your class, my expectations,
and chemistry in the world around you.
```

<a> tags to point to other files

5. Save your changes to **chem.htm**.

6. Using your Web browser, view **chem.htm**. The two new, external text links are displayed below the four internal links, as shown in Figure 2-18.

Figure 2-18   BROWSER DISPLAYING LINKS TO OTHER DOCUMENTS

links to the Contact
and Links pages

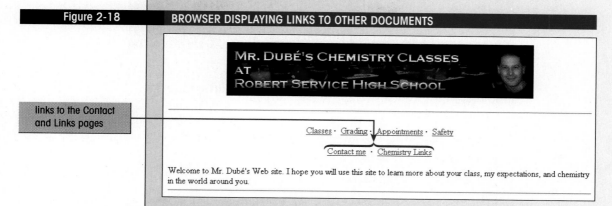

Welcome to Mr. Dubé's Web site. I hope you will use this site to learn more about your class, my expectations, and chemistry in the world around you.

7. Click the **Contact me** link to verify that you navigate to the Contact page as shown in Figure 2-19.

Figure 2-19   CONTACT PAGE IN THE BROWSER

MR. DUBÉ'S CHEMISTRY CLASSES
AT
ROBERT SERVICE HIGH SCHOOL

How to Contact Mr. Dubé

Office Hours

I'm in my room, H113, during the following times each day:

- 6:45 a.m. until Period 1 begins at 7:30 a.m.
- lunch hour (11:10 a.m. to 11:50 a.m.)
- 2:30 p.m. until at least 3:00 p.m.

I am often there earlier in the morning and later in the afternoon, so stop by to check! You can also make an appointment to see me if those times don't work for you.

Address and Phone

You can write me at 5587 Abbot Road, Edmonton, Alberta T5H 4G9.

My phone number is 780-555-0955, ext. 230. I am unreachable during class hours, but I return phone calls within one school day of receiving a message.

E-mail

E-mail is a great way to reach me. I answer e-mails from students and parents within one school day of receiving the e-mail. My address is sdube@eps.edmonton.ab.ca.

TROUBLE? If the link doesn't work, check to see that **chem.htm** and **contact.htm** are in the same folder on your Data Disk.

8. Go back to the Chemistry page (usually by clicking a Back button on the tool-bar of your browser), and then click **Chemistry Links** to verify that you navigate to the Links page as shown in Figure 2-20.

Figure 2-20   LINKS PAGE IN THE BROWSER

MR. DUBÉ'S CHEMISTRY CLASSES AT ROBERT SERVICE HIGH SCHOOL

Cool (and helpful) Chemistry Links

Help with homework

Homework Central No, this site won't do your homework for you, but it has some helpful links.

Academic Assistance A free service offering help in a variety of disciplines.

Practice tests and quizzes

Aufbaul An extensive and somewhat unconventional on-line resource for tutorials and exercises. Although aimed at British middle-school students, this will likely be suitable for high school and college students in North America.

ChemTutor Basic help for high school and college chemistry students.

Research resources

ChemTeam A solid chemistry course with plenty of links.

Chemistry Coach A collection of great links for high school chemistry.

The next step is to add similar links in the contact.htm and links.htm files that point to the other two pages. Specifically, in contact.htm, you need to add one link to chem.htm and another to links.htm; in links.htm you need one link to chem.htm and another to contact.htm. This way, each page will have links that point to the other two pages.

To add links in the Contact page to the Chemistry and Links pages:

1. Using your text editor, open **contact.htm** from the tutorial folder in the tutorial.02 folder on your Data Disk.

2. Locate the <hr> tag near the top of the page, and then in the blank line below it, type the following:

```
<p align="center">
<a href="chem.htm">Mr. Dub&#233;'s Home page</a>
 &#183; 
<a href="links.htm">Chemistry Links</a></p>
```

3. Compare your code to Figure 2-21.

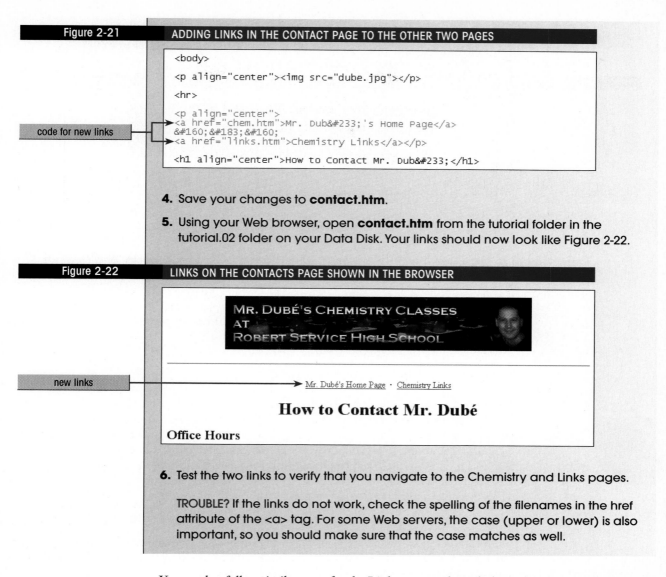

| Figure 2-21 | ADDING LINKS IN THE CONTACT PAGE TO THE OTHER TWO PAGES |

code for new links

```
<body>

<p align="center"><img src="dube.jpg"></p>

<hr>

<p align="center">
<a href="chem.htm">Mr. Dub&#233;'s Home Page</a>
 &#183; 
<a href="links.htm">Chemistry Links</a></p>

<h1 align="center">How to Contact Mr. Dub&#233;</h1>
```

4. Save your changes to **contact.htm**.

5. Using your Web browser, open **contact.htm** from the tutorial folder in the tutorial.02 folder on your Data Disk. Your links should now look like Figure 2-22.

| Figure 2-22 | LINKS ON THE CONTACTS PAGE SHOWN IN THE BROWSER |

new links

> MR. DUBÉ'S CHEMISTRY CLASSES
> AT
> ROBERT SERVICE HIGH SCHOOL
>
> Mr. Dubé's Home Page · Chemistry Links
>
> ### How to Contact Mr. Dubé
>
> **Office Hours**

6. Test the two links to verify that you navigate to the Chemistry and Links pages.

TROUBLE? If the links do not work, check the spelling of the filenames in the href attribute of the <a> tag. For some Web servers, the case (upper or lower) is also important, so you should make sure that the case matches as well.

You need to follow similar steps for the Links page so that it links to the two other Web pages.

To add links in the Links page to the Chemistry and Contact pages:

1. Using your text editor, open **links.htm** from the tutorial folder in the tutorial.02 folder on your Data Disk. You can close contact.htm.

2. Locate the <hr> tag near the top of the page, and then in the blank line below it, type the following:

```
<p align="center">
<a href="chem.htm">Mr. Dub&#233;'s Home Page</a>
 &#183; 
<a href="contact.htm">Contact me</a></p>
```

3. Save your changes to **links.htm**.

4. Using your Web browser, open **links.htm** from the tutorial folder in the tutorial.02 folder on your Data Disk. You should see the links shown in Figure 2-23.

| Figure 2-23 | NEW LINKS ON THE LINKS PAGE |

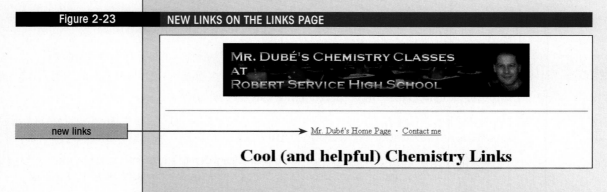

new links

MR. DUBÉ'S CHEMISTRY CLASSES AT ROBERT SERVICE HIGH SCHOOL

Mr. Dubé's Home Page · Contact me

Cool (and helpful) Chemistry Links

5. Click the two links to verify that you navigate to the Chemistry and Contact Web pages.

Now that you have established links among the three Web pages, users can easily navigate to and from each of the three pages.

Linking to a Section of a Document

When testing your links, you may have noticed that you always navigate to the top of the destination page. What if you'd like to navigate to a specific location elsewhere in a document, rather than to the top of the page? To do this, you can set anchors as you did in Session 2.1 and link to an anchor you create within the document. For example, to create a link to a section in the Web page home.htm marked with an anchor name of "interests," you create an anchor in home.htm in the section on Interests, and then enter the following HTML code in your current document:

```
<a href="home.htm#interests">View my interests</a>
```

In this example, the entire text, "View my interests," is linked to the Interests section in the home.htm file, via the anchor name "interests." Note that the pound symbol (#) in this tag distinguishes the filename from the anchor name (that is why you included the # symbol earlier when linking to anchors within the same document).

Stephen wants to link three of the topics in his Grading section to specific sections in the Links page. The links.htm file already has these anchors in place:

- "home," for the chemistry links related to help with homework
- "test," for the chemistry links on practice tests and quizzes
- "search," for the chemistry links that are helpful in preparing research projects

Now you need to link the phrases listed in the Grading section of the Chemistry file ("Homework," "Tests and quizzes," and "small research projects") to these three anchors in the Links Web page.

To add links to the Chemistry Web page that navigate to anchors located in the Links Web page:

1. Using your text editor, open **chem.htm**. You can close the Links file at this time.

2. Locate the Grading section near the middle of the chemistry file.

   As you enter the following code, be sure not to alter any other code, such as the <p>, <i>, and <b> tags.

3. Locate the word "Homework" and replace it with the following code:

   ```
   <p><i><b><a href="links.htm#home">Homework</a></b></i>
   ```

4. Locate the phrase "Tests and quizzes" and replace it with the following code:

   ```
   <p><i><b><a href="links.htm#test">Tests and quizzes</a>
   </b></i>
   ```

5. Locate the phrase "small research projects" and replace it with the following code:

   ```
   <i><b><a href="links.htm#search">small research
   projects</a></b></i>
   ```

   See Figure 2-24.

Figure 2-24   **ADDING LINKS TO SPECIFIC LOCATIONS IN A PAGE**

```
<h2><a name="gra">Grading</a></h2>
<p><i><b><a href="links.htm#home">Homework</a></b></i> will be given
daily, is due at the beginning of the period the school day
after it was assigned, and will be worth 5 to 10 points.
A periodic quiz consisting of 1 or 2 homework problems from the past
week may be given in lieu of collecting homework.</p>

<p><i><b><a href="links.htm#test">Tests and quizzes</a></b></i> will
be used to check your understanding of concepts, procedures, and
information. Quizzes will be worth 10 to 25 points and will be given
at least once a month. Tests will be worth up to 100 points
and will be given 2 or 3 times a quarter.</p>

<p><i><b>Labs</b></i> will be worth 10 to 30 points
and will be graded on safety, participation, and write-up.
I expect neat handwritten or typed reports. I'll also assign
<i><b><a href="links.htm#search">small research projects</a></b></i>
throughout the semester.</p>

<p>You must <i><b>make up</b></i> missed tests and quizzes
the day you return, and you must submit missed homework assignments
and labs within two days for every one day you missed.
Failure to make up work within these time frames will result
in a 0 for that test or assignment.</p>

<hr>
```

6. Save your changes to **chem.htm**.

7. Using your Web browser, refresh or reload **chem.htm**. The phrases in the Grading section are now displayed as text links, as shown in Figure 2-25.

Figure 2-25   **LINKS IN THE CHEMISTRY PAGE THAT POINT TO ANCHORS IN THE LINKS PAGE**

Grading

Homework will be given daily, is due at the beginning of the period the school day after it was assigned, and will be worth 5 to 10 points. A periodic quiz consisting of 1 or 2 homework problems from the past week may be given in lieu of collecting homework.

links

Tests and quizzes will be used to check your understanding of concepts, procedures, and information. Quizzes will be worth 10 to 25 points and will be given at least once a month. Tests will be worth up to 100 points and will be given 2 or 3 times a quarter.

Labs will be worth 10 to 30 points and will be graded on safety, participation, and write-up. I expect neat handwritten or typed reports. I'll also assign *small research projects* throughout the semester.

You must **make up** missed tests and quizzes the day you return, and you must submit missed homework assignments and labs within two days for every one day you missed. Failure to make up work within these time frames will result in a 0 for that test or assignment.

8. Click the three links you created to verify that you navigate to the appropriate places in the Links page.

TROUBLE? If you are having problems with your links, remember that anchors are case sensitive. Be sure you typed "home", "test", and "search" in all lower-case letters.

9. If you are continuing to Session 2.3, you can leave your browser and text editor open. Otherwise, close them.

With these last hypertext links in place, you have given users of Stephen's Web page easy access to additional information. In the next session, you'll learn how to create hypertext links that navigate to documents and resources located throughout the Internet.

Session 2.2 QUICK CHECK

1. What is storyboarding? Why is it important in creating a Web page system?

2. What is a linear structure?

3. What is a hierarchical structure?

4. What is the purpose of the pound symbol (#) when creating a link to an anchor in a separate Web page?

5. What code would you enter to link the text "Sports info" to the HTML file sports.htm?

6. What code would you enter to link the text "Basketball news" to the HTML file sports.htm at a place in the file with the anchor name "bball"?

SESSION 2.3

In Session 2.2 you created links to other documents located within the same folder as chem.htm. In this session you'll learn to create hypertext links to documents located in other folders as well as to other locations on the Internet. You'll also see how to display linked documents in separate browser windows.

Stephen wants to add a new link in the Chemistry page that points to the College Board's Web page on Advanced Placement tests. This Web page provides an overview of the Advanced Placement program and provides help for preparing for the AP tests. Before you can create this link for Stephen, you need to review the way HTML links to files located in different folders and computers.

Linking to Documents in Other Folders

Until now you've worked with documents located in the same folder. When you created links to other files in that folder, you specified the filename in the link tag but not its location. Browsers assume that if no folder information is given, the file is in the same folder as the current document. In some situations, such as when working with large multidocument systems that span several topics, you might want to place different files in different folders to help you stay organized.

When referencing a file located in a different folder than the link tag, you must include the location, or **path**, for the file. HTML supports two kinds of paths: absolute paths and relative paths.

Absolute Pathnames

An **absolute path** provides a precise location for a file. With HTML, absolute pathnames begin with a slash (/) and are followed by a sequence of folders beginning with the highest-level folder and proceeding to the folder that contains the file. Each folder is separated by a slash. Finally, after you type the name of the folder that contains the file, you type a final slash and then the filename itself.

For example, consider the folder structure shown in Figure 2-26.

Figure 2-26	FOLDER TREE

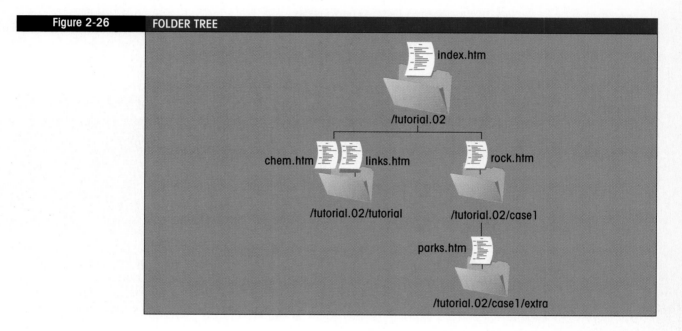

Figure 2-26 shows five HTML files that are located in four different folders. The topmost folder is the tutorial.02 folder. Within the tutorial.02 folder are the tutorial and case1 folders, and within the case1 folder is the extra folder. Figure 2-27 shows absolute pathnames for the five files.

Figure 2-27	ABSOLUTE PATHNAMES

ABSOLUTE PATHNAME	INTERPRETATION
/tutorial.02/index.htm	The index.htm file in the tutorial.02 folder
/tutorial.02/tutorial/chem.htm	The chem.htm file in the tutorial folder, a subfolder of the tutorial.02 folder
/tutorial.02/tutorial/links.htm	The links.htm file in the same folder as the chem.htm file
/tutorial.02/case1/rock.htm	The rock.htm file in the case1 folder, another subfolder of the tutorial.02 folder
/tutorial.02/case1/extra/parks.htm	The parks.htm file in the extra folder, a subfolder of the /tutorial.02/case1 folder

Even the absolute pathnames for files located on different computers begin with a slash. To differentiate these files, HTML requires you to include the drive letter followed by a vertical bar (|). For example, a file named "chem.htm" in the tutorial.02 folder on drive C of your computer has the absolute pathname "/C|/tutorial.02.chem.htm".

Relative Pathnames

When there are many folders and subfolders involved, absolute pathnames can be cumbersome and confusing. For that reason, most Web designers use **relative pathnames** in their hypertext links. A relative path specifies the location for a file in relation to the folder containing the current Web document. As with absolute pathnames, folder names are separated by slashes. Unlike absolute pathnames, however, a relative pathname does not begin with a slash. To reference a file in a folder directly above the current folder in the folder hierarchy, relative pathnames use two periods (..).

For example, if the current folder is the tutorial.02/tutorial folder shown in Figure 2-26, the relative pathnames and their interpretations for the other four files in the folder tree are displayed in Figure 2-28.

Figure 2-28	RELATIVE PATHNAMES
RELATIVE PATHNAME	**INTERPRETATION**
../index.htm	The index.htm file in the folder one level up in the folder tree from the current folder
../tutorial/chem.htm	The chem.htm file in the tutorial subfolder one level up in the folder tree from the current folder
rock.htm	The rock.htm file in the current folder
extra/parks.htm	The parks.htm file in the extra subfolder, one level down from the current folder

A second reason to use relative pathnames is that they make your hypertext links portable. If you have to move your files to a different computer or server, you can move the entire folder structure and still use the relative pathnames you've specified for the hypertext links. If absolute pathnames are used, each link has to be revised. This can be a very tedious process.

Linking to Documents on the Internet

Now you can turn your attention to creating a link on Stephen's chemistry page to the Advanced Placement page. To create a hypertext link to a document on the Internet, you need to know its URL. A **URL**, or **Uniform Resource Locator**, specifies a precise location on the Web for a file. The URL for the College Board Web page, for example, is *http://www.collegeboard.com/ap/students/*. You can find the URL of a Web page in the Location or Address box of your browser's document window.

Once you know a document's URL, you can create a link to it by adding the URL to the <a> tag along with the href attribute in your text file. For example, to create a link to a document on the Internet with the URL *http://www.mwu.edu/course/info.html*, you use this HTML code:

```
<a href="http://www.mwu.edu/course/info.html">Course
Information</a>
```

This example links the text "Course Information" to the Internet document located at *http://www.mwu.edu/course/info.html*. As long as your computer is connected to the Internet, clicking the text within the tag navigates you to the document located at the specified URL. Note that this link is for illustrative purposes only.

REFERENCE WINDOW   **RW**

Linking to a Document on the Internet
- Using your text editor, locate the text or image you want to designate as the link.
- Before the text or image, place the tag <a href="url"> where url is the URL of the Web page you are linking to.
- Following the text or image, insert the </a> closing tag.

Displaying **Linked Documents in a New Window**

By default, each Web page you open is displayed in the main browser window, replacing the one you were viewing last. This means that when users click Stephen's AP Chemistry link, they will leave his Web site; to get back, they would have to click their browser's Back button. He would prefer that his Web site stay open, and that when a link navigates to a page outside of his chemistry site, a second browser window opens. This will allow students and parents to "stay" with his chemistry Web site, even as they're browsing other sites.

To force a document to appear in a new window, you use the target attribute in the href tag. The general syntax is:

```
<a href="url" target="window">Hypertext</a>
```

where *url* is the URL of the page, and *window* is a name assigned to the new browser window. The value you use for the target attribute doesn't affect the appearance or content of the window; it's simply used by the browser to identify the different open windows in the current browser session.

You can set up your external hyperlinks to open in the same browser window by using the same value for the target attribute.

If you do, the first hyperlink clicked opens the new window and displays the contents of the external file. As subsequent external hyperlinks are clicked, they replace the contents of the already opened window, and the contents of the main browser window remain unaffected.

If you want your external documents to be displayed in their own browser window, you can assign a unique target value for each hyperlink, or you can assign the _blank keyword to the target attribute as follows:

```
<a href="url" target=_blank>Hypertext</a>
```

Note that you do *not* enclose the _blank keyword in quotation marks.

In the links at the top of the page, Stephen wants to add the link text "College Board AP" to navigate to the College Board Advanced Placement page. Because this is a page outside of his chemistry site, he wants it to appear in a new browser window. He'll give the new browser window the target name "new_window".

To add a link to the College Board AP page from Stephen's Chemistry page:

1. Using your text editor, open **chem.htm**, the file you worked on in Session 2.2 of this tutorial.

2. Locate the links section near the top of the page.

3. In the code containing "Contact me" and "Chemistry Links", place the insertion point just before the closing </p> tag, press the **Enter** key to create a blank line, and then type the following code:

```
 &#183;&160;
<a href="http://www.collegeboard.org/ap/students/"
target="new_window">
AP Information</a>
```

Be sure to leave the closing </p> tag intact.

4. Save your changes to **chem.htm**.

5. Using your Web browser while connected to the Internet, open **chem.htm**. The College Board entry should look like the text link shown in Figure 2-29.

| Figure 2-29 | LINK TO ANOTHER PAGE ON THE WEB |

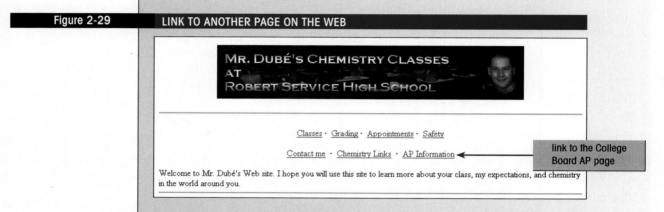

6. Click the **AP Information** link to navigate to the College Board Web site. The page is displayed in a new window as shown in Figure 2-30.

| Figure 2-30 | COLLEGE BOARD AP PAGE |

Stephen's Chemistry page remains open in the original browser window

AP page in a separate browser window

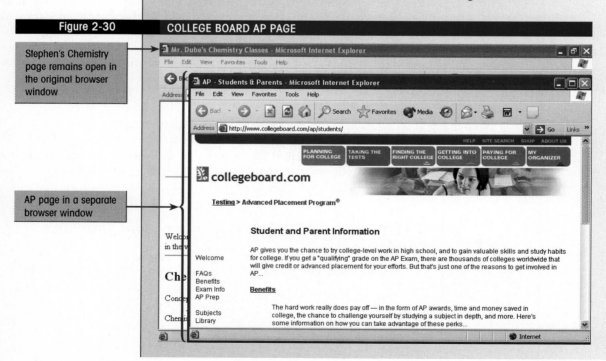

> TROUBLE? If the College Board AP page doesn't display right away, it might just be loading slowly on your system. If the page fails to display, verify that your computer is connected to the Internet. Also, since Web pages are updated regularly, the page may look quite different from the one shown in Figure 2-30.
>
> **7.** Close the second browser window and return to Stephen's Web page in the main browser window.

Linking to Other Internet Objects

Occasionally you see a URL for an Internet object other than a Web page. Remember that one reason for the World Wide Web's success is that it allows users to access several types of Internet resources with a browser. The method you used to create a link to the College Board Advanced Placement page is the same method you use to create links to other Internet resources, such as FTP servers or Usenet newsgroups (you'll learn what these are in the sections that follow). Only the URL for each object is required.

Each URL follows the same format. The first portion of the URL identifies the **communication protocol**, which is a set of rules that governs how information is exchanged. Web pages use the communication protocol **HTTP**, short for **Hypertext Transfer Protocol**, so all Web page URLs begin with the letters "http". Other Internet resources use different communication protocols. Following the communication protocol, there is typically a separator, such as a colon and two slashes (://). The exact separator depends on the Internet resource. The rest of the URL identifies the location of the document or resource on the Internet. Figure 2-31 interprets a Web page with the URL

```
http://www.mwu.edu/course/info.html#majors
```

Figure 2-31	INTERPRETING PARTS OF A URL
PART OF URL	**INTERPRETATION**
http://	The communication protocol
www.mwu.edu	The Internet host name for the computer storing the document
/course/info.html	The pathname and filename of the document on the computer
#majors	An anchor in the document

You may have noticed that many URLs don't seem to have any path or file information (such as *www.course.com*). By convention, if the path and filename are left off the URL, the browser searches for a file named "index.html" or "index.htm" in the root folder of the Web server; this file is often the home page of the Web site. Note that the path can be expressed in relative or absolute terms.

Before you walk Stephen through the task of creating the final link for his Web page, you take the time to show him how to create links to other Internet resources. It is not the objective of this tutorial to teach you about these resources in detail, but rather to show you how to reference them in your HTML files.

Linking to FTP Servers

FTP servers can store files that Internet users can download, or transfer, to their computers. **FTP**, short for **File Transfer Protocol**, is the communications protocol these file servers use to transfer information. URLs for FTP servers follow the same format as those for Web pages, except that they use the FTP protocol rather than the HTTP protocol: ftp://ftp.hostname. For example, to create a link to the FTP server located at *ftp.microsoft.com*, you use the following HTML code:

```
<a href="ftp://ftp.microsoft.com">Microsoft FTP server</a>
```

In this example, clicking the text "Microsoft FTP server" navigates the user to the Microsoft FTP server page as shown in Figure 2-32. Note that different browsers can display the contents of the FTP site in different ways. Figure 2-32 shows what it might look like with Internet Explorer.

| Figure 2-32 | FTP SERVER AT FTP.MICROSOFT.COM |

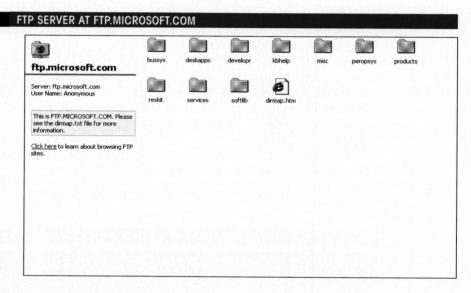

Linking to Usenet News

Usenet is a collection of discussion forums called **newsgroups** that let users exchange messages with other users on a wide variety of topics. The URL for a newsgroup is news:newsgroup. To access the surfing newsgroup alt.surfing, you place this line in your HTML file:

```
<a href="news:alt.surfing">Go to the surfing newsgroup</a>
```

When you click a link to a newsgroup, your computer starts your newsgroup software and accesses the newsgroup. For example, if you have the Outlook Newsreader program installed, clicking the link opens the window shown in Figure 2-33.

Figure 2-33	ACCESSING THE ALT.SURFING NEWSGROUP

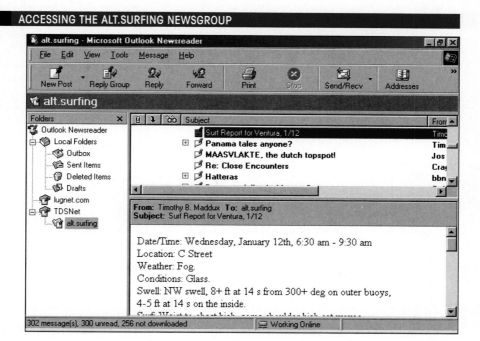

Linking to E-mail

Many Web designers include their e-mail addresses on their Web pages so that users who access the page can send feedback. You can identify e-mail addresses as hypertext links. When a user clicks the e-mail address, the browser starts a mail program and automatically inserts the e-mail address into the "To" field of the outgoing message. The URL for an e-mail address is mailto:*e-mail_address*. To create a link to the e-mail address davis@mwu.edu, for example, enter the following code into your document:

```
<a href="mailto:davis@mwu.edu">davis@mwu.edu</a>
```

If a user on the Web clicks the text davis@mwu.edu and has Microsoft Outlook installed as the default e-mail program, the window shown in Figure 2-34 is displayed.

Figure 2-34　　MAIL MESSAGE WINDOW

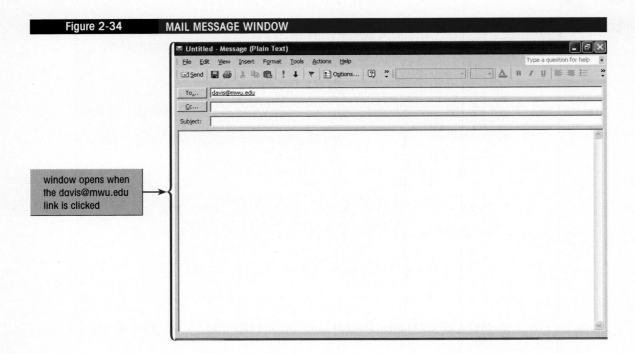

window opens when
the davis@mwu.edu
link is clicked

Adding an E-mail Link to Stephen's Chemistry Page

The last thing Stephen wants you to add to his Web pages is a link to his e-mail address. With this link, students and their parents can quickly send him messages via the Internet.

Stephen placed his e-mail address on his Contact page. You need to designate that text as a link so that when a user clicks it, an e-mail program window opens similar to the one shown in Figure 2-34.

To add an e-mail link to Stephen's Contact page:

1. Using your text editor, open **contact.htm**. You can close **chem.htm**.

2. Delete the text "My address is sdube@eps.ab.ca." located near the bottom of the file in the e-mail section.

   Students no longer need to know what Stephen's e-mail address is, because the link will insert it automatically into the "To" field in the mail message window.

3. After the text "...receiving the e-mail.", press the **Enter** key to create a blank line, and then type the following code:

   ```
   <a href="mailto:sdube@eps.edmonton.ab.ca">Click here</a>
   to send me an e-mail.
   ```

   Be sure to leave the closing </p> tag intact.

4. Save your changes to **contact.htm**.

5. Using your Web browser, open **contact.htm**.

6. Scroll to the bottom of the page. The link should look like the one shown in Figure 2-35.

Figure 2-35	BROWSER SHOWING LINK TO STEPHEN'S E-MAIL ADDRESS

the address itself is in the code for the mailto: URL

E-mail

E-mail is a great way to reach me. I answer e-mails from students and parents within one school day of receiving the e-mail. Click here to send me an e-mail.

TROUBLE? Some browsers do not support the mailto: URL. If you use a browser other than Netscape Navigator or Internet Explorer, check to see if it supports this feature.

7. Click the **Click here** hypertext link to Stephen's e-mail address. An e-mail message window opens, similar to the one in Figure 2-36.

Figure 2-36	TESTING STEPHEN'S E-MAIL LINK

mail message window opens with Stephen's e-mail address already inserted

Untitled - Message (Plain Text)

File   Edit   View   Insert   Format   Tools   Actions   Help   Type a question for help

Send   Options...   B I U

To...   sdube@eps.edmonton.ab.ca

Cc...

Subject:

TROUBLE? Your e-mail window may look different, depending on the mail program you are using.

8. Cancel the mail message by clicking the Close button in the upper-right corner of the window. Stephen's e-mail address is fictional, so you can't send him mail anyway.

9. Close your Web browser and text editor.

You show Stephen the final version of the three Web pages you have been collaborating on. He's thrilled with the results. You explain to him that the next step is to contact an Internet service provider and transfer the files to an account on that provider's server. When that's done, Stephen's Web pages become available online to anyone with Internet access.

Session 2.3 QUICK CHECK

1. What's the difference between an absolute path and a relative path?

2. Refer to Figure 2-26. If the current file is parks.htm in the tutorial.02/case1/extra folder, what are the relative pathnames for the four other files?

3. What tag would you enter to link the text "White House" to the URL *http://www.whitehouse.gov*? Have this link displayed in a new browser window named "GovWin".

4. What tag would you enter to link the text "Washington" to the FTP server at *ftp.uwash.edu*?

5. What tag would you enter to link the text "Boxing" to the newsgroup *rec.sports.boxing.pro*?

6. What tag would you enter to link the text "President" to the e-mail address president@whitehouse.gov?

REVIEW ASSIGNMENTS

Stephen would like you to add a few more items to his chemistry Web pages. Since the main Chemistry page is quite long, he wants to add a link at the bottom of the page so that users can easily return to the top of the page. Additionally, in the Chemistry Classes section, he'd like to add a phrase to the Advanced Placement Chemistry course, "click for AP resources," that links to an anchor in the Links page. He's added links to some pages that will be especially helpful for AP Chemistry students. Finally, in the Appointments section, he would like the text "I can meet with you" to link to his Contact page so that students can quickly reach him for help. The final page is shown in Figure 2-37.

Figure 2-37

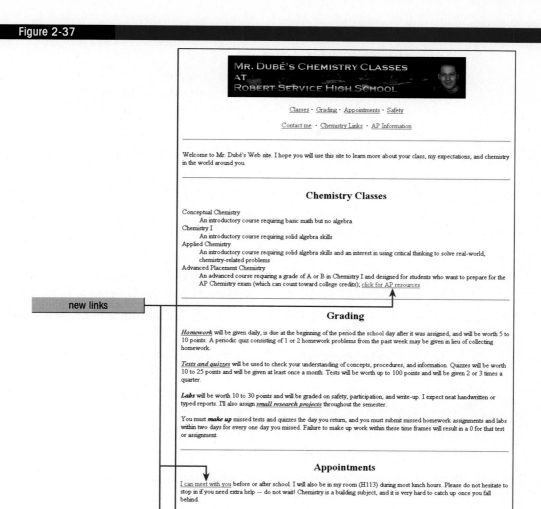

1. Using your text editor, open the **chem2txt.htm** file located in the review folder in the tutorial.02 folder on your Data Disk.

2. Save the file as **chem2.htm** in the review folder on your data disk.

3. Add an anchor tag around the image file at the top of the page (**dube.jpg**), and give the anchor the name "top."

4. After the HTML line at the bottom of the page containing Stephen's "spoonful of sugar" sentence, and just before the </body> tag, type a new paragraph with the line "Return to the top of the page."

5. Use the <small> tag to format the sentence you entered in Step 4 with smaller text.

6. Create a hyperlink using the text you entered in Step 4 and pointing to the "top" anchor you created in Step 3.

7. In the Chemistry Classes list, locate the Advanced Placement Chemistry list item. After the phrase in parentheses, but before the closing </p> tag, enter the text

```
; click for AP resources
```

so that the semicolon immediately follows the closing parenthesis, with no space between.

8. Change the phrase "click for AP resources" to a hyperlink pointing to the "ap" anchor in the Links page. You'll create this anchor shortly.

9. In the Appointments section, change the phrase "I can meet with you" to a hyperlink pointing to **contact2.htm**.

10. Save **chem2.htm**.

11. Using your text editor, open **cont2txt.htm**, located in the review folder of the tutorial.02 folder on your Data Disk, and save it as **contact2.htm**. You can close **chem2.htm**.

12. Using your text editor, open **link2txt.htm**, located in the review folder of the tutorial.02 folder on your Data Disk, and save it as **links2.htm**. You can close **contact2.htm**.

13. In the **links2.htm** file, add the "ap" anchor to the heading "AP Resources," and then save **links2.htm**.

14. Using your browser, view **chem2.htm**, and compare it to Figure 2-37. (Make sure you open **chem2.htm** from the review folder of the tutorial.02 folder.)

15. Verify that all of the new links work correctly.

16. Using your text editor, fix any errors if necessary.

17. When you are satisfied with the results, use your browser to print **chem2.htm**, **contact2.htm**, and **links2.htm**.

18. Using your text editor, print **chem2.htm**, **contact2.htm**, and **links2.htm**.

19. Close your text editor.

CASE PROBLEMS

Case 1. Rock Hotel You are the Marketing Manager for the Rock Hotel, located in Green River, Utah. The hotel's owner has asked you to create a Web page listing nearby attractions, with a hyperlink for each attraction. You decide to first organize the links with appropriate <h2> headings, and then add the links. You have chosen a logo and background, provided on your Data Disk in the following files: **grrock.jpg** and **grback.jpg**.

Figure 2-38 lists the URLs you need to include in the page, and Figure 2-39 shows the page you'll create.

Figure 2-38

ATTRACTION	URL
Canyonlands National Park	http://www.nps.gov/cany/
Arches National Park	http://www.nps.gov/arch/
Capitol Reef National Park	http://www.nps.gov/care/
Green River State Park	http://parks.state.ut.us/parks/www1/gree.htm
Adventure Bound River Expeditions	http://www.raft-utah.com
Way Out West Tours	http://www.wayoutwesttours.com
Fly Fishing the Green River	http://quickbyte.com/greenriver/
City of Green River	http://www.greenriver-utah.com
Emery County	http://www.emerycounty.com/

Figure 2-39

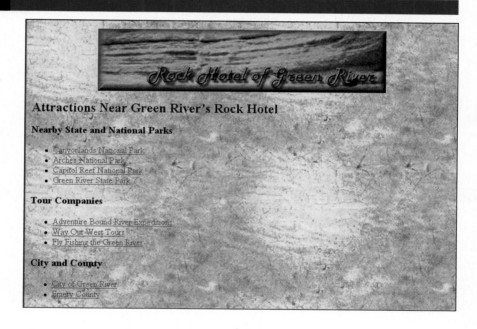

1. Using your text editor, create a new document.

2. Enter the <html>, <head>, and <body> tags to identify different sections of the page.

3. Save the file as **rock.htm** in the case1 folder of the tutorial.02 folder on your Data Disk.

4. Within the head section, insert a <title> tag with the text "Green River Attractions".

5. With the <body> tag and background attribute, add the background image **grback.jpg**, located in the case1 folder of the tutorial.02 folder on your Data Disk.

6. Within the body section, create a centered level 2 heading containing the image file, **grrock.jpg**, located in the tutorial.02/case1 folder.

7. Below the level 2 heading, insert another level 2 heading with the text "Attractions Near Green River's Rock Hotel" as shown in Figure 2-39.

8. After the second level 2 heading, create three level 3 headings with the text "Nearby State and National Parks", "Tour Companies", and "City and County" as shown in Figure 2-39.

9. Below each heading, create an unordered list of the appropriate Web site names shown in the left column of Figure 2-38. The first four sites go under the first heading, the second three go under the second heading, and the last two sites go under the third heading.

10. Link each Web site name with its URL, shown in the right column of Figure 2-38. Because these are external links, use the target attribute to have the pages open in a new window. Use the same target name "SiteWin" for each link so the pages all open in a single separate window.

11. Save the file in your text editor.

12. View the file with your Web browser, compare it to Figure 2-39, testing the links, and then return to your text editor to fix any errors.

13. When you are satisfied with the result, print the page and close your browser.

14. Print a copy of the file from your text editor, and then close your text editor.

Case 2. Western College for the Arts You are a graduate assistant in the Music Department who has been assigned the task of creating Web pages for topics in classical music. Previously, you created a Web page that showed the different sections of the fourth movement of Beethoven's Ninth Symphony. Now that you've learned to link multiple HTML files together, you have created pages for all four movements.

The four Web pages are in the case2 folder of the tutorial.02 folder on your Data Disk. Their names are: **move1a.htm**, **move2a.htm**, **move3a.htm**, and **move4a.htm**. You'll rename them **move1.htm**, **move2.htm**, **move3.htm**, and **move4.htm**, so that the originals remain intact. Figure 2-40 shows the Web page for the third movement.

Figure 2-40

Beethoven's Ninth Symphony

🖎 **The Third Movement** 🖎

Sectional Form

1. A-Section
2. B-Section
3. A-Section varied
4. B-Section
5. Interlude
6. A-Section varied
7. Coda

View the Classical Net Home Page.

You now need to link the pages. You've already placed graphic elements—the hands pointing to the previous or next movement of the symphony—in each file. You decide to mark each image as a hypertext link that navigates the user to the previous or next movement.

1. Using your text editor, open **move1a.htm**, **move2a.htm**, **move3a.htm**, and **move4a.htm**, and save the files as **move1.htm**, **move2.htm**, **move3.htm**, and **move4.htm** in the tutorial.02/case2 folder on your Data Disk.

2. Within each of the HTML files you created in Step 1, edit the inline images **right.jpg** and **left.jpg** so that the **right.jpg** inline image is a hyperlink pointing to the next movement in the symphony, and **left.jpg** points to the previous movement in the symphony.

3. Within each of the four HTML files, change the text "View the Classical Net Home page." to a hyperlink pointing to the URL *http://www.classical.net/*. Use the target attribute and the target name "classic_site" so the page opens in a new browser window.

4. Save all four HTML files.

5. Using your Web browser, open the pages and verify that all of the links work as you expect them to.

6. Using your text editor, print each page and then close the program.

7. Using your Web browser, print each page and then close the browser.

Case 3. *Diamond Health Club, Inc.* You work for Diamond Health Club, a family-oriented health club in Seattle, Washington that has been serving active families for 25 years. You've been asked to help create a Web site describing the club, its classes, and its membership options. There are three pages: the main page describing the club, a page listing classes offered, and a page describing the various membership options. You need to add links within the main page and add other links connecting the pages. The completed main page is shown in Figure 2-41.

Figure 2-41

Diamond Health Club

Your Source for Year-Round, Fun Family Health

Amenities · Staff · Links

At Diamond Health Club, you can stay healthy year-round and have fun doing it! We offer something for everyone.

Amenities

- 2 workout rooms
- 2 swimming pools
  - Olympic size pool with at least 3 laps always open
  - warm 3-foot deep pool perfect for therapeutic swimming (also open for children's open swim and lessons)
- gymnasium with full size basketball court
- private men's, women's, and family locker rooms
- on-site child care
- weight management programs
- personal training

Staff

Ty Stoven, General Manager, ext. 300

Yosef Dolen, Assistant Manager, ext 301

Sue Myafin, Child Care, ext 302

James Michel, Health Services, ext 303

Ron Chi, Membership, ext 304

Marcia Lopez, Classes, ext 305

To contact our staff members, click the appropriate name to send an e-mail, or call 404-555-4874 and dial the extension above.

Links

Check out our great classes, for everyone from children and teens to adults and seniors.

We have the right membership option for you!

- Individual – day-time or all hours
- Family – with or without child care
- Punch cards – try the Club or give a healthy gift!

1. Using your text editor, open **clubtxt.htm**, **classtxt.htm**, and **membtxt.htm** in the tutorial.02/case3 folder of your Data Disk, and then save the files as **club.htm**, **classes.htm,** and **members.htm** in the case3 folder.

2. Using your text editor, open **club.htm** and add anchor names to the three <h3> headings ("Amenities", "Staff", and "Links"). Use the anchor names amen, staff, and links.

3. Link the text at the top of the page (located just below the image) to the anchors you created in Step 2.

4. Link each of the names (do not include the titles or phone extensions) in the Staff section to the appropriate e-mail address, using "first initial_last name@dmond-health.com" as a template, so the first link would be to TStoven@dmond-health.com.

5. In the Links section, link the word "classes" to **classes.htm**, and then change the text "children", "teens", "adults", and "seniors" to links pointing to the child, teen, adult, and sen anchors in **classes.htm**. You'll create the anchors in a moment.

6. In the last bulleted list item in the Links section, change the text "Individual", "Family", and "Punch cards" to links pointing to the ind, fam, and punch anchors in the **members.htm** file. You'll create the anchors in a moment.

7. Save your changes to **club.htm**.

8. Using your text editor, open **classes.htm**. Create anchors for each of the <h2> headings with the names sen, adult, teen, and child.

9. Change the text "Return to Main page" at the top of the page to a hyperlink pointing to **club.htm**, and the text "Membership Options" to a link pointing to the **members.htm** file.

10. Near the top of the page, change the text "e-mail Marcia Lopez" to a link pointing to the e-mail address MLopez@dmond-health.com. Save your changes to **classes.htm**.

11. Using your text editor, open **members.htm** and create anchors to the three <h2> headings with the names ind, fam, and punch.

12. Change the text "Return to Main page" at the top of the page to a hyperlink pointing to **club.htm**, and the text "Classes for Everyone" to a link pointing to **classes.htm**.

13. Change the text "e-mail Ron Chi" to a link pointing to the e-mail address RChi@dmond-health.com. Save your changes.

14. Using your Web browser, open **club.htm** and verify that all of your links work correctly.

15. When you've fixed any errors, use your Web browser to print each of the three Web pages, and then close the program.

16. Using your text editor, print each of the three pages and then close the program.

Case 4. Create Your Own Home Page   Now that you've completed this tutorial, you are ready to create your own Web page. The page should include information about you and your interests. If you like, you can create a separate page devoted entirely to one of your favorite hobbies. Be sure to include the following elements:

- section headings
- bold and/or italic fonts
- paragraphs
- an ordered, unordered, or definition list
- an inline image that is either a link or the destination of a link
- links to some of your favorite Internet pages; have these open in a single secondary window
- a hypertext link that moves the user from one section of your page to another

1. Create a file called **myweb.htm** in the case4 folder of the tutorial.02 folder on your Data Disk, and then enter HTML code to set up the document.

2. Add heading and character attribute tags to make your Web page readable and attractive.

3. Test your code as you develop your home page by viewing **myweb.htm** in your browser.

4. Insert images you think will enhance your page.

5. Use at least one image as either a link or the destination of a link.

6. Use your Web browser to explore other Web pages. Record the URLs of pages that you like, and list them in your document. Then create links to those URLs. Remember to make them all appear in a single new browser window.

7. When you finish entering and checking your code, save and print **myweb.htm**, and then close your text editor.

8. View the final version in your browser, print the Web page, and then close your browser.

QUICK | CHECK ANSWERS

Session 2.1

1. <a name="csu">Colorado State University</a>
2. <a href="#csu">Universities</a>
3. Anchor tags should be placed within style tags such as the <h3> heading tag.
4. <a name="photo"> <img src="photo.jpg"></a>
5. <a href="#links"> <img src="button.jpg"></a>
6. True. Anchor names are case-sensitive.

Session 2.2

1. Storyboarding is diagramming a series of related Web pages, taking care to identify all hypertext links between the various pages. Storyboarding is an important tool in creating Web sites that are easy to navigate and understand.
2. A linear structure is one in which Web pages are linked from one to another in a direct chain. Users can go to the previous page or the next page in the chain, but not to a page in a different section of the chain.
3. A hierarchical structure is one in which Web pages are linked from general to specific topics. Users can move up and down the hierarchy tree.
4. It distinguishes the file name from the anchor name.
5. <a href="sports.htm">Sports info</a>
6. <a href="sports.htm#bball">Basketball news</a>

Session 2.3

1. An absolute path gives the location of a file on the computer's hard disk. A relative path gives the location of a file relative to the active Web page.
2. ../../index.htm

   ../../tutorial/chem.htm

   ../tutorial/links.htm

   ../rock.htm
3. <a href="http://www.whitehouse.gov" target="GovWin">White House</a>
4. <a href="ftp://ftp.uwash.edu">Washington</a>
5. <a href=news:rec.sports.boxing.pro>Boxing</a>
6. <a href=mailto:president@whitehouse.gov>President</a>

New Perspectives on

CREATING WEB PAGES
WITH HTML

3rd Edition

TUTORIAL 3   HTML 3.03

Designing a Web Page
Working with Fonts, Colors, and Graphics

TUTORIAL 4   HTML 4.01

Designing a Web Page with Tables
Creating a News Page

TUTORIAL 5   HTML 5.01

Using Frames in a Web Site
Using Frames to Display Multiple Web Pages

Read This Before You Begin

To the Student

Data Disks

To complete the Level II tutorials, Review Assignments, and Case Problems, you need four Data Disks. Your instructor will either provide you with these Data Disks or ask you to make your own.

If you are making your own Data Disks, you will need **four** blank, formatted high-density disks. You will need to copy a set of files and/or folders from a file server, standalone computer, or the Web onto your disks. Your instructor will tell you which computer, drive letter, and folders contain the files you need. You could also download the files by going to **www.course.com** and following the instructions on the screen.

The information below shows you the Data Disks you need so that you will have enough disk space to complete all the tutorials, Review Assignments, and Case Problems:

Data Disk 2

Write this on the disk label:
Data Disk 1: HTML Tutorial 3

Put these folders on the disk:
tutorial.03/tutorial
tutorial.03/review
tutorial.03/case1
tutorial.03/case2
tutorial.03/case3
tutorial.03/case4

Data Disk 2

Write this on the disk label:
Data Disk 2: HTML Tutorial 4

Put these folders on the disk:
tutorial.04/tutorial
tutorial.04/review
tutorial.04/case1
tutorial.04/case2
tutorial.04/case3
tutorial.04/case4

Data Disk 3

Write this on the disk label:
Data Disk 3: HTML Tutorial 5 and Review Assignment

Put these folders on the disk:
tutorial.05/tutorial
tutorial.05/review

Data Disk 4

Write this on the disk label:
Data Disk 4: HTML Tutorial 5 Case Problems

Put these folders on the disk:
tutorial.05/case1
tutorial.05/case2
tutorial.05/case3
tutorial.05/case4

When you begin each tutorial, Review Assignment, or Case Problem, be sure you are using the correct Data Disk. Refer to the "File Finder" chart at the back of this text for more detailed information on which files are used in which tutorials. See the inside front cover of this book for more information on Data Disk files, or ask your instructor or technical support person for assistance.

Using Your Own Computer

If you are going to work through this book using your own computer, you need:

- **Computer System** A text editor and a Web browser (preferably Netscape Navigator or Internet Explorer, versions 4.0 or higher) must be installed on your computer. If you are using a non-standard browser, it must support frames and HTML 4.0 or higher.

- **Data Disks** You will not be able to complete the tutorials or exercises in this book using your own computer until you have your Data Disks.

Visit Our World Wide Web Site

Additional materials designed especially for you are available on the World Wide Web. Go to **www.course.com/ NewPerspectives**.

To the Instructor

The Data Disk Files are available on the Instructor's Resource Kit for this title. Follow the instructions in the Help file on the CD-ROM to install the programs to your network or standalone computer. For information on creating Data Disks, see the "To the Student" section above.

In this tutorial you will:

- Learn how HTML handles color

- Create a color scheme for a Web page

- Work with font sizes, colors, and types

- Place a background image on a Web page

- Define colors for a Web page and for specific characters

- Learn about different image file formats

- Control the placement and appearance of images on a Web page

- Work with client-side image maps

DESIGNING A WEB PAGE

Working with Fonts, Colors, and Graphics

CASE

Arcadium Amusement Park

Arcadium is a new amusement park located in northern Georgia. The park contains a wealth of rides, including roller coaster, water rides, go-kart racetracks, and gentler rides more appropriate for young children. Tom Calloway is the director of advertising for the park. In addition to radio, newspaper, and television spots, Tom is also overseeing the development of the park's Web site. He has asked you to join his Web site development team.

The content of the site has already been determined. Tom wants you to concentrate on the site's design. He wants the design to convey a sense of fun and excitement to the reader. The Web pages you create should be colorful and should include a variety of images and even animation, if possible. Tom has provided some of the graphic files you'll need to complete the site's design.

The park is scheduled to open in three months, so Tom is very anxious to see your first draft.

In this session you'll explore how HTML handles and defines color, and you'll learn how to add color to text and to the background of a Web page. You'll also work with different fonts and type sizes. Finally, you'll learn how to create a background image for a Web page.

Working with Color in HTML

The grand opening of the park is rapidly approaching, and Tom has called you to discuss the appearance of the park's Web page. As you can see in Figure 3-1, a copywriter has written the text of the site's home page.

Figure 3-1	THE ARCADIUM WEB PAGE

Arcadium

Georgia's Newest and Best Amusement Park

Exciting adventures await you at **Arcadium**, Georgia's family fun center. The park is located 5 miles northwest of Derby - close to many of Georgia's scenic wonders. Arcadium supports over 70 rides, including some of the state's most exciting roller coasters and water rides. There's also plenty of fun for the younger kids. The park provides two separate kiddie pools and special rides for the kids.

Arcadium is open seven days a week:

- April 1 to Memorial Day weekend: 10am to 5pm
- Memorial Day weekend through Labor Day weekend: 9am to 11pm
- Labor Day weekend to October 31: 10am to 5pm
- November 1 to March 31: closed

Arcadium is easy on your budget. Compare our low daily rates to the big chain parks. Special off-season and large group rates are available.

Water Park

Arcadium's water rides constitute a park within the park. You can experience the thrill of the *Big Dipper*, Arcadium's 10-story-high water slide. Or enjoy the twisting, curving ride of Arcadium's underground water ride, the *Black Hole*. For a ride gentler on the stomach, take a few laps on the *Lazy River* in a one-, two-, or four-person inner tube. No day is complete without a visit of one of our two wavepools.

Fun Rides

Enjoy some of the most exciting roller coaster rides in the area. Start off with the *Dragon*, our double looping roller coaster more than 12 stories high. Get a great view of the park from the *Skywheel*, a 120-foot-high gondola capable of holding up to 115 people. The *Missouri Breaks* will get your heart pumping at speeds of greater than 55 mph and forces up to 2.8 g's.

Vroooom

Put yourself behind the wheel for a change, by enjoying one of our three go-kart tracks. For those with a little more aggression, you can take it out on our bumper car or bumper boat tracks. All rides support the highest safety standards in the industry.

Arcadium • Hwy 12, Exit 491 • Derby, GA 20010 • 1 (800) 555-5431

Tom is satisfied with the page's content, but he wants you to work on the design of the page. He'd like you to add a colorful background or background image to the page for visual interest, modify the appearance of some of the text, and add the Arcadium logo and photographs of people enjoying themselves at the park. Tom wants this Web page to be as eye-catching as possible, which is why he has contacted you for this job.

You decide to start this project by working on an overall color scheme for the page. The first step is to learn how to select colors using HTML. If you've worked with illustration or desktop publishing applications, you've probably made your color choices without much difficulty due to the WYSIWYG (What you see is what you get) graphical user interface those programs employ. Selecting color with HTML is somewhat less intuitive because HTML is a text-based language, requiring you to define your colors in textual terms.

HTML identifies a color in one of two ways: either by the color's name or by color values. Both methods have their advantages and disadvantages. You'll first learn about identifying a color by its name.

Using Color Names

There are 16 basic **color names** that are recognized by all versions of HTML. These color names are shown in Figure 3-2.

Figure 3-2	THE 16 BASIC COLOR NAMES		

Aqua	Gray	Navy	Silver
Black	Green	Olive	Teal
Blue	Lime	Purple	White
Fuchsia	Maroon	Red	Yellow

As long as you keep to this fundamental list of colors, you can rely on these color names to create a color scheme that can be accurately displayed across different browsers and operating systems.

However, a list of only 16 colors is limiting to Web designers. In response to this need, Netscape and Internet Explorer began to support an extended list of color names in early versions of their browsers. Figure 3-3 shows a partial list of these additional color names. The extended color name list allows you to create color schemes with greater color variation. A more complete list is provided in Appendix A, "HTML Color Names."

Figure 3-3	PARTIAL LIST OF EXTENDED COLOR NAMES		

Blueviolet	Gold	Orange	Seagreen
Chocolate	Hotpink	Paleturquoise	Sienna
Darkgoldenrod	Indigo	Peachpuff	Snow
Firebrick	Mintcream	Salmon	Tan

One practical problem with using a color name list is that, while it's easy to specify a blue background, "blue" might not be specific enough for the purposes of your design. How do you specify a background of "light blue with a touch of green"? To do so, you would have to look through a long list of color names before discovering that "Paleturquoise" is close to the color you want. Even so, some users might try to access your page with older browsers that do not support the long list of color names. Your page might end up being unreadable on those browsers.

When you want to have more control and more choices regarding the colors in your Web page, you need to specify colors using color values.

Using Color Values

A **color value** is a numerical expression that precisely describes a color. To better understand how HTML uses numbers to represent colors, it will help to review some of the basic principles of color theory and how they relate to the colors displayed by your monitor.

Any color can be thought of as a combination of three primary colors: red, green, and blue. You are probably familiar with the color diagram shown in Figure 3-4, in which the colors yellow, magenta, cyan, and white are produced by adding the three primary colors. By varying the intensity of each primary color, you can create almost any color and any shade of color that you want. This principle allows your computer monitor to combine pixels of red, green, and blue light to create the array of colors you see on your screen.

Figure 3-4	ADDING THE THREE PRIMARY COLORS

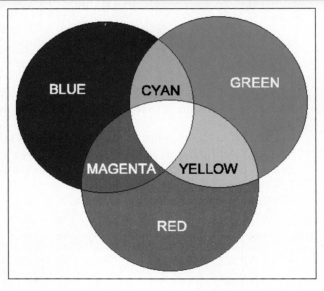

Software programs, such as your Web browser, define color mathematically. The intensity of each of the three colors (RGB) is assigned a number from 0 (absence of color) to 255 (highest intensity). In this way, 255^3, or more than 16.7 million, distinct colors can be defined. Each color is represented by a triplet of numbers, called an **RGB triplet**, based on the strength of its **R**ed, **G**reen, and **B**lue components. For example, white has a triplet of (255,255,255), indicating that red, green, and blue are equally mixed at the highest intensity. Yellow has the triplet (255,255,0) because it is an equal mixture of red and green with no presence of blue. In most programs, you make your color choices with visual clues, usually without being aware of the underlying RGB triplet. Figure 3-5 shows a typical dialog box in which you would make color selections based on the appearance of the color, rather than on the RGB values.

Figure 3-5   **A TYPICAL COLORS DIALOG BOX**

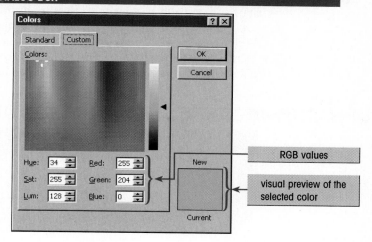

RGB values

visual preview of the selected color

HTML requires that such color values be entered as hexadecimals. A **hexadecimal** is a number based on base-16 mathematics rather than base-10 mathematics that we use every day. In base 10 counting, you use combinations of 10 characters (0 through 9) to represent numerical values, whereas hexadecimals include six extra characters: A (for 10), B (for 11), C (for 12), D (for 13), E (for 14), and F (for 15). For values above 15, you use a combination of the 16 characters; 16 is expressed as "10," 17 is expressed as "11," and so forth. To represent a number in hexadecimal terms, you convert the value to multiples of 16 plus a remainder. For example, 21 is equal to (16 x 1) + 5, so its hexadecimal representation is 15. The number 255 is equal to (16 x 15) + 15, or FF in hexadecimal format (remember that F = 15 in hexadecimal). In the case of the number 255, the first F represents the number of times 16 goes into 255 (which is 15), and the second F represents the remainder of 15.

Once you know the RGB triplet of a color you want to use in your Web page, you need to convert that triplet to the hexadecimal format and express it in a single string of six characters. For example, the color yellow has the RGB triplet (255,255,0) and is represented by the hexadecimal string FFFF00. Figure 3-6 shows the RGB triplets and hexadecimal equivalents for the 16 basic color names presented earlier.

Figure 3-6   **COLOR NAMES, RGB TRIPLETS, AND HEXADECIMAL VALUES**

Color Name	RGB Triplet	Hexadecimal	Color Name	RGB Triplet	Hexadecimal
Aqua	(0,255,255)	00FFFF	Navy	(0,0,128)	000080
Black	(0,0,0)	000000	Olive	(128,128,0)	808000
Blue	(0,0,255)	0000FF	Purple	(128,0,128)	800080
Fuchsia	(255,0,255)	FF00FF	Red	(255,0,0)	FF0000
Gray	(128,128,128)	808080	Silver	(192,192,192)	C0C0C0
Green	(0,128,0)	008000	Teal	(0,128,128)	008080
Lime	(0,255,0)	00FF00	White	(255,255,255)	FFFFFF
Maroon	(128,0,0)	800000	Yellow	(255,255,0)	FFFF00

At this point you might be wondering if you have to become a math major before you can start adding color to your Web pages! Because of the popularity of the Web, most graphics programs display the hexadecimal value of the colors in their color selection dialog boxes. Web page designers can also rely on tools, such as the ones shown in Figure 3-7, to generate the hexadecimal values that HTML requires for specific colors. Once you've chosen your colors, you can use the code generated by these tools in your HTML document.

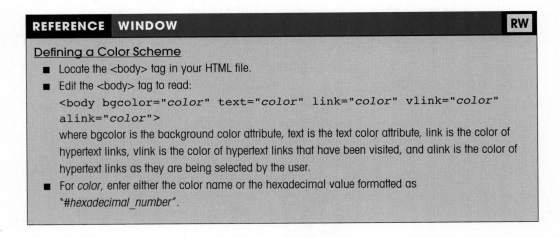

Figure 3-7	COLOR SELECTION RESOURCES AVAILABLE ON THE WEB

TITLE	URL
ColorMix	http://www.colormix.com/
Palette Man	http://www.paletteman.com/
Two4U's Color Page	http://www.two4u.com/color/
ZSPC Super Color Chart	http://www.zspc.com/color/index-e.html

However you decide to work with color in your Web pages, it's important to understand how HTML handles color, if for no other reason than to be able to interpret the HTML source code of the pages you explore on the Web.

Specifying a Color Scheme for Your Page

After reviewing the issues surrounding color and HTML, you are ready to add color to the Web page that Tom has given you. Web browsers have a default color scheme that they apply to the background and text of the pages they retrieve. In most cases, the default scheme involves black text on a white or gray background, with hypertext links highlighted in purple and blue. When you want to use different colors than these, you need to modify the attributes of the page, defined within the <body> tag.

REFERENCE WINDOW   **RW**

Defining a Color Scheme
- Locate the <body> tag in your HTML file.
- Edit the <body> tag to read:
  ```
  <body bgcolor="color" text="color" link="color" vlink="color"
  alink="color">
  ```
  where bgcolor is the background color attribute, text is the text color attribute, link is the color of hypertext links, vlink is the color of hypertext links that have been visited, and alink is the color of hypertext links as they are being selected by the user.
- For color, enter either the color name or the hexadecimal value formatted as "#hexadecimal_number".

In your work with HTML, you've used the <body> tag to identify the section of the HTML file containing the content that users see in their browsers. The <body> tag can also be used to indicate the colors on your page. The syntax for controlling a page's color scheme through the <body> tag is:

```
<body bgcolor="color" text="color" link="color" vlink="color" alink="color">
```

Here, the bgcolor attribute sets the background color, the text attribute controls text color, the link attribute defines the color of hypertext links, the vlink attribute defines the color of links that have been visited by the user, and the alink attribute determines the color of an active hyperlink (the color of the link as it is clicked by the user). The value of *color* will be either one of the accepted color names or the color's hexadecimal value. If you use the hexadecimal value, you must preface the hexadecimal string with the pound symbol (#) and enclose the string in double or single quotation marks. For example, the HTML tag to create a background color with the hexadecimal value FFCO88 is:

```
<body bgcolor="#FFCO88">
```

After viewing various color combinations, Tom has decided that he'd like you to use a color scheme consisting of dark blue text on a light blue background. He also wants the hypertext links and active hypertext links to be red with visited links displayed in dark blue. Using color values obtained from a Web design application, Tom wants to use the RGB triplet of (220, 240, 255) for the background color. This color has the hexadecimal value of "#CDFOFF". You'll use color names for the colors of the other items on the Web page.

To change the color scheme of the Arcadium Web page:

1. Using your text editor, open **arcatxt.htm** from the tutorial.03/tutorial folder on your Data Disk, and then save the file in the same folder as **arcadium.htm**.

2. Within the <body> tag at the top of the file, type **bgcolor="#CDFOFF" text="darkblue" link="red" vlink="darkblue" alink="red"**.

Your HTML code should look like Figure 3-8.

Figure 3-8	MODIFIED <BODY> TAG

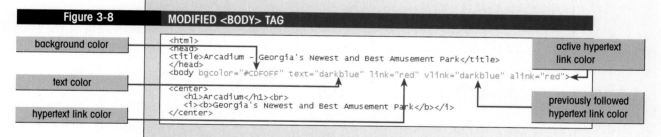

background color

text color

hypertext link color

active hypertext link color

previously followed hypertext link color

```
<html>
<head>
<title>Arcadium - Georgia's Newest and Best Amusement Park</title>
</head>
<body bgcolor="#CDFOFF" text="darkblue" link="red" vlink="darkblue" alink="red">

<center>
    <h1>Arcadium</h1><br>
    <i><b>Georgia's Newest and Best Amusement Park</b></i>
</center>
```

3. Save your changes to arcadium.htm, but leave the text editor open. You'll be revising this file throughout this session.

4. Using your Web browser, open the arcadium.htm file. See Figure 3-9.

Figure 3-9	THE ARCADIUM PAGE WITH THE NEW COLOR SCHEME

Arcadium

Georgia's Newest and Best Amusement Park

Exciting adventures await you at **Arcadium,** Georgia's family fun center. The park is located 5 miles northwest of Derby - close to many of Georgia's scenic wonders. Arcadium supports over 70 rides, including some of the state's most exciting roller coasters and water rides. There's also plenty of fun for the younger kids. The park provides two separate kiddie pools and special rides for the kids.

Arcadium is open seven days a week:

- April 1 to Memorial Day weekend: 10am to 5pm
- Memorial Day weekend through Labor Day weekend: 9am to 11pm
- Labor Day weekend to October 31: 10am to 5pm
- November 1 to March 31: closed

Arcadium is easy on your budget. Compare our low daily rates to the big chain parks. Special off-season and large group rates are available.

Water Park

Arcadium's water rides constitute a park within the park. You can experience the thrill of the *Big Dipper*, Arcadium's 10-story-high water slide. Or enjoy the twisting, curving ride of Arcadium's underground water ride, the *Black Hole*. For a ride gentler on the stomach, take a few laps on the *Lazy River* in a one-, two-, or four-person inner tube. No day is complete without a visit of one of our two wavepools.

Fun Rides

Enjoy some of the most exciting roller coaster rides in the area. Start off with the *Dragon*, our double looping roller coaster more than 12 stories high. Get a great view of the park from the *Skywheel*, a 120-foot-high gondola capable of holding up to 115 people. The *Missouri Breaks* will get your heart pumping at speeds of greater than 55 mph and forces up to 2.8 g's.

Vroooom

Put yourself behind the wheel for a change, by enjoying one of our three go-kart tracks. For those with a little more aggression, you can take it out on our bumper car or bumper boat tracks. All rides support the highest safety standards in the industry.

Arcadium • Hwy 12, Exit 491 • Derby, GA 20010 • 1 (800) 555-5431

The Arcadium Web page now has dark blue text on a light blue background. Hypertext links are red and dark blue. By adding the color scheme to the <body> tag of the HTML file, you've superseded the browser's default color scheme with one of your own.

Modifying Text with the <font> Tag

Specifying the text color in the <body> tag of your Web page changed the color of all the text on the Web page. Occasionally you may want to change the color of individual words or characters. This is an effective way to make specific sections of text stand out. HTML allows you to use the <font> tag with specific sections of text to override the color specified in the <body> tag.

REFERENCE WINDOW   RW

Modifying Text Appearance with the <font> Tag
- Using your text editor, locate the text you want to modify.
- Insert the <font> tag as follows:

  `<font size="size" color="color" face="face"> text </font>`

  where *size* is the actual size of the text or the amount by which you want to increase or decrease the text size; *color* is the color name or color value you want to apply to the text; and *face* is the name of the font you want to use for the text.

You've worked with some character tags that allow you to bold or italicize individual characters. The <font> tag gives you even more control by allowing you to specify the color, the size, and even the font to be used for the text on your Web page. The syntax for the <font> tag is:

`<font size="size" color="color" face="face"> text </font>`

The <font> tag has three attributes: size, color, and face. Your primary concern right now is to use the <font> tag to change text color, but it's worthwhile exploring the other attributes of the tag at this time.

Changing the Font Size

The size attribute of the <font> tag allows you to specify the font size of the text. The size value can be expressed in either absolute or relative terms. For example, if you want your text to have a size of 2, you enter size="2" in the <font> tag. On the other hand, if you want to increase the font size by 2 relative to the surrounding text, you enter size="+2" in the tag. What is the value "size" in absolute terms? Remember that in HTML we define things such as font size in a fairly general way, allowing the browser to render the page. This means that text formatted with size 7 font in one browser might be slightly different in size than the same text in another browser. Figure 3-10 provides a representation of the various font sizes for a typical browser.

Figure 3-10   **EXAMPLES OF DIFFERENT FONT SIZES**

This is size 1 text
This is size 2 text
This is size 3 text
This is size 4 text
This is size 5 text
This is size 6 text
This is size 7 text

For comparison, text formatted with the <h1> tag corresponds to bold, size 6 text; the <h2> tag is equivalent to bold, size 5 text, and so forth. Figure 3-11 presents a complete comparison of header tags and font sizes.

Figure 3-11	EXAMPLES OF HEADING TAGS AND FONT SIZES

TAG	FORMAT
<h1>	Size 6, Bold
<h2>	Size 5, Bold
<h3>	Size 4, Bold
<h4>	Size 3, Bold
<h5>	Size 2, Bold
<h6>	Size 1, Bold
Normal text (no <h*i*> tag)	Size 3, Not Bold

So, if you use the attribute size="+1" to increase the size of text enclosed within an <h3> tag, the net effect will be to produce text that is size 5 and bold. The largest value for the size attribute supported by browsers is 7. Note that font sizes in HTML do not correspond to point sizes that you may be familiar with if you have experience in graphic design.

Changing the Font Color

The color attribute of the <font> tag allows you to change the color of individual characters or words. Just as you did when defining color in the <body> tag, you specify the color in the <font> tag by using either an accepted color name or the color value. For example, to change the color of the word "Arcadium" to the hexadecimal color value 8000C0, you would enter the following HTML tag:

```
<font color="#8000C0"> Arcadium</font>
```

The text surrounding the word "Arcadium" is still formatted in the color scheme specified in the <body> tag. If there is no color specified in the <body> tag, the default colors of the Web browser are used.

Changing the Font Face

The final attribute of the <font> tag we're going to examine is the face attribute. You use the face attribute to specify a particular font for a section of text. The introduction of this attribute in HTML 4.0 (although it was supported early on by Internet Explorer 1.0 and Netscape 3.0) was a bit of a departure from earlier versions of HTML, in which the browser alone determined the font used in the Web page. With the face attribute you can override the browser's font choice. For this to work, you must either specify a font that is installed on the user's computer or use one of the following five generic font names: serif, sans-serif, monospace, cursive, and fantasy. The exact depiction of these fonts depends on what fonts have been installed on the user's computer. Figure 3-12 shows some of the possible ways each of these generic fonts could be displayed.

Figure 3-12   **EXAMPLES OF GENERIC FONTS**

Generic Names	Font Samples		
serif	defg	defg	defg
sans-serif	defg	defg	defg
monospace	defg	defg	defg
cursive	defg	defg	defg
fantasy	DEFG	DEFG	defg

within each generic font there can be a wide range of appearances

Because you have no way of knowing which fonts have been installed on the user's computer, the face attribute allows you to specify a list of potential font names. The browser tries to use the first font in the list; if that fails, it will try the second font, and so on until the list is exhausted. It's a good idea to have a generic font name as the last item in the list so that if the browser cannot find any of the specific fonts, it will still have the generic font to fall back on.

For example, to display the word "Arcadium" in a sans-serif, you could enter the following HTML tag:

```
<font face="Arial, Helvetica, sans-serif">Arcadium</font>
```

In this example, each of the three fonts is a sans-serif font. The browser first tries to display the word "Arcadium" using the Arial font. If the user's computer doesn't have that font installed, the browser tries to apply the Helvetica font, and after that it will use whatever generic sans-serif font is available.

Now that you've learned how to use the face attribute of the <font> tag, you decide to change some of the headings in the Web page to a sans-serif font.

To change the appearance of some of the page headings:

1. Return to **arcadium.htm** in your text editor.

2. Locate the h3 heading for the Water Park, located halfway through the document.

3. Enclose the heading within the <font> tag as follows:

   <font face="Arial, Helvetica, sans-serif">Water Park</font>

4. Enclose the h3 headings for the Fun Rides and Vroooom headings within the same set of <font> tags. Figure 3-13 shows the revised code for arcadium.htm.

5. Save your changes to arcadium.htm.

Figure 3-13 **APPLYING A SANS-SERIF FONT TO A SECTION OF TEXT**

text appears in
a sans-serif font

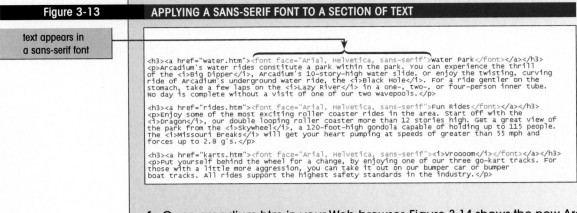

```
<h3><a href="water.htm"><font face="Arial, Helvetica, sans-serif">Water Park</font></a></h3>
<p>Arcadium's water rides constitute a park within the park. You can experience the thrill
of the <i>Big Dipper</i>, Arcadium's 10-story-high water slide. or enjoy the twisting, curving
ride of Arcadium's underground water ride, the <i>Black Hole</i>. For a ride gentler on the
stomach, take a few laps on the <i>Lazy River</i> in a one-, two-, or four-person inner tube.
No day is complete without a visit of one of our two wavepools.</p>

<h3><a href="rides.htm"><font face="Arial, Helvetica, sans-serif">Fun Rides</font></a></h3>
<p>Enjoy some of the most exciting roller coaster rides in the area. Start off with the
<i>Dragon</i>, our double looping roller coaster more than 12 stories high. Get a great view of
the park from the <i>Skywheel</i>, a 120-foot-high gondola capable of holding up to 115 people.
The <i>Missouri Breaks</i> will get your heart pumping at speeds of greater than 55 mph and
forces up to 2.8 g's.</p>

<h3><a href="karts.htm"><font face="Arial, Helvetica, sans-serif"><i>Vroooom</i></font></a></h3>
<p>Put yourself behind the wheel for a change, by enjoying one of our three go-kart tracks. For
those with a little more aggression, you can take it out on our bumper car or bumper
boat tracks. All rides support the highest safety standards in the industry.</p>
```

6. Open arcadium.htm in your Web browser. Figure 3-14 shows the new Arcadium page with the sans-serif headings.

Figure 3-14 **HEADINGS IN A SANS-SERIF FONT**

Water Park

Arcadium's water rides constitute a park within the park. You can experience the thrill of the *Big Dipper*, Arcadium's 10-story-high water slide. Or enjoy the twisting, curving ride of Arcadium's underground water ride, the *Black Hole*. For a ride gentler on the stomach, take a few laps on the *Lazy River* in a one-, two-, or four-person inner tube. No day is complete without a visit of one of our two wavepools.

Fun Rides

Enjoy some of the most exciting roller coaster rides in the area. Start off with the *Dragon*, our double looping roller coaster more than 12 stories high. Get a great view of the park from the *Skywheel*, a 120-foot-high gondola capable of holding up to 115 people. The *Missouri Breaks* will get your heart pumping at speeds of greater than 55 mph and forces up to 2.8 g's

Vroooom

Put yourself behind the wheel for a change, by enjoying one of our three go-kart tracks. For those with a little more aggression, you can take it out on our bumper car or bumper boat tracks. All rides support the highest safety standards in the industry.

Using the <font> Tag to Specify Color

As you can see, the <font> tag gives you significant control over the appearance of individual blocks of text. Tom wants the subtitle of the page, "Georgia's Newest and Best Amusement Park," to stand out on the page. To accomplish this, you'll format the line of text to be red using the <font> tag.

To change the color of the page's subtitle:

1. Return to arcadium.htm in your text editor.

2. Insert the <font> tag around the park's motto as follows:

<font color="red">Georgia's Newest and Best Amusement Park</font>

The arcadium.htm file should now appear as shown in Figure 3-15.

3. Save your changes to arcadium.htm.

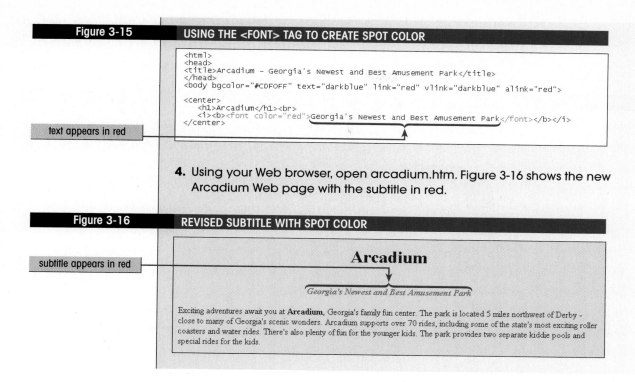

Figure 3-15 | **USING THE <FONT> TAG TO CREATE SPOT COLOR**

```
<html>
<head>
<title>Arcadium - Georgia's Newest and Best Amusement Park</title>
</head>
<body bgcolor="#CDF0FF" text="darkblue" link="red" vlink="darkblue" alink="red">

<center>
    <h1>Arcadium</h1><br>
    <i><b><font color="red">Georgia's Newest and Best Amusement Park</font></b></i>
</center>
```

text appears in red

4. Using your Web browser, open arcadium.htm. Figure 3-16 shows the new Arcadium Web page with the subtitle in red.

Figure 3-16 | **REVISED SUBTITLE WITH SPOT COLOR**

Arcadium

subtitle appears in red

Georgia's Newest and Best Amusement Park

Exciting adventures await you at **Arcadium**, Georgia's family fun center. The park is located 5 miles northwest of Derby - close to many of Georgia's scenic wonders. Arcadium supports over 70 rides, including some of the state's most exciting roller coasters and water rides. There's also plenty of fun for the younger kids. The park provides two separate kiddie pools and special rides for the kids.

You show the revised page to Tom and he likes the new subtitle color. However, he feels that the background needs some enhancement. He's seen Web pages that use images for backgrounds, and he'd like you to try something similar for this project.

Inserting a Background Image

Another attribute of the <body> tag is the background attribute. With this attribute you can use an image file for the background of your Web page. The syntax for inserting a background image is:

```
<body background="URL">
```

where *URL* is the location and filename of the graphic file you want to use for the background of the Web page. For example, to use an image named "bricks.gif" as your background image, you would use the tag:

```
<body background="bricks.gif">
```

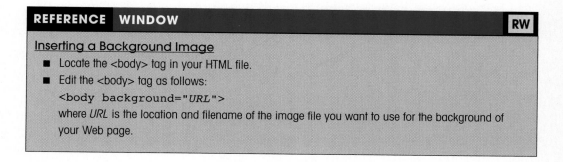

REFERENCE WINDOW   **RW**

Inserting a Background Image
- Locate the <body> tag in your HTML file.
- Edit the <body> tag as follows:
  ```
  <body background="URL">
  ```
  where *URL* is the location and filename of the image file you want to use for the background of your Web page.

When the browser retrieves your image file, it repeatedly inserts the image into the background, in a process called **tiling**, until the entire display window is filled up, as shown in Figure 3-17.

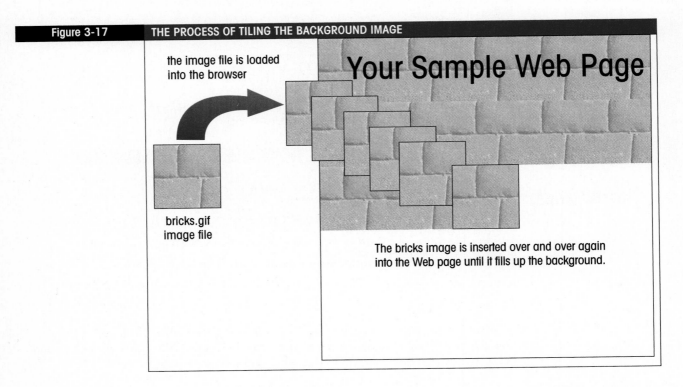

| Figure 3-17 | THE PROCESS OF TILING THE BACKGROUND IMAGE |

the image file is loaded into the browser

bricks.gif image file

Your Sample Web Page

The bricks image is inserted over and over again into the Web page until it fills up the background.

In choosing a background image, you should remember the following:

- Use an image that will not detract from the text on the Web page, making it hard to read.
- Do not use a large image file (more than 20 kilobytes). Large and complicated backgrounds will increase the time it takes a page to load.
- Be sure to take into consideration how an image file looks when it is tiled in the background.

Figure 3-18 shows some examples of well-designed and poorly designed Web page backgrounds.

Figure 3-18	WEB PAGE BACKGROUNDS

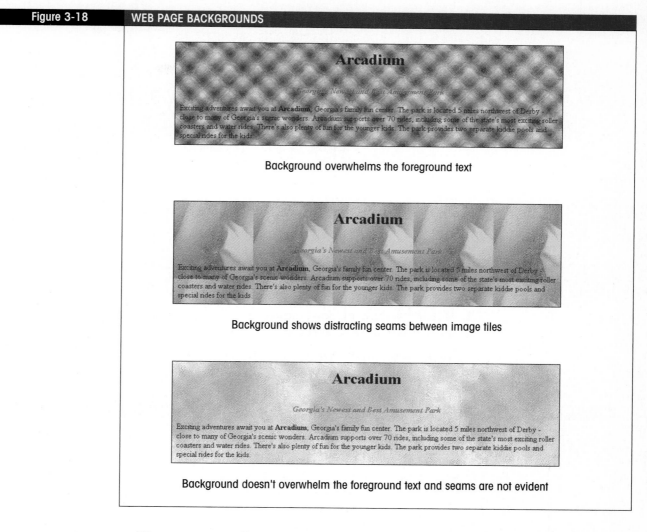

Background overwhelms the foreground text

Background shows distracting seams between image tiles

Background doesn't overwhelm the foreground text and seams are not evident

There are many collections of background images available on the Web. The only restriction is that you cannot sell or distribute the images in a commercial product. Figure 3-19 provides a list of some of these collections. Finding the right background image is a process of trial and error. You won't know for certain whether a background image works well until you actually view it in a browser.

Figure 3-19	SOURCE OF WEB BACKGROUNDS

TITLE	URL
Absolute Backgrounds Textures Archive	http://www.grsites.com/textures/
Free Backgrounds	http://www.free-backgrounds.com/
Texture Station	http://www.nepthys.com/textures/
WebGround	http://www.ip.pt/webground/

After searching, Tom has found a background image he thinks will work well for the Arcadium Web site. The image, **clouds.jpg**, is shown in Figure 3-20.

Figure 3-20	CLOUDS.JPG WEB BACKGROUND

The next step is to replace the light blue background of the Arcadium Web page with the Clouds image that Tom has selected.

To add clouds.jpg to the background:

1. Return to arcadium.htm in your text editor

2. Modify the <body> tag, replacing the bgcolor attribute with:
background="clouds.jpg"

The revised <body> tag should now appear as shown in Figure 3-21.

3. Save your changes to arcadium.htm.

Figure 3-21	ENTERING CLOUDS.JPG AS THE BACKGROUND

setting the image file for the page's background

```
<html>
<head>
<title>Arcadium - Georgia's Newest and Best Amusement Park</title>
</head>
<body background="clouds.jpg" text="darkblue" link="red" vlink="darkblue" alink="red">

<center>
    <h1>Arcadium</h1><br>
    <i><b><font color="red">Georgia's Newest and Best Amusement Park</font></b></i>
</center>
```

4. Reload arcadium.htm in your web browser.

Figure 3-22 shows the new background for the Arcadium page.

Figure 3-22	THE ARCADIUM PAGE WITH THE CLOUDS.JPG BACKGROUND

Arcadium

Georgia's Newest and Best Amusement Park

Exciting adventures await you at **Arcadium**, Georgia's family fun center. The park is located 5 miles northwest of Derby - close to many of Georgia's scenic wonders. Arcadium supports over 70 rides, including some of the state's most exciting roller coasters and water rides. There's also plenty of fun for the younger kids. The park provides two separate kiddie pools and special rides for the kids.

Tom is pleased with the impact of the new background. He notes that the size of the image file is not too large (only about 3 kilobytes) and that it does not show any obvious seams between the image tiles. Also, the background does not overwhelm the content of the Web page.

Extensions to the <font> and <body> Tags

Both Netscape and Internet Explorer support some attributes for the <font> and <body> tags that are not part of the specifications from the World Wide Web Consortium (W3C). Netscape supports the following two extensions to the <font> tag:

```
<font point-size="size" weight="boldness">
```

where *size* is the point size of the font and *boldness* is a measure of the weight or boldness of the font. The point-size attribute operates the same way that point sizes work in word processing and graphic design applications. This attribute provides Web designers with greater control over font sizes than can be obtained by using the size attribute. Values for the weight attribute range from 100 to 900 in increments of 100, with 900 being the heaviest, or "most bold" font. For example, to display text in a 12 point font with a weight of 700, you would use the following <font> tag:

```
<font point-size="12" weight="700">
```

Both of these attributes are supported only by Netscape 4.0 or higher. They are not supported by Internet Explorer, so you should not rely on them if you intend your Web page to be viewed by browsers other than Netscape 4.0 or higher.

Internet Explorer does not support any extensions for the <font> tag, but it does support the following additional attributes for the <body> tag:

```
<body bgproperties="properties" bottommargin="value"
leftmargin="value" rightmargin="value" topmargin="value">
```

where the bgproperties attribute is used to determine whether the background image can scroll along with the page, and the bottommargin, leftmargin, rightmargin, and topmargin attributes specify the size of the margin between the Web page and the edge of the browser window in pixels. If bgproperties attribute is set to the value "fixed", the background image will not scroll with the page. Any other value for this attribute will cause the background to scroll (the default behavior). Both of these attributes are supported by Internet Explorer 4.0 or above. They are not supported by Netscape.

Deprecated Tags

The <font> tag and the attributes of the <body> tag discussed in this session have both been **deprecated** by the W3C, which means that they are considered to be outdated by newer methods. Web page authors are encouraged to use other approaches, such as cascading style sheets, to format the appearance of their Web pages. However, in practical terms, most of the deprecated tags and attributes are still supported by the major browsers. Indeed, many applications that generate HTML code will include deprecated tags like the <font> tag.

In time, tags like the <font> tag will be completely replaced, but for now they are still a heavily used tool of the Web page author. As you review the source code of other Web documents (an excellent way to learn HTML) you will run across these deprecated tags, and it's important to understand what they do. Moreover, if you need to design a Web page that supports older browsers, you may have to use those tags and attributes that have been deprecated in the latest HTML specifications.

In the next session, you'll learn more about handling graphics with HTML as you add inline images to the Arcadium Web page.

Session 3.1 QUICK CHECK

1. What are the two ways of specifying a color in an HTML file? What are the advantages and disadvantages of each?

2. What HTML tag would you use in your HTML file to use a color scheme of red text on a gray background, with hypertext links displayed in blue, and previously visited hypertext links displayed in yellow?

3. What HTML tag would you use to format the words "Major Sale" in red, with a font of size 5 larger than the surrounding text?

4. What HTML tag would you use to display the text "Major Sale" in the Times New Roman font and, if that font is not available, in the MS Serif font?

5. What HTML tag would you use to define "stars.gif" as the background image for a Web page?

6. Name three things you should avoid when choosing a background image for your Web page.

SESSION 3.2

In this session you'll learn about different image file formats and how you can use them to add special effects to your Web page. You'll also explore the advantages and disadvantages of each format. Finally, you'll learn how to control the size, placement, and appearance of inline images on your Web page.

Having added color to the Arcadium Web page, you now turn to the task of adding images in order to make the Web page more interesting to tourists. The two image file formats supported by most Web browsers are GIF and JPEG. Choosing the appropriate image format is an important part of Web page design. You must balance the goal of creating an interesting and attractive page against the need to keep the size of your page small and easy to retrieve. Each file format has its advantages and disadvantages, and you will probably use a combination of both formats in your Web page designs. First, let's look at the advantages and disadvantages of using GIF image files.

Working with GIF Files

GIF (Graphics Interchange Format) is the most commonly used image format on the Web, being compatible with virtually all browsers. GIF files are limited to displaying 256 colors, so they are more often used for graphics requiring fewer colors, such as clip art images, line art, logos, and icons. Images that require more color depth, such as photographs, can appear grainy when saved as GIF files.

There are actually two GIF file formats: GIF87 and GIF89a. The **GIF89a** format, the newer standard, includes enhancements such as interlacing, transparent colors, and animation. You'll explore these enhancements now and learn how to use them in your Web page design.

Interlaced and Noninterlaced GIFs

Interlacing refers to the way the GIF file is saved by the graphics software. Normally, with a **noninterlaced GIF** the image is saved one line at a time, starting from the top of the graphic and moving downward. Figure 3-23 shows how a noninterlaced GIF appears as it is slowly retrieved by the Web browser. If the graphic is large, it might take several minutes for the entire image to appear, which can frustrate the visitors to your Web page.

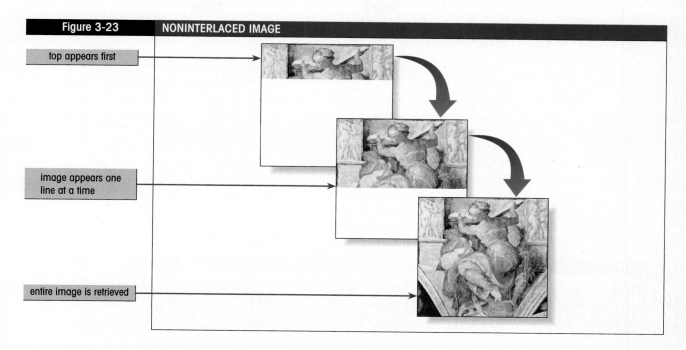

Figure 3-23   NONINTERLACED IMAGE

top appears first

image appears one line at a time

entire image is retrieved

With **interlaced GIFs**, the image is saved and retrieved "stepwise." For example, every fifth line of the image might appear first, followed by every sixth line, and so forth through the remaining rows. As shown in Figure 3-24, the effect of interlacing is that the image starts out as a blurry representation of the final image, then gradually comes into focus–unlike the noninterlaced image, which is always a sharp image as it's being retrieved, although an incomplete one.

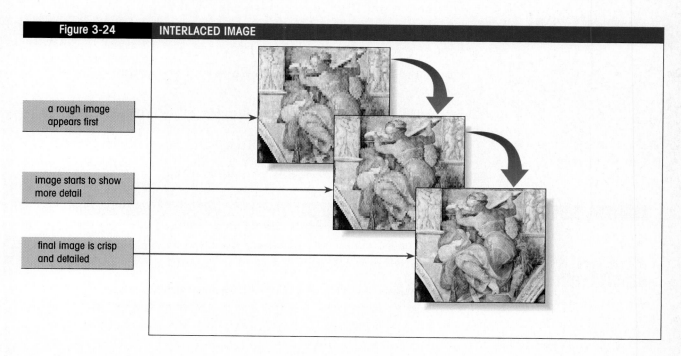

Figure 3-24   INTERLACED IMAGE

a rough image appears first

image starts to show more detail

final image is crisp and detailed

Interlacing is an effective format if you have a large graphic and want to give users a preview of the final image as it loads. They get an immediate idea of what the image looks like and can decide whether to wait for it to come into focus. The downside of interlacing is that it increases the size of the GIF file by anywhere from 3 to 20 kilobytes, depending on the image.

Transparent GIFs

Another enhancement of the GIF89a format is the ability to use transparent colors. A **transparent color** is a color from the image that is not displayed when the image is viewed in an application. In place of a transparent color, the browser will display whatever is on the page background, whether that is white, a background color, or a background image.

The process by which you create a transparent color depends on the graphics software you are using. Many applications include the option to designate a transparent color when saving the image, while other packages include a transparent color tool, which you use to click the color from the image that you want saved as transparent.

Tom has saved the Arcadium logo in the GIF89a format. He wants you to replace the text heading from arcadium.htm with the logo. The logo, saved as **aclogo1.gif**, is shown in Figure 3-25.

Figure 3-25	THE ACLOGO1.GIF FILE

the green background will be transparent when displayed in the browser

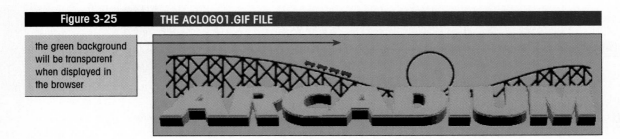

When the logo was created, the green background color was designated as transparent. This means that when you insert the graphic into your Web page, the background image you inserted in the previous session will show through in places where green now appears. To see how this works, you'll replace the text heading with the logo.

To insert the logo in your HTML file:

1. Using your text editor, open the **arcadium.htm** file that you worked on in the last session.

2. Navigate to the top of the page and replace the entire h1 heading with the <img> tag.

   ```
   <img src="aclogo1.gif">
   ```

   Figure 3-26 shows the modified code for arcadium.htm.

Figure 3-26	REPLACING THE HEADING TEXT WITH A GRAPHIC LOGO

tag for the logo image file

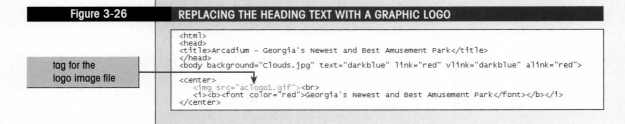

```
<html>
<head>
<title>Arcadium - Georgia's Newest and Best Amusement Park</title>
</head>
<body background="Clouds.jpg" text="darkblue" link="red" vlink="darkblue" alink="red">

<center>
    <img src="aclogo1.gif"><br>
    <i><b><font color="red">Georgia's Newest and Best Amusement Park</font></b></i>
</center>
```

3. Save your changes to arcadium.htm.

4. Using your Web browser, open arcadium.htm.

The browser displays the revised page with the logo, as shown in Figure 3-27.

Figure 3-27	ARCADIUM LOGO DISPLAYED IN THE WEB PAGE

logo background
is transparent

Note that the background image is visible beneath the logo in those locations
where the green background appeared in the original image.

Transparent GIFs can be used as layout tools to help Web page designers to place elements on a Web page. To accomplish this, a GIF is created that is one pixel in size, with the color of the pixel specified as transparent. This type of image is sometimes referred to as a **spacer**. A Web designer can then size the spacer image in order to position objects in specific locations on the page. Using the height and width attributes, you can place another object at any coordinate within the page. For example, to position an object 100 pixels from the top of the page, insert the spacer at the top of the page and assign it a height of 100 pixels. Place your object directly after the spacer in the HTML file. Because the spacer is transparent, it will appear that the object has been placed, magically, 100 pixels from the page's top margin. You'll have a chance to work with spacers in a case problem at the end of the tutorial.

Animated GIFs

One of the most popular uses of GIFs is to create animated images. Compared to video clips, animated GIFs are easier to create and smaller in size. An **animated GIF** is composed of several images that are displayed one after the other in rapid succession. Animated GIFs are an effective way to compose slide shows or to simulate motion. Figure 3-28 provides a list of programs available on the Web that you can use to create your own animated GIFs.

Figure 3-28	ANIMATED GIF PROGRAMS

TITLE	URL
AniMagic	http://www.rtlsoft.com
Gif Construction Set	http://www.mindworkshop.com
Gif.glf.giF	http://www.peda.com
GIFMation	http://www.boxtopsoft.com/GIFmation/
ImageMagik	http://www.imagemagick.org/
Xara	http://www.xara.com/products/

Most animated GIF software allows you to control the rate at which the animation plays (as measured by frames per second) and to determine the number of times the animation is repeated before stopping. You can also set the animation to repeat without stopping. You can combine individual GIF files into a single animated file and create special transitions between images.

If you don't want to take the time to create your own animated GIFs, many animated GIF collections are available on the Web. Figure 3-29 lists a few of them.

Figure 3-29	ANIMATED GIF COLLECTIONS	
TITLE	**URL**
Animated GIFs	http://www.webdeveloper.com/animations/
Animation Express	http://www.animationexpress.co.uk/
Animation Factory	http://www.animfactory.com/
Animation Library	http://www.animationlibrary.com/
Web Animation Library	http://webwizards.hypermart.net/

Because an animated GIF is typically larger than a static GIF image, the use of animated GIFs can greatly increase the size of your Web page. You should also be careful not to overwhelm the user with animated images. Animated GIFs can quickly become a source of irritation to the user once the novelty has worn off, especially because there is no way for the user to turn them off! As with other GIF files, animated GIFs are limited to 256 colors. This makes them ideal for small icons and logos, but not for photographic images.

To see whether an animated GIF enhances the appearance of your Web page, you'll replace the existing Arcadium logo with an animated version.

To insert the animated logo in your HTML file:

1. Return to **arcadium.htm** in your text editor.

2. Replace "aclogo1.gif" in the <img> tag at the top of the document with the filename "**aclogo2.gif**".

3. Save your changes to arcadium.htm and open the file using your Web browser.

The revised Web page now shows a moving train of cars on the roller coaster. Note that animated GIFs, like static GIFs, can use transparent colors. Early browser versions may not support animated GIFs. If a user tries to access your Web page with a browser that does not support animated GIFs, a static image of the first frame of the animation is displayed.

The GIF Controversy

The future of GIFs as a preferred file format on the World Wide Web is in doubt. The problem is that GIFs employ an image compression method known as **Lempel-Ziv-Welch**, or **LZW**. When the GIF format became hugely popular, CompuServe released the format as a free and open file specification, meaning that people could create and distribute GIFs without purchasing the rights from CompuServe. Between 1987 and 1994, GIF became the most popular image format on the Internet, and later, on the World Wide Web. However, the LZW compression method at the heart of the GIF format is patented by the Unisys Corporation. In 1994, Unisys and CompuServe announced that software developers would have to pay a license fee to continue to use LZW compression. This included developers of GIFs.

Because the Web relies so heavily on free and open standards, the possibility that GIFs would be licensed caused an uproar. Unisys is not asking for any licenses for GIFs themselves, but only for software that incorporates the LZW algorithm. Most commercial programs that create GIF files already have a GIF/LZW license from Unisys, so users and Web authors creating GIF files with these programs do not need to worry about getting a separate license.

Still, uncertainty about the patent issue and how Unisys might try to enforce its patent in the future has caused many in the Web community to move away from GIFs as a preferred file format. In its place, a new file format called **PNG (portable network graphics)** has been offered. PNG files use a free and open file format and can display more colors than GIFs. However, PNGs cannot be used for animated graphics. PNGs do allow transparent colors, but not all browsers support this feature. The PNG format may eventually replace GIFs as the primary image type of the World Wide Web, but for the moment, to ensure compatibility across the widest range of browsers, GIFs are still the preferred standard. A detailed summary of this issue and its history can be found in the article "The GIF Controversy: A Software Developer's Perspective" at http://cloanto.com/users/mcb/19950127giflzw.html.

To provide more flexibility for the Web page author, Internet Explorer and Netscape have expanded the types of graphic formats they can display. Internet Explorer can display graphic files in the BMP format, while Netscape can display XPM and XBM files. Be aware that if you use one of these formats, your image might not be viewable in all browsers or browser versions.

Working **with JPEG Files**

The other main image file format is the JPEG format. **JPEG** stands for **Joint Photographic Experts Group**. JPEGs differ from GIFs in several ways. In the JPEG format you can create images that use the full 16.7 million colors available in the color palette. Because of this, JPEG files are most often used for photographs and images that cover a wide spectrum of color.

Another feature of JPEG files is that their image compression algorithm yields image files that are usually (though not always) smaller than their GIF counterparts. For example, in the previous session you used the JPEG file **clouds.jpg** as your background image. The size of that file was only 3.53 KB. If that image were converted to a GIF file, the file size would increase to 43.6 KB. There are situations in which the GIF format creates a smaller and better-looking image—such as when the image has large sections covered with a single color—but as a general rule, JPEGs are smaller.

You can control the size of a JPEG by controlling the degree of image compression applied to the file. Increasing the compression reduces the file size, but it might do so at the expense of image quality. Figure 3-30 shows the effect of compression on a JPEG file. As you can see, the increased compression cuts the file size to one-tenth that of the original, but the resulting image is less well-defined than the image with low compression.

Figure 3-30 | THE EFFECTS OF COMPRESSION ON JPEG FILE SIZE AND QUALITY

minimal compression: file size = 84.3 KB

moderate compression: file size = 20.7 KB

medium compression: file size = 14.2 KB

heavy compression: file size = 8.6 KB

By testing different compression levels with your image editing software, you can reduce the size of your JPEG files while maintaining an attractive image. Note that a smaller file size does not always mean that your page will load faster. The browser has to decompress the JPEG image when it retrieves it, and for a heavily compressed image this can take more time than retrieving and displaying a less compressed file.

There are some other differences between JPEGs and GIFs. You cannot use transparent colors or animation with JPEG files. A JPEG format called **progressive JPEG** does allow JPEG files to be interlaced. However, not all design applications and Web browsers support progressive JPEGs.

Tom wants you to add an image of a roller coaster ride to the Arcadium Web page. The photo has been saved as a JPEG file named **ride.jpg** on your Data Disk. You will insert the image below the title and date on the Web page.

To insert the roller coaster image in your Web page:

1. Return to **arcadium.htm** in your text editor.

2. Locate the paragraph that begins "Exciting adventures await you at" and then insert the following <img> tag after the <p> tag:

```
<img src="ride.jpg">
```

Figure 3-31 shows how the revised HTML code should look.

| Figure 3-31 | ADDING THE RIDE.JPG IMAGE TO THE ARCADIUM PAGE |

```
<p><img src="ride.jpg">Exciting adventures await you at
<b>Arcadium</b>, Georgia's family fun center. The park is located 5 miles
northwest of Derby - close to many of Georgia's scenic wonders. Arcadium supports over 70 rides,
including some of the state's most exciting roller coasters and water rides. There's also
plenty of fun for the younger kids. The park provides two separate kiddie pools and special
rides for the kids.</p>
```

3. Save your changes to the file and reload the file using your Web browser. Figure 3-32 shows the revised page with the newly inserted JPEG image.

| Figure 3-32 | RIDE INLINE IMAGE |

TROUBLE? If the image appears blurry or grainy, it could be because your monitor is capable of displaying only 256 colors, and not the full palette of 16.7 million colors.

Controlling **Image Placement and Size**

You show Tom the progress you've made on the Web page. Although he's pleased with the image of the ride, he doesn't like how the image is positioned on the page. With the current design, there is a large blank space between the park logo and the first paragraph. Tom wonders if you could control the way text flows around the image so that there is less blank space. You can, using the align attribute of the <img> tag.

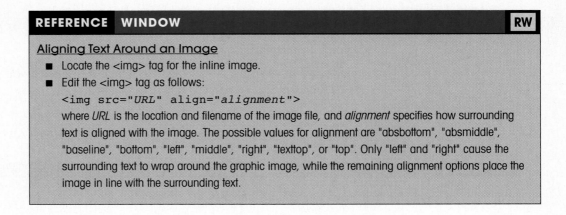

Controlling Image Alignment

As you know, the align attribute can be used to control the alignment of paragraph tags. The align attribute fulfills a similar function in the <img> tag. The syntax for the align attribute is:

```
<img src="URL" align="alignment">
```

where *URL* is the location and filename of the graphic file, and *alignment* indicates how you want the image aligned in relation to the surrounding text. Figure 3-33 describes the possible values of the align attribute.

Figure 3-33	ALIGNMENT OPTIONS
ALIGN=	**DESCRIPTION**
absbottom	Aligns the bottom of the object with the absolute bottom of the surrounding text. The absolute bottom is equal to the baseline of the text minus the height of the largest descender in the text.
absmiddle	Aligns the middle of the object with the middle of the surrounding text. The absolute middle is the midpoint between the absolute bottom and text top of the surrounding text.
baseline	Aligns the bottom of the object with the baseline of the surrounding text.
bottom	Aligns the bottom of the object with the bottom of the surrounding text. The bottom is equal to the baseline minus the standard height of a descender in the text.
left	Aligns the object to the left of the surrounding text. All preceding and subsequent text flows to the right of the object.
middle	Aligns the middle of the object with the surrounding text.
right	Aligns the object to the right of the surrounding text. All subsequent text flows to the left of the object.
texttop	Aligns the top of the object with the absolute top of the surrounding text. The absolute top is the baseline plus the height of the largest ascender in the text.
top	Aligns the object to the right of the surrounding text. All subsequent text flows to the left of the object.

The seven align values—absbottom, absmiddle, baseline, bottom, middle, texttop, and top—place the image in line with the surrounding text. The distinctions between absbottom and bottom, absmiddle and middle, and texttop and top, are subtle. In most cases you can simply use bottom, middle, and top to align the image with the bottom, middle, and top of the surrounding text.

The align values left and right do not place the image in line with the surrounding text; instead, the image is aligned with either the left or right margin of the Web page, and the text is wrapped around the image.

Figure 3-34 shows the effect of each of these alignment options on text surrounding the roller coaster image.

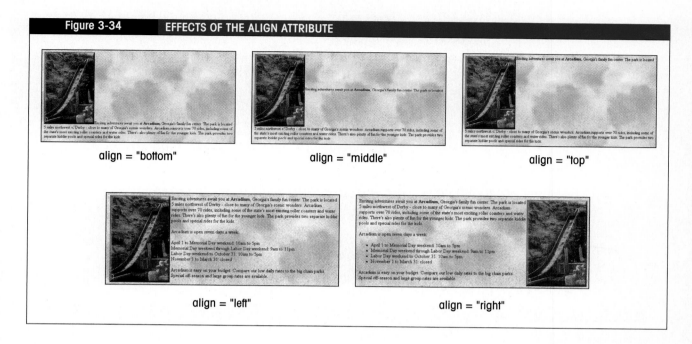

Figure 3-34   EFFECTS OF THE ALIGN ATTRIBUTE

Tom would like you to align the ride.jpg image with the right margin of the Web page so that the text wraps around the left edge of the image.

> ## To align the image on the right margin of the Web page:
>
> 1. Within the <img> tag for the ride.jpg image, insert the attribute: **align="right"**.
> 2. Save your changes to the file and reload it in your Web browser.

The image is now aligned with the right margin of the page, and the text wraps around the image.

Controlling Vertical and Horizontal Space

Wrapping the text around the image has solved one problem: the large blank space has been removed. However, a second problem has surfaced. There's not enough space separating the image and the opening paragraph, which makes the page appear crowded. You can increase the horizontal and vertical space around the image with the hspace and vspace attributes, as follows:

```
<img src="URL" vspace="value" hspace="value" >
```

The hspace (horizontal space) attribute indicates the amount of space to the left and right of the image. The vspace (vertical space) attribute controls the amount of space above and below the image.

Increasing the Space Around an Image

■ Add the following attributes to the <img> tag:

hspace="*value*" vspace="*value*"

where the hspace attribute indicates the amount of space to the left or the right of the image, and the vspace attribute indicates the amount of space above or below the image. All space values are measured in pixels.

You decide to set the horizontal space to 15 pixels and the vertical space to 5 pixels.

To increase the space around the ride image:

1. Return to **arcadium.htm** in your text editor.

2. Within the <img> tag for ride.jpg, add the following attributes and values: **hspace="15" vspace="5"**.

   Your revised <img> tag should appear as shown in Figure 3-35.

Figure 3-35	USING THE HSPACE AND VSPACE ATTRIBUTES

set the horizontal space around the image to 15 pixels and the vertical space to 5 pixels

```
<p><img src="ride.jpg" align="right" hspace="15" vspace="5">Exciting adventures await you at
<b>Arcadium</b>, Georgia's family fun center. The park is located 5 miles
northwest of Derby – close to many of Georgia's scenic wonders. Arcadium supports over 70 rides,
including some of the state's most exciting roller coasters and water rides. There's also
plenty of fun for the younger kids. The park provides two separate kiddie pools and special
rides for the kids.</p>
```

3. Save your changes to the file and reload it in your Web browser.

   As shown in Figure 3-36, the revised page shows increased space between the image and the surrounding text and appears less crowded.

Figure 3-36   INCREASING THE SPACE AROUND THE RIDE IMAGE

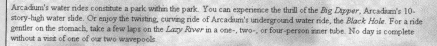

Controlling Image Size

Another set of attributes for the <img> tag are the height and width attributes. Height and width attributes instruct the browser to display an image at a specific size. These attributes can be used to increase or decrease the size of the image on your page. The syntax for setting the height and width attributes is:

```
<img src="URL" height="value" width="value">
```

where *value* is the height or width of the image either in pixels or as a percentage of the page's height or width.

REFERENCE WINDOW   **RW**

<u>Specifying the Size of an Inline Image</u>
- Add the following attributes to the <img> tag:
  ```
  height="value" width="value"
  ```
  where the height and width attributes specify the dimensions of the image as measured in pixels or as a percentage of the height or width of the Web page.

Generally, if you want to decrease the size of an image, you should do so using an image editing application so that the file size is reduced as well as the dimensions of the image. Changing the size of the image within the <img> tag does not affect the file size, it merely makes the image look smaller without improving the performance of the Web page. It is a good idea to specify the height and width of an image even if you're not trying to change the dimensions. Why? Because of the way browsers work with inline images. When a browser encounters an inline image, it calculates the image size and then uses this information to format the page. If you include the dimensions of the image, the browser does not have to perform that calculation, and the page is displayed, or loaded, that much faster. You can obtain the height and width of an image as measured in pixels using an image editing application such as Adobe Photoshop.

The logo image, aclogo.gif, is 517 pixels wide by 119 pixels high, and the roller coaster image, ride.jpg, is 201 pixels wide by 300 pixels high. Add this information for each of the <img> tags in the document.

To specify the width and height of the two images:

1. Return to **arcadium.htm** in your text editor.

2. Within the <img> tag for the aclogo2.gif graphic, add the following attributes and values: **width="517" height="119"**.

3. Within the <img> tag for the ride.jpg image, add the following attributes and values: **width="201" height="300"**.

   The revised arcadium.htm file should appear as shown in Figure 3-37.

Figure 3-37 | INCREASING THE SPACE AROUND THE RIDE IMAGE

```
<html>
<head>
<title>Arcadium – Georgia's Newest and Best Amusement Park</title>
</head>
<body background="clouds.jpg" text="darkblue" link="red" vlink="darkblue" alink="red">

<center>
    <img src="aclogo2.gif" width="517" height="119"><br>
    <i><b><font color="red">Georgia's Newest and Best Amusement Park</font></b></i>
</center>

<p><img src="ride.jpg" align="right" hspace="15" vspace="5" width="201" height="300">Exciting adventures await you at
<b>Arcadium</b>, Georgia's family fun center. The park is located 5 miles
northwest of Derby – close to many of Georgia's scenic wonders. Arcadium supports over 70 rides,
including some of the state's most exciting roller coasters and water rides. There's also
plenty of fun for the younger kids. The park provides two separate kiddie pools and special
rides for the kids.</p>
```

4. Save your changes to arcadium.htm and reload it in your Web browser.

5. Confirm that the layout is the same as the last time you viewed the page because you have not changed the dimensions of the inline images; you've simply included their dimensions in the HTML file.

Using the alt Attribute

Another attribute available with the <img> tag is the alt attribute. The alt attribute allows you to specify text to display in place of your inline images, either temporarily or for the entire time a viewer has your page loaded. Alternate image text is important because it allows users who have nongraphical browsers to know the content of your images. Alternate image text also appears as a placeholder for the image while the page is loading. This can be particularly important for users accessing your page through a slow dial-up connection.

REFERENCE   WINDOW

Specifying Alternate Text for an Inline Image
■ Add the following attribute to the <img> tag:
  alt="*alternate text*"
  where *alternate text* is the text that nongraphical browsers will display in place of the image.

The syntax for specifying alternate text is:

```
<img src="URL" alt="alternate text">
```

Because you replaced the heading text with the Arcadium logo, you decide it would be a good idea to place the text of the logo into the alt attribute for users who are not using graphical browsers.

To insert alternate image text into your Web page:

1. Return to **arcadium.htm** in your text editor.

2. Within the <img> tag for the Arcadium logo image, insert the text: **alt="Arcadium Amusement Park"**.

   Figure 3-38 shows the revised <img> tag.

| Figure 3-38 | SPECIFYING ALTERNATIVE TEXT FOR AN INLINE IMAGE |

```
<html>
<head>
<title>Arcadium - Georgia's Newest and Best Amusement Park</title>
</head>
<body background="clouds.jpg" text="darkblue" link="red" vlink="darkblue" alink="red">

<center>
    <img src="aclogo2.gif" width="517" height="119" alt="Arcadium Amusement Park"><br>
    <i><b><font color="red">Georgia's Newest and Best Amusement Park</font></b></i>
</center>
```

3. Save your changes to the file and close your text editor.

General Tips for Working with Color and Images

You've completed much of the layout for the Arcadium Web page. When working with color and images, keep in mind that the primary purpose of the page is to convey information. "A picture is worth a thousand words," and if an image can convey an idea quickly, by all means use it. If an image adds visual interest to your page and makes the user interested in what you have to say, include it. However, always be aware that overusing images can make your page difficult to read and cumbersome to display. With that in mind, this section provides some tips to remember as you design your Web pages.

Reduce the Size of Your Pages

You should strive to make your page quick and easy to retrieve; particularly for users with dial-up connections. A user with a 56Kbps dial-up modem can retrieve information at a rate of about 7 kilobytes per second. If you have 100 Kilobytes of information on your page, that user will wait, on average, 15 to 20 seconds to see the page in its entirety. To get a feeling how long that can be, sit quietly and patiently count to 20. When users are used to quick responses from their computers, 20 seconds can seem like a long time. That's a problem when a user is a potential customer whose business you don't want to lose. A general rule of thumb is that the total size of the images on your Web page should be no more than 40 to 50 kilobytes. There are several ways to achieve this:

- Reduce the size of the images using an image editing application; don't simply reduce the height and width of the image with the <img> tag

- Experiment with different image file types. Is the file size smaller with the JPEG format or the GIF? Can you compress an image without losing image quality?

- Use **thumbnails**—reduced versions of your images. Place the thumbnail image within a hypertext link to the larger, more detailed image, so that clicking the reduced image loads the higher-quality image. This gives users who want to view the better image the option to do so. Note that the thumbnail has to be a different, smaller file than the original image. If you simply use the height and width attributes to reduce the original image file, you won't be saving your browser any time in rendering the page.

- Reuse your images. If you are creating a Web presentation containing several pages, consider using the same background image for each page. Once a browser has retrieved the image file for the background, it stores the image locally on the user's computer and can quickly display it again. This can also give your Web site a consistent look and feel.

Finally, you can provide an alternate, text-only version of your Web page for those users who are either using a text-based browser or want to quickly load the information stored on your page without viewing inline images.

Manage Your Colors

Color can add a lot to your page, but it can also detract from it. Make sure that you have enough contrast between the text and the background. In other words, don't put dark text on a dark background or light text on a light background. Color is handled differently on different browsers, so you should try to view your page in most of the popular browsers. Certainly you should check to see how Netscape Navigator and Internet Explorer render your page before going live to the Web.

You should also check to see how your Web page is displayed on monitors with different color depth capabilities. Your monitor might be capable of displaying 24-bit color (millions), but users viewing your page might not be so lucky. View your page with your display set to 8-bit color to see how it is rendered. When an image that contains millions of colors (JPEGs) or a GIF image that contains custom colors is displayed on an 8-bit monitor, the browser goes through a process called **dithering**, in which the colors in the image are converted to a fixed palette. As shown in Figure 3-39, dithered images can sometimes appear grainy. Even if your computer is capable of displaying full-color images, you might want to consider creating all your images in 256 colors to control, and if possible eliminate, the effects of dithering.

Figure 3-39	IMAGE DITHERING

original image   dithered image

To completely eliminate dithering, some Web designers recommend that you use the Safety Palette. The **Safety Palette**, also referred to as the **browser-safe palette**, **web palette**, or **216 color palette**, is a collection of 216 colors that display consistently on different browsers and operating systems.

By limiting your color selections to the colors of the Safety Palette, you can be assured that your images will appear the same to all users regardless of the browser they are using. You can search the Web and find several pages devoted to the use of the Safety, or browser-safe, Palette.

The only reason to use a Safety Palette of 216 colors is to accommodate those in your audience who have 8-bit (256 color) systems. Given the growth of 24-bit (millions of colors) color systems, this is rapidly becoming less of an issue for Web designers.

You're finished working with the inline images on your Web page. You've learned about the different image formats supported by most browsers and their advantages and disadvantages. You've also seen how to control the appearance and placement of images on your Web page. In the next session, you'll learn how to create an image that links to other Web pages.

Session 3.2 QUICK CHECK

1. List three reasons for using the GIF image format instead of the JPEG format.

2. List three reasons for using the JPEG image format instead of the GIF format.

3. What HTML tag would you use to display the alternate text "MidWest University" in place of the image mwu.jpg?

4. What HTML tag would you use to align mwu.jpg with the top of the surrounding text?

5. What HTML tag would you use to place the surrounding text on the left side of mwu.jpg?

6. What HTML tag would you use to increase the horizontal and vertical space around mwu.jpg to 10 pixels?

7. The mwu.jpg image is 120 pixels wide by 85 pixels high. Using this information, what would you enter into your HTML file to increase the speed at which the page is rendered by the browser?

8. What is dithering? What is the Safety Palette?

SESSION 3.3

In this session you'll learn about different types of image maps, and you'll create an image map and test it for the Arcadium Web site.

Understanding Image Maps

Tom has reviewed your Arcadium Web page and is pleased with the progress you're making. He's decided that the page should also include a park map so that visitors can easily find their way to all of the different attractions.

Tom wants the map to be interactive so that, for example, when a user clicks the section of the map on roller coaster rides a page describing the roller coaster rides at Arcadium is displayed. Figure 3-40 shows how these links work on the map.

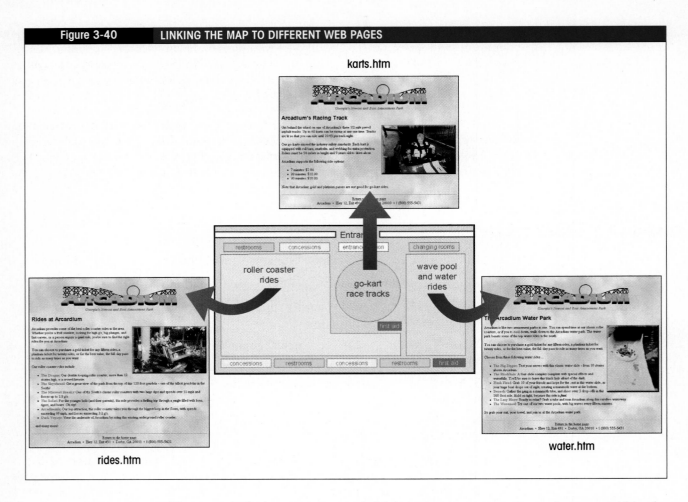

Figure 3-40   LINKING THE MAP TO DIFFERENT WEB PAGES

To use a single image to access multiple targets, you must set up hotspots within the image. A **hotspot** is a defined area of the image that acts as a hypertext link. Any time a user clicks within a hotspot, the hypertext link is activated.

Hotspots are defined through the use of **image maps**, which list the positions of all hotspots within a particular image. As a Web designer, you can use two types of image maps: server-side image maps and client-side image maps. Each has advantages and disadvantages.

Server-Side Image Maps

In a **server-side image map**, the image map is stored on the Web server (see Figure 3-41). When a user clicks a hotspot, the coordinates where the user clicked are sent to a program running on the server. The program uses the coordinates to determine which hotspot was clicked and then activates the corresponding hypertext link.

Figure 3-41 | SERVER-SIDE IMAGE CROP

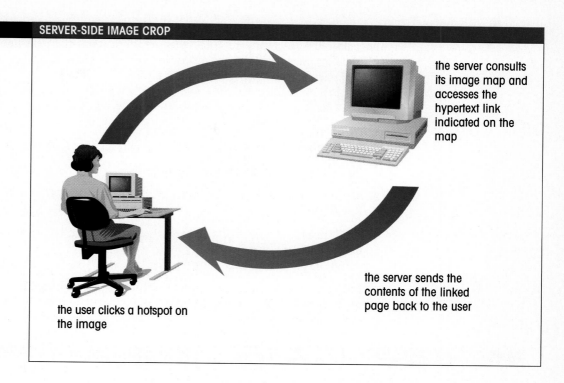

the server consults
its image map and
accesses the
hypertext link
indicated on the
map

the server sends the
contents of the linked
page back to the user

the user clicks a hotspot on
the image

Server-side image maps are supported by most graphical browsers, but there are some limitations to their use. Because a program on the server must process the image map, you cannot test your HTML code using local files. Additionally, server-side image maps can be slow to operate, since every time a user clicks the inline image, the request is sent to the Web server for processing. With most Web browsers, the target of a hypertext link is indicated in the browser's status bar, providing valuable feedback to the user. This is not the case with hotspots of a server-side image map. Because it is the server and not the Web browser that handles the hotspots, no feedback is given to the user regarding the location of the hotspots and their targets.

Client-Side Image Maps

With a **client-side image map**, you insert the image map into the HTML file, and the Web browser locally processes the image map. Because all of the processing is done locally, and not on the Web server, you can easily test your Web pages using the HTML files stored on your computer. Another advantage of client-side image maps is that they tend to be more responsive than server-side maps, because the information does not have to be sent over the network or dial-up connection. Finally, when a user moves the pointer over the inline image, the browser's status bar displays the target of each hotspot. The downside of client-side image maps is that older browsers do not support them. This is much less of a problem than it once was, so you can now use client-side image maps with confidence.

As you become more experienced with HTML, you may want to support both server-side and client-side image maps in your Web pages. For the purposes of this tutorial, you'll concentrate solely on client-side image maps.

The first step in creating the image map is to add the park map image to the Arcadium Web page. In addition to the image, you'll add a note that describes what the user should do to activate hypertext links within the image map. This note should appear directly above the image. To achieve this, you can use the <br> tag, which creates a line break and forces the following image or text to appear on its own line.

The clear attribute is often used within the <br> tag to create the effect of starting a paragraph below the inline image. The clear attribute starts the next line at the first point at which the page margin is clear of text or images. For example, using <br clear="left"> starts the next line when the left page margin is clear.

In this case, you'll use just the <br> tag to force the park map image to appear directly below the text describing how to activate the hypertext links in the image map.

To add the park map image to arcadium.htm:

1. Using your text editor, open **arcadium.htm**.

2. At the bottom of the file, directly above the <hr> tag, enter the following HTML code:

   ```
   <h5 align="center"> Click each location for a list of
   attractions <br>
   <img src="parkmap.gif" width="520" height="309"> </h5>
   ```

   The <br> tag creates a line break, causing the parkmap.gif image to be displayed directly below the explanatory text. Your revised file should appear as shown in Figure 3-42.

Figure 3-42	INSERTING THE PARK MAP IMAGE

```
<h5 align="center">Click each location for a list of attractions<br>
<img src="parkmap.gif" width="520" height="309"></h5>

<hr>

<center>
 Arcadium  &#149;  Hwy 12, Exit 491  &#149; 
 Derby, GA 20010  &#149; 1 (800) 555-5431
</center>

</body>
</html>
```

the <br> tag creates a line break

3. Save your changes to the file and reload it in your Web browser.

   Figure 3-43 shows the park map image as it appears in the Web page.

Figure 3-43	PARK MAP IMAGE AS IT APPEARS IN THE BROWSER

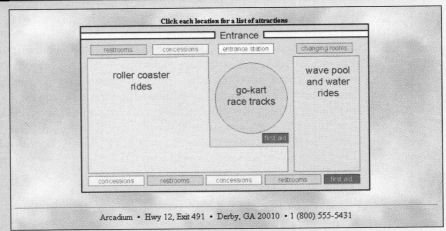

Your next task is to convert parkmap.gif to an image map.

Defining **Image Map Hotspots**

To create the image map, you could open the image in an image editing application and record the coordinates of the points corresponding to the hotspot boundaries. However, this is a difficult and time-consuming procedure. Instead, a Web designer typically uses a special program that determines the image map coordinates. Most image map programs generate the coordinates for hotspots as well as the necessary HTML code. There are several programs available for this purpose, some of which are listed in Figure 3-44.

Figure 3-44	PROGRAMS FOR CREATING IMAGE MAPS

TITLE	URL
CompuPic Pro	http://www.photodex.com/products/pro/
Image Mapper	http://www.coffeecup.com/mapper/
LiveImage	http://www.mediatec.com/
MapEdit	http://www.boutell.com/mapedit/
Visual Imagemapper	http://www.sofasitters.net/imagemap/

To help you understand the syntax of image maps better, you'll be given the coordinates and then use that information to create your own HTML code.

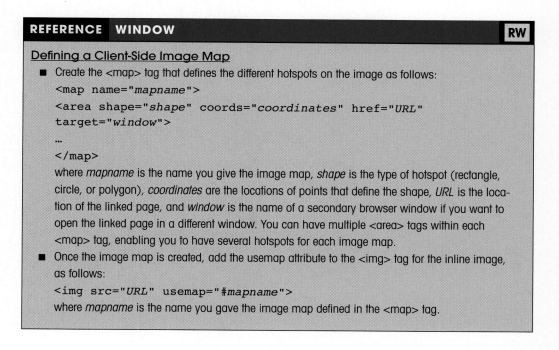

REFERENCE WINDOW   **RW**

<u>Defining a Client-Side Image Map</u>

■ Create the <map> tag that defines the different hotspots on the image as follows:

```
<map name="mapname">
<area shape="shape" coords="coordinates" href="URL"
target="window">
…
</map>
```

where *mapname* is the name you give the image map, *shape* is the type of hotspot (rectangle, circle, or polygon), *coordinates* are the locations of points that define the shape, *URL* is the location of the linked page, and *window* is the name of a secondary browser window if you want to open the linked page in a different window. You can have multiple <area> tags within each <map> tag, enabling you to have several hotspots for each image map.

■ Once the image map is created, add the usemap attribute to the <img> tag for the inline image, as follows:

```
<img src="URL" usemap="#mapname">
```

where *mapname* is the name you gave the image map defined in the <map> tag.

The general syntax for an image map tag is:

```
<map name="mapname">
<area shape="shape" coords="coordinates" href="URL"
target="window">
</map>
```

The <map> tag gives the name of the image map. Within the <map> tag, you use the <area> tag to specify the areas of the image that act as hotspots. You can include as many <area> tags within the <map> tags as you need for the image map.

The shape attribute refers to the shape of the hotspot. It has three possible values: "rect" for a rectangular hotspot, "circle" for a circular hotspot, and "poly" or " Polygon" for irregularly-shaped polygon hotspots.

In the coords attribute, you enter coordinates to specify the location of the hotspot. The values you enter depend on the shape of the hotspot. As you'll see, you need to enter different coordinates for a rectangular hotspot than you would for a circular one. Coordinates are expressed as a point's distance in pixels from the left and the top edges of the image. For example, the coordinates (123,45) refer to a point 123 pixels from the left edge and 45 pixels down from the top. If the coordinates of your <area> tags overlap, the browser uses the first tag in the list for the hotspot.

In the href attribute you enter the location of the page opened by the hotspot. In the target attribute, you can specify the name of a secondary browser window in which to open the linked page. You can use the value "nohref" in place of a URL if you do not want the hotspot to activate a hypertext link. This is a useful technique when you are first developing your image map, without all the hypertext links in place. The <area> tag then acts as a placeholder until the time when you have the hypertext links ready for use.

REFERENCE   WINDOW   **RW**

Defining Image Map Hotspots

- Within the <map> tag, enter the code for the type of hotspot(s) and the coordinates.
  The syntax for a rectangular hotspot is:

  ```
  <area shape="rect" coords="x_left, y_upper, x_right, y_lower"
  href="URL" target="window">
  ```

  where x_left, y_upper are the coordinates of the upper-left corner of the rectangle, and x_right, y_lower are the coordinates of the lower-right corner.
  The syntax for a circular hotspot is:

  ```
  <area shape="circle" coords="x_center, y_center, radius"
  href="URL" target="window">
  ```

  where x_center, y_center is the center of the circle, and radius is the circle's radius.
  The syntax for a polygonal hotspot is:

  ```
  <area shape="polygon" coords="x1, y1, x2, y2, x3, y3, … "
  href="URL" target="window">
  ```

  where x1, y1, x2, y2, x3, y3, … are the coordinates of the vertices of the polygon.

Before creating your <area> tags, you'll add the <map> tag to arcadium.htm and assign the name "ParkMap" to the image map.

To insert the <map> tag:

1. Return to **arcadium.htm** in your text editor.

2. Navigate to the bottom of the file and enter the following directly above the </body>tag:

```
<map name="ParkMap">
</map>
```

With the <map> tag in place, you must next determine the hotspot areas for the image. Tom wants the image map to include hotspots for the roller coaster rides (a polygonal hotspot), the go-kart track (a circular hotspot), and the water park (a rectangular hotspot). You'll start by creating the rectangular hotspot for the water park.

Creating a Rectangular Hotspot

Two points define a rectangular hotspot: the upper-left corner and the lower-right corner. These points for the waterpark hotspot are located at (384,61) and (499,271). In other words, the upper-left corner is 384 pixels to the right and 61 pixels down from the left and top edges of the image, and the lower-right corner is 499 pixels to the right and 271 pixels down. The hotspot links to water.htm, a Web page that contains information on all the rides in the water park.

To insert the waterpark <area> tag:

1. Insert a blank line between the opening and closing <map> tags you just entered. The blank line is necessary only to make your code more readable.

2. Type the following code in the blank line:

```
<area shape="rect" coords="384,61,499,271"
href="water.htm">
```

Note that the coordinates are entered as a series of four numbers separated by commas. Because this is a rectangular hotspot, HTML expects that the first two numbers represent the coordinates for the upper-left corner of the rectangle, and the second two numbers indicate the location of the lower-right corner.

Next you'll enter the <area> tag for the go-kart race track, a circular hotspot.

Creating a Circular Hotspot

The coordinates required for a circular hotspot differ from those of a rectangular hotspot. A circular hotspot is defined by the location of its center and its radius. The circle representing the go-kart racing area hotspot is centered at the coordinates (307,137), and it has a radius of 66 pixels. The hotspot is a hypertext link to karts.htm.

To insert the go-kart <area> tag:

1. Insert a blank line directly above the waterpark <area> tag.

2. Type the following in the new blank line:

```
<area shape="circle" coords="307,137,66"
href="karts.htm">
```

The final hotspot you need to define is for the roller coaster rides. Because of its irregular shape, you need to create a polygonal hotspot.

Creating a Polygonal Hotspot

To create a polygonal hotspot, you enter the coordinates for each vertex in the shape.

The coordinates for the vertices of the roller coaster hotspot are shown in Figure 3-45. The link for this hotspot is rides.htm.

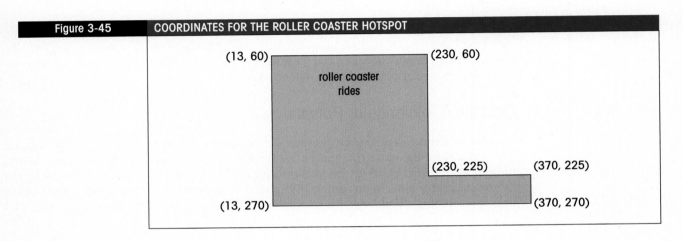

Figure 3-45   COORDINATES FOR THE ROLLER COASTER HOTSPOT

With the coordinate information in hand, you can create the final <area> tag for your image map.

To insert the roller coaster <area> tag:

1. Insert a blank line directly above the go-kart <area> tag.

2. Type the following in the new blank line:

```
<area shape="poly" coords="13,60,13,270,370,270,370,
225,230,225,230,60" href="rides.htm">
```

Figure 3-46 shows the completed list of <area> tags for the ParkMap image map. Compare these values with the values you entered to confirm that you entered them correctly.

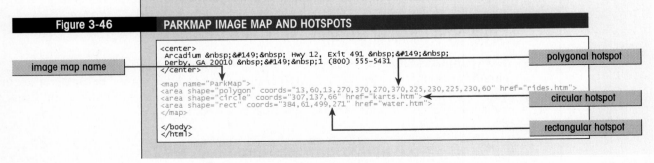

Figure 3-46   PARKMAP IMAGE MAP AND HOTSPOTS

With all of the <area> tags in place, you're finished defining the image map. Your next task is to instruct the browser to use the ParkMap image map with the inline image. Then you'll test the image to confirm that it works properly.

Using an Image Map

The final step in adding an image map to a Web page is to add the usemap attribute to the <img> tag for the image map graphic. The usemap attribute tells the browser the name of the image map to associate with the inline image. The syntax for adding the usemap attribute is:

```
<img src="URL" usemap="#mapname">
```

Here, *mapname* is the name assigned to the name attribute in the <map> tag. Note that you have to place a pound sign (#) before the image map name. You named your image map ParkMap and you inserted the image into your Web page. Now you have to add the usemap attribute to the <img> tag to associate parkmap.gif with the ParkMap image map.

> ## To assign the ParkMap image map to parkmap.gif and test the image map:
>
> **1.** Navigate to the parkmap.gif <img> tag.
>
> **2.** Add the following attribute to the tag: **usemap="#ParkMap"**.
>
> The completed <img> tag should appear as shown in Figure 3-47.

Figure 3-47	PARKMAP IMAGE MAP AND HOTSPOTS

```
<h5 align="center">Click each location for a list of attractions<br>
<img src="parkmap.gif" width="520" height="309" usemap="#ParkMap"></h5>

<hr>

<center>
Arcadium  &#149;  Hwy 12, Exit 491  &#149; 
Derby, GA 20010  &#149; 1 (800) 555-5431
</center>

<map name="ParkMap">
<area shape="polygon" coords="13,60,13,270,370,270,370,225,230,225,230,60" href="rides.htm">
<area shape="circle" coords="307,137,66" href="karts.htm">
<area shape="rect" coords="384,61,499,271" href="water.htm">
</map>

</body>
</html>
```

name of image to use

properties of image map

> **3.** Save your changes to the file and reload arcadium.htm in your Web browser.
>
> **4.** Scroll to the park map image, positioning your mouse pointer over the image.
>
> Note that the pointer changes to a hand when it is positioned over a hotspot, and the status bar displays the URL for that particular hotspot. See Figure 3-48.

Figure 3-48   **PARKMAP IMAGE MAP AND HOTSPOTS**

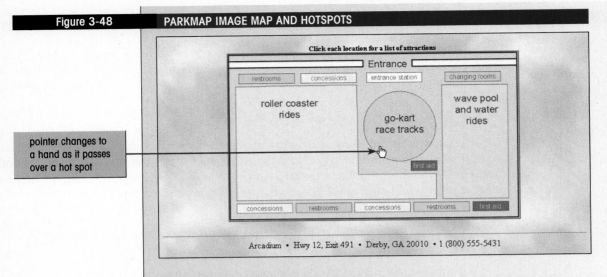

pointer changes to
a hand as it passes
over a hot spot

TROUBLE? If your image does not have a red border around it, don't worry. The border is created by some browsers and not others and is discussed in the following section.

5. Click anywhere within the roller coaster rides section of the map.
The Web browser opens a Web page describing the different rides at the Arcadium theme park.

6. Click the **Back** button in your Web browser to return to the Arcadium Web page.

7. Test the other hotspots in the image map to confirm that they navigate to the appropriate Web pages.

8. When you're finished testing the hotspots, return to the Arcadium Web page.

With some browsers, you'll notice that an image map is displayed with a red border. Where did this border come from? Some browsers use the border to identify the image as a hypertext link. The border color is red because that is the color you specified earlier for hypertext links. You can remove that border using the <img> tag's border attribute.

Using the border Attribute

The border attribute specifies the size of the border surrounding your inline images. The syntax for setting the border width is:

```
<img src="URL" border="value">
```

where *value* is the width of the border in pixels. An inline image that does not contain hypertext links to other documents will, by default, not have a border. However, if the image does contain hypertext links, some browsers create a two-pixel-wide border. If you want to either create or remove a border, you can do so by specifying the appropriate border width.

Tom thinks that the map would look better without a border, so you'll remove it from the image by specifying a border width of 0 pixels. Even if your browser did not display a red border, you should complete the following steps for those browsers that do add borders around image maps.

To remove the border from the ParkMap graphic:

1. Return to **arcadium.htm** in your text editor.

2. Locate the <img> tag for the park map and insert the attribute **border="0"**.

3. Save your changes to the file, and then close the file and your text editor.

4. Open **arcadium.htm** in your Web browser and verify that the border is not displayed around the park map.

5. Close your Web browser.

Tom reviews the completed Arcadium page. He's pleased with the work you've done and will get back to you with any changes he wants you to make. For now you can close your browser and text editor.

Figure 3-49 shows the finished Web page of the Arcadium amusement park.

Figure 3-49   COMPLETED ARCADIUM WEB PAGE

Georgia's Newest and Best Amusement Park

Exciting adventures await you at **Arcadium**, Georgia's family fun center. The park is located 5 miles northwest of Derby - close to many of Georgia's scenic wonders. Arcadium supports over 70 rides, including some of the state's most exciting roller coasters and water rides. There's also plenty of fun for the younger kids. The park provides two separate kiddie pools and special rides for the kids.

Arcadium is open seven days a week:

- April 1 to Memorial Day weekend: 10am to 5pm
- Memorial Day weekend through Labor Day weekend: 9am to 11pm
- Labor Day weekend to October 31: 10am to 5pm
- November 1 to March 31: closed

Arcadium is easy on your budget. Compare our low daily rates to the big chain parks. Special off-season and large group rates are available.

Water Park

Arcadium's water rides constitute a park within the park. You can experience the thrill of the *Big Dipper*, Arcadium's 10-story-high water slide. Or enjoy the twisting, curving ride of Arcadium's underground water ride, the *Black Hole*. For a ride gentler on the stomach, take a few laps on the *Lazy River* in a one-, two-, or four-person inner tube. No day is complete without a visit of one of our two wavepools.

Fun Rides

Enjoy some of the most exciting roller coaster rides in the area. Start off with the *Dragon*, our double looping roller coaster more than 12 stories high. Get a great view of the park from the *Skywheel*, a 120-foot-high gondola capable of holding up to 115 people. The *Missouri Breaks* will get your heart pumping at speeds of greater than 55 mph and forces up to 2.8 g's.

Vroooom

Put yourself behind the wheel for a change, by enjoying one of our three go-kart tracks. For those with a little more aggression, you can take it out on our bumper car or bumper boat tracks. All rides support the highest safety standards in the industry.

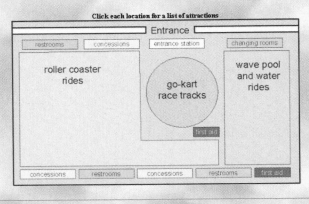

Arcadium • Hwy 12, Exit 491 • Derby, GA 20010 • 1 (800) 555-5431

You've done an effective job enhancing the Arcadium Web page with images. You've seen how to create an image map so that a single image can provide links to multiple Web pages. You've also learned about some of the design issues and challenges involved in adding images to a Web page, and how to choose the correct file type for a particular image. Using the knowledge you've gained, you're ready to work on new design challenges that Tom has in store for you.

Session 3.3 QUICK CHECK

1. What is a hotspot? What is an image map?

2. What are the two types of image maps? List the advantages and disadvantages of each.

3. What HTML tag would you use to define a rectangular hotspot with the upper-left edge of the rectangle at the point (5,20) and the lower-right edge located at (85,100) and with oregon.htm displayed when the hotspot is activated?

4. What HTML tag would you use for a circular hotspot centered at (44,81) with a radius of 23 pixels to be linked to la.htm?

5. What HTML tag would you use for a hotspot that connects the points (5,10), (5,35), (25,35), (30,20), and (15,10) and that you want linked to hawaii.htm?

6. What HTML tag would you use to assign an image map named States to westcoast.gif?

7. What HTML tag would you use to increase the border around westcoast.gif to 5 pixels?

REVIEW ASSIGNMENTS

Tom has come back to you with some more changes and additions he wants made to the Arcadium Web pages. The park has a new area called the Toddler Park, specially designed for very young children. Tom needs you to revise the hotspots for the new park map, and he also needs you to design a Web page for the toddler park. Figure 3-50 shows a preview of the toddler page you'll create.

Figure 3-50

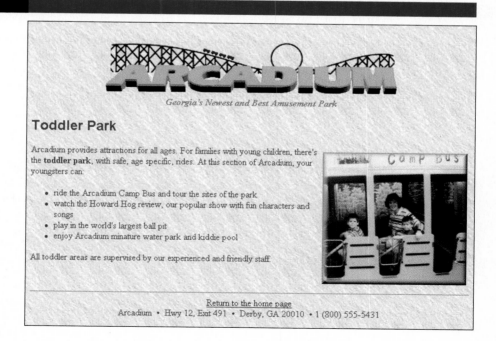

Toddler Park

Arcadium provides attractions for all ages. For families with young children, there's the **toddler park**, with safe, age specific, rides. At this section of Arcadium, your youngsters can:

- ride the Arcadium Camp Bus and tour the sites of the park
- watch the Howard Hog review, our popular show with fun characters and songs
- play in the world's largest ball pit
- enjoy Arcadium minature water park and kiddie pool

All toddler areas are supervised by our experienced and friendly staff.

Return to the home page
Arcadium • Hwy 12, Exit 491 • Derby, GA 20010 • 1 (800) 555-5431

To complete this task:

1. Using your text editor, open **arcatxt2.htm** located in the tutorial.03/review folder of your Data Disk and save it as **arca2.htm**.

2. At the bottom of the file, before the </body> tag, create an image map named pmap2 with the following hotspots:

   ■ a polygonal hotspot for **rides.htm**. The coordinates of the polygon's vertices are: (13, 54), (13, 245), (294, 245), (294, 204), (184, 204), and (184, 54).

   ■ a circular hotspot for **karts.htm**. The circle is centered at the coordinate (246,125) and has a radius of 59 pixels.

   ■ a polygonal hotspot for **water.htm**. The coordinates of the polygon's vertices are: (310,55), (310, 246),(503, 246), (503, 186), (423, 186), and (423, 55).

   ■ a rectangular hotspot for **toddler.htm**. The coordinates of the rectangle's corners are (428, 55) and (502, 182).

3. Associate the **pmap2.jpg** image with the image map. Set the size of the image border to 0 pixels.

4. Save your changes to the file, and print the code.

5. Using your text editor, open **toddtxt.htm** and save it as **toddler.htm**.

6. Use **wall.jpg** for the background of the Web page. Set the link color to blue. Set the text, previously followed links, and active link color to dark red.

7. Replace the h1 heading with the **aclogo1.gif** image and display the text "Arcadium" for browsers that don't support inline graphics.

8. Change the font of the Toddler Park heading to the following font list: Arial, Helvetica, and sans-serif.

9. At the top of the Toddler Park paragraph, insert **toddler.jpg** and align it with the right margin of the page. Set the width of the graphic to 250 pixels and the height to 234 pixels. Set the horizontal space around the graphic to 5 pixels and the vertical space to 10 pixels.

10. Above the <hr> tag, modify the <br> tag so that the line break clears any object on the right margin of the page.

11. Using your text editor, save your changes to toddler.htm. Print the HTML code.

12. Using your Web browser, open **arca2.htm**. Verify that the image map works properly and opens all four files.

13. Hand in your files and printouts to your instructor.

Case 1. **Midwest University Center for Diversity.** Stewart Findlay is a project coordinator for the Midwest University Center for Diversity. He is currently working on a Web site highlighting the words and deeds of minorities in America. He's asked you to help develop a page on Martin Luther King, Jr. The page shows an excerpt from one of Dr. King's speeches, along with a photo of Dr. King. Stewart has created the text for the page, but he needs your help in improving the page's design. Figure 3-51 shows a preview of the page you'll create in this assignment.

Figure 3-51

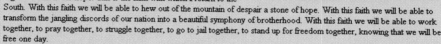

Martin Luther King, Jr.

I have a dream that one day this nation will rise up and live out the true meaning of its creed: "We hold these truths to be self-evident: that all men are created equal." I have a dream that one day on the red hills of Georgia the sons of former slaves and the sons of former slaveowners will be able to sit down together at a table of brotherhood. I have a dream that one day even the state of Mississippi, a desert state, sweltering with the heat of injustice and oppression, will be transformed into an oasis of freedom and justice. I have a dream that my four children will one day live in a nation where they will not be judged by the color of their skin but by the content of their character. I have a dream today.

I have a dream that one day the state of Alabama, whose governor's lips are presently dripping with the words of interposition and nullification, will be transformed into a situation where little black boys and black girls will be able to join hands with little white boys and white girls and walk together as sisters and brothers. I have a dream today. I have a dream that one day every valley shall be exalted, every hill and mountain shall be made low, the rough places will be made plain, and the crooked places will be made straight, and the glory of the Lord shall be revealed, and all flesh shall see it together. This is our hope. This is the faith with which I return to the South. With this faith we will be able to hew out of the mountain of despair a stone of hope. With this faith we will be able to transform the jangling discords of our nation into a beautiful symphony of brotherhood. With this faith we will be able to work together, to pray together, to struggle together, to go to jail together, to stand up for freedom together, knowing that we will be free one day.

This will be the day when all of God's children will be able to sing with a new meaning, "My country, 'tis of thee, sweet land of liberty, of thee I sing. Land where my fathers died, land of the pilgrim's pride, from every mountainside, let freedom ring." And if America is to be a great nation, this must become true. So let freedom ring from the prodigious hilltops of New Hampshire. Let freedom ring from the mighty mountains of New York. Let freedom ring from the heightening Alleghenies of Pennsylvania! Let freedom ring from the snowcapped Rockies of Colorado! Let freedom ring from the curvaceous peaks of California! But not only that; let freedom ring from Stone Mountain of Georgia! Let freedom ring from Lookout Mountain of Tennessee! Let freedom ring from every hill and every molehill of Mississippi. From every mountainside, let freedom ring.

When we let freedom ring, when we let it ring from every village and every hamlet, from every state and every city, we will be able to speed up that day when all of God's children, black men and white men, Jews and Gentiles, Protestants and Catholics, will be able to join hands and sing in the words of the old Negro spiritual, "Free at last! free at last! thank God Almighty, we are free at last!"

Created by the Midwest University Center for Diversity

To complete this task:

1. Using your text editor, open **kingtext.htm** in the tutorial.03/case1 folder of your Data Disk and save it as **king.htm**.

2. Change the background color of the Web page to tan.

3. Format the h1 heading so it appears in one of the following fonts: Arial, Helvetica, or sans-serif.

Explore

4. Change the color of the heading to the RGB triplet (73, 111, 197). Note that you will need to convert this RGB triplet to a hexadecimal value using one of the resources mentioned in this tutorial.

5. At the top of the first paragraph, insert the image **mlk.gif** and align it with the right margin of the Web page. Set the dimensions of the image to 336 pixels wide by 400 pixels high. Set the horizontal and vertical space around the image to 5 pixels.

6. Replace the letter "I" in the first line of the Dr. King's speech with **i.gif** and align the image with the left margin of the Web page.

7. Display the closing sentence of Dr. King's speech using the same color you used for the Web page heading. Set the font size to 4.

Explore   8. Replace the <hr> tag at the bottom of the page with **line.gif** and set the width of the image to 100% of the Web page width. Set the height of the image to 3 pixels.

9. Display the text below the line in the same color you used for the Web page heading.

10. Save your changes and print a copy of the HTML code.

11. Using your Web browser, open **king.htm** and verify that you've changed the design correctly.

12. Hand in your printouts and files to your instructor.

Case 2. Kelsey's Diner. You've been asked to create an online menu for Kelsey's Diner, a well-established restaurant in Worcester, Massachusetts, so that patrons can order carryout dishes via the Web. Cindy Towser is the manager and she has provided you with a text file that contains the current carryout breakfast menu. She wants you to spice it up with an effective color scheme and some images. She also wants you to create hypertext links to the lunch and dinner carryout menus. A preview of the page that you'll create is shown in Figure 3-52.

Figure 3-52

To create the Web menu for Kelsey's Diner:

1. Using your text editor, open **breaktxt.htm** from the tutorial.03/case2 folder on your Data Disk, and save it as **breakfst.htm** in the same folder.

2. Use **tan.jpg** for the background of the Web page.

3. Insert **breakfst.jpg** at the top of the page within a set of <h5> heading tags and center the image on the page. Directly below the image, after a line break, insert the text "Click the Breakfast, Lunch, or Dinner menu" (within the <h5> tags used for the inline image).

Explore   4. Change the text of the title "Breakfast Menu" to green, and increase the point size of the text by three.

5. For the name of each dish in the menu, make the text boldface, change the color of the text to green, and specify that the text should appear in either the Arial, Helvetica, or sans-serif font (in that order).

6. At the bottom of the page, insert an image map named Menu. The image map should have three rectangular hotspots. The first hotspot has the coordinates (20,40) and (156,77) and points to **breakfst.htm**; the second has coordinates at (241,40) and (336,77) and points to **lunch.htm**; the third has coordinates at (464,40) and (568,77) and points to **dinner.htm**. Apply this image map to **breakfst.jpg** and set the border width of the image to 0 pixels.

7. Repeat Steps 2 through 6 with **lunchtxt.htm**, but place **lunch.jpg** at the top of the page and save the file as **lunch.htm**.

8. Repeat Steps 2 through 6 with **dinnrtxt.htm**, but place **dinner.jpg** at the top of the page and save the file as **dinner.htm**.

9. Using your Web browser, open **breakfst.htm** and test the hypertext links. Verify that the pages look correct and that the inline image changes to reflect the change in the menu.

10. Using your text editor, print the source code for all three files.

11. Hand in your printouts and files to your instructor.

Case 3. Pixal Digital Products, Inc.   PDP, Inc. is a leading manufacturer and distributor of digital cameras. You've been hired by Plant Manager Maria Sanchez to work on the Web site for PDP.

Maria would like you to develop a **splash screen**, an opening Web page that provides some animation and visual interest to the reader. Maria suggests that you use an animation that displays the Pixal logo on the Web page. A PDP designer has already created the animated GIF file that Maria would like to use. The animated GIF image is to be centered and offset 250 pixels from the top margin of the Web page. Figure 3-53 shows a preview of how Maria wants the splash screen to look.

Figure 3-53

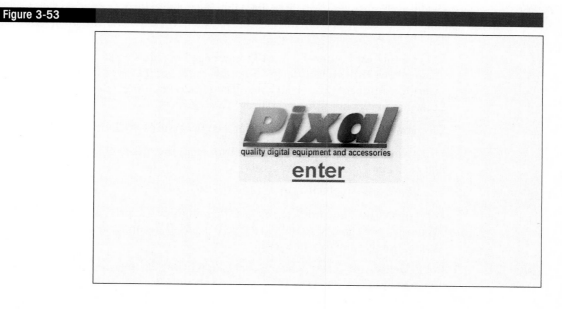

When users click on the logo in the splash screen, Maria would like the browser to display the home page of the PDP Web site. She has created text for the home page and three other Web pages describing Pixal's DC100, DC250, and DC500 digital cameras. Figure 3-54 shows a preview of one of the Web pages you'll create for Maria.

Figure 3-54

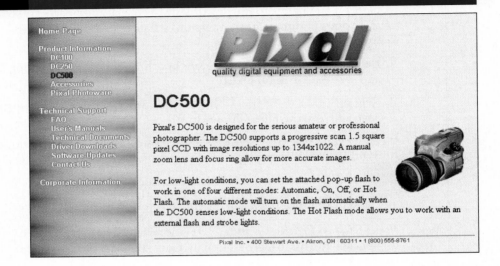

To create a Web page for PDP, Inc.:

1. Using your text editor, open **introtxt.htm** located in the tutorial.03/case3 folder of your Data Disk and save it as **intro.htm**.

Explore

2. Set the background color of the page to ivory. Instead of using the color name, use the hexadecimal value for the ivory color as listed in Appendix A.

Explore

3. Replace the <br> tag with **spacer.gif** and set the dimensions of the image to 1 pixel wide by 250 pixels high. Note that **spacer.gif** is a transparent image, 1 pixel in size, used as a layout tool.

4. Replace the text "Enter the Pixal Home Page" with **intro.gif**. Set the dimensions of the image file to 281 pixels wide by 140 pixels high. Set the size of the border to 0 pixels. Insert the alternate text, "Enter the Pixal Home Page" into the <img> tag for the benefit of those users not using graphical Web browsers.

5. Save your changes to intro.htm. Print a copy of the HTML code.

6. Using your text editor, open **pixaltxt.htm** from the tutorial.03/case3 folder of your Data Disk and save it as **pixal.htm**.

7. Use **pback.jpg** for the background of the Web page.

8. Directly below the <body> tag, insert **dclist1.gif** and align it with the left margin of the Web page. Set the size of the border to 0 pixels. This image contains a menu of Pixal Web pages that the user can visit.

Explore

9. Below **dclist1.gif**, insert **spacer.gif** and align it with the left margin of the page. Set the dimensions of this image to 120 pixels wide by 90 pixels high. The effect of this spacer image is to position the company name precisely 120 pixels to the right of the page menu.

10. Replace the entire h2 heading (include the opening and closing <h2> tags), "Pixal Digital Products," with the **plogo.jpg** image. Set the dimensions of the image to 281 pixels wide by 96 pixels high. Specify the alternate text "Pixal Digital Products" for this image.

Explore ▶ 11. Below **plogo.jpg**, insert another **spacer.gif** image. Align this spacer with the left margin of the Web page, and set the dimensions of the spacer image to 20 pixels wide by 400 pixels high. The effect of this spacer is to position the paragraph text precisely 20 pixels to the right of the page menu.

12. Scroll to the bottom of the file and replace the <hr> tag with the inline image **red.jpg**. Set the dimensions of the inline image to 1 pixel in height and 100% of the width of the Web page.

13. Display the company name, address, and phone number at the bottom of the page in an Arial, Helvetica, or sans-serif font. Set the color of this text to blue and the font size to 1.

14. Create an image map named dcpages with the following hotspots:

- a rectangular hotspot for **pixal.htm** with the coordinates (1, 1) and (81, 15)
- a rectangular hotspot for **dc100.htm** with the coordinates (23, 50) and (64, 62)
- a rectangular hotspot for **dc250.htm** with the coordinates (23, 64) and (64, 79)
- a rectangular hotspot for **dc500.htm** with the coordinates: (23, 81) and (64, 95)

15. Apply the dcpages image map to **dclist1.gif**, located at the top of the page.

16. Using your text editor, save your changes to pixal.htm and print the HTML code.

17. Using your text editor, open **dc100txt.htm** and save it as **dc100.htm**.

18. Apply the same design to this file as you applied to **pixal.htm**, with the following additions:

- Change the image file for the page menu to **dclist2.gif**.
- Display the h1 heading, DC100, in an Arial, Helvetica, or sans-serif font and specify the color as blue.
- Insert **dc100.jpg** into the first paragraph and align it with the right margin of the Web page.

19. Using your text editor, save your changes to dc100.htm and print the HTML code.

20. Using your text editor, open **dc250txt.htm** and save it as **dc250.htm**. Apply the same design to this page as you applied to **dc100.htm**, except use **dclist3.gif** for the menu on the Web page, and insert **dc250.jpg** into the first paragraph of the page. Save your changes and print the HTML code.

21. Using your text editor, open **dc500txt.htm** and save it as **dc500.htm**. Apply the same design to this page as you applied to the other two product pages, except use **dclist4.gif** for the menu on the Web page, and insert **dc500.jpg** into the first paragraph of the page. Save your changes and print the HTML code.

22. Open **intro.htm** with your Web browser and view the Pixal Web site. Verify that all hotspots work correctly and that the page design resembles the design shown in Figure 3-57.

23. Hand in your printouts and files to your instructor.

Case 4. Tri-State Realty. Tri-State Realty is in the process of putting its listings on the World Wide Web. You've been asked to create some Web pages for its Web site. The marketing manager at Tri-State has provided you with the information for your first Web page: a property listing located at 22 North Shore Drive.

"This is a must see. Large waterfront home overlooking Mills Lake. It comes complete with three bedrooms, a huge master bedroom, hot tub, family room, large office or den, and three-car garage. Wood boat ramp. Great condition!"

In addition, the owners have included the following main selling points that they want featured on the Web page:

- 2900 sq. feet
- 15 years old
- updated electrical, plumbing, and heating systems
- central air conditioning
- near school, park, and shopping center
- nice, quiet neighborhood
- asking price: $280,000

Finally, you've been given the following files to complete your task that are located in the case4 subfolder of the tutorial.03 folder on your Data Disk:

- **house.jpg**, which contains a photo of the property; size is 243x163
- **tristate.gif**, the company logo; size is 225x100
- **listings.gif**, an image showing the various listing categories; size is 600x100
- **tsback.gif**, the background image used on all Tri-State Web pages

Using this information, you'll create a Web page for the property at 22 North Shore Drive. The design of the page is up to you, but it should include the following:

- an appropriately titled heading
- a paragraph describing the house
- a list of the main points of interest
- the photo of the house, the logo, and the image of the different listing categories
- the background image for the background on all the Web pages you design
- at least one example of a color other than the color specified in the <body> tag or default browser colors
- at least one example of a font displaying a different face and size from the surrounding text
- alternate text for the logo and house photo images
- height and width information for all inline images
- the listings image converted to an image map, with the following hotspots (target files are blank, except for some placeholder text):
  - rectangular hotspot at (5,3) (182,44) that points to **newhome.htm**
  - rectangular hotspot at (12,62) (303,95) that points to **mansions.htm**
  - rectangular hotspot at (210,19) (374,60) that points to **business.htm**
  - rectangular hotspot at (375,1) (598,44) that points to **family.htm**
  - rectangular hotspot at (378,61) (549,96) that points to **apartmnt.htm**
  - appropriately labeled hypertext links that point to the same files as indicated in the image map
  - your name, as Web designer, in italics

Save the page as **tristate.htm** in the tutorial.03/case4 folder, and then print a copy of your page and the HTML code. Close your Web browser and your text editor when you're finished.

QUICK CHECK ANSWERS

Session 3.1

1. Color names and color values. Color names are easier to work with, but the color name may not exist for exactly the color you want to use. Also your color name may not be supported by all browsers. Color values allow you to precisely describe a color, but they can be difficult to work with.

2. <body bgcolor="gray" text="red" link="blue" vlink="yellow">

3. <font color="red" size="+5">Major Sale</font>

4. <font face="Times New Roman, MS Serif">Major Sale</font>

5. <body background="stars.gif">

6. Overwhelming the page's text, using a large image file that will make the page take longer to load, and using an image that displays visible seams.

Session 3.2

1. Use GIF when you want to use transparent colors, when you want to use an animated image, and when your image has 256 colors or less.

2. Use JPEG for photographic images, for images that contain more than 256 colors, to reduce file size through compression, and to avoid the problem of the legal issues of using GIFs.

3. <img src="mwu.jpg" alt="MidWest University">

4. <img src="mwu.jpg" align="top">

5. <img src="mwu.jpg" align="right">

6. <img src="mwu.jpg" hspace="10" vspace="10">

7. <img src="mwu.jpg" height="85" width="120">

8. When an image with many colors is displayed on a monitor that does not support all those colors, the monitor will attempt to approximate the appearance of those colors by "dithering". The Safety Palette, or browser-safe palette, is a palette of 216 colors that display consistently on different browsers and operating systems.

Session 3.3

1. A hotspot is a defined area of the image that acts as a hypertext link. An image map lists the coordinates on the image that define the boundaries of the hotspots.

2. Server-side and client-side. The server-side is the older, more accepted method of creating image maps and relies on the Web server to interpret the image map and create the hypertext link. The client-side image map is newer and is not supported by some older browsers. Because the user's browser interprets the image map, the image map is interpreted more quickly; it can be tested on the local machine, and information about various hotspots appear in the status bar of the Web browser.

3. <area shape="rect" coords="5,20,85,100" href="oregon.htm">

4. <area shape="circle" coords="44,81,23" href="la.htm">

5. <area shape="poly" coords="5,10,5,35,25,35,30,20,15,10" href="hawaii.htm">

6. <img src="westcoast.gif" usemap="#States">

7. <img src="westcoast.gif" border="5">

OBJECTIVES

In this tutorial you will:

- Create a text table

- Create a table using the <table>, <tr>, and <td> tags

- Create table headers and captions

- Control the appearance of a table and table text

- Create table cells that span several rows or columns

- Use nested tables to enhance page design

- Learn about Internet Explorer extensions for use with tables

DESIGNING A WEB PAGE WITH TABLES

Creating a News Page

CASE

The Park City Gazette

Park City, Colorado, is a rural mountain community located near a popular national park. The town's primary attraction is tourism as visitors from around the world come to Park City to enjoy its natural beauty, hike and climb in the national park, and ski at the many area resorts. During the busy tourist season, the population of Park City can triple in size.

Kevin Webber is the editor of the weekly Park City Gazette. Kevin knows that the newspaper is a valuable source of information for tourists as well as year-round residents, and he would like to publish a Web edition.

He has approached you about designing a Web site for the paper. He would like the design of the Web site to have the same look and feel as the printed Gazette, which has been published for over 100 years. The Gazette has a classic and traditional design and a large and loyal readership.

In order to implement the design that Kevin is looking for, you'll need to learn how to work with tables in HTML.

SESSION 4.1

In this session you'll learn how to add tables to a Web page, starting with simple text tables and progressing to graphical tables, and you'll learn the advantages of each approach. You'll also learn how to define table rows, cells, and headings with HTML tags. Finally, you'll add a caption to your table and learn how to control the caption's placement on a Web page.

Tables on the World Wide Web

Kevin has his first assignment for you. The annual Front Range Marathon in Boulder has just been run, and a local woman, Laura Blake, won the women's open division. Kevin wants you to place the marathon story on the Web. With the story, he would like to see a table that lists the top three male and female finishers. Kevin presents you with a table of the race results shown in Figure 4-1.

Figure 4-1   MARATHON RESULTS

GROUP	RUNNER	TIME	ORIGIN
Men	1. Peter Teagan	2:12:34	San Antonio, Texas
Men	2. Kyle Wills	2:13:05	Billings, Montana
Men	3. Jason Wu	2:14:28	Cutler, Colorado
Women	1. Laura Blake	2:28:21	Park City, Colorado
Women	2. Kathy Lasker	2:30:11	Chicago, Illinois
Women	3. Lisa Peterson	2:31:14	Seattle, Washington

A table can be stored on a Web page either in a text or a graphical format. A **text table**, like the one shown in Figure 4-2, contains only text, evenly spaced on the Web page in rows and columns. Text tables use only standard word processing characters, so cell borders and lines must be created using such characters as hyphens or equal signs.

Figure 4-2   A TEXT TABLE

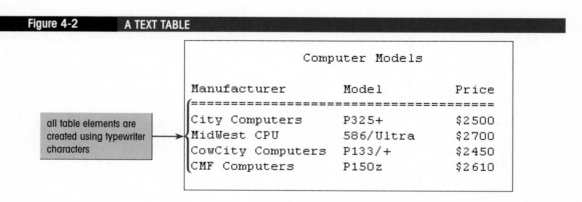

```
                    Computer Models

         Manufacturer        Model          Price
        ╔═══════════════════════════════════════════
        ║City Computers       P325+          $2500
        ║MidWest CPU          586/Ultra      $2700
        ║CowCity Computers    P133/+         $2450
        ║CMF Computers        P150z          $2610
```

all table elements are created using typewriter characters

A **graphical table**, as shown in Figure 4-3, is displayed using graphical elements to distinguish the table components. You can include such design elements as background colors and colored borders with shading. You can also control the size of individual table cells and align text within those cells. You can even create cells that span several rows or columns.

Figure 4-3   **A GRAPHICAL TABLE**

the table can contain graphical elements such as color, borders, and shading

color background

a table cell

graphical borders and shading

Computer Models		
Manufacturer	Model	Price
City Computers	P325+	$2500
MidWest CPU	586/Ultra	$2700
CowCity Computers	P133/+	$2450
CMF Computers	P150z	$2610

Although graphical tables are more flexible and attractive than text tables, there are some situations when you'll want to use a text table. Some browsers, such as the text-based Lynx browser used on many UNIX systems, can display only text characters. Also, working with the tags for graphical tables can be complicated and time-consuming. For these reasons, you might want to create two versions of your Web page: one that uses only text elements and text tables, and another that takes advantage of graphical elements. Due to the wide variety of Gazette readers, this is the approach Kevin suggests that you take. First you'll create a text table of the marathon results, and then you'll work on the graphical version of the table.

Creating a Text Table

Information for the text table version of the race results page has been created for you and is stored on your Data Disk as racetxt1.htm. To begin, you'll open this text file and save it with a new name.

To open racetxt1.htm and save it with a new name:

1. Using your text editor, open **racetxt1.htm** from the tutorial.04/tutorial folder on your Data Disk.

2. Save the file as **race1.htm** in the same folder.

Figure 4-4 shows a preview of the page as it is displayed in a browser.

Figure 4-4   **THE RACE1 PAGE**

Local Woman Wins Marathon

Park City native, **Laura Blake**, won the 27th Front Range Marathon over an elite field of the best long distance runners in the country. Laura's time of 2 hr. 28 min. 21 sec. was only 2 minutes off the women's course record set last year by Sarah Rawlings. Kathy Lasker and Lisa Peterson finished second and third, respectively. Laura's victory came on the heels of her performance at the NCAA Track and Field Championships, in which she placed second running for Colorado State.

In an exciting race, **Peter Teagan** of San Antonio, Texas, used a finishing kick to win the men's marathon for the second straight year, in a time of 2 hr. 12 min. 34 sec. Ahead for much of the race, Kyle Wills of Billings, Montana, finished second, when he could not match Teagan's finishing pace. Jason Wu of Cutler, Colorado, placed third in a very competitive field.

This year's race through downtown Boulder boasted the largest field in the marathon's history, with over 9500 men and 6700 women competing. Race conditions were perfect with low humidity and temperatures that never exceeded 85°.

The page consists of an article that Kevin has written about the marathon. You'll place the race results table between the first and second paragraphs.

Using Fixed-Width Fonts

When you create a text table, the font you use is important. A text table relies on spaces and the characters that fill those spaces to create its column boundaries. To accomplish this, you need to use a **fixed-width**, or **mono-space**, font so that the columns align properly. Fixed-width fonts use the same amount of space for each character.

Most typeset documents, including the one you're reading now, use **proportional fonts**. Proportional fonts assign a different amount of space for each character depending on the width of that character. For example, since the character "m" is wider than the character "l," a proportional font assigns it more space.

Because of the variable spacing, proportional fonts are more visually attractive, and typically easier to read, than fixed-width fonts. However, proportional fonts are less suitable for text tables. The distinction between fixed-width and proportional fonts is important. If you use a proportional font in a text table, the varying width of the characters and the spaces between characters can cause errors when the page is rendered in the user's browser. Figure 4-5 shows how a text table that uses a proportional font loses alignment when the font size is increased or decreased.

Figure 4-5   COLUMN ALIGNMENT PROBLEMS WITH PROPORTIONAL FONTS

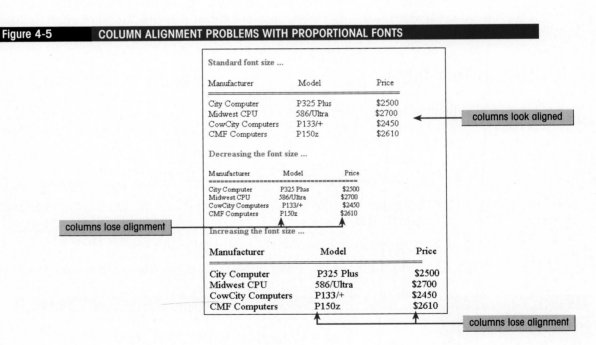

By contrast, the table shown in Figure 4-6 uses fixed-width fonts. Note that the columns remain aligned regardless of font size.

Figure 4-6   **COLUMN ALIGNMENT WITH FIXED-WIDTH FONTS**

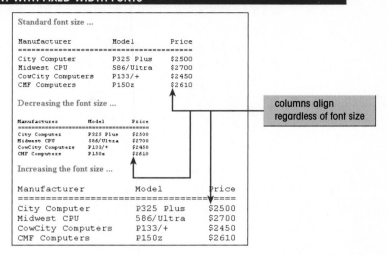

Different browsers and operating systems may use different font sizes to display your page's text, so you should always use a fixed-width font to ensure that the columns in your text tables remain in alignment.

Using the <pre> Tag

Remember that HTML ignores blank spaces, blank lines, and tabs. However, to control the appearance of a text table, you need to use spaces and other characters for alignment. You can use the <pre> tag to display preformatted text, which is text formatted in ways that HTML would otherwise not recognize. Any text formatted with the <pre> tag retains any spaces or lines you want to display on your Web page. The <pre> tag also displays text using a fixed-width font, which makes it effective for building text tables.

REFERENCE WINDOW   **RW**

Creating a Text Table Using the <pre> Tag
- Before the table, insert the tag <pre>.
- Enter the table text, aligning the columns of the table by inserting blank spaces as needed.
- Immediately following the table, insert the tag </pre> to turn off the preformatted text tag.

You'll use the <pre> tag to enter the table data from Figure 4-1 into race1.htm. When you use this tag, you insert blank spaces by pressing the spacebar to align the columns of text in the table.

To create a text table using the <pre> tag:

1. Place the insertion point in the blank line located between the first and second paragraphs of Kevin's article.

2. Type **<pre>** and press the **Enter** key to create a blank line.

3. Type **Group** and press the spacebar 4 times.

4. Type **Runner** and press the spacebar 15 times.

5. Type **Time** and press the spacebar 10 times.

6. Type **Origin** and press the **Enter** key to create a blank line.

7. Underline each heading (Group, Runner, Time, Origin) using the equal sign symbol (see Figure 4-7) and press the **Enter** key.

8. Complete the table by entering the information from Figure 4-1 about the runners, their times, and their places of origin. Place a blank line between the men's and women's results, and align each entry with the left edge of the column headings.

9. Below the women's results, type **</pre>** to turn off the preformatted text tag. Figure 4-7 shows the complete preformatted text as it appears in the file.

Figure 4-7 | **TEXT TABLE CREATED WITH THE <PRE> TAG**

text will appear in the browser as it appears here →

```
<p>
Park City native, <b>Laura Blake</b>, won the 27<sup>th</sup> Front Range Marathon
over an elite field of the best long distance runners in the country. Laura's
time of 2 hr. 28 min. 21 sec. was only 2 minutes off the women's course record
set last year by Sarah Rawlings. Kathy Lasker and Lisa Peterson finished second
and third, respectively. Laura's victory came on the heels of her performance at
the NCAA Track and Field Championships, in which she placed second running for
Colorado State.
</p>
<pre>
Group      Runner          Time        Origin
=====      ======          ====        ======
Men        1. Peter Teagan 2:12:34     San Antonio, Texas
Men        2. Kyle Wills   2:13:05     Billings, Montana
Men        3. Jason Wu     2:14:28     Cutler, Colorado

Women      1. Laura Blake  2:28:21     Park City, Colorado
Women      2. Kathy Lasker 2:30:11     Chicago, Illinois
Women      3. Lisa Peterson 2:31:14    Seattle, Washington
</pre>
<p>
In an exciting race, <b>Peter Teagan</b> of San Antonio, Texas, used a finishing
kick to win the men's marathon for the second straight year, in a time of
2 hr. 12 min. 34 sec. Ahead for much of the race, Kyle Wills of Billings, Montana,
finished second, when he could not match Teagan's finishing pace. Jason Wu of
Cutler, Colorado, placed third in a very competitive field.
</p>
```

10. Save your changes to race1.htm and close the file.

11. Using your Web browser, open **race1.htm**. Figure 4-8 displays the page as it appears in the browser.

Figure 4-8 | **TEXT TABLE AS IT APPEARS IN THE BROWSER**

Local Woman Wins Marathon

Park City native, **Laura Blake**, won the 27th Front Range Marathon over an elite field of the best long distance runners in the country. Laura's time of 2 hr. 28 min. 21 sec. was only 2 minutes off the women's course record set last year by Sarah Rawlings. Kathy Lasker and Lisa Peterson finished second and third, respectively. Laura's victory came on the heels of her performance at the NCAA Track and Field Championships, in which she placed second running for Colorado State.

table text appears in a fixed width font →

```
Group      Runner          Time        Origin
=====      ======          ====        ======
Men        1. Peter Teagan 2:12:34     San Antonio, Texas
Men        2. Kyle Wills   2:13:05     Billings, Montana
Men        3. Jason Wu     2:14:28     Cutler, Colorado

Women      1. Laura Blake  2:28:21     Park City, Colorado
Women      2. Kathy Lasker 2:30:11     Chicago, Illinois
Women      3. Lisa Peterson 2:31:14    Seattle, Washington
```

In an exciting race, **Peter Teagan** of San Antonio, Texas, used a finishing kick to win the men's marathon for the second straight year, in a time of 2 hr. 12 min. 34 sec. Ahead for much of the race, Kyle Wills of Billings, Montana, finished second, when he could not match Teagan's finishing pace. Jason Wu of Cutler, Colorado, placed third in a very competitive field.

This year's race through downtown Boulder boasted the largest field in the marathon's history, with over 9500 men and 6700 women competing. Race conditions were perfect with low humidity and temperatures that never exceeded 85°.

using the <pre> tag, you've created a text table that can be displayed by all browsers, and you've ensured that the columns will retain their alignment no matter what font the browser is using.

You show the completed table to Kevin. He's pleased with your work and would like you to create a similar page using a graphical table. To create that table, you'll start by studying how HTML defines table structures.

Defining Table Structure

Creating graphical tables with HTML can be a complicated process because a lot of information is required to define the layout and appearance of a table. The first step is to specify the table structure: the number of rows and columns, the location of column headings, and the placement of a table caption. Once the table structure is in place, you can start entering data into the table.

The contents for the graphical table have been created for you and stored on your Data Disk, as racetxt2.htm. The first step is to open the file using your text editor and save it with a new name.

To open racetxt2.htm and save it with a new name:

1. Using your text editor, open **racetxt2.htm** from the tutorial.04/tutorial folder on your Data Disk and save it as **race2.htm** in the same folder.

Figure 4-9 shows a preview of the page as it appears in the browser. Note that Kevin has added more graphical features to this page because he intends it to be viewed by graphical Web browsers.

| 4-9 | THE RACE2 PAGE |

Local Woman Wins Marathon

Park City native, **Laura Blake**, won the 27th Front Range Marathon over an elite field of the best long distance runners in the country. Laura's time of 2 hr. 28 min. 21 sec. was only 2 minutes off the women's course record set last year by Sarah Rawlings. Kathy Lasker and Lisa Peterson finished second and third, respectively. Laura's victory came on the heels of her performance at the NCAA Track and Field Championships, in which she placed second running for Colorado State.

In an exciting race, **Peter Teagan** of San Antonio, Texas, used a finishing kick to win the men's marathon for the second straight year, in a time of 2 hr. 12 min. 34 sec. Ahead for much of the race, Kyle Wills of Billings, Montana, finished second, when he could not match Teagan's finishing pace. Jason Wu of Cutler, Colorado, placed third in a very competitive field.

This year's race through downtown Boulder boasted the largest field in the marathon's history, with over 9500 men and 6700 women competing. Race conditions were perfect with low humidity and temperatures that never exceeded 85°.

Using the <table>, <tr>, and <td> Tags

Graphical tables are enclosed within a two-sided <table> tag that identifies the start and ending of the table structure. Each row of the table is indicated using a two-sided <tr> (for table row) tag. Finally, within each table row, a two-sided <td> (for table data) tag indicates the presence of individual table cells. The general syntax of a graphical table is therefore:

```
<table>
     <tr>
          <td> First Cell </td>
          <td> Second Cell </td>
```

```
        </tr>
        <tr>
                <td> Third Cell </td>
                <td> Fourth Cell </td>
        </tr>
    </table>
```

This example creates a table with two rows and two columns. Fig[...] shows the layout of a table with this HTML code.

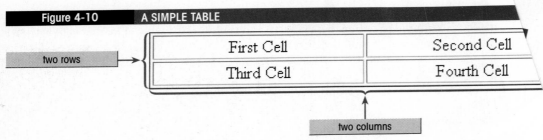

Figure 4-10   A SIMPLE TABLE

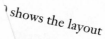

two rows

| First Cell | Second Cell |
| Third Cell | Fourth Cell |

two columns

REFERENCE   WINDOW

Defining Table Structure with HTML
- Enter the <table> and </table> tags to identify the beginning and end of the table.
- Enter <tr> and </tr> tags to identify the beginning and end of each table row.
- Enter <td> and </td> tags to identify the beginning and end of each table cell.
- Enter <th> and </th> tags to identify text to be table headers.

You may have noticed that there is no HTML tag for table columns. In the orig[...] HTML specifications, the number of columns is determined by how many cells are insert[...] within each row. For example, if you have four <td> tags in each table row, that table ha[...] four columns. Later versions of HTML have provided increased support for controlling the[...] appearance of table columns. You'll learn about those tags later in the tutorial.

Let's return to the table that Kevin outlined in Figure 4-1. His table requires seven rows and four columns. The first row contains column titles; the remaining six rows display the table's data. HTML provides a special tag for column titles, which you'll learn about shortly. For now you'll create the table structure for the table data.

To create the structure for the race results table:

1. Place the insertion point in the blank line between the first and second paragraphs of Kevin's article.

2. Type **<table>** to identify the beginning of the table structure, and then press the **Enter** key.

3. Type the entries for the first row of the table as follows:

```
<tr>
    <td></td>
    <td></td>
```

```
        <td></td>
        <td></td>
    </tr>
```

Note that you do not need to indent the <td> tags or place them on separate lines, but you may find it easier to interpret your code if you do so.

4. Press the **Enter** key and then repeat Step 3 five times to create the six rows of the table. You might want to use the copy and paste function of your text editor to save time.

5. Press the **Enter** key and then type **</table>** to complete the code for the table structure. See Figure 4-11.

Figure 4-11   **STRUCTURE OF THE RACE RESULTS TABLE**

beginning of the table structure

first row of six in the table

table cells

end of the table structure

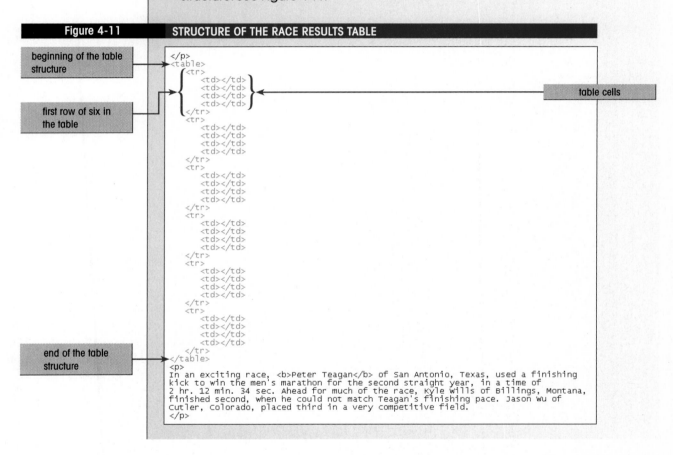

With the table structure in place, you're ready to add the text for each cell.

To insert the table text:

1. Locate the first <td> tag in the table structure and type **Men** between the opening and closing <td> tags.

2. Within the next three <td> tags, type the remaining entries for the first row of the table as follows:

```
<td>1. Peter Teagan</td>
<td>2:12:34</td>
<td>San Antonio, Texas</td>
```

3. Continue entering the text for the cells for the remaining five rows of the table. Figure 4-12 shows the completed text for the body of the table.

Figure 4-12 COMPLETED TABLE TEXT

```
<table>
    <tr>
        <td>Men</td>
        <td>1. Peter Teagan</td>
        <td>2:12:34</td>
        <td>San Antonio, Texas</td>
    </tr>
    <tr>
        <td>Men</td>
        <td>2. Kyle Wills</td>
        <td>2:13:05</td>
        <td>Billings, Montana</td>
    </tr>
    <tr>
        <td>Men</td>
        <td>3. Jason Wu</td>
        <td>2:14:28</td>
        <td>Cutler, Colorado</td>
    </tr>
    <tr>
        <td>Women</td>
        <td>1. Laura Blake</td>
        <td>2:28:21</td>
        <td>Park City, Colorado</td>
    </tr>
    <tr>
        <td>Women</td>
        <td>2. Kathy Lasker</td>
        <td>2:30:11</td>
        <td>Chicago, Illinois</td>
    </tr>
    <tr>
        <td>Women</td>
        <td>3. Lisa Peterson</td>
        <td>2:31:14</td>
        <td>Seattle, Washington</td>
    </tr>
</table>
```

With the text for the body of the table entered, the next step is to add the column headings.

Creating Headings with the <th> Tag

Instead of the <td> tag, HTML provides the <th> tag for the table headings. The difference between the <th> and <td> tags is that text formatted with the <th> tag is centered within the cell and displayed in a boldface font. The <th> tag is most often used for column headings, but you can use it for any cell that you want to contain centered boldfaced text.

In the race results table, Kevin has specified a single row of table headings. You'll enter them using the <th> tag.

To insert the table headings:

1. Place the insertion point after the <table> tag and press the **Enter** key to create a blank line.

2. Type the following HTML code and content:

```
<tr>
    <th>Group</th>
    <th>Runner</th>
    <th>Time</th>
    <th>Origin</th>
</tr>
```

Figure 4-13 shows the <th> tags as they appear in your file.

Figure 4-13 ADDING TABLE HEADINGS TO THE TABLE

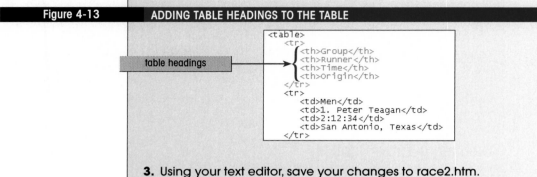

table headings

```
<table>
    <tr>
        <th>Group</th>
        <th>Runner</th>
        <th>Time</th>
        <th>Origin</th>
    </tr>
    <tr>
        <td>Men</td>
        <td>1. Peter Teagan</td>
        <td>2:12:34</td>
        <td>San Antonio, Texas</td>
    </tr>
```

3. Using your text editor, save your changes to race2.htm.

4. Using your Web browser, open **race2.htm**. The table is shown in Figure 4-14.

Figure 4-14 RACE RESULTS TABLE AS DISPLAYED IN THE BROWSER

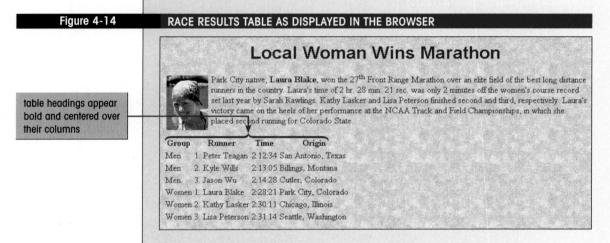

table headings appear bold and centered over their columns

Note that the text in cells formatted with the <th> tag is bold and centered above each table column.

Identifying the Table Heading, Body, and Footer

HTML allows you to identify the different parts of your table using the <thead>, <tbody>, and <tfoot> tags, which are used for the table's heading, body, and footer, respectively. These tags do not format the table, but they do contain collections of rows called **row groups**. The general syntax for these tags is:

```
<table>
    <thead>
        <tr>heading information ...
    </thead>
    <tfoot>
        <tr>footer  information ...
    </tfoot>
    <tbody>
        <tr>first group of table rows ...
    </tbody>
    <tbody>
        <tr>second group of table rows ...
    </tbody>
...
</table>
```

Note that a single table can contain several <tbody> tags to identify different parts of the table. The <thead> and <tfoot> sections *must* appear before any <tbody> sections in the table structure. These tags are most often used in a table that draws its data from an external data source, or for tables that span several Web pages. By identifying which rows belong to the table's header or footer, the browser can be made to repeat those sections across multiple pages, while changing the contents of the table's main body. Not all browsers support this capability, and since it does not apply to the Web page that Kevin wants you to design, we won't use these tags in the table.

Creating a Table Caption

HTML allows you to specify a caption for your table. The syntax for creating a caption is:

```
<caption align="alignment">caption text</caption>
```

where *alignment* indicates the caption placement.

- A value of "bottom" centers the caption below the table.
- A value of "top" or "center" centers the caption above the table.
- Values of "left" or "right" place the caption above the table to the left or right.

Only Internet Explorer supports all caption values. Netscape supports only the "top" and "bottom" values. Because the <caption> tag works only with tables, the tag must be placed within the table structure.

Captions are shown as normal text without special formatting, but you can format the caption by embedding the caption text within other HTML tags. For example, placing the caption text within a pair of <b> and <i> tags causes the caption to display as bold and italic.

REFERENCE WINDOW   **RW**

Creating a Table Caption
- Within the <table> tags enter the following tag:
  ```
  <caption align="alignment">caption text</caption>
  ```
  where *alignment* can be "bottom", "top", "left", "right", or "center". A value of "bottom" centers the caption below the table. A value of "top" or "center" centers the caption above the table. The values "left" or "right" place the caption above the table to the left or right.

Kevin asks you to add the caption "Race Results" above the table, centered and bold.

To add the caption to the race results table:

1. Return to **race2.htm** in your text editor.

2. Insert the following code below the <table> tag (see Figure 4-15):

   ```
   <caption align="top"><b>Race Results</b></caption>
   ```

Figure 4-15   **INSERTING A TABLE CAPTION**

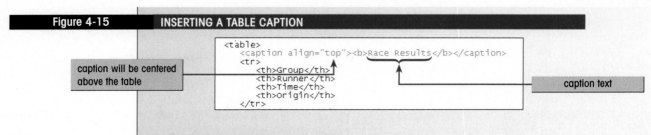

caption will be centered above the table

caption text

```
<table>
    <caption align="top"><b>Race Results</b></caption>
    <tr>
        <th>Group</th>
        <th>Runner</th>
        <th>Time</th>
        <th>Origin</th>
    </tr>
```

3. Save your changes to the file.

4. Using your Web browser, reload or refresh race2.htm. Figure 4-16 shows the table with the newly added caption.

Figure 4-16   **RACE RESULTS TABLE WITH CAPTION**

table caption

Race Results			
Group	Runner	Time	Origin
Men	1. Peter Teagan	2:12:34	San Antonio, Texas
Men	2. Kyle Wills	2:13:05	Billings, Montana
Men	3. Jason Wu	2:14:28	Cutler, Colorado
Women	1. Laura Blake	2:28:21	Park City, Colorado
Women	2. Kathy Lasker	2:30:11	Chicago, Illinois
Women	3. Lisa Peterson	2:31:14	Seattle, Washington

You've completed your work with the initial structure of the race results table. Kevin is pleased with your progress, but he would like you to make some improvements in the table's appearance. In the next session, you'll learn how to modify the appearance and placement of your table and the text contained in it.

Session 4.1 QUICK CHECK

1. What are the two kinds of tables you can place in a Web page? What are the advantages and disadvantages of each?

2. What is the difference between a proportional font and a fixed-width font? Which should you use in a text table, and why?

3. What HTML tag would you use to create a text table?

4. Define the purpose of the following HTML tags in defining the structure of a table:

```
<tr>
<td>
<th>
```

5. How do you specify the number of rows in a graphical table? How do you specify the number of columns?

6. How does the <th> tag differ from the <td> tag?

7. What HTML code would you use to place the caption "Product Catalog" below a table? Where must this HTML code be placed in relation to the <table> and </table> tags?

SESSION 4.2

In this session you'll learn how to customize the appearance of your tables, including how to specify the size of the table and the space between and within the cells. You'll learn how to place the table on your Web page, how to align the text within the table, and also how to merge several cells into a single cell. Finally, this session shows you how to create a color scheme for your table by modifying the background and border colors.

Modifying the Appearance of a Table

After viewing the race results table in the browser, Kevin notes that the text is displayed with properly aligned columns, but the lack of gridlines and borders makes the table difficult to read. Kevin asks you to enhance the table's design by adding borders, gridlines, and a background color. He also wants you to control the placement and size of the table. HTML provides tags and attributes to do all of these things.

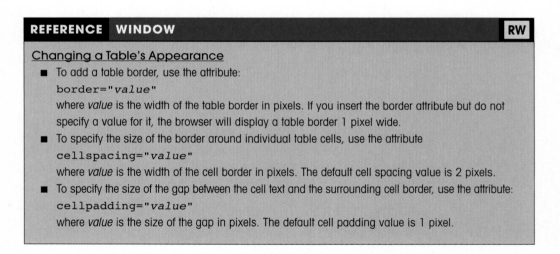

REFERENCE WINDOW   RW

Changing a Table's Appearance

- To add a table border, use the attribute:

  border="*value*"

  where *value* is the width of the table border in pixels. If you insert the border attribute but do not specify a value for it, the browser will display a table border 1 pixel wide.
- To specify the size of the border around individual table cells, use the attribute

  cellspacing="*value*"

  where *value* is the width of the cell border in pixels. The default cell spacing value is 2 pixels.
- To specify the size of the gap between the cell text and the surrounding cell border, use the attribute:

  cellpadding="*value*"

  where *value* is the size of the gap in pixels. The default cell padding value is 1 pixel.

You'll begin enhancing the race results table by adding a table border.

Adding a Table Border

By default, browsers display tables without table borders. You can create a table border by adding the border attribute to the <table> tag. The syntax for creating a table border is:

```
<table border="value">
```

where *value* is the width of the border in pixels. The size attribute is optional; if you don't specify a size, but simply insert the border attribute without a value, the browser creates a table border 1 pixel wide. Figure 4-17 shows the effect on a table's border when the border size is varied. Note that only the outside border is affected by the border attribute; the internal gridlines are not affected. You'll see how to change the size of these gridlines later on.

Figure 4-17   **TABLES WITH DIFFERENT BORDER VALUES**

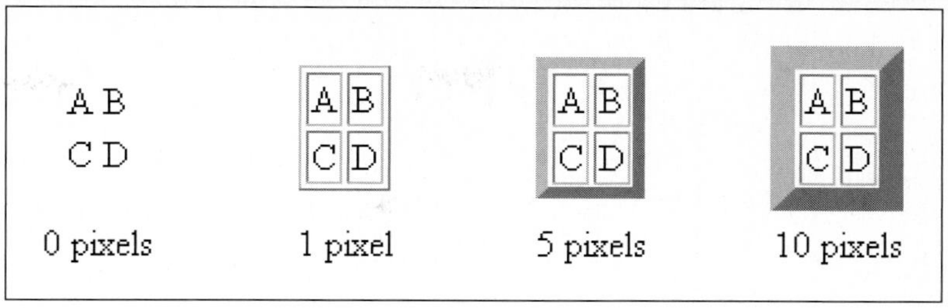

A B
C D

| A B | | A B | | A B |
| C D | | C D | | C D |

0 pixels   1 pixel   5 pixels   10 pixels

Kevin wants a wide border around the race results table, so you'll format the table with a 5-pixel-wide border.

To insert a table border:

1. Using your text editor, open **race2.htm**, if it is not currently open.

2. Locate the <table> tag, and within the tag, type **border="5"**. See Figure 4-18.

Figure 4-18   **ADDING A 5-PIXEL BORDER TO THE RACE RESULTS TABLE**

```
<table border="5">
    <caption align="top"><b>Race Results</b></caption>
    <tr>
        <th>Group</th>
        <th>Runner</th>
        <th>Time</th>
        <th>origin</th>
    </tr>
```

3. Save your changes to race2.htm.

4. Using your Web browser, reload or refresh race2.htm. Figure 4-19 shows the new border.

Figure 4-19   **RACE RESULTS TABLE WITH A BORDER VALUE OF 5**

Race Results

Group	Runner	Time	Origin
Men	1. Peter Teagan	2:12:34	San Antonio, Texas
Men	2. Kyle Wills	2:13:05	Billings, Montana
Men	3. Jason Wu	2:14:28	Cutler, Colorado
Women	1. Laura Blake	2:28:21	Park City, Colorado
Women	2. Kathy Lasker	2:30:11	Chicago, Illinois
Women	3. Lisa Peterson	2:31:14	Seattle, Washington

You've modified the outside border of the table, and now Kevin would like you to change the width of the gridlines within the table. He feels that the table would look better if the interior borders were less prominent.

Controlling Cell Spacing

The cellspacing attribute controls the amount of space inserted between table cells. The syntax for specifying the cell spacing is:

```
<table cellspacing="value">
```

where *value* is the width of the interior borders in pixels. The default cell spacing is 2 pixels. Figure 4-20 shows how different cell spacing values affect a table's appearance.

Figure 4-20   **TABLES WITH DIFFERENT CELL SPACING VALUES**

| A B | | A B | | A B | | A B |
| C D | | C D | | C D | | C D |

0 pixels   1 pixel   5 pixels   10 pixels

Kevin has decided that he wants the width of the borders between individual table cells to be as small as possible, so you'll decrease the width to 0 pixels. This will not remove the border between the cells. As long as you have a border around the entire table, there will be gridlines separating individual table cells, but it will reduce the interior border width to a minimal size. This is because the interior border includes a drop shadow, and even if cell spacing is set to 0, the drop shadow remains to give the effect of an interior border.

To change the cell spacing:

1. Return to **race2.htm** in your text editor.

2. Type **cellspacing="0"** within the <table> tag, as shown in Figure 4-21.

Figure 4-21   **SETTING THE CELL SPACING TO 0 PIXELS**

```
<table border="5" cellspacing="0">
    <caption align="top"><b>Race Results</b></caption>
    <tr>
        <th>Group</th>
        <th>Runner</th>
        <th>Time</th>
        <th>Origin</th>
    </tr>
```

3. Save your changes to the file.

4. Using your Web browser, reload or refresh race2.htm. The new cell spacing is shown in Figure 4-22. Note that the line that separates the cells has been reduced, but not eliminated. Compare Figure 4-19 with Figure 4-22.

Figure 4-22   RACE RESULTS TABLE WITH A CELLSPACING VALUE OF 0

Race Results

Group	Runner	Time	Origin
Men	1. Peter Teagan	2:12:34	San Antonio, Texas
Men	2. Kyle Wills	2:13:05	Billings, Montana
Men	3. Jason Wu	2:14:28	Cutler, Colorado
Women	1. Laura Blake	2:28:21	Park City, Colorado
Women	2. Kathy Lasker	2:30:11	Chicago, Illinois
Women	3. Lisa Peterson	2:31:14	Seattle, Washington

Kevin feels that the race results table is too crowded. He would like you to increase the space between the table text and the surrounding gridlines. You can do this by increasing the amount of cell padding in the table.

Defining Cell Padding

To control the space between the table text and the cell borders, add the cellpadding attribute to the table tag. The syntax for this attribute is:

```
<table cellpadding="value">
```

where *value* is the distance from the table text to the cell border, as measured in pixels. The default cell padding value is 1 pixel. Figure 4-23 shows the effect of changing the cell padding value for a table.

Figure 4-23   TABLES WITH DIFFERENT CELL PADDING VALUES

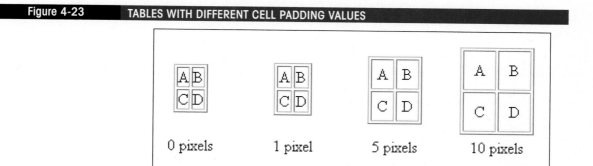

It is easy to confuse the terms cell spacing and cell padding. Just remember that cell spacing refers to the space between the cells, and cell padding refers to the space within the cells. You need to increase the amount of space within your table cells because the default value of 1 pixel is too small and results in crowded text. You'll increase the cell padding to 4 pixels to satisfy Kevin's request.

To increase the amount of cell padding:

1. Return to **race2.htm** in your text editor.

2. Type the attribute **cellpadding="4"** within the <table> tag, as shown in Figure 4-24.

Figure 4-24	SETTING THE CELL PADDING TO 4 PIXELS

```
<table border="5" cellspacing="0" cellpadding="4">
   <caption align="top"><b>Race Results</b></caption>
   <tr>
      <th>Group</th>
      <th>Runner</th>
      <th>Time</th>
      <th>Origin</th>
   </tr>
```

3. Save your changes to the file, and then reload **race2.htm** in your Web browser. Figure 4-25 shows the table with the increased amount of cell padding.

Figure 4-25	RACE RESULTS TABLE WITH A CELLPADDING VALUE OF 4

Race Results

Group	Runner	Time	Origin
Men	1. Peter Teagan	2:12:34	San Antonio, Texas
Men	2. Kyle Wills	2:13:05	Billings, Montana
Men	3. Jason Wu	2:14:28	Cutler, Colorado
Women	1. Laura Blake	2:28:21	Park City, Colorado
Women	2. Kathy Lasker	2:30:11	Chicago, Illinois
Women	3. Lisa Peterson	2:31:14	Seattle, Washington

By increasing the cell padding, you added needed space to the table.

Creating Frames and Rules

Two additional table attributes introduced in HTML 4.0 are the frame and rule attributes. As you've seen, when borders are displayed, they surround the entire table, and gridlines are automatically applied between cells. With the frame and rule attributes you can control how borders and gridlines are applied to the table.

The frame attribute allows you to determine which sides of the table will have borders. The syntax is:

```
<table frame="type">
```

where *type* is either "box" (the default), "above", "below", "hsides", "vsides", "lhs", "rhs", or "void". Figure 4-26 describes each of these options.

Figure 4-26 | VALUES OF THE FRAME ATTRIBUTE

FRAME VALUE	DESCRIPTION
"box"	Border is drawn around all four sides of the table
"above"	Border is drawn only above the table
"below"	Border is drawn only below the table
"hsides"	Border is drawn on the top and bottom sides of the table (the horizontal sides)
"lhs"	Border is drawn only on the left-hand side
"rhs"	Border is drawn only on the right-hand side
"vsides"	Border is drawn on the left and right sides of the table (the vertical sides)
"void"	No border is drawn around the table

Figure 4-27 shows the effect of each of these values on the table grid. The frames attribute is supported by Internet Explorer version 4.0 and above. It is supported by Netscape version 6.2, but not by earlier versions of Netscape.

Figure 4-27 | EFFECT OF DIFFERENT FRAME VALUES

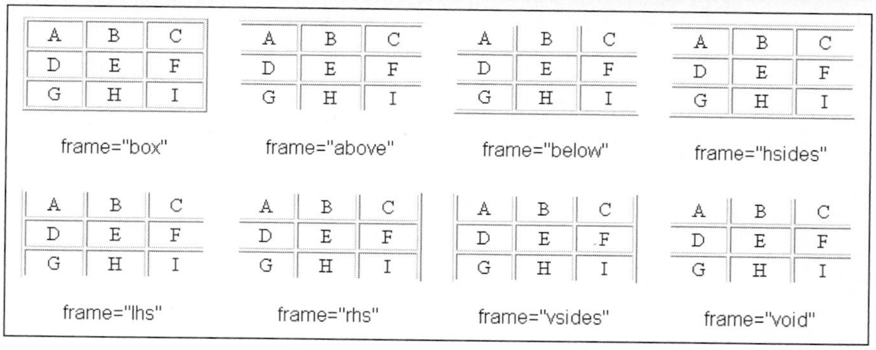

The rules attribute lets you control how the table gridlines are drawn. The syntax of this attribute is:

```
<table rules="type">
```

where *type* is either "all", "rows", "cols", or "none". Figure 4-28 shows the effect of each of the attribute values on a table.

Figure 4-28 | EFFECT OF DIFFERENT RULES VALUES

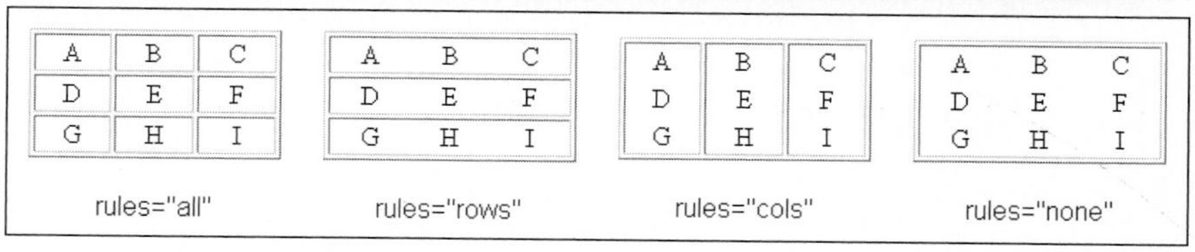

The rules attribute is supported by Internet Explorer version 4.0 and above. It is not supported by any versions of Netscape.

Working with Table and Cell Size

Unless you specify differently, the size of a table is determined by the text it contains in its cells. By default, HTML places text on a single line. As you add text in a cell, the width of the column and the table expands to the edge of the page while keeping text on a single line unless you've inserted a line break, paragraph, or heading tag within the cell. Once the page edge is reached, the browser reduces the size of the remaining columns to keep the text to a single line. The browser wraps the text to a second line within the cell only when it can no longer increase the size of the column and table or decrease the size of the remaining columns. As more text is added, the height of the table expands to accommodate the additional text.

To gain control over what your table looks like, it is important to manually define the size of the table cells and the table as a whole.

REFERENCE WINDOW   **RW**

Choosing Table and Cell Size
- Limit your table size to approximately 600 pixels to prevent the table from expanding beyond the viewing area of many browsers.
- Specify a cell width, either absolute or relative, for all of your table cells, so that you can be sure that the table will be rendered accurately in the browser.
- Test the appearance of your Web page under several different monitor resolutions, from 640 x 480 on up.

Defining the Table Size

The syntax for specifying the table size is:

```
<table width="size" height="size">
```

where *size* is the width and height of the table as measured in pixels or as a percentage of the display area. If you want your table to fill the entire width of the display area, regardless of the resolution of the user's monitor, set the width attribute to 100%. Note that the percent value should be placed within double quotation marks (use width="100%" not width=100%). Similarly, to create a table whose height is equal to the entire height of the display area, enter the attribute height="100%".

On the other hand, if you specify an absolute size for a table in pixels, its size remains constant, regardless of the browser or monitor settings used. If you use this approach, remember that some monitors display your page at a resolution of 640 by 480 pixels. If it's important that the table not exceed the browser's display area, you should specify a table width of less than 610 pixels to allow space for other window elements such as scroll bars.

Specifying a Table Size

■ To create a table of a specific size, enter the following attributes to the <table> tag:
```
width="value" height="value"
```
where *value* is the table's height or width, either in pixels or as a percentage of the browser's display area.

Kevin feels that the race results table appears too crowded and would like you to increase its width to 500 pixels. This will ensure that the table will not extend beyond the display area, but it will also provide more room in the table cells if you want to insert additional text. You don't need to specify the height of the table, because the table's height expands if additional race entries are added.

To specify the width of the race results table:

1. Return to **race2.htm** in your text editor.

2. Type **width="500"** within the <table> tag, as shown in Figure 4-29.

Figure 4-29   **SETTING THE WIDTH OF THE RACE RESULTS TABLE TO 500 PIXELS**

```
<table border="5" cellspacing="0" cellpadding="4" width="500">
    <caption align="top"><b>Race Results</b></caption>
    <tr>
        <th>Group</th>
        <th>Runner</th>
        <th>Time</th>
        <th>Origin</th>
    </tr>
```

3. Save your changes to the file and then reload it in your Web browser. Figure 4-30 shows the revised page with the table width increased to 500 pixels.

Figure 4-30   **RACE RESULTS TABLE WITH A WIDTH OF 500 PIXELS**

Park City native, **Laura Blake**, won the 27th Front Range Marathon over an elite field of the best long distance runners in the country. Laura's time of 2 hr. 28 min. 21 sec. was only 2 minutes off the women's course record set last year by Sarah Rawlings. Kathy Lasker and Lisa Peterson finished second and third, respectively. Laura's victory came on the heels of her performance at the NCAA Track and Field Championships, in which she placed second running for Colorado State.

Race Results

Group	Runner	Time	Origin
Men	1. Peter Teagan	2:12:34	San Antonio, Texas
Men	2. Kyle Wills	2:13:05	Billings, Montana
Men	3. Jason Wu	2:14:28	Cutler, Colorado
Women	1. Laura Blake	2:28:21	Park City, Colorado
Women	2. Kathy Lasker	2:30:11	Chicago, Illinois
Women	3. Lisa Peterson	2:31:14	Seattle, Washington

Now that you've set the width of the table, you can set the width of individual cells and columns.

Defining Cell and Column Sizes

To set the width of an individual cell, add the width attribute to either the <td> or <th> tags using the syntax:

```
width="value"
```

where *value* can be expressed either in pixels or as a percentage of the table width. For example, a width value of 30% displays a cell that is 30% of the total width of the table. To create a cell that is always 35 pixels wide, you enter width="35" within the <td> or <th> tag. Whether you enter a pixel value or a percentage depends on whether you're trying to create a table that will be a specific size or fill a relative space.

Specifying a width for an individual cell does not guarantee that the cell will be that width when displayed in the browser. The reason for this is that the cell is part of a column containing other cells. If another cell in the column is set to a different width or expands because of the text in it, the widths of all cells in the column change accordingly. Setting a width for one cell guarantees only that the cell width will not be less than that value. If you want to ensure that the cells do not change in size, you must set the width of all the cells in the column to the same value.

The height attribute can also be used in the <td> or <th> tags to set the height of individual cells. Like the width attribute, the height attribute is expressed either in pixels or as a percentage of the height of the table. If you include more text than can be displayed within that height value you specify, the cell expands to display the additional text. For this reason, the height value is seldom used.

Kevin notices that the Group column is slightly wider than it needs to be. He suggests that you reduce the size of the column to 50 pixels. To accomplish this, you need only add the width attribute to the <th> tag of the first column.

To set a column width for the Group column:

1. Using your text editor, open **race2.htm** if it is not currently open.

2. Type the attribute **width="50"** within the <th> tag for the Group column.

3. Save your changes to race2.htm.

4. Using your Web browser, reload **race2.htm**.

   Note that the first column is narrower than before.

Next you'll work with the alignment of a table and the text it contains.

Aligning a Table and Its Contents

By default, a browser places a table on the left margin of a Web page, with surrounding text placed above and below the table. Kevin would like the table to be placed so that surrounding text wraps around it. He likes the way the text wraps around the photo of Laura Blake, and he wants the table to have a similar appearance.

Aligning a Table on the Web Page

To align a table with the surrounding text, use the align attribute as follows:

```
align="alignment"
```

where *alignment* equals "left", "right", or "center". The align attribute is similar to the align attribute used with the <img> tag, except that images have more alignment options. As with inline images, using left or right alignment places the table on the margin of the Web page and wraps surrounding text to the side. Center alignment places the table in the horizontal center of the page, but does not allow text to wrap around it.

The align attribute is available only with browsers that support HTML 3.2 or later. Earlier browsers ignore the align attribute, placing the table on the left margin of the Web page without text wrapping.

REFERENCE WINDOW **RW**

Aligning a Table on the Page

■ To align a table on a Web page, use the align attribute within the <table> tag as follows:
```
align="alignment"
```
where *alignment* is either "left", "right", or "center". Using a value of "left" or "right" places the table on the left or right margin of the Web page and wraps the text around the table. Using a value of "center" centers the table on the page and does not wrap text around the table.

Kevin wants the race results table to be placed on the right margin of the Web page.

To align the race results table to the right margin:

1. Return to **race2.htm** in your text editor.

2. Type the attribute **align="right"** within the <table> tag as shown in Figure 4-31.

Figure 4-31 | **ALIGNING THE RACE RESULTS TABLE WITH THE PAGE'S RIGHT MARGIN**

```
<table border="5" cellspacing="0" cellpadding="4" width="500" align="right">
   <caption align="top"><b>Race Results</b></caption>
   <tr>
      <th width="50">Group</th>
      <th>Runner</th>
      <th>Time</th>
      <th>Origin</th>
   </tr>
```

3. Save your changes to the file and then reload it in your Web browser.

The race results table is now displayed on the right margin of the Web page as shown in Figure 4-32.

Figure 4-32   RIGHT-ALIGNED RACE RESULTS TABLE

Local Woman Wins Marathon

Park City native, **Laura Blake**, won the 27th Front Range Marathon over an elite field of the best runners in the country. Laura's time of 2 hr. 28 min. 21 sec. was only 2 minutes off the women's course set last year by Sarah Rawlings. Kathy Lasker and Lisa Peterson finished second and third, respectively. victory came on the heels of her performance at the NCAA Track and Field Championships, in which sh placed second running for Colorado State.

In an exciting race, **Peter Teagan** of San Antonio, Texas, used a finishing kick to win the men's marathon for the second straight year, in a time of 2 hr. 12 min. 34 sec. Ahead for much of the race, Kyle Wills of Billings, Montana, finished second, when he could not match Teagan's finishing pace. Jason Wu of Cutler, Colorado, placed third in a very competitive field.

This year's race through downtown Boulder boasted the largest field in the marathon's history, with over 9500 men and 6700 women competing. Race conditions were perfect with low humidity and temperatures that never exceeded 85°.

Race Results

Group	Runner	Time	Origin
Men	1. Peter Teagan	2:12:34	San Antonio, Texas
Men	2. Kyle Wills	2:13:05	Billings, Montana
Men	3. Jason Wu	2:14:28	Cutler, Colorado
Women	1. Laura Blake	2:28:21	Park City, Colorado
Women	2. Kathy Lasker	2:30:11	Chicago, Illinois
Women	3. Lisa Peterson	2:31:14	Seattle, Washington

Aligning the Contents of a Table

By default cell text is placed in the middle of the cell, aligned with the cell's using the align and valign attributes, you can specify the text's horizontal and v ment. Figure 4-33 shows how the combination of the align and valign attribu the position of the cell text in relation to the cell borders.

Figure 4-33   VALUES OF THE ALIGN AND VALIGN ATTRIBUTES

align="left" valign="top"	align="left" valign="middle"	align="left" valign="bottom"
align="center" valign="top"	align="center" valign="middle"	align="center" valign="bottom"
align="right" valign="top"	align="right" valign="middle"	align="right" valign="bottom"

After reviewing the table, Kevin decides that the values in the Time column would look better if they were right-aligned. Because of the way HTML works with table columns, if you want to align the text for a single column, you must apply the align attribute to every cell in that column.

To right-align the Time column values:

1. Return to **race2.htm** in your text editor.

2. Type the attribute **align="right"** within each <td> tag in the Time column. Figure 4-34 shows the revised HTML code.

Figure 4-34 **RIGHT-ALIGNING THE VALUES IN THE TIME COLUMN**

```
<table border="5" cellspacing="0" cellpadding="4" width="500" align="right">
    <caption align="top"><b>Race Results</b></caption>
    <tr>
        <th width="50">Group</th>
        <th>Runner</th>
        <th>Time</th>
        <th>Origin</th>
    </tr>
    <tr>
        <td>Men</td>
        <td>1. Peter Teagan</td>
        <td align="right">2:12:34</td>
        <td>San Antonio, Texas</td>
    </tr>
    <tr>
        <td>Men</td>
        <td>2. Kyle Wills</td>
        <td align="right">2:13:05</td>
        <td>Billings, Montana</td>
    </tr>
    <tr>
        <td>Men</td>
        <td>3. Jason Wu</td>
        <td align="right">2:14:28</td>
        <td>Cutler, Colorado</td>
    </tr>
    <tr>
        <td>women</td>
        <td>1. Laura Blake</td>
        <td align="right">2:28:21</td>
        <td>Park City, Colorado</td>
    </tr>
    <tr>
        <td>women</td>
        <td>2. Kathy Lasker</td>
        <td align="right">2:30:11</td>
        <td>Chicago, Illinois</td>
    </tr>
    <tr>
        <td>women</td>
        <td>3. Lisa Peterson</td>
        <td align="right">2:31:14</td>
        <td>Seattle, washington</td>
    </tr>
</table>
```

3. Save your changes to the file and reload it in your Web browser. The race times should now be aligned with the right edge of the Time column. See Figure 4-35.

Figure 4-35 **RACE RESULTS TABLE WITH TIME VALUES RIGHT-ALIGNED**

Race Results			
Group	**Runner**	**Time**	**Origin**
Men	1. Peter Teagan	2:12:34	San Antonio, Texas
Men	2. Kyle Wills	2:13:05	Billings, Montana
Men	3. Jason Wu	2:14:28	Cutler, Colorado
Women	1. Laura Blake	2:28:21	Park City, Colorado
Women	2. Kathy Lasker	2:30:11	Chicago, Illinois
Women	3. Lisa Peterson	2:31:14	Seattle, Washington

You can also use the align and valign attributes with the <tr> tag to align all the text within a single row in the same manner as you did with columns.

Spanning Rows and Columns

Kevin has reviewed your table and would like to make a few more changes. He feels that repeating the group information for each row in the table is redundant and wonders if you can merge several cells into a single cell. He draws a proposed layout for the table, which is displayed in Figure 4-36.

Figure 4-36	KEVIN'S PROPOSED TABLE LAYOUT

	Runner	Time	Origin
Men	1. Peter Teagan	2:12:34	San Antonio, Texas
	2. Kyle Wills	2:13:05	Billings, Montana
	3. Jason Wu	2:14:28	Cutler, Colorado
Women	1. Laura Blake	2:28:21	Park City, Colorado
	2. Kathy Lasker	2:30:11	Chicago, Illinois
	3. Lisa Peterson	2:31:14	Seattle, Washington

To merge several cells into one, you need to create a **spanning cell**, which is a cell that occupies more than one row or column in a table. Figure 4-37 shows a table of opinion poll data in which some of the cells span several rows and/or columns.

Figure 4-37	EXAMPLE OF SPANNING CELLS

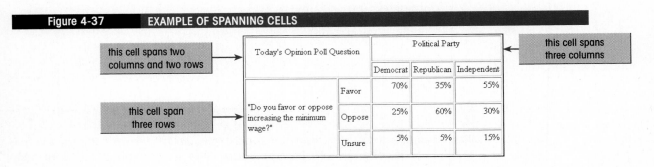

this cell spans two columns and two rows

this cell span three rows

this cell spans three columns

Spanning cells are created by inserting the rowspan and colspan attributes in a <td> or <th> tag. The syntax for these attributes is:

```
rowspan="value" colspan="value"
```

where *value* is the number of rows or columns that the cell spans in the table. The direction of the spanning is downward and to the right of the cell containing the rowspan and colspan attributes. For example, to create a cell that spans two columns in the table, you enter the <td> tag as:

```
<td colspan="2">
```

For a cell that spans two rows, the tag is:

```
<td rowspan="2">
```

and to span two rows and two columns at the same time, the tag is:

```
<td rowspan="2" colspan="2">
```

The important thing to remember when you have a cell that spans several rows or columns is that you must adjust the number of cell tags used in the table row. For example, if a row has five columns, but one of the cells in the row spans three columns, you only need three <td> tags within the row: two <td> tags for the cells that occupy a single column and the third for the cell spanning three rows.

When a cell spans several rows, the rows below the spanning cell must also be adjusted. Consider the table, shown in Figure 4-38, with three rows and four columns. The first cell in the first row is a spanning cell that spans three rows. You need four <td> tags for the first row, but only three <td> tags for rows two and three. This is because the spanning cell from row one occupies the cells that would normally appear in rows two and three.

Figure 4-38	TABLE STRUCTURE WITH A ROW-SPANNING CELL

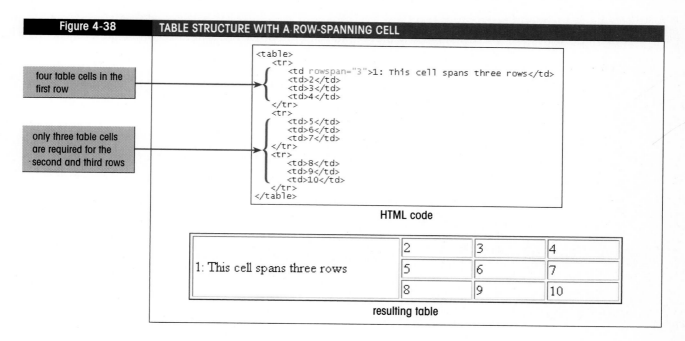

four table cells in the first row

only three table cells are required for the second and third rows

```
<table>
  <tr>
    <td rowspan="3">1: This cell spans three rows</td>
    <td>2</td>
    <td>3</td>
    <td>4</td>
  </tr>
  <tr>
    <td>5</td>
    <td>6</td>
    <td>7</td>
  </tr>
  <tr>
    <td>8</td>
    <td>9</td>
    <td>10</td>
  </tr>
</table>
```

HTML code

1: This cell spans three rows	2	3	4
	5	6	7
	8	9	10

resulting table

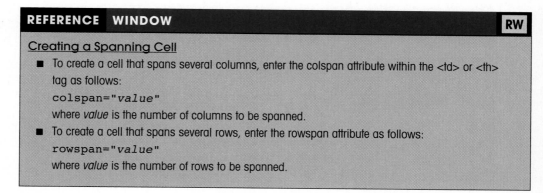

REFERENCE WINDOW   **RW**

Creating a Spanning Cell

- To create a cell that spans several columns, enter the colspan attribute within the <td> or <th> tag as follows:

  colspan="*value*"

  where *value* is the number of columns to be spanned.
- To create a cell that spans several rows, enter the rowspan attribute as follows:

  rowspan="*value*"

  where *value* is the number of rows to be spanned.

To make the changes that Kevin has requested, delete the table heading for the Group column, and then span the Runner table heading across two columns.

To create a cell that spans two columns:

1. Return to **race2.htm** in your text editor.

2. Delete the **Group** table heading, including both the opening and closing <th> tags.

3. Type the attribute **colspan="2"** within the <th> tag for the Runner table heading.

Next, you'll delete the second and third occurrences of the "Men" and "Women" cells in the table, keeping only the first occurrences. You'll also span those two cells over three rows of the table.

To span two cells over three rows:

1. Insert the attribute **rowspan="3"** in the first <td> tag that contains the text "Men".

2. Delete the next two <td> tags that contain the text "Men".

3. Insert the attribute **rowspan="3"** in the first <td> tag that contains the text "Women".

4. Delete the next two <td> tags that contain the text "Women". Figure 4-39 shows the revised table structure.

Figure 4-39	ADDING SPANNING CELLS TO THE RACE RESULTS TABLE

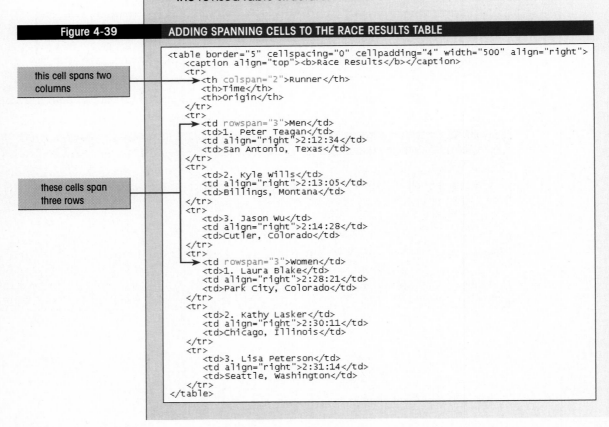

this cell spans two columns

these cells span three rows

```
<table border="5" cellspacing="0" cellpadding="4" width="500" align="right">
   <caption align="top"><b>Race Results</b></caption>
   <tr>
      <th colspan="2">Runner</th>
      <th>Time</th>
      <th>Origin</th>
   </tr>
   <tr>
      <td rowspan="3">Men</td>
      <td>1. Peter Teagan</td>
      <td align="right">2:12:34</td>
      <td>San Antonio, Texas</td>
   </tr>
   <tr>
      <td>2. Kyle Wills</td>
      <td align="right">2:13:05</td>
      <td>Billings, Montana</td>
   </tr>
   <tr>
      <td>3. Jason Wu</td>
      <td align="right">2:14:28</td>
      <td>Cutler, Colorado</td>
   </tr>
   <tr>
      <td rowspan="3">Women</td>
      <td>1. Laura Blake</td>
      <td align="right">2:28:21</td>
      <td>Park City, Colorado</td>
   </tr>
   <tr>
      <td>2. Kathy Lasker</td>
      <td align="right">2:30:11</td>
      <td>Chicago, Illinois</td>
   </tr>
   <tr>
      <td>3. Lisa Peterson</td>
      <td align="right">2:31:14</td>
      <td>Seattle, Washington</td>
   </tr>
</table>
```

5. Save your changes to race2.htm and reload it in your Web browser. Figure 4-40 shows the revised table.

Figure 4-40

RACE RESULTS TABLE WITH SPANNING CELLS

	Runner	Time	Origin
	Race Results		
	Runner	Time	Origin
Men	1. Peter Teagan	2:12:34	San Antonio, Texas
	2. Kyle Wills	2:13:05	Billings, Montana
	3. Jason Wu	2:14:28	Cutler, Colorado
Women	1. Laura Blake	2:28:21	Park City, Colorado
	2. Kathy Lasker	2:30:11	Chicago, Illinois
	3. Lisa Peterson	2:31:14	Seattle, Washington

The text in the two cells that span three rows is centered vertically, but Kevin feels it would look better if it were placed at the top of those cells. You can do this using the valign attribute that was discussed earlier.

To align the text with the top of the spanning cell:

1. Return to **race2.htm** in your text editor.

2. Type the attribute **valign="top"** within the <td> tag for the Men and Women spanning cells that you edited in the last set of steps.

Applying a Color Scheme to a Table

Kevin is pleased with the structure you've created for the race results table. He does have some concern that the table may be difficult to read due to the color scheme and would like you to apply a different one. He would like you to apply colors to the table background and to the table cells.

Applying a Background Color

Table elements support the same bgcolor attribute that can be applied to an entire Web page. You can specify a background color for all of the cells in a table, all of the cells in a row, or for individual cells, by adding the bgcolor attribute to either the <table>, <tr>, <td>, or <th> tags as follows:

```
<table bgcolor="color">
<tr bgcolor="color">
<td bgcolor="color">
<th bgcolor="color">
```

where *color* is either a color name or hexadecimal color value. Note that you cannot set a background color for a column with a single attribute; to set the background color for an entire column, you must define the background color for each cell in that column.

The color defined for a cell overrides the color defined for a row, and the color defined for a row overrides the color defined for a table. Keep this hierarchy in mind as you develop color schemes for tables.

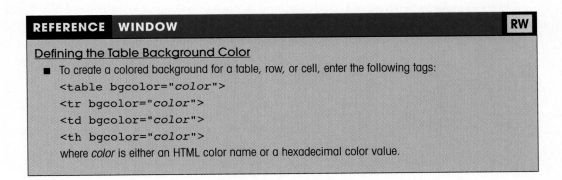

REFERENCE   WINDOW   **RW**

<u>Defining the Table Background Color</u>

■ To create a colored background for a table, row, or cell, enter the following tags:

`<table bgcolor="color">`

`<tr bgcolor="color">`

`<td bgcolor="color">`

`<th bgcolor="color">`

where *color* is either an HTML color name or a hexadecimal color value.

After considering many different colors, Kevin tells you to change the color of the table cells to white, the table heading to yellow, the cell containing the text "Men" to light blue, and the cell containing the text "Women" to light green.

To apply a color scheme to the table:

1. Type the attribute **bgcolor="white"** within the <table> tag.

2. Type the attribute **bgcolor="yellow"** within the <tr> tag for the table heading.

3. Type the attribute **bgcolor="lightblue"** within the <td> tag for the cell containing the text "Men".

4. Type the attribute **bgcolor="lightgreen"** within the <td> tag for the cell containing the text "Women". Figure 4-41 shows the revised HTML code for the table.

Figure 4-41   **SPECIFYING TABLE, ROW, AND CELL COLORS**

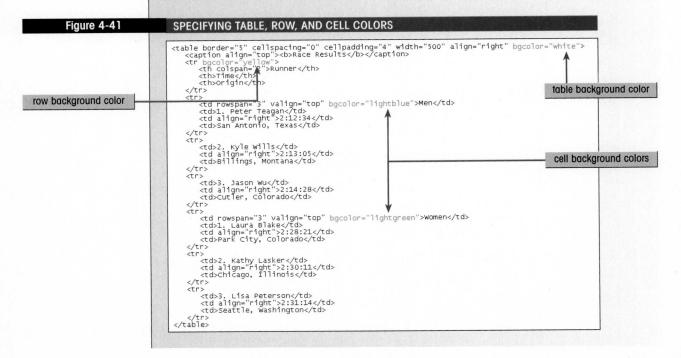

```
<table border="5" cellspacing="0" cellpadding="4" width="500" align="right" bgcolor="white">
   <caption align="top"><b>Race Results</b></caption>
   <tr bgcolor="yellow">
      <th colspan="2">Runner</th>
      <th>Time</th>
      <th>Origin</th>
   </tr>
   <tr>
      <td rowspan="3" valign="top" bgcolor="lightblue">Men</td>
      <td>1. Peter Teagan</td>
      <td align="right">2:12:34</td>
      <td>San Antonio, Texas</td>
   </tr>
   <tr>
      <td>2. Kyle Wills</td>
      <td align="right">2:13:05</td>
      <td>Billings, Montana</td>
   </tr>
   <tr>
      <td>3. Jason Wu</td>
      <td align="right">2:14:28</td>
      <td>Cutler, Colorado</td>
   </tr>
   <tr>
      <td rowspan="3" valign="top" bgcolor="lightgreen">Women</td>
      <td>1. Laura Blake</td>
      <td align="right">2:28:21</td>
      <td>Park City, Colorado</td>
   </tr>
   <tr>
      <td>2. Kathy Lasker</td>
      <td align="right">2:30:11</td>
      <td>Chicago, Illinois</td>
   </tr>
   <tr>
      <td>3. Lisa Peterson</td>
      <td align="right">2:31:14</td>
      <td>Seattle, Washington</td>
   </tr>
</table>
```

row background color

table background color

cell background colors

5. Save your changes to race2.htm and reload it in your Web browser. Figure 4-42 shows the table's new appearance.

Figure 4-42 | RACE RESULTS TABLE WITH COLORED BACKGROUND

	Race Results		
	Runner	**Time**	**Origin**
Men	1. Peter Teagan	2:12:34	San Antonio, Texas
	2. Kyle Wills	2:13:05	Billings, Montana
	3. Jason Wu	2:14:28	Cutler, Colorado
Women	1. Laura Blake	2:28:21	Park City, Colorado
	2. Kathy Lasker	2:30:11	Chicago, Illinois
	3. Lisa Peterson	2:31:14	Seattle, Washington

By default, table borders are displayed in two shades of gray that create a three-dimensional effect. You can change these colors by using the bordercolor attribute as follows:

```
<table bordercolor="color">
```

where *color* is an HTML color name or hexadecimal color value. Be aware that Internet Explorer and Netscape apply this attribute differently. As shown in Figure 4-43, Internet Explorer applies the same color to all parts of the border, thus removing the 3-D effect; Netscape does not.

Figure 4-43 | USING THE BORDERCOLOR ATTRIBUTE 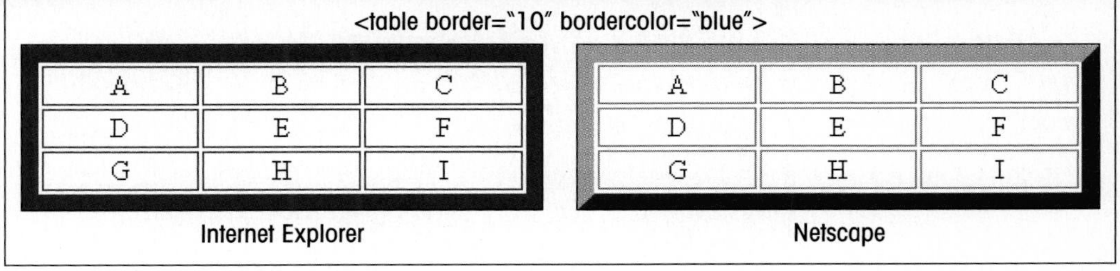

`<table border="10" bordercolor="blue">`

A	B	C
D	E	F
G	H	I

Internet Explorer

A	B	C
D	E	F
G	H	I

Netscape

To get around this problem, you can use two additional attributes supported by Internet Explorer: bordercolorlight and bordercolordark. These attributes allow you to specify light and dark colors of the 3-D border. Figure 4-44 shows an example of the use of the bordercolor and bordercolorlight attributes to create a 3-D colored border in Internet Explorer. Note that Netscape does not support these attributes.

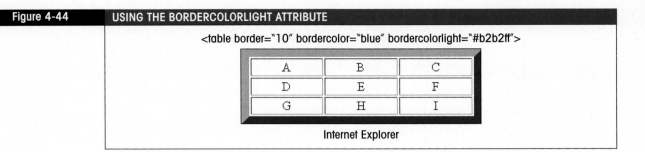

Figure 4-44 | **USING THE BORDERCOLORLIGHT ATTRIBUTE**

`<table border="10" bordercolor="blue" bordercolorlight="#b2b2ff">`

A	B	C
D	E	F
G	H	I

Internet Explorer

Kevin would also like you to change the color of the table border to brown. In order to maintain the 3-D border effect for Internet Explorer users, you'll also set the bordercolorlight attribute value to tan.

To change the color of a table border:

1. Return to **race2.htm** in your text editor.

2. Insert the attribute **bordercolor="brown" bordercolorlight="tan"** within the `<table>` tag.

3. Save your changes to race2.htm and reload it in your Web browser. Figure 4-45 shows the final version of the Web page.

4. Exit from your text editor and Web browser.

Figure 4-45 | **FINAL VERSION OF THE RACE2 PAGE**

Local Woman Wins Marathon

 Park City native, **Laura Blake**, won the 27th Front Range Marathon over an elite field of the best long distance runners in the country. Laura's time of 2 hr. 28 min. 21 sec. was only 2 minutes off the women's course record set last year by Sarah Rawlings. Kathy Lasker and Lisa Peterson finished second and third, respectively. Laura's victory came on the heels of her performance at the NCAA Track and Field Championships, in which she placed second running for Colorado State.

In an exciting race, **Peter Teagan** of San Antonio, Texas, used a finishing kick to win the men's marathon for the second straight year, in a time of 2 hr. 12 min. 34 sec. Ahead for much of the race, Kyle Wills of Billings, Montana, finished second, when he could not match Teagan's finishing pace. Jason Wu of Cutler, Colorado, placed third in a very competitive field.

This year's race through downtown Boulder boasted the largest field in the marathon's history, with over 9500 men and 6700 women competing. Race conditions were perfect with low humidity and temperatures that never exceeded 85°.

Race Results

	Runner	Time	Origin
Men	1. Peter Teagan	2:12:34	San Antonio, Texas
	2. Kyle Wills	2:13:05	Billings, Montana
	3. Jason Wu	2:14:28	Cutler, Colorado
Women	1. Laura Blake	2:28:21	Park City, Colorado
	2. Kathy Lasker	2:30:11	Chicago, Illinois
	3. Lisa Peterson	2:31:14	Seattle, Washington

Applying a Table Background

Though not needed for the race results table, you can add a background image to your tables using the same background attribute you used for the entire Web page. A background can be applied to the entire table, to a single row (Netscape 6.2 only), or to an individual cell. Figure 4-46 shows an example of the background attribute applied to three sample tables.

Figure 4-46   **APPLYING A BACKGROUND IMAGE TO A TABLE, ROW, AND CELL**

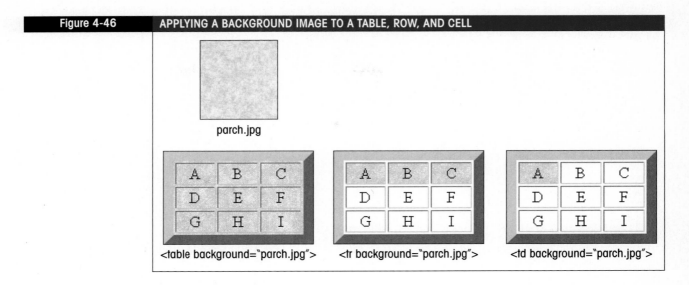

Note that certain browser versions may not support the use of background images in tables.

Working **with Column Groups**

Thus far, you've formatted columns by manipulating the attributes of individual cells within a column. HTML 4.0 supports tags that allow you to manipulate the features of entire columns and groups of columns. This feature is currently only supported by Internet Explorer 4.0 or above, and not at all by Netscape. Therefore it shouldn't be used if your page is to be viewed by multiple browsers and browser versions.

To define a column, add the following tag to the top of the table structure:

```
<col span="value">
```

where *value* is the number of columns in the group. The <col> tag supports many of the attributes you've applied to tables, rows, and cells, including the align, bgcolor, valign, and width attributes. Figure 4-47 shows an example of the <col> tag used to format the appearance of entire table columns.

Figure 4-47   USING THE <COL> TAG

```
<table width="200" border="10" cellspacing="5" cellpadding="5">
    <col span="2" align="left" bgcolor="lightblue">
    <col align="right" bgcolor="lightgreen">

    <tr>
        <td width="50">A</td>
        <td width="50">B</td>
        <td width="50">C</td>
    </tr>
    <tr>
        <td width="50">D</td>
        <td width="50">E</td>
        <td width="50">F</td>
    </tr>
    <tr>
        <td width="50">G</td>
        <td width="50">H</td>
        <td width="50">I</td>
    </tr>
</table>
```

HTML code

resulting table

In this example, setting the span attribute to "2" modifies the first <col> tag and the first two table columns. The second <col> tag modifies the appearance of the third column.

Another way of grouping columns is by using the <colgroup> tag. The syntax of the <colgroup> tag is:

```
<colgroup span="value">
        columns
</colgroup>
```

where *value* is the number of columns in the group, and *columns* are definitions for individual columns within the group (defined using the <col> tag.) Figure 4-48 shows an example of a column group used to center the text of all columns in the table. Background colors for the individual columns are specified using a series of <col> tags.

Figure 4-48   USING THE <COLGROUP> TAG

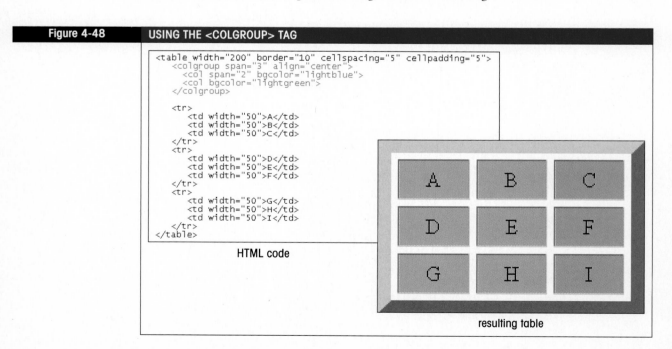

```
<table width="200" border="10" cellspacing="5" cellpadding="5">
    <colgroup span="3" align="center">
        <col span="2" bgcolor="lightblue">
        <col bgcolor="lightgreen">
    </colgroup>

    <tr>
        <td width="50">A</td>
        <td width="50">B</td>
        <td width="50">C</td>
    </tr>
    <tr>
        <td width="50">D</td>
        <td width="50">E</td>
        <td width="50">F</td>
    </tr>
    <tr>
        <td width="50">G</td>
        <td width="50">H</td>
        <td width="50">I</td>
    </tr>
</table>
```

HTML code

resulting table

In the event of a conflict between the attributes in the <col> and <colgroup> tags, the <col> tag attributes take precedence.

You've completed your work on the race results table and the story that Kevin wanted you to work on. In the next session, you'll use tables to create a layout for this story and other features of the Park City Gazette.

Session 4.2 QUICK CHECK

1. What HTML code would you use to create a table with a 5-pixel-wide outside border, a 3-pixel-wide border between table cells, and 4 pixels of padding between the cell text and the cell border?

2. What HTML code would you use to align text with the top of a table heading cell?

3. What HTML code would you use to center all of the text within a given row?

4. What are the two ways of expressing table width? What are the advantages and disadvantages of each?

5. What HTML code would you use to create a table that fills half the width of the browser's display area, regardless of the resolution of the user's monitor?

6. What HTML code would you use to set the width of a cell to 60 pixels? Will this keep the cell from exceeding 60 pixels in width? Will this keep the cell from being less than 60 pixels wide? How can you guarantee that the cell width will be exactly 60 pixels?

7. What HTML code would you use to set the background color of your table to yellow? What are some limitations of this code?

8. What HTML code would you use to create a cell that spans three rows and two columns?

SESSION 4.3

In this session you'll work with tables to create a newspaper-style layout for a Web page. You'll learn how to create comments for your HTML document to assist in the design process. You'll also learn how to nest one table within another, and how to format the text within table cells using the <font> tag.

Designing a Page Layout with Tables

In the first two sessions, you used the <table> tag to create a table of products that was part of a larger Web page. In practice, however, HTML tables are most often used to define the layout of an entire Web page. If you want to design a page that displays text in newspaper-style columns, or separates the page into distinct sections, you'll find tables an essential and useful tool. One of the most useful features of tables is that you can use any of the HTML layout tags you've learned so far for individual table cells. For example, you can format your cell text as an h1 heading, or the cell can store an unordered list of bulleted items. You can even nest one table inside another.

Kevin is satisfied with the layout of the article on the marathon results. He now wants you to create a newspaper-style Web page for the entire Gazette. The Web page will contain the Gazette logo, a list of links to other pages, and a few articles, one of which is the race results article you've been working on. Figure 4-49 displays the layout that Kevin has created.

Figure 4-49 **KEVIN'S DESIGN SKETCH FOR THE GAZETTE HOME PAGE**

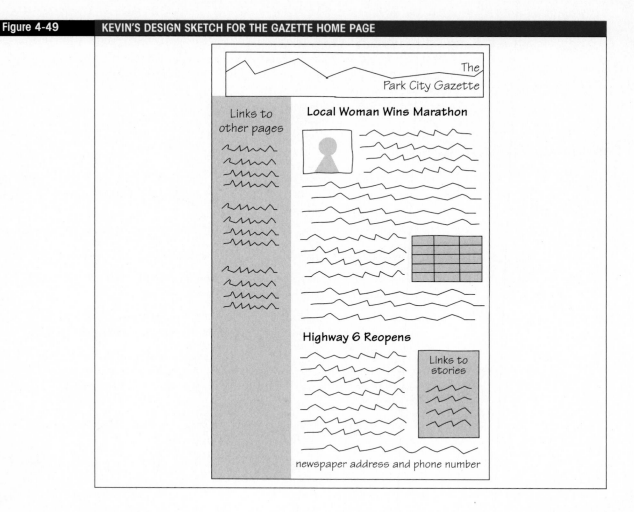

One way to lay out the page specified in Kevin's sketch is to create two tables, one nested inside the other. The outer table, shown in Figure 4-50, consists of four cells that are contained in two columns and three rows. The first cell, containing the Gazette logo, occupies the first row of the table and spans two columns. The second cell, displaying the list of links, occupies one column and spans the remaining two rows. The articles and newspaper address are placed in the remaining two cells, each occupying a single row and column.

You'll set the width of the table to 620 pixels to ensure that the entire Web page can be viewed by monitors with resolutions as low as 640 x 480 pixels. The first column's width will be set to 120 pixels. The second column, containing the articles and the paper's address, will be 500 pixels wide.

Figure 4-50   **TABLE LAYOUT OF THE GAZETTE HOME PAGE**

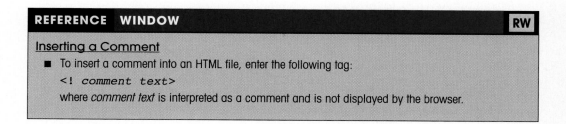

Creating the Outer Table

Kevin has created the initial part of the file for the front page, setting the page background and text color. Your job is to create the table structure displayed in Figure 4-50.

HTML code for pages like this one can be long and complex. **Comment tags** can aid you and others viewing your HTML file by describing the different sections of the code. The syntax for creating a comment tag is:

```
<! comment text>
```

where *comment text* is the text that you want to insert into the comment. Any text appearing within the comment tag is ignored by the browser and not displayed in the page.

REFERENCE   WINDOW   **RW**

Inserting a Comment

- To insert a comment into an HTML file, enter the following tag:
  ```
  <! comment text>
  ```
  where *comment text* is interpreted as a comment and is not displayed by the browser.

To create the outer table and comments:

1. If you took a break after the previous session, use your text editor to open **page1txt.htm** located in the tutorial.04/tutorial folder of your Data Disk and save it as **page1.htm**.

2. Enter the following code in a new line immediately following the <body> tag:

```
<table width="620" cellpadding="5">
<tr>
 <td colspan="2">
 <!-- Newspaper logo -->
 </td>
</tr>

<tr>
 <td width="120" rowspan="2" valign="top">
 <!- List of links ->
 </td>
 <td width="500" valign="top">
 <!-- Articles -->
 </td>
</tr>

<tr>
 <td width="500" valign="top" align="center">
 <!-- Newspaper address -->
 </td>
</tr>

</table>
```

Figure 4-51 displays what page1.htm should look like.

Figure 4-51	TABLE STRUCTURE OF THE PAGE1 WEB PAGE

```
<html>
<head>
<title>The Park City Gazette</title>
</head>
<body background="parch2.jpg" text="#524020" link="#524020" vlink="#524020" alink="#524020">
<table width="620" cellpadding="5">

<tr>
 <td colspan="2">
 <!-- Newspaper logo -->
 </td>
</tr>

<tr>
 <td width="120" rowspan="2" valign="top">
 <!-- List of links -->
 </td>

 <td width="500" valign="top">
 <!-- Articles -->
 </td>
</tr>

<tr>
 <td width="500" valign="top" align="center">
 <!-- Newspaper address -->
 </td>
</tr>

</table>
</body>
</html>
```

Note that in three of the cells of this outer table, you've set the vertical alignment to top, rather than using the default value of middle. This is because the cells in this table act as newspaper columns. The tables in this layout don't display any borders.

Now you place the Gazette logo, pclogo.jpg, on the Web page.

To insert the logo in a table cell:

1. Insert the code **<img src="pcglogo.jpg" alt="The Park City Gazette">** immediately after the comment <!--- Newspaper logo --->.

2. Save your changes to page1.htm and open the file in your Web browser. Your page should appear as shown in Figure 4-52.

Figure 4-52 **INITIAL CONTENTS OF PAGE1**

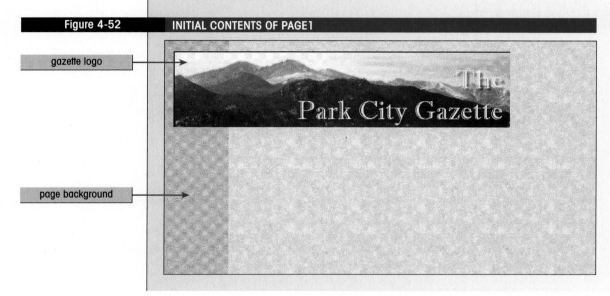

gazette logo

page background

Next you'll insert the list of links into the second table cell. The contents of this cell have been created for you and stored in a file named links.htm. You'll copy the information from that document and paste into the table cell. If you don't know how to copy and paste with your text editor, ask your instructor or technical support person for assistance.

To insert the contents of the links.htm file:

1. Using your text editor, open **links.htm** from the tutorial.04/tutorial folder of your data disk.

2. Copy the HTML code within the <body> tags of links.htm, but do *not* include the opening and closing <body> tags.

3. Close links.htm and return to **page1.htm** in your text editor.

4. Paste the HTML code you copied from links.htm directly after the comment tag, <!-- List of links --> as shown in Figure 4-53.

Figure 4-53   **INSERTING THE CONTENTS OF LINKS.HTM**

contents of the links.htm
file pasted here

```
<tr>
    <td width="120" rowspan="2" valign="top">
    <!-- List of links -->
    <font face="Arial, Helvetica, sans-serif" size="2">
        <h5><a href="parkcity.htm">Home Page</a></h5>
        <h5>News</h5>
            <a href="#">Local</a><br>
            <a href="#">State</a><br>
            <a href="#">National</a><br>
            <a href="#">International</a><br>
            <a href="#">Sports</a><br>
            <a href="#">Weather</a>

        <h5>Classifieds</h5>
            <a href="#">For Sale</a><br>
            <a href="#">Wanted</a><br>
            <a href="#">Employment</a><br>
            <a href="#">Real Estate</a><br>
            <a href="#">Personal</a>

        <h5>Tourism</h5>
            <a href="#">Attractions</a><br>
            <a href="#">Events</a><br>
            <a href="#">Parks</a><br>
            <a href="#">Camping</a>

        <h5><a href="#">Subscriptions</a></h5>
        <h5><a href="#">Contact Us</a></h5>
    </font>
    </td>

    <td width="500" valign="top">
    <!-- Articles -->
    </td>
</tr>
```

5. Save your changes to page1.htm and reload it in your Web browser. Figure 4-54 shows the current state of the home page of the Park City Gazette.

Figure 4-54   **PAGE1 WITH LINKS**

TROUBLE? At this point, the links on this page point to page1.htm and are acting as placeholders. Kevin will add the actual links as more work is done on the Gazette's Web site.

The next piece of the outer table you'll add is the newspaper address and phone number located at the bottom of the page. The content for this cell has been created for you, stored in the address.htm file.

To insert the contents of address.htm into a table:

1. Using your text editor, open **address.htm** from the tutorial.04/tutorial folder of your data disk.

2. Copy the HTML code within the <body> tags of address.htm, not including the opening and closing <body> tags.

3. Close address.htm and return to **page1.htm** in your text editor.

4. Paste the HTML code you copied from address.htm directly after the comment tag, <!-- Newspaper address --> as shown in Figure 4-55.

Figure 4-55   INSERTING THE CONTENTS OF ADDRESS.HTM

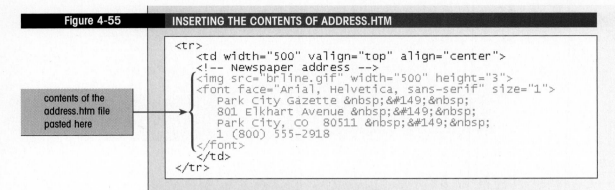

contents of the
address.htm file
pasted here

```
<tr>
   <td width="500" valign="top" align="center">
   <!-- Newspaper address -->
   <img src="brline.gif" width="500" height="3">
   <font face="Arial, Helvetica, sans-serif" size="1">
      Park City Gazette  &#149; 
      801 Elkhart Avenue  &#149; 
      Park City, CO  80511  &#149; 
      1 (800) 555-2918
   </font>
   </td>
</tr>
```

5. Save your changes to page1.htm and reload it in your Web browser. See Figure 4-56.

Figure 4-56   PAGE1 WITH THE NEWSPAPER ADDRESS

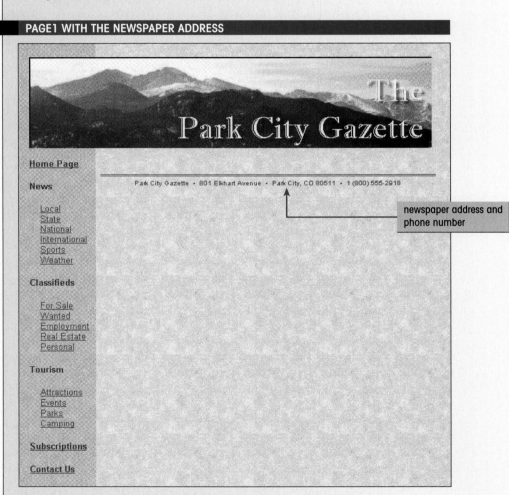

newspaper address and
phone number

At this point, you've populated all of the table cells with information except one, the articles cell. Essentially, the articles cell is the only cell with content that changes on a weekly basis. When Kevin wants to update this Web page, he need only edit the contents of a single cell. Therefore, it makes sense to separate the articles content from the rest of the front page by placing it in a separate cell.

Creating the Nested Table

Kevin has decided on the stories he wants you to use for today's front page articles. The main story is the results of the marathon, and another story concerns the reopening of Highway 6 (one of Park City's main roads over the Continental Divide). He also wants the Web page to have a sidebar with links to some of the other important stories and features of the day. In Figure 4-57, Kevin has sketched a layout to assist you with the design of the Web page.

Figure 4-57	DESIGN SKETCH FOR TODAY'S ARTICLES

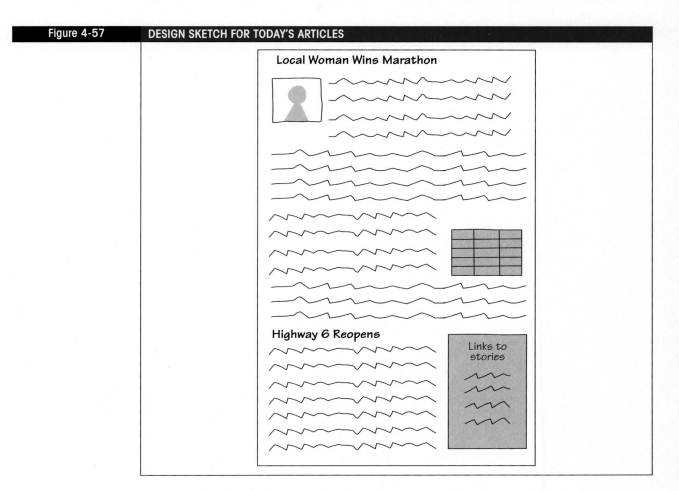

This material is best organized in a second table, an outline of which is shown in Figure 4-58. The width of this table is 500 pixels, since it has to match the width assigned to the third cell from Figure 4-50. The first cell contains the marathon story and spans two columns. The second cell, 300 pixels wide, contains the Highway 6 story. The third cell contains a list of links to other stories and is 200 pixels wide. For this third cell, you'll use the parch3.jpg graphic for a background image.

Figure 4-58   **TABLE LAYOUT OF TODAY'S ARTICLES**

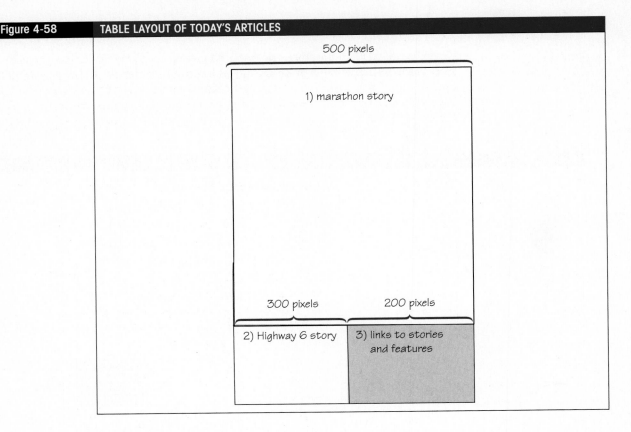

Kevin has begun creating the Web page for this table, artcltxt.htm, and you can open that file now.

To create the outer table and comments:

1. Using your text editor, open **artcltxt.htm** located in the tutorial.04/tutorial folder of your Data Disk and save it as **articles.htm** in the sam...

2. Type the following HTML code immediately following t...

```
<table width="500" cellpadding="5" cel
<tr>
  <td colspan="2" valign="top">
  <!-- Marathon story -->
  </td>
</tr>

<tr>
  <td width="300" valign="top">
  <!-- Highway story -->
  </td>

  <td width="200" valign="top" background="parch3.jpg">
  <!-- Features -->
  </td>
</tr>

</table>
```

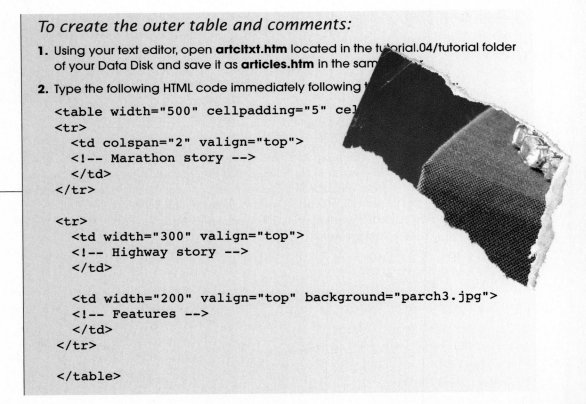

Figure 4-59 displays what articles.htm should look like.

Figure 4-59	TABLE STRUCTURE OF THE ARTICLES WEB PAGE

```
<html>
<head>
<title>Today's Headlines</title>
</head>

<body background="parch.jpg" text="#524020" link=""#524020" vlink="#524020" alink="#524020">
<table width="500" cellpadding="5" cellspacing="5">

<tr>
   <td colspan="2" valign="top">
   <!-- Marathon story -->
   </td>
</tr>

<tr>
   <td width="300" valign="top">
   <!-- Highway story -->
   </td>

   <td width="200" valign="top" background="parch3.jpg">
   <!-- Features -->
   </td>
</tr>

</table>
</body>

</html>
```

3. Save your changes to the file.

The next step is to copy the code for the marathon article that you created in race2.htm and paste it in the first cell of the table. You will also have to edit some of the contents of this material to fit the size of the cell.

To insert the contents of race2.htm into the first cell:

1. Using your text editor, open **race2.htm** from the tutorial.04/tutorial folder of your Data Disk.

2. Copy the HTML code within the <body> tags of race2.htm, but do *not* include the <body> tags themselves.

3. Close the file and return to **articles.htm** in your text editor.

4. Paste the HTML code you copied from race2.htm directly after the comment tag <!-- Marathon story--> as shown in Figure 4-60. Save your changes to articles.htm.

Figure 4-60	INSERTING THE CONTENTS OF RACE2.HTM

contents of the race2.htm file pasted here

```
<tr>
   <td colspan="2" valign="top">
   <!-- Marathon story -->
<h1 align="center"><font face="Arial, Helvetica, sans-serif">
   Local Woman Wins Marathon
</font></h1>

<p>
<img src="blake.jpg" align="left" hspace="5" vspace="5" width="75" height="101">
Park City native, <b>Laura Blake</b>, won the 27<sup>th</sup> Front Range Marathon
over an elite field of the best long distance runners in the country. Laura's
time of 2 hr. 28 min. 21 sec. was only 2 minutes off the women's course record
set last year by Sarah Rawlings. Kathy Lasker and Lisa Peterson finished second
and third, respectively. Laura's victory came on the heels of her performance at
the NCAA Track and Field Championships, in which she placed second running for
Colorado State.
</p>

<table border="5" cellspacing="0" cellpadding="4" width="500" align="right" bgcolor="white"
   bordercolor="brown" bordercolorlight="tan">
   <caption align="top"><b>Race Results</b></caption>
   <tr bgcolor="yellow">
      <th colspan="2">Runner</th>
      <th>Time</th>
      <th>Origin</th>
   </tr>
```

One problem you have with the current layout is that the total width of the article is limited to 500 pixels, yet the race results table alone is 500 pixels. In order to make the text wrap around the results table, you need to reduce the width of the table. Kevin suggests a new width of 300 pixels. However, with a smaller table, the text entries no longer fit as neatly into the individual cells. One solution is to use the <font> tag to reduce the size of the text in the table.

It would be convenient if you could apply the <font> tag to all of the text in the table at once, but the <font> tag cannot be applied that way. In order to change the size of the table text, you need to insert a <font> tag into each cell. You decide to set the size of the caption, table headings, and the Men and Women cells to size "2", and all other text in the table to size "1". You may find the following steps easier to complete by using the copy and paste feature of your text editor.

To change the size of the text in the race results table:

1. Within articles.htm, locate the **<table>** tag for the race results table and change the width of the table from "500" to **"300"**.

   Please refer to Figure 4-61 as you enter the code specified in the following steps.

2. Insert the tag **<font size="2">** immediately before the <b> tag in the table caption, and then insert a closing **</font>** tag immediately after the closing </b> tag in the table caption.

3. Enclose the text for all of the table headings in **<font size="2">** tags.

4. Locate the table cell containing the text "Men", and enclose that text with the **<font size="2">** tag.

5. Locate the table cell containing the text "Women", and enclose that text with the **<font size="2">** tag.

6. Enclose the remaining text in the race results table with the **<font size="1">** tags. Figure 4-61 shows the revised code for the table.

Figure 4-61	CHANGING THE FONT SIZE IN THE RACE RESULTS TABLE

```
<table border="5" cellspacing="0" cellpadding="4" width="300" align="right" bgcolor="white"
bor, bordercolor="brown" bordercolorlight="tan">
    <caption align="top"><font size="2"><b>Race Results</b></font></caption>
    <tr bgcolor="yellow">
        <th colspan="2"><font size="2">Runner</font></th>
        <th><font size="2">Time</font></th>
        <th><font size="2">Origin</font></th>
    </tr>
    <tr>
        <td rowspan="3" valign="top" bgcolor="lightblue"><font size="2">Men</font></td>
        <td><font size="1">1. Peter Teagan</font></td>
        <td align="right"><font size="1">2:12:34</font></td>
        <td><font size="1">San Antonio, Texas</font></td>
    </tr>
    <tr>
        <td><font size="1">2. Kyle Wills</font></td>
        <td align="right"><font size="1">2:13:05</font></td>
        <td><font size="1">Billings, Montana</font></td>
    </tr>
    <tr>
        <td><font size="1">3. Jason Wu</font></td>
        <td align="right"><font size="1">2:14:28</font></td>
        <td><font size="1">Cutler, Colorado</font></td>
    </tr>
    <tr>
        <td rowspan="3" valign="top" bgcolor="lightgreen"><font size="2">Women</font></td>
        <td><font size="1">1. Laura Blake</font></td>
        <td align="right"><font size="1">2:28:21</font></td>
        <td><font size="1">Park City, Colorado</font></td>
    </tr>
    <tr>
        <td><font size="1">2. Kathy Lasker</font></td>
        <td align="right"><font size="1">2:30:11</font></td>
        <td><font size="1">Chicago, Illinois</font></td>
    </tr>
    <tr>
        <td><font size="1">3. Lisa Peterson</font></td>
        <td align="right"><font size="1">2:31:14</font></td>
        <td><font size="1">Seattle, Washington</font></td>
    </tr>
</table>
```

7. Save your changes to articles.htm and reload it in your Web browser. Figure 4-62 shows the current appearance of the page.

Figure 4-62   **ARTICLES PAGE WITH THE MARATHON STORY**

Local Woman Wins Marathon

 Park City native, **Laura Blake**, won the 27th Front Range Marathon over an elite field of the best long distance runners in the country. Laura's time of 2 hr. 28 min. 21 sec. was only 2 minutes off the women's course record set last year by Sarah Rawlings. Kathy Lasker and Lisa Peterson finished second and third, respectively. Laura's victory came on the heels of her performance at the NCAA Track and Field Championships, in which she placed second running for Colorado State.

In an exciting race, **Peter Teagan** of San Antonio, Texas, used a finishing kick to win the men's marathon for the second straight year, in a time of 2 hr. 12 min. 34 sec. Ahead for much of the race, Kyle Wills of Billings, Montana, finished second, when he could not match Teagan's finishing pace. Jason Wu of Cutler, Colorado, placed third in a very competitive field.

Race Results

	Runner	Time	Origin
Men	1. Peter Teagan	2:12:34	San Antonio, Texas
	2. Kyle Wills	2:13:05	Billings, Montana
	3. Jason Wu	2:14:28	Cutler, Colorado
Women	1. Laura Blake	2:28:21	Park City, Colorado
	2. Kathy Lasker	2:30:11	Chicago, Illinois
	3. Lisa Peterson	2:31:14	Seattle, Washington

This year's race through downtown Boulder boasted the largest field in the marathon's history, with over 9500 men and 6700 women competing. Race conditions were perfect with low humidity and temperatures that never exceeded 85°.

TROUBLE? It's easy to make a mistake in the set of steps outlined here. Make sure that each <font> tag is placed *inside* the <td>, <th>, or <caption> tags and that you've included the closing </font> tag within each cell. Another possible source of error is to neglect to include a closing double quotation mark around the attribute values. Carefully compare your HTML code to the code shown in Figure 4-61.

Next you need to insert the article about the reopening of Highway 6 in the second table cell. The text for this file has been created for you and is in highway.htm.

To insert the contents of highway.htm in the second table cell:

1. Open **highway.htm** from the tutorial.04/tutorial folder of your Data Disk in your text editor.

2. Copy the HTML code contained between the <body> tags of highway.htm.

3. Close highway.htm and open **articles.htm** with your text editor if it is not currently open.

4. Paste the copied HTML code into articles.htm immediately after the comment tag, <!-- Highway story--> as shown in Figure 4-63.

Figure 4-63	INSERTING THE CONTENTS OF HIGHWAY.HTM

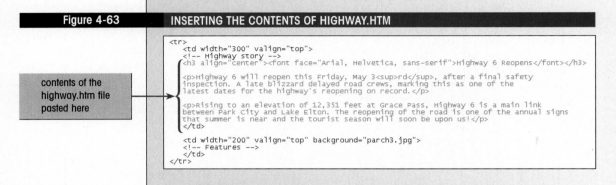

contents of the
highway.htm file
pasted here

```
<tr>
  <td width="300" valign="top">
  <!-- Highway story -->
  <h3 align="center"><font face="Arial, Helvetica, sans-serif">Highway 6 Reopens</font></h3>

  <p>Highway 6 will reopen this Friday, May 3<sup>rd</sup>, after a final safety
  inspection. A late blizzard delayed road crews, marking this as one of the
  latest dates for the highway's reopening on record.</p>

  <p>Rising to an elevation of 12,351 feet at Grace Pass, Highway 6 is a main link
  between Park City and Lake Elton. The reopening of the road is one of the annual signs
  that summer is near and the tourist season will soon be upon us!</p>
  </td>

  <td width="200" valign="top" background="parch3.jpg">
  <!-- Features -->
  </td>
</tr>
```

5. Save your changes to articles.htm and reload it in your Web browser (see Figure 4-64).

Figure 4-64   ARTICLES PAGE WITH THE HIGHWAY STORY

Local Woman Wins Marathon

 Park City native, **Laura Blake**, won the 27th Front Range Marathon over an elite field of the best long distance runners in the country. Laura's time of 2 hr. 28 min. 21 sec. was only 2 minutes off the women's course record set last year by Sarah Rawlings. Kathy Lasker and Lisa Peterson finished second and third, respectively. Laura's victory came on the heels of her performance at the NCAA Track and Field Championships, in which she placed second running for Colorado State.

In an exciting race, **Peter Teagan** of San Antonio, Texas, used a finishing kick to win the men's marathon for the second straight year, in a time of 2 hr. 12 min. 34 sec. Ahead for much of the race, Kyle Wills of Billings, Montana, finished second, when he could not match Teagan's finishing pace. Jason Wu of Cutler, Colorado, placed third in a very competitive field.

Race Results

	Runner	Time	Origin
Men	1. Peter Teagan	2:12:34	San Antonio, Texas
	2. Kyle Wills	2:13:05	Billings, Montana
	3. Jason Wu	2:14:28	Cutler, Colorado
Women	1. Laura Blake	2:28:21	Park City, Colorado
	2. Kathy Lasker	2:30:11	Chicago, Illinois
	3. Lisa Peterson	2:31:14	Seattle, Washington

This year's race through downtown Boulder boasted the largest field in the marathon's history, with over 9500 men and 6700 women competing. Race conditions were perfect with low humidity and temperatures that never exceeded 85°.

Highway 6 Reopens

Highway 6 will reopen this Friday, May 3rd, after a final safety inspection. A late blizzard delayed road crews, marking this as one of the latest dates for the highway's reopening on record.

Rising to an elevation of 12,351 feet at Grace Pass, Highway 6 is a main link between Park City and Lake Elton. The reopening of the road is one of the annual signs that summer is near and the tourist season will soon be upon us!

The final piece you'll add to articles.htm is the code for the links to stories and features. The code for this cell is stored in features.htm.

To insert the contents of features.htm in a table cell:

1. Using your text editor, open **features.htm** from the tutorial.04/tutorial folder.

2. Copy the HTML code located between the <body> tags of the file.

3. Close features.htm and return to **articles.htm** in your text editor.

4. Paste the copied HTML code directly after the comment tag <!-- Features --> as shown in Figure 4-65.

| Figure 4-65 | INSERTING THE CONTENTS OF FEATURES.HTM |

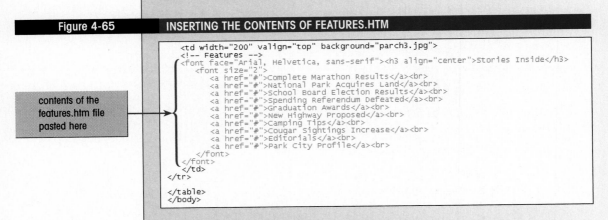

contents of the features.htm file pasted here

```
<td width="200" valign="top" background="parch3.jpg">
<!-- Features -->
<font face="Arial, Helvetica, sans-serif"><h3 align="center">Stories Inside</h3>
    <font size="2">
        <a href="#">Complete Marathon Results</a><br>
        <a href="#">National Park Acquires Land</a><br>
        <a href="#">School Board Election Results</a><br>
        <a href="#">Spending Referendum Defeated</a><br>
        <a href="#">Graduation Awards</a><br>
        <a href="#">New Highway Proposed</a><br>
        <a href="#">Camping Tips</a><br>
        <a href="#">Cougar Sightings Increase</a><br>
        <a href="#">Editorials</a><br>
        <a href="#">Park City Profile</a><br>
    </font>
</font>
    </td>
</tr>

</table>
</body>
```

5. Save your changes to articles.htm and reload the file in your Web browser. The completed page appears in Figure 4-66.

Figure 4-66 COMPLETED ARTICLES PAGE

Local Woman Wins Marathon

Park City native, **Laura Blake**, won the 27th Front Range Marathon over an elite field of the best long distance runners in the country. Laura's time of 2 hr. 28 min. 21 sec. was only 2 minutes off the women's course record set last year by Sarah Rawlings. Kathy Lasker and Lisa Peterson finished second and third, respectively. Laura's victory came on the heels of her performance at the NCAA Track and Field Championships, in which she placed second running for Colorado State.

In an exciting race, **Peter Teagan** of San Antonio, Texas, used a finishing kick to win the men's marathon for the second straight year, in a time of 2 hr. 12 min. 34 sec. Ahead for much of the race, Kyle Wills of Billings, Montana, finished second, when he could not match Teagan's finishing pace. Jason Wu of Cutler, Colorado, placed third in a very competitive field.

Race Results

	Runner	Time	Origin
Men	1. Peter Teagan	2:12:34	San Antonio, Texas
	2. Kyle Wills	2:13:05	Billings, Montana
	3. Jason Wu	2:14:28	Cutler, Colorado
Women	1. Laura Blake	2:28:21	Park City, Colorado
	2. Kathy Lasker	2:30:11	Chicago, Illinois
	3. Lisa Peterson	2:31:14	Seattle, Washington

This year's race through downtown Boulder boasted the largest field in the marathon's history, with over 9500 men and 6700 women competing. Race conditions were perfect with low humidity and temperatures that never exceeded 85°.

Highway 6 Reopens

Highway 6 will reopen this Friday, May 3rd, after a final safety inspection. A late blizzard delayed road crews, marking this as one of the latest dates for the highway's reopening on record.

Rising to an elevation of 12,351 feet at Grace Pass, Highway 6 is a main link between Park City and Lake Elton. The reopening of the road is one of the annual signs that summer is near and the tourist season will soon be upon us!

Stories Inside

Complete Marathon Results
National Park Acquires Land
School Board Election Results
Spending Referendum Defeated
Graduation Awards
New Highway Proposed
Camping Tips
Cougar Sightings Increase
Editorials
Park City Profile

Combining the Outer and Inner Tables

It's now time to place the code from articles.htm into page1.htm. You'll use the same copy and paste techniques that you've used to populate the other table cells.

To insert the contents of articles.htm into page1.htm:

1. Return to **articles.htm** in your text editor.

2. Copy the HTML code between the <body> tags.

3. Close articles.htm and open **page1.htm** using your text editor if it is not currently open.

4. Paste the copied HTML code from Step 2 directly after the comment tag <! -- Articles --> as shown in Figure 4-67.

Figure 4-67　INSERTING THE CONTENTS OF ARTICLES.HTM INTO PAGE1.HTM

contents of the articles.htm file pasted here →

```
        <h5><a href="#">Subscriptions</a></h5>
        <h5><a href="#">Contact Us</a></h5>
    </font>
    </td>

    <td width="500" valign="top">
    <!-- Articles -->
<table width="500" cellpadding="5" cellspacing="5">

<tr>
    <td colspan="2" valign="top">
    <!-- Marathon story -->
<h1 align="center"><font face="Arial, Helvetica, sans-serif">
 Local Woman Wins Marathon
</font></h1>

<p>
<img src="blake.jpg" align="left" hspace="5" vspace="5" width="75" height="101">
Park City native, <b>Laura Blake</b>, won the 27<sup>th</sup> Front Range Marathon
over an elite field of the best long distance runners in the country. Laura's
time of 2 hr. 28 min. 21 sec. was only 2 minutes off the women's course record
set last year by Sarah Rawlings. Kathy Lasker and Lisa Peterson finished second
and third, respectively. Laura's victory came on the heels of her performance at
the NCAA Track and Field Championships, in which she placed second running for
Colorado State.
</p>
```

5. Save your changes to page1.htm and reload it in your Web browser. Figure 4-68 shows the final appearance of the front page of the Park City Gazette.

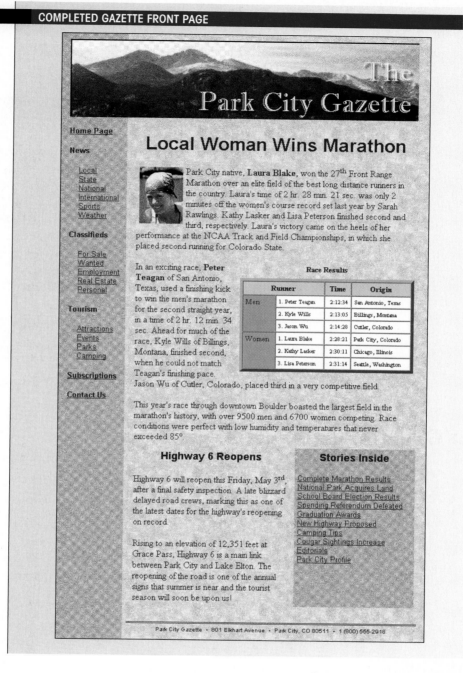

You've finished designing the Park City Gazette's front page. Using tables, you've managed to create an interesting and attractive layout. The process you followed used several principles you should keep in mind as you gain experience as a Web designer:

1. Diagram the layout before you start writing the HTML code.

2. Create the text for various columns and cells in separate files to be inserted later.

3. Create the table structure for the outer table first, and then gradually work inward.

4. Insert comment tags to identify the different sections of a Web page.

5. Indent the code for the various levels of nested tables, to make your code easier to read.

6. Test and review your code as you proceed to catch errors early in the design process.

REFERENCE WINDOW   **RW**

Using Tables to Control Page Layout
- Use cell padding and cell spacing to keep your columns from being too crowded.
- Add background colors to table cells to provide visual interest and variety.
- Use the valign="top" attribute in cells containing articles, to ensure that the text flows from the top down.
- Use row spanning to vary the size and starting point of articles within your columns. Having all articles start and end within the same row creates a static layout that can be difficult to read.
- If possible, avoid using more than three columns of text. Too many columns can make column widths too narrow and make the text hard to read.

You show the final version of the Web page to Kevin and he's pleased you were able to create a Web page that closely resembles his original design sketch. He decides to use this layout for future issues of the Gazette. As he compiles new articles, he may look for your help in providing design assistance.

Session 4.3 QUICK CHECK

1. What HTML code would you use to create a 2 × 2 table nested inside the upper-left cell of another 2 × 2 table?

2. What HTML code is used to insert the comment "Nested table starts here"?

3. If you wanted to change the font color of all cells in a table to red, how would you enter the HTML code?

4. What HTML code would you use to insert the text "Headlines" into a table cell in an h1 heading with an Arial, Helvetica, or sans-serif font?

5. What is the first thing you should do when creating a table layout?

REVIEW ASSIGNMENTS

Kevin has another page of the Park City Gazette to place on the Web site. Cougar sightings have recently increased in the Park City area, causing great concern for both local residents and tourists. Kevin has written an article describing the sightings and providing safety tips for effectively handling a cougar encounter. Kevin has also created a table, shown in Figure 4-69, listing local cougar sightings for the last six months. Kevin would like you to include this table with his article.

Figure 4-69

LOCATION	APRIL	MAY	JUNE	JULY	AUGUST	TOTAL
Park City	0	2	1	3	4	10
Riley	2	1	1	3	2	9
Dixon	0	2	3	1	4	10
TOTAL	2	5	5	7	10	29

The articles should employ the same layout you designed for the paper's front page. Figure 4-70 shows a preview of the Web page you'll create for Kevin.

Figure 4-70

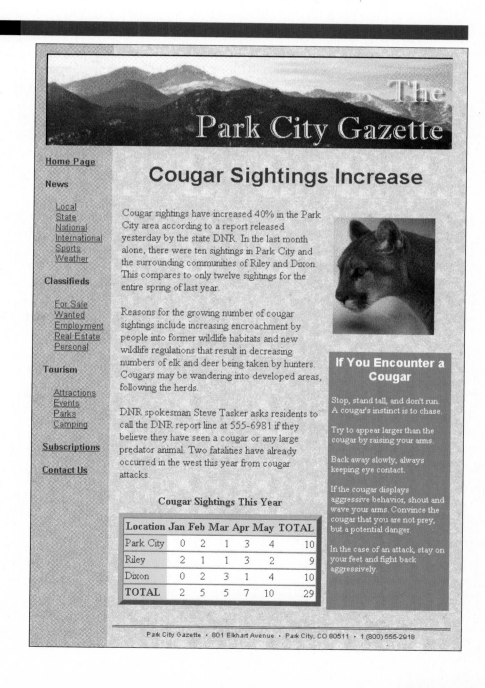

To complete this task:

1. Using your text editor, open **sighttxt.htm** located in the tutorial.04/review folder of your Data Disk and save it as **sighting.htm**.

2. Below the last paragraph in the story, insert a table with the following attributes:

   ■ The table should be 300 pixels wide with a 7-pixel-wide border.
   ■ The cell spacing should be set to 0 pixels. The cell padding should be set to 2 pixels.
   ■ The table should have a white background. The color of the table border should be brown. The light border color should be tan.
   ■ The table should be centered on the page.

Explore ▶ 3. Apply gridlines to the rows of the table only (HINT: Use the rules attribute).

4. Insert the caption "Cougar Sightings This Year" in a bold font above the table.

5. Insert the table entries shown in Figure 4-69. Create the cells in the table's first row using the <th> tag. Give the table headings and the table's first column a pink background. Display the text, "TOTAL", in the last row of the first column in a bold font.

6. Right-align all numeric values in the table.

7. Save your changes to sighting.htm and print the HTML code.

8. Using your text editor, open **art2txt.htm** and save it as **article2.htm**.

9. Below the <body> tag, insert a table that is 500 pixels wide with a cell spacing value of 3 and a cell padding value of 5.

10. Create a cell on the first row of the table that spans two columns, and identify this cell with the comment "Cougar headline". Within this cell, insert a centered h1 heading that contains the text "Cougar Sightings Increase". Display the headline in an Arial, Helvetica, or sans-serif font.

11. In the second row of the table, insert a cell that is 300 pixels wide and spans two rows. Vertically align the text of this cell with the cell's top border. Identify this cell with the comment "Cougar story". Insert the contents of the **sighting.htm** file (excluding the <body> tags) into this cell.

12. Also in the table's second row, insert a cell that is 200 pixels wide. Identify this cell with the comment "Cougar photo". Display the image, cougar.jpg, in the cell.

13. In the table's third row, insert a cell that is 200 pixels wide, has a red background, and align the cell text with the cell's top border. Insert the comment "Cougar tips" for this cell. Insert the contents of the **tips.htm** file (excluding the <body> tags) into this cell.

14. Save your changes to article2.htm and print the HTML code.

15. Using your text editor, open **page2txt.htm** and save it as **page2.htm**.

16. Locate the Articles cell in the main table of this file (it will be the third cell). Insert the contents of **article2.htm**. Save your changes to the file and view its contents with your Web browser.

17. Hand in your files and printouts to your instructor.

CASE PROBLEMS

Case 1. dHome, Inc. dHome is one of the nation's leading manufacturers of geodesic dome houses. Olivia Moore, the director of advertising for dHome, has hired you to work on the company's Web site. She has provided you with all of the text you need for the Web page, and your job is to design the page's layout. Olivia would like each page in the Web site to display the company logo, a column of links, a footer displaying additional hypertext links, and another footer displaying the company's address and phone number. In the center of the page, she would like you to place the appropriate text for the topic of that particular Web page. Figure 4-71 shows a preview of the company's Web page.

Figure 4-71

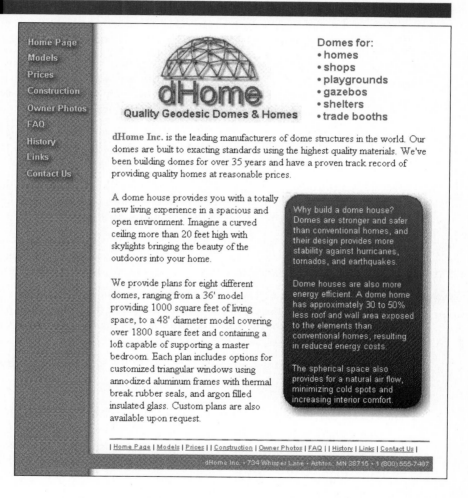

To create the dHome Web page:

1. Using your text editor, open **introtxt.htm** from the tutorial.04/case1 folder of your Data Disk and save it as **intro.htm**.

2. Between the first and the second paragraphs, create a table 224 pixels wide and 348 pixels high. Set the cell padding and cell spacing values to zero. Align the table with the right margin of the Web page.

Explore 3. The table should have a single row with three columns. The first cell should be 20 pixels wide, using the **back3.jpg** file for its background.

4. The second cell should be 200 pixels wide, using the **back4.jpg** file as a background. Insert the contents of the uses.htm file into this cell. Display the contents of the uses.htm file in a size 2 white Arial, Helvetica, or sans-serif font.

5. The third cell should be 30 pixels wide and use the **back5.jpg** file as its background.

6. Save your changes to intro.htm and print the file.

7. Using your text editor, open **dhometxt.htm** and save it as **dhome.htm**.

8. Within the file, create a table 620 pixels wide with a cell padding of 5 and a cell spacing of zero.

9. The first row of the table should have three cells. The first cell should be 120 pixels wide and span 3 rows. Within this cell, insert the **links.jpg** image, aligning it with the cell's top border. Identify this cell with the comment tag "List of links".

10. The second cell should be 300 pixels wide. Within this cell insert the company's logo, found in the dhome.jpg file. Align the logo with the cell's top border. For non-graphical browsers, provide the alternate text "dHome Quality Geodesic Domes & Homes". Identify this cell with the comment tag "Company logo".

11. The third cell should be 200 pixels wide. Insert the contents of the textbox.htm file into this cell. Align the text of the cell with the cell's top border. Identify the cell with the comment "Text box".

12. In the table's second row, create a single cell 500 pixels wide that spans two columns. Insert the contents of the intro.htm file into this cell. Align the text with the top of the cell. Identify the cell with the comment "Intro text".

13. In the table's third row, create another cell 500 pixels wide that spans two columns. Within this cell, insert the contents of the footer.htm file, aligning the contents with the top of the cell. Identify the contents of this cell with the comment "Footer".

Explore 14. In the fourth and last row of the table, create a cell 620 pixels wide and 15 pixels high, that spans three columns. Use **back2.jpg** as the background image for the cell. Insert the contents of the **address.htm** file into the cell, aligned with the cell's right border. Identify the cell with the comment, "Address".

15. Save your changes to the file, and print the final version of the code.

16. Hand in your printouts and files to your instructor.

Case 2. Chamberlain Civic Center. The Chamberlain Civic Center of Chamberlain, Iowa, is in the process of designing a Web page to advertise its events and activities. Stacy Dawes, the director of the publicity, has asked you to create a Web page describing the events in February shown in the following list. Ticket prices are provided in parentheses.

- Every Sunday, the Carson Quartet plays at 1 p.m. ($8)
- February 1, 8 p.m.: Taiwan Acrobats ($16/$24/$36)
- February 5, 8 p.m.: Joey Gallway ($16/$24/$36)
- February 7–8, 7 p.m.: Joey Gallway ($24/$36/$64)
- February 10, 8 p.m.: Jazz Masters ($18/$24/$32)
- February 13, 8 p.m.: Harlem Choir ($18/$24/$32)
- February 14, 8 p.m.: Chamberlain Symphony ($18/$24/$32)
- February 15, 8 p.m.: Edwin Drood ($24/$36/$44)
- February 19, 8 p.m.: The Yearling ($8/$14/$18)

■ February 21, 8 p.m.: An Ellington Tribute ($24/$32/$48)

■ February 22, 8 p.m.: Othello ($18/$28/$42)

■ February 25, 8 p.m.: Madtown Jugglers ($12/$16/$20)

■ February 28, 8 p.m.: Robin Williams ($32/$48/$64)

Figure 4-72 shows a preview of the Web page you'll create for Stacy.

Figure 4-72

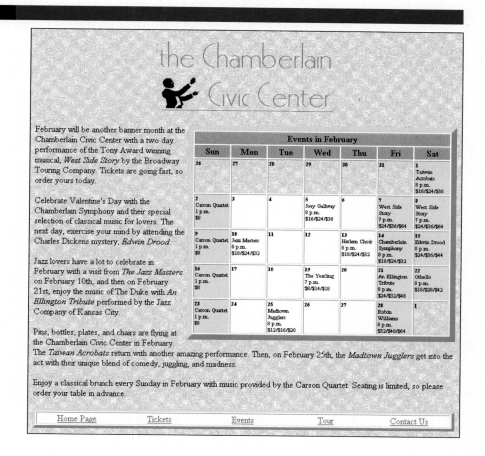

To create the CCC calendar:

1. Using your text editor, open **febtxt.htm** from the tutorial.04/case2 folder of your Data Disk and save it as **feb.htm**.

2. Below the first <p> tag, insert a table with the following attributes:

   ■ The table should be aligned with the right margin of the Web page.

   ■ The table border should be 10 pixels wide. The color of the table border should be red and pink.

   ■ The background color of the table should be white.

Explore 3. Within the table, create a column group spanning seven columns. These columns represent the seven days of the week in the calendar table. Set the width of the columns to 60 pixels and align the text in the column group with the top of each cell.

Explore 4. Within the column group, assign the first column a background color of pink. Assign a background color of white to the next four columns, and assign a background color of pink to the last two columns.

5. In the table's first row, create a heading that spans seven columns. Insert the text "Events in February" centered horizontally within the cell. Make the background color light blue.

6. In the table's second row, insert the following table headings: "Sun", "Mon", "Tue", "Wed", "Thu", "Fri", and "Sat". Make the background color light blue.

7. The next five rows contain the individual days from the calendar, each placed in a separate table cell. Format the dates as follows:

   ■ The font size of each cell should be "1". (HINT: Enclose the contents of the cell in a <font> tag.)
   ■ Display the day of the month on its own line, formatted with a boldfaced font.
   ■ If there is an event for that date, display the name of the event on one line, the time the event takes place on the second line, and the ticket price on a third line. Separate one line from another using the <br> tag.
   ■ If the date is not in the month of February, use the back.jpg image as the cell's background.

Explore   8. At the bottom of the Web page, insert a table with the following attributes:

   ■ The width of the table should be 100% of the width of the Web page.
   ■ The table should have a 5-pixel-wide border in red and pink.
   ■ The background color of the table should be white.

Explore   9. The bottom table should contain a single row with five columns. Make the width of each cell 20% of the width of the table. Enter the following text into the five cells: "Home Page", "Tickets", "Events", "Tour", and "Contact Us". Make each entry a hypertext link that, for the moment, points to the current file.

Explore   10. Use the <col> tag to horizontally center the contents of five cells in the bottom table.

Explore   11. Remove all gridlines from the bottom table. (HINT: Use the rules attribute.)

12. Save your changes to the file and print your HTML code. Using your Web browser, verify that the table displays correctly. Note that Netscape users will not see the results of creating a column group or removing the gridlines from the bottom table.

13. Hand in your printouts and files to your instructor.

Case 3. Dunston Retreat Center. The Dunston Retreat Center, located in northern Wisconsin, offers weekends of quiet and solitude for all who visit. The center, started by a group of Trappist monks, has grown in popularity over the last few years as more people have become aware of its services. The director of the center, Benjamin Adams, wants to advertise the center on the Internet and has asked you to create a Web site for the center. The Web site includes a welcome message from Benjamin Adams, a list of upcoming events, a letter from one of the center's guests, and a description of the current week's events. The Web page you'll create is shown in Figure 4-73.

Figure 4-73

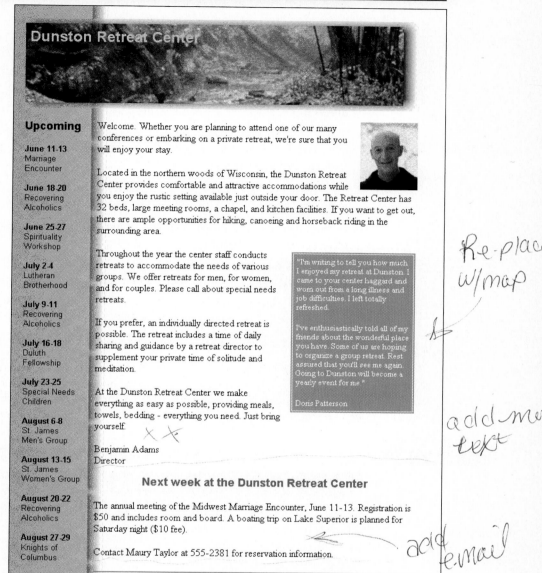

To create the Dunston Retreat Center Web page:

1. Using your text editor, open **welctxt.htm** located in the tutorial.04/case3 folder of your Data Disk and save it as **welcome.htm**.

2. At the top of the third paragraph, insert a table with the following attributes:

   ■ Align the table with the page's right margin
   ■ The table's border and cell padding should be 5 pixels
   ■ The border color should be white. The table background should be equal to the hexadecimal color value 8080FF.

3. Within the table insert a single cell 180 pixels wide, with the text aligned with the top of the cell. Insert the contents of the **letter.htm** file into the cell.

4. Save your changes to welcome.htm and print the code.

5. Using your text editor, open **dunsttxt.htm** and save it as **dunston.htm**.

6. Create a table 620 pixels wide with cell spacing and cell padding values of 5 within the file.

7. In the first row of the table, insert a single cell two columns wide containing the image **dlogo.jpg**. Center the contents of the cell.

8. The second row of the table should contain two cells. The first cell should be 100 pixels wide, spanning three rows. It should contain the contents of the events.htm file, aligned with the cell's top border.

9. The second cell should be 520 pixels wide. It should contain the contents of **welcome.htm** that you just created and be aligned with the top border of the cell.

10. In the third row of the table, insert a single cell 520 pixels wide containing the contents of **next.htm**, and align the text with the top of the cell.

11. The table's fourth row contains a single cell 520 pixels wide. In this cell, insert the contents of **address.htm** and center it horizontally within the cell.

12. Save your changes to the file and print the HTML code. Open the file in your Web browser and verify that the layout displays correctly.

13. Hand in your files and printouts to your instructor.

Case 4. TravelWeb E-ZineMagazine. TravelWeb provides useful material to online subscribers. You have joined the staff of TravelWeb, which publishes travel information and tips, and you have been asked to work on the layout for the Web page. You've been given files that you should use in creating the page that are listed and described in Figure 4-74.

Figure 4-74

FILE	DESCRIPTION
luxair.txt	Article about LuxAir reducing airfares to Europe
photo.txt	Article about the Photo of the Week
ppoint.jpg	Large version of the Photo of the Week (320 x 228)
ppoint2.jpg	Small version of the Photo of the Week (180 x 128)
toronto.txt	Article about traveling to Toronto
twlinks.htm	Links to other TravelWeb pages (list version)
twlinks2.htm	Links to other TravelWeb pages (table version)
twlogo.jpg	Image file of the TravelWeb logo (425 x 105)
yosemite.txt	Article about limiting access to Yosemite National Park
yosemite.jpg	Image file of Yosemite National Park (112 x 158)

To create a Web page for TravelWeb:

1. Use the files listed in Figure 4-74 to create a newspaper-style page. All of these files are stored in the tutorial.04/case4 folder on your Data Disk. The page should include several columns, but the number, size, and layout of the columns is up to you.

2. Use all of the files on the page, with the following exceptions: use only one of the two files twlinks.htm or twlinks2.htm, and use only one of the two image files ppoint.jpg or ppoint2.jpg. Note that not all of the links on this Web page point to existing files.

3. Use background colors to give the Web page an attractive and interesting appearance.

4. Include comment tags to describe the different parts of your page layout.

5. Save your page as **tw.htm** in the tutorial.04/case4 folder.

6. Print a copy of the Web page and the HTML code.

QUICK CHECK ANSWERS

Session 4.1

1. Text tables and graphical tables. Text tables are supported by all browsers and are easier to create. The graphical table is more difficult to create but provides the user with a wealth of formatting options.

2. A proportional font assigns different widths to each character based on the width of the character. A fixed-width font assigns the same width to each character regardless of width.

3. The <pre> tag

4. The <table> tag identifies the beginning of a table. The <tr> tag identifies the start of a table row. The <td> tag identifies individual table cells, and the <th> tag identifies table cells that act as table headings.

5. The number of rows in a table is determined by the number of <tr> tags. The number of columns is equal to the largest number of <td> and <th> tags within a single table row.

6. Text within the <th> tag is automatically bolded and centered within the table cell.

7. <caption align="bottom">Product Catalog</caption>

   Place this tag anywhere between the <table> and </table> tags.

Session 4.2

1. <table border="5" cellspacing="3" cellpadding="4">

2. <td valign="top">

   or

   <th valign="top">

3. <tr align="center">

4. In pixels or as a percentage of the display area. Use pixels if you want to control the size of the table. Use percentages if you want your table to adapt to the user's monitor resolution.

5. <table width="50%">

6. <td width="60">

   or

   <th width="60">

   This keeps the cell from exceeding 60 pixels in width. The only way to guarantee that all cells will be exactly 60 pixels wide is to set the width of all cells in that table column to 60 pixels.

7. <table bgcolor="yellow">

This attribute is not supported by earlier browsers.

8. <td rowspan="3" colspan="2">

or

<th rowspan="3" colspan="2">

Session 4.3

1. ```
<table>

<tr>
        <td>
        <table><tr><td></td><td></td></tr>
             <tr><td></td><td></td></tr>
        </table>
        </td>
        <td></td>
</tr>
<tr>
        <td></td>
        <td></td>
</tr>
</table>
```

2. &lt;! Nested table starts here&gt;

3. Separate &lt;font&gt; tags would have to be placed within each table cell.

4. &lt;td&gt;&lt;h1&gt;&lt;font face="Arial, Helvetica, sans-serif"&gt;Headlines&lt;/font&gt;&lt;/h1&gt;&lt;/td&gt;

5. Diagram the layout.
```

In this tutorial you will:

- Create frames for a Web site

- Control the appearance and placement of frames

- Control the behavior of hypertext links on a Web page with frames

- Use reserved target names to specify a target for a hypertext link

- Create a Web page that is viewable by browsers that support frames and by those that do not

- Modify the appearance of your frame borders

- Create and implement floating frames

USING FRAMES IN A WEB SITE

Using Frames to Display Multiple Web Pages

CASE

The Yale Climbing School

One of the most popular climbing schools and touring agencies in Colorado is the Yale Climbing School (YCS). Located in Vale Park, outside Rocky Mountain National Park, YCS specializes in teaching beginning and advanced climbing techniques. The school also sponsors several tours, leading individuals on some of the most exciting, challenging, and picturesque climbs in North America. The school has been in business for 15 years and, in that time, it has helped thousands of people experience the mountains in ways they never thought possible.

Yale Climbing School has a lot of competition from other climbing schools and touring groups in the area. Debbie Chen is the owner of the school and is always looking for ways to market her programs and improve the visibility of the school. Early on, she decided to use the Internet and the World Wide Web as a means of promoting the school, and she has already created many Web pages.

Debbie has seen other Web sites use frames to display several Web pages in a single browser window. She feels that frames would be a good way to highlight all that the school has to offer potential students. She asks you to help develop a frame-based Web site for the YCS.

SESSION 5.1

In this session you'll create a Web site that contains frames. You'll use the HTML tags that control the placement and appearance of frames, and you'll learn how to specify a source document for each frame and how to nest one set of frames inside another.

Introducing Frames

Typically, as a Web site grows in size and complexity, each page is dedicated to a particular topic or group of topics. One page might contain a list of hypertext links, another page might display contact information for the company or organization, and another page might describe the business philosophy. As more pages are added to the site, the designer might wish for a way to display information from several pages at the same time.

One solution is to duplicate that information across the Web site, but that presents problems as well. It requires a great deal of time and effort to repeat (or copy and paste) the same information over and over again. Also, each time a change is required, you need to repeat your edit for each page in the site—a process that could easily result in error.

Such considerations contributed to the creation of frames. A **frame** is a section of the browser window capable of displaying the contents of an entire Web page. Figure 5-1 shows an example of a browser window containing two frames. The frame on the left displays the contents of a Web page containing a list of hypertext links. The frame on the right displays a Web page with product information.

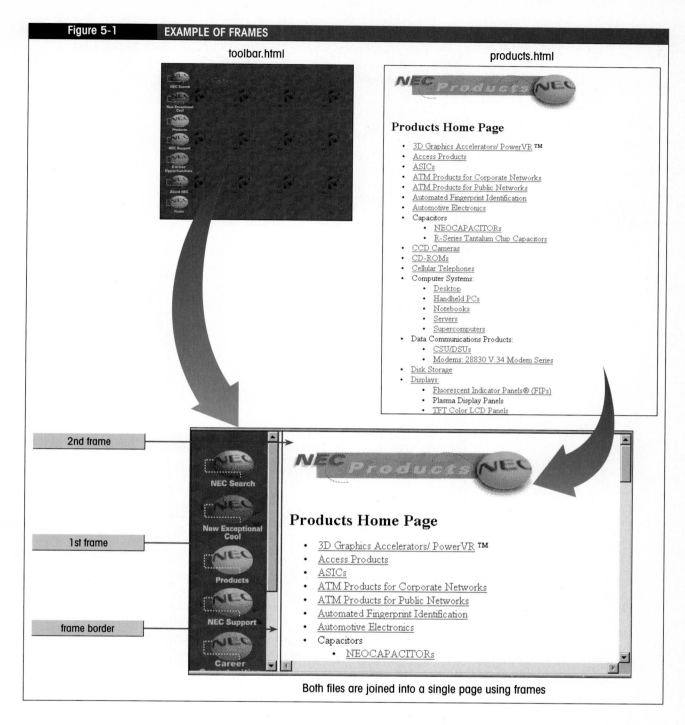

Figure 5-1   EXAMPLE OF FRAMES

toolbar.html

products.html

Both files are joined into a single page using frames

This example illustrates a common use of frames: displaying a table of contents in one frame, while showing individual pages from the site in another. Figure 5-2 illustrates how a list of hypertext links can remain on the screen while the user navigates through the contents of the site. An advantage for the designer is that the list of links can be easily updated because it is stored on only one page.

Figure 5-2	ACTIVATING A HYPERTEXT LINK WITHIN FRAMES

When the user clicks the Support hypertext link...

... the frame containing the document page is updated, but the list of hypertext links remains unchanged.

A consequence of a frame-based Web site is that the browser has to load multiple HTML files before a user can view the contents of the site. This can result in increased waiting time for potential customers. In addition, some older browsers cannot display frames, although this is less of an issue than it once was. Finally, some users simply do not like using frames and prefer Web page designs where the entire browser window is devoted to a single page. For these reasons, some Web designers advocate creating both framed and non-framed versions for a Web site and giving users the option of which one to use.

Planning **Your Frames**

Before you start creating your frames, it is a good idea to plan their appearance and how they are to be used. There are several issues to consider:

- What information will be displayed in each of the frames?
- How do you want the frames placed on the Web page? What is the size of each frame?
- Which frames will be static, that is, always showing the same content?
- Which frames will change in response to hypertext links being clicked?
- What Web pages will users first see when they access the site?
- Should users be permitted to resize the frames to suit their needs?

As you progress with your design for the Web site for the Yale Climbing School, you'll consider each of these questions. Debbie has already created the Web pages for the YCS Web site. Figure 5-3 describes the different Web pages you'll work with in this project.

Figure 5-3	DOCUMENTS AT THE YCS WEB SITE	
TOPIC	**FILENAME**	**CONTENT**
Biographies	staff.htm	Links to biographical pages of the YCS staff
Home page	home.htm	The YCS home page
Lessons	lessons.htm	Climbing lessons offered by the YCS
Logo	head.htm	A page containing the company logo
Philosophy	philosoph.htm	Statement of the YCS's business philosophy
Table of contents	links.htm	Links to the YCS pages
Tours	diamond.htm	Description of the Diamond climbing tour
Tours	eldorado.htm	Description of the Eldorado Canyon tour
Tours	grepon.htm	Description of the Petit Grepon climbing tour
Tours	kieners.htm	Description of the Kiener's Route climbing tour
Tours	lumpy.htm	Description of the Lumpy Ridge climbing tour
Tours	nface.htm	Description of the North Face climbing tour

Debbie has organized the pages by topic, such as tour descriptions, climbing lessons, and company philosophy. Two of the files, links.htm and staff.htm, do not focus on a particular topic but contain hypertext links to other YCS Web pages. How should this material for YCS be organized on the Web site, and what information should the user see first?

Debbie has considered these questions carefully and has sketched a layout that illustrates how she would like the frames to be organized. See Figure 5-4.

| Figure 5-4 | FRAMES FOR THE YCS WEB SITE |

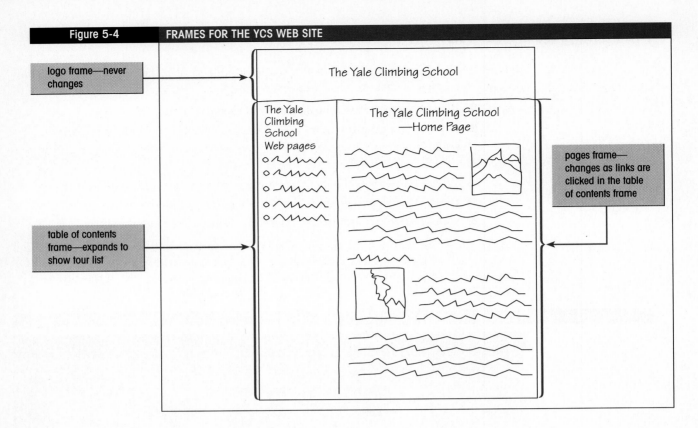

Debbie would like you to create three frames. The top frame displays the school's logo and address. The frame on the left displays a list of the Web pages at the YCS Web site. Finally, the frame on the lower-right displays the content of those pages.

Your first task is to enter the HTML code for the frame layout Debbie has described.

Creating a Frame Layout

The general syntax for creating an HTML file with frames is:

```
<html>
<head>
<title>Page Title</title>
</head>
<frameset>
    Frame Definitions
</frameset>
</html>
```

In this code, the <frameset> tag is used to store the definitions of the various frames in the file. These definitions will typically include the size and location of the frames, as well as the Web pages the frames display.

Note that the code does not include an opening and closing <body> tag. The reason for this is that this HTML file displays the contents of other Web pages; technically, it is not a Web page. Later in the tutorial, we'll explore situations where you would include a <body> tag in order to support browsers that do not display frames. For now, we'll concentrate on defining the appearance and content of the frames.

Specifying Frame Size and Orientation

To create a frame layout, you use the rows and cols attributes of the <frameset> tag. The rows attribute creates a row of frames, while the cols attribute creates a column of frames. You cannot use both attributes within a single <frameset> tag. You must choose to lay out your frames in either rows or columns (see Figure 5-5).

Figure 5-5	FRAMES DEFINED IN EITHER ROWS OR COLUMNS

Frames laid out in columns

The first frame	The second frame	The third frame

Frames laid out in rows

The first frame
The second frame
The third frame

The syntax for creating a row or column frame layout is:

```
<frameset rows="row height 1, row height 2, row height 3,
. . .">
```

or

```
<frameset cols="column width 1, column width 2, column
width 3, . . .">
```

where *row height* is the height of each row, and *column width* is the width of each column. There is no limit to the number of rows or columns you can specify for a frameset.

Row and column sizes can be specified in three ways: in pixels, as a percentage of the total size of the frameset, or by an asterisk (*). The asterisk instructs the browser to allocate any unclaimed space in the frameset to the particular row or column. For example, the tag <frameset rows="160,*"> creates two rows of frames. The first row has a height of 160 pixels, and the height of the second row is equal to whatever space remains in the display area. You can combine the three methods. The tag <frameset cols="160,25%,*"> lays out the frames in the columns shown in Figure 5-6. The first column is 160 pixels wide, the second column is 25% of the width of the display area, and the third column covers whatever space is left.

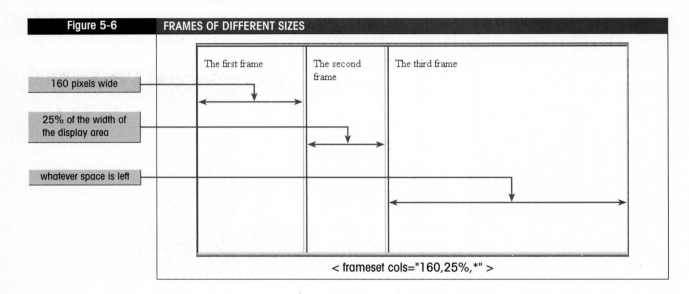

Figure 5-6   **FRAMES OF DIFFERENT SIZES**

160 pixels wide

25% of the width of the display area

whatever space is left

The first frame

The second frame

The third frame

< frameset cols="160,25%,*" >

It is a good idea to specify at least one of the rows or columns of your <frameset> tag with an asterisk to ensure that the frames fill up the screen regardless of a user's monitor settings. You can also use multiple asterisks. In that case, the browser divides the remaining display space equally among the frames with the asterisks. For example, the tag <frameset rows="*,*,*"> creates three rows of frames with equal heights.

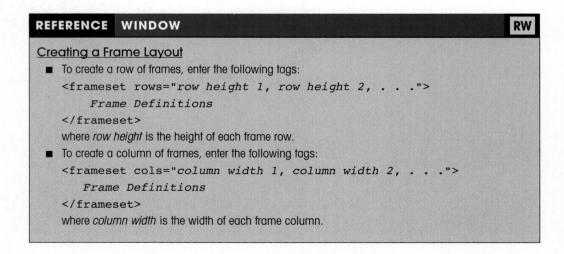

REFERENCE   WINDOW   **RW**

Creating a Frame Layout

■ To create a row of frames, enter the following tags:

```
<frameset rows="row height 1, row height 2, . . .">
    Frame Definitions
</frameset>
```

where *row height* is the height of each frame row.

■ To create a column of frames, enter the following tags:

```
<frameset cols="column width 1, column width 2, . . .">
    Frame Definitions
</frameset>
```

where *column width* is the width of each frame column.

Debbie has created an HTML file that she wants you to edit in order to create the frame layout she's described.

To edit Debbie's file:

1. Using your text editor, open **yaletxt.htm** from the tutorial.05/tutorial folder on your Data Disk.

2. Save the file in the same folder as **yale.htm**.

The first set of frames you'll create for the Yale Climbing School page has two rows. The top row is used for the company logo, and the second row is used for the remaining content of the Web page. A frame that is 85 pixels high should provide enough space to display the logo. The rest of the display area is occupied by the second row.

To create the first set of frames:

1. Create a blank line directly below the </head> tag in yale.htm.

2. Insert the following HTML code:

```
<frameset rows="85,*">
</frameset>
```

This code specifies a height of 85 pixels for the top row and allocates the remaining space to the second row. Figure 5-7 shows the revised yale.htm file.

Figure 5-7   **CREATING TWO ROWS OF FRAMES**

tag creates two rows of frames: the first 85 pixels high and the second occupying the remaining display area

```
<html>
<head>
<title>The Yale Climbing School</title>
</head>
<frameset rows="85,*">
</frameset>
</html>
```

The initial frame layout is now defined, and you'll augment this design later to include the third frame as Debbie has specified. For now, you need to specify the source for the two frame rows that you have created.

Specifying a Frame Source

To specify a source for a frame, use the <frame> tag with the syntax:

```
<frame src="URL">
```

where *URL* is the filename and location of the page that you want to load. You must insert the <frame> tag between the opening and closing <frameset> tags.

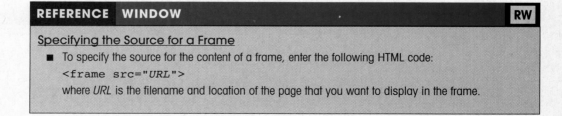

REFERENCE   WINDOW   **RW**

Specifying the Source for a Frame

■ To specify the source for the content of a frame, enter the following HTML code:

```
<frame src="URL">
```

where *URL* is the filename and location of the page that you want to display in the frame.

The company logo is to be displayed in the top frame. Figure 5-8 provides you with a preview of the logo and its placement.

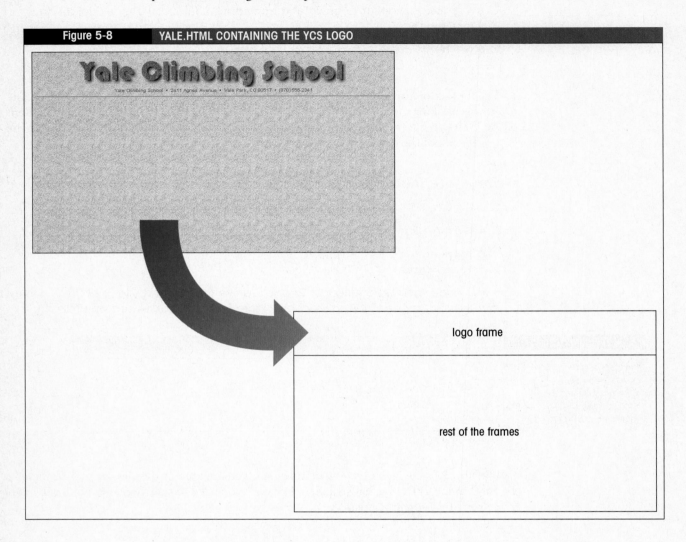

| Figure 5-8 | YALE.HTML CONTAINING THE YCS LOGO |

logo frame

rest of the frames

To define the YCS logo as a frame source:

1. Insert a blank line after the opening <frameset> tag line.

2. Type the following HTML code (see Figure 5-9):

```
<!-- Company Logo -->
<frame src="head.htm">
```

| Figure 5-9 | INSERTING A FRAME FOR THE HEAD.HTM FILE |

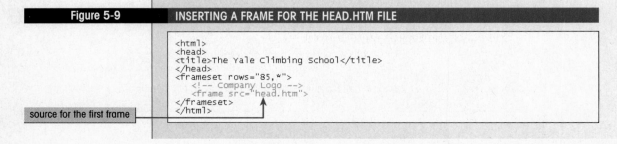

```
<html>
<head>
<title>The Yale Climbing School</title>
</head>
<frameset rows="85,*">
    <!-- Company Logo -->
    <frame src="head.htm">
</frameset>
</html>
```

source for the first frame

> Because this is the first <frame> tag, the browser displays head.htm in the first frame row. Note that using the comment tag and indenting the <frame> tag a few spaces helps make your HTML code easier to follow and interpret.

You have successfully specified the source for the first row, but what about the second row? Looking at Debbie's sketch in Figure 5-4, you notice that the second row contains two additional frames. So rather than specify a source for the second row, you need to create another set of frames.

Nesting <frameset> Tags

A frameset is defined by rows or columns, but not both. To create frames using both rows *and* columns, one frameset must be nested inside another. When you use this technique, the interpretation of the rows and cols attributes changes slightly. For example, a row height of 25% does not mean 25% of the display area, but rather 25% of the height of the frame into which that row has been inserted (or nested).

Debbie wants the second row of your current frame layout to contain two frames in separate columns. The first column displays a table of contents, and the second column displays a variety of YCS documents. You'll specify a width of 140 pixels for the first column, and whatever remains in the display area will be allotted to the second column.

To create the second set of frames:

1. Create a blank line immediately below the <frame> tag line that you just inserted.

2. Type the following HTML code:

```
<!-- Nested Frames -->
<frameset cols="140,*">
</frameset>
```

Your file should appear as shown in Figure 5-10. It is not necessary to indent the code as shown in the figure, but it makes the code easier to read and interpret.

Figure 5-10	CREATING A NESTED SET OF FRAMES IN THE SECOND FRAME ROW

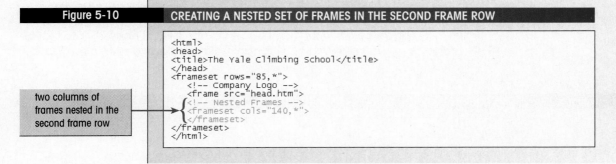

two columns of frames nested in the second frame row

```
<html>
<head>
<title>The Yale Climbing School</title>
</head>
<frameset rows="85,*">
   <!-- Company Logo -->
   <frame src="head.htm">
   <!-- Nested Frames -->
   <frameset cols="140,*">
   </frameset>
</frameset>
</html>
```

Next, you'll specify the sources for the two frames in the frameset. The frame in the first column displays the contents of links.htm. The Yale Climbing School home page, home.htm, is displayed in the second frame. Figure 5-11 shows the content of these two pages and their placement on the Web page.

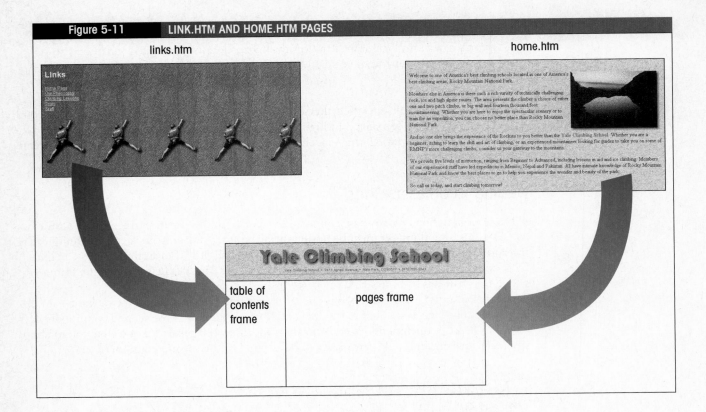

Figure 5-11   LINK.HTM AND HOME.HTM PAGES

links.htm

home.htm

To insert the sources for the two frames:

1. Create a blank line immediately below the nested <frameset> tag you just inserted.

2. Type the following HTML code:

```
<!-- List of YCS Links -->
<frame src="links.htm">
<!-- YCS Home Page -->
<frame src="home.htm">
```

Figure 5-12 shows the code for the two new frames. It is not necessary to indent the code as shown in the figure, but it can make the code easier to read and interpret.

Figure 5-12   SOURCES FOR THE TWO FRAMES IN THE SECOND ROW

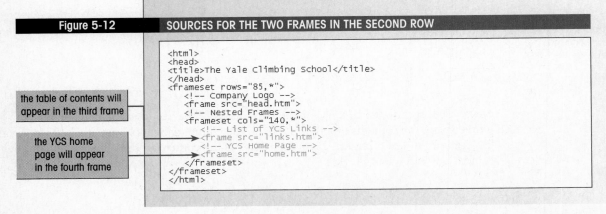

```
<html>
<head>
<title>The Yale Climbing School</title>
</head>
<frameset rows="85,*">
   <!-- Company Logo -->
   <frame src="head.htm">
   <!-- Nested Frames -->
   <frameset cols="140,*">
      <!-- List of YCS Links -->
      <frame src="links.htm">
      <!-- YCS Home Page -->
      <frame src="home.htm">
   </frameset>
</frameset>
</html>
```

the table of contents will appear in the third frame

the YCS home page will appear in the fourth frame

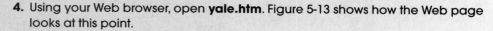

3. Save your changes to the file.

4. Using your Web browser, open **yale.htm**. Figure 5-13 shows how the Web page looks at this point.

Figure 5-13 | YCS WEB SITE WITH FRAMES

heading extends beyond the frame border, causing a vertical scroll bar to be displayed

table of contents frame

home page frame

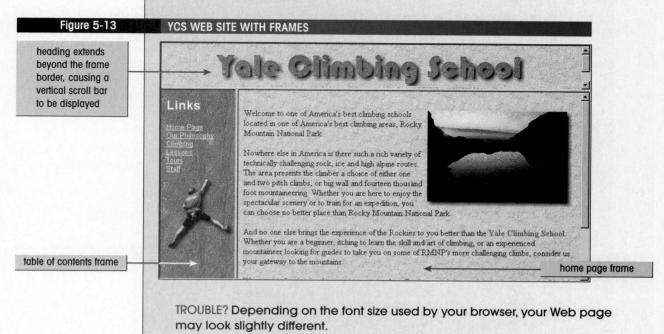

TROUBLE? Depending on the font size used by your browser, your Web page may look slightly different.

The browser window displays three Web pages from the YCS Web site. However, the design of the frame layout could use some refinement. Notice that the address information has been cut off in the logo frame. Because not all of the contents of this page fit into the frame, scroll bars have been added to the frame. Scroll bars do not appear in the links frame, because the entire list of links is visible. Debbie doesn't mind the appearance of scroll bars for the school's home page—she realizes that entire page won't fit into the frame—but she doesn't want scroll bars for the frame containing the school's logo and address.

Controlling **the Appearance of Your Frames**

You can control three attributes of a frame: scroll bars, the size of the margin between the source document and the frame border, and whether or not the user is allowed to change the size of the frame.

REFERENCE WINDOW   **RW**

Modifying the Appearance of Frames

- To control the appearance of scroll bars in a frame, add the scrolling attribute to the frame tag as follows:

  ```
  <frame src="URL" scrolling="scrolling">
  ```

  where *scrolling* can be either "yes" (scroll bars) or "no" (no scroll bars). If you do not specify the scrolling attribute, scroll bars appear only when the content of the frame source cannot fit within the boundaries of the frame.

- To control the amount of space between the frame source and the frame boundary, add the marginwidth and/or the marginheight attributes to the frame tag:

  ```
  <frame src="URL" marginwidth="value" marginheight="value">
  ```

  where the width and height *value* is expressed in pixels. The margin width is the space to the left and right of the frame source. The margin height is the space above and below the frame source. If you do not specify a margin height or width, the browser assigns dimensions based on the content of the frame source.

- To keep users from resizing frames, add the noresize attribute to the frame tag:

  ```
  <frame src="URL" noresize>
  ```

The first attribute you'll work with is the scroll bar attribute.

Controlling the Appearance of Scroll Bars

By default, scroll bars are displayed when the content of the source page cannot fit within the frame. You can override this setting using the scrolling attribute. The syntax for this attribute is:

```
<frame src="URL" scrolling="scrolling">
```

where *scrolling* can either be "yes" (to always display scroll bars) or "no" (to never display scroll bars). If you don't specify a setting for the scrolling attribute, the browser displays scroll bars when necessary.

Debbie feels that scroll bars are inappropriate for the logo frame, and she wants to ensure that they are never displayed for that frame. Therefore, you need to add the scrolling="no" attribute to the <frame> tag. However, Debbie does want scroll bars for the other two frames, as needed, so the default value for this frame is sufficient. Note that if you are using Netscape you need to close and then open the file for the changes to the frames to take effect. If you simply click the Reload button, your changes are not displayed. This is not the case with Internet Explorer 3.0 and above, in which you can view changes to the page by clicking the Refresh button.

To remove the scroll bars from the logo frame:

1. Return to **yale.htm** in your text editor.

2. Within the <frame> tag in the logo frame, enter the attribute **scrolling="no"**, as shown in Figure 5-14.

Figure 5-14	REMOVING THE SCROLL BARS FROM THE LOGO FRAME

set the scrolling
attribute to "no" to
remove the scroll bars

```
<frameset rows="85,*">
    <!-- Company Logo -->
    <frame src="head.htm" scrolling="no">
    <!-- Nested Frames -->
    <frameset cols="140,*">
        <!-- List of YCS Links -->
        <frame src="links.htm">
        <!-- YCS Home Page -->
        <frame src="home.htm">
    </frameset>
</frameset>
```

3. Save your changes to yale.htm and reload it in your Web browser. Note that if you are using Netscape you might have to close and then open yale.htm for the changes to take effect.

Although the scroll bars for the logo frame have been removed, you still cannot see all of the text that is contained in head.htm. This problem can be corrected by modifying the frame margins.

When working with frames, keep in mind that you should remove scroll bars from a frame only when you are convinced that the entire Web page will be visible in the frame. To do this, you should view your Web page using several different monitor settings. Few things are more irritating to Web site visitors than to discover that some content is missing from a frame with no scroll bars available to reveal the missing content.

With that in mind, your next task is to solve the problem of the missing text from the logo frame. To do so, you need to modify the internal margins of the frame.

Controlling Frame Margins

When your browser retrieves the frame's Web page, it determines the amount of space between the content of the page and the frame border. Occasionally the browser sets the margin between the border and the content too large. Generally, you want the margin to be big enough to keep the source's text or images from running into the frame's borders. However, you do not want the margin to take up too much space, because you typically want to display as much of the source as possible.

You've already noted that the margin height for the logo frame is too large, and this has shifted some of the text beyond the border of the frame. To fix this problem, you need to specify a smaller margin for the frame so that the logo can move up and allow all of the text to be displayed in the frame.

The syntax for specifying margins for a frame is:

```
<frame src="URL" marginheight="value" marginwidth="value">
```

where, marginheight is the amount of space, in pixels, above and below the content of the page in the frame, and marginwidth is the amount of space to the left and right of the page. You do not have to specify both the margin height and width. However, if you specify only one, the browser assumes that you want to use the same value for both. Setting margin values is a process of trial and error as you determine what combination of margin sizes looks best.

To correct the problem with the logo frame, you'll decrease its margin size to 0 pixels. This setting will allow the entire page to be displayed within the frame. Also, to keep the home page from running into the borders of its frame, you'll set the frame's margin width to 10 pixels, and Debbie wants you to decrease the frame's margin height to 0 pixels. The links frame margin does not require any changes.

To set the margin sizes for the frames:

1. Return to the **yale.htm** file in your text editor.

2. Within the <frame> tag for the logo frame, enter the attribute **marginheight="0"**. This will, by default, set both the margin height and the margin width to 0.

3. Within the <frame> tag for the home page frame, enter the attributes **marginheight="0" marginwidth="10"**.

   Figure 5-15 shows the revised HTML code for yale.htm.

| Figure 5-15 | SPECIFYING THE MARGIN SIZES FOR THE FRAMES |

height of the margin text for the logo frame will be 0 pixels

height of the margin for the home page will be 0 pixels and the width of the margin will be 10 pixels

```
<frameset rows="85,*">
    <!-- Company Logo -->
    <frame src="head.htm" scrolling="no" marginheight="0">
    <!-- Nested Frames -->
    <frameset cols="140,*">
        <!-- List of YCS Links -->
        <frame src="links.htm">
        <!-- YCS Home Page -->
        <frame src="home.htm" marginheight="0" marginwidth="10">
    </frameset>
</frameset>
```

4. Save your changes to yale.htm and reload or refresh it in your Web browser. The revised frames are shown in Figure 5-16.

| Figure 5-16 | YCS WEB SITE WITH RESIZED FRAME MARGINS |

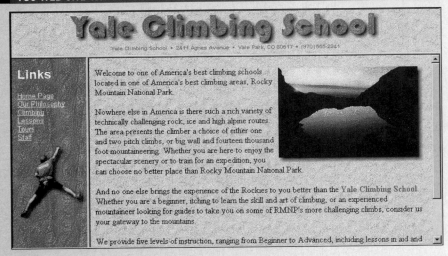

Debbie is satisfied with the changes you've made to the Web page. Your next task is to "lock in" the sizes and margins for each frame on the page to prevent users from resizing the frames.

Controlling Frame Resizing

By default, users can resize frame borders in the browser by simply dragging a frame border. However, some Web designers prefer to freeze, or lock, frames, so that users cannot resize them. This insures that the Web site displays as the designer intended. Debbie would like you to do this for the YCS Web site. The syntax for controlling frame resizing is:

```
<frame src="URL" noresize>
```

The noresize attribute is included within the <frame> tag to prevent users from modifying the sizes of your frames. You'll add this attribute now to all the frames in yale.htm.

To prevent the frames in the YCS Web site from being resized:

1. Return to **yale.htm** in your text editor.

2. Within each of the three <frame> tags in the file, add the attribute **noresize**.

3. Save your changes to yale.htm and reload it in your Web browser.

4. Verify that the frames are now "locked in" and cannot be resized by the user.

You're ready to take a break from working on the YCS Web site. Debbie is pleased with the progress you've made to the site, although there are a few things left to accomplish before your work is complete. For example, you haven't specified how the targets of the site's hypertext links should be displayed. You'll deal with this question and others in the next session.

Session 5.1 QUICK CHECK

1. What are frames, and why are they useful in displaying and designing a Web page?

2. Why is the <body> tag unnecessary for pages that contain frames?

3. What HTML code do you use to create three rows of frames with the height of the first row set to 200 pixels, the height of the second row set to 50% of the display area, and the height of the third row set to occupy the remaining space?

4. What HTML code do you use to specify home.htm as a source for a frame?

5. What HTML code do you use to remove the scroll bars from the frame for home.htm?

6. What HTML code do you use to set the size of the margin above and below the home.htm frame to 3 pixels?

7. What is the size of the margins to the right and left of the frame in Question 6?

8. What code would you use to prevent users from moving the frame borders in home.htm?

SESSION 5.2

In this session you'll learn how hypertext links work within frames, and you'll control which frame displays the source of an activated hypertext link. You'll also learn how to create a Web page that can be used by browsers that support frames and browsers that don't. Finally, you'll examine some extensions to the <frame> and <frameset> tags, and you'll learn how to create internal frames using the <iframe> tag.

Working with Frames and Hypertext Links

Now that you've created frames for the Yale Climbing School Web site, you're ready to work on the hypertext links for the Web page. The table of contents page contains the following five hypertext links (see Figure 5-17):

- The Home Page link points to home.htm
- The Our Philosophy link points to philosph.htm
- The Climbing Lessons link points to lessons.htm
- The Tours link points to tours.htm
- The Staff link points to staff.htm

Figure 5-17	PAGES IN THE YCS WEB SITE

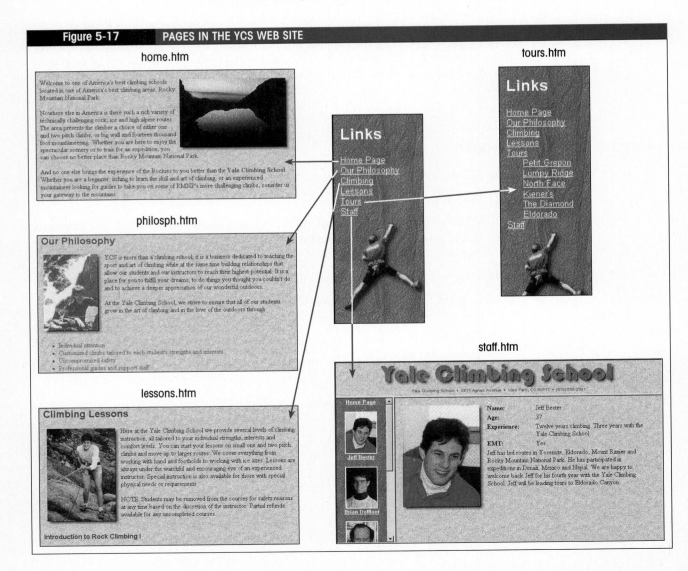

By default, clicking a hypertext link within a frame opens the linked file inside the same frame. However, this is not the way Debbie wants each of the hypertext links to work. She wants:

- the Home, Our Philosophy, and Climbing Lessons pages to display in the bottom-right frame
- the Tours page to display in the table of contents frame
- the Staff page to occupy the entire browser window

When you want to control the behavior of hyperlinks in a framed page, there are two required steps: you need to give each frame on the page a name, and then point each hypertext link to one of the named frames.

REFERENCE WINDOW   **RW**

Retrieving a Page in a Specific Frame
- Assign a name to the frame by editing the <frame> tag as follows:
  ```
  <frame src="URL" name="frame_name">
  ```
  where *frame_name* is a single word you choose to describe the content and purpose of the frame.
- Edit the <a> tag for the hyperlink, specifying a target for the link as follows:
  ```
  <a href="URL" target="frame_name">
  ```
  where *frame_name* is the name you assigned to the frame.
- To use the same target for all links in a page, insert the <base> tag between the file's <head> and </head> tags as follows:
  ```
  <base target="frame_name">
  ```
- All links on the page direct their output to the frame specified by "*frame_name*".

Assigning a Name to a Frame

To assign a name to a frame, add the name attribute to the frame tag. The syntax for this attribute is:

```
<frame src="URL" name="frame_name">
```

where *frame_name* is any single word you assign to the frame. Case is important in assigning names: "information" is considered a different name than "INFORMATION."

You'll name the three frames in the YCS Web site: "logo," "links," and "pages."

To assign names to the frames:

1. Using your text editor, open **yale.htm** if it is not currently open.

2. Within the tag for the logo frame, enter the attribute **name="logo"**.

3. Within the tag for the links frame, enter the attribute **name="links"**.

4. Within the tag for the home page frame, enter the attribute **name="pages"**.

   Figure 5-18 shows the revised code for yale.htm.

Figure 5-18 ASSIGNING A NAME TO EACH FRAME

```
<frameset rows="85,*">
    <!-- Company Logo -->
    <frame src="head.htm" scrolling="no" marginheight="0" noresize name="logo">
    <!-- Nested Frames -->
    <frameset cols="140,*">
        <!-- List of YCS Links -->
        <frame src="links.htm" noresize name="links">
        <!-- YCS Home Page -->
        <frame src="home.htm" marginheight="0" marginwidth="10" noresize name="pages">
    </frameset>
</frameset>
```

5. Save your changes to yale.htm.

Now that you've named the frames, the next task is to specify the "pages" frame as the target for the Home Page, Our Philosophy, and Climbing Lessons hyperlinks, so that clicking each of these links opens the corresponding file in the home page frame.

Specifying a Link Target

Previously you may have used the target attribute to open a page in a new browser window. You can also use the target attribute to open a page in a specific frame. The syntax for this is:

```
<a href="URL" target="frame_name">
```

where *frame_name* is the name you've assigned to a frame on your Web page. In this case, the target name for the frame you need to specify is "documents." To change the targets for the links, edit the <a> tags in links.htm. You'll start by editing only the <a> tags pointing to the Home Page, Our Philosophy, and Climbing Lessons pages. These are the hyperlinks to be displayed in the "pages" frame of yale.htm. You'll work with the other hyperlinks later.

To specify the targets for the hypertext links:

1. Using your text editor, open **links.htm** from the tutorial.05/tutorial folder on your Data Disk.

2. Within the <a> tag for the Home Page, Our Philosophy, and Climbing Lessons hypertext links, enter the attribute **target="pages"**. The revised code is shown in Figure 5-19.

Figure 5-19 ASSIGNING A TARGET TO A HYPERTEXT LINK

```
<html>
<head>
<title>Yale Climbing School Links</title>
</head>
<body background="wall2.jpg" text="white" link="white" vlink="white" alink="white">
<font face="Arial, Helvetica, sans-serif" color="white">
<h2>Links</h2>
<font size="2">
<a href="home.htm" target="pages">Home Page</a><br>
<a href="philosph.htm" target="pages">Our Philosophy</a><br>
<a href="lessons.htm" target="pages">Climbing Lessons</a><br>
<a href="tours.htm">Tours</a><br>
<a href="staff.htm">Staff</a>
</font>
</body>
</html>
```

the Web page will appear in the pages frame

3. Save your changes to links.htm.

TROUBLE? If you need to return to the original version of the file, you can open linkstxt.htm in the tutorial.05/tutorial folder of your Data Disk.

Now test the first three hyperlinks in the list.

4. Using your Web browser, open **yale.htm**

5. Click the **Our Philosophy** link in the Links frame. The Our Philosophy Web page should display in the lower-right frame. See Figure 5-20.

Figure 5-20 ASSIGNING A TARGET TO A HYPERLINK

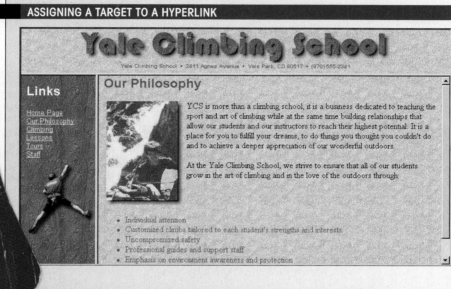

TROUBLE? If the Our Philosophy page displays in the left frame instead, you may need to close and open yale.htm for your changes to take effect.

6. Click the **Home Page** and **Climbing Lessons** links, verifying that the links are working properly and the pages are displaying in the "pages" frame.

There are occasions when a page contains dozens of hypertext links that should all open in the same frame. It would be tedious to insert target attributes for each link. Fortunately, HTML provides a way to specify a target frame for all the hypertext links within a single page.

Using the <base> Tag

The <base> tag is used within the <head> tags of your HTML file and is used to specify global options for the page. One of the attributes of the <base> tag is the target attribute, which identifies a default target for all of the hypertext links in a page. The syntax for this attribute is:

```
<base target="frame_name">
```

where *frame_name* is the name of the target frame. The <base> tag is useful when your page contains a lot of hypertext links that all point to the same target. Rather than adding the target attribute to each <a> tag, you can enter the information once with the <base> tag.

You can still use the <base> tag even if your file contains links that point to a different target than the one specified in the <base> tag. The target in the <a> tag overrides any target specified in the <base> tag.

To see how the <base> tag works, you'll use it to indicate that the "pages" frame is the default target for all hyperlinks in the links.htm file.

To specify a default target using the <base> tag:

1. Return to **links.htm** in your text editor.

2. Delete the **target="pages"** attributes within the <a> tags that you previously entered.

3. Insert the line **<base target="pages">** directly above the </head> tag, as shown in Figure 5-21.

Figure 5-21	SPECIFYING A DEFAULT TARGET FOR ALL HYPERTEXT LINKS

```
<html>
<head>
<title>Yale Climbing School Links</title>
<base target="pages">
</head>
<body background="wall2.jpg" text="white" link="white" vlink="white" alink="white">
<font face="Arial, Helvetica, sans-serif" color="white">
<h2>Links</h2>
<font size="2">
<a href="home.htm" target="pages">Home Page</a><br>
<a href="philosph.htm" target="pages">Our Philosophy</a><br>
<a href="lessons.htm" target="pages">Climbing Lessons</a><br>
<a href="tours.htm">Tours</a><br>
<a href="staff.htm">Staff</a>
</font>
</body>
</html>
```

the target of all links will be the page frame

4. Save your changes to links.htm.

5. Using your Web browser, reload or refresh yale.htm. Verify that the links for the Home, Our Philosophy, and Climbing Lessons pages still work correctly.

   TROUBLE? If any of the hyperlinks do not work correctly, check the frame name and target name to verify that they match exactly, both in spelling and in the use of uppercase and lowercase letters.

So far you've worked with the first three hypertext links in the list. The remaining two links require different targets.

Using **Reserved Target Names**

The remaining two tags in the list of hypertext links point to a list of the tours offered by the Yale Climbing School (tours.htm) and to a staff information page, respectively. The tours.htm file does not contain information about individual tours; instead, it is an expanded table of contents of YCS Web pages, some of which are devoted to individual tours. Each tour has its own Web page, as shown in Figure 5-22.

Figure 5-22   **TOURS PAGES**

grepon.htm

The Petit Grepon

The Petit Grepon is one of Rocky Mountain National Park's most challenging and awesome climbs. Nestled in the middle of the Cathedral Spires, the summit of the Petit Grepon is a mere ten by thirty foot perch, but "placemat" may be a better term. For those who are more interested in a less intimidating climb, we also offer tours up Sharkstooth, a nearby summit offering excellent views of the Petit Grepon.

Difficulty Level:	Expert
Time:	Full day
Physical Stress:	Extreme

lumpy.htm

Lumpy Ridge

Located north of Vale Park, Lumpy Ridge is a veritable garden of interesting and challenging routes for climbers of all ages and abilities. Lumpy Ridge is a three mile long granite ridge containing over 400 different climbing routes with names ranging from the "Bowels of the Owls" to the "J Crack." Guides from the Yale Climbing School will be happy to lead you and your party to some of the most sought-after climbing routes in the country.

Difficulty Level	Beginner to expert, depending on climber
Time:	Half day and full day options
Physical Stress:	Mild to extreme, depending upon climb

nface.htm

Longs Peak: North Face

The North Face route of Longs Peak is the perfect tour for the beginner hiker/climber who wants to reach the summit following a different route from the main trail. The North Face is the most direct and shortest route and does not have the crowds you'd find in the more popular Keyhole route. The views from the North Face are spectacular and provide some of the finest scenery in the park.

Difficulty Level:	Beginner
Time:	Allow for one day
Physical Stress:	Mild to moderate

Links

Home Page
Our Philosophy
Climbing
Lessons
Tours
　　Petit Grepon
　　Lumpy Ridge
　　North Face
　　Kiener's
　　The Diamond
　　Eldorado
Staff

kieners.htm

Longs Peak: Kiener's Route

One of the most awesome climbs in the park, yet still very accessible to the beginning climber, Kiener's Route is a YCS favorite. The route starts at Mills Glacier and proceeds up a 1000 foot couloir known as Lamb's Slide (ice axes and crampons required to climb Lamb's Slide). Moving off Lamb's Slide, you are led across Broadway, a narrow ledge varying in width from several feet to six inches. The ledge overlooks a sheet of granite plunging down to Chasm Lake far below. Proceeding up from Broadway, you will climb to the summit of Longs Peak following a route requiring climbing gear and climbing technique. Kiener's is one of North America's classic climbs.

Difficulty Level:	Beginner to moderate
Time:	Allow for one day
Physical Stress:	Moderate

eldorado.htm

Eldorado Canyon

Eldorado Canyon is not actually in Rocky Mountain National Park, but if you're willing to take a 60 minute drive to this awesome state park, we can provide some of the best climbing in Colorado. Choose from beginner climbs to more advanced routes. Eldorado offers climbs of 400 to 600 feet, high on a solid rock wall. All climbs are only a short distance from the parking lot. No matter what your skill and experience, we'll tailor the Eldorado Canyon tour to fit you.

Difficulty Level:	Beginner to expert, depending on climber
Time:	Allow for one day
Physical Stress:	Mild to extreme, depending upon climb

diamond.htm

Longs Peak: The Diamond

The pinnacle of climbing in Rocky Mountain National Park, the Diamond starts at 13,100 feet and rises nearly 1000 vertical feet to the upper slopes of Longs Peak. The left side of the Diamond offers several different routes, none easier than 5.10 (extreme difficulty). The right half of the Diamond is primarily used by aid climbers. Due to the strenuous nature of the Diamond, all participants will have to pass a physical examination and climbing evaluation.

Difficulty Level:	Expert
Time:	Two days
Physical Stress:	Extreme

Debbie wants tours.htm to display in the links frame in order to give the effect of expanding the table of contents whenever a user clicks the Tours hypertext link. You can specify Links (the name of the frame) as the target. However, there is another way to do this using reserved target names.

Reserved target names are special names that can be used in place of a frame name as the target. They are useful in situations where the name of the frame is unavailable, when you want the page to appear in a new window, or when you want the page to replace the current browser window. Figure 5-23 describes the reserved target names.

Figure 5-23	RESERVED TARGET NAMES	
RESERVED TARGET NAME	**DESCRIPTION**	
_blank	Loads the document into a new browser window	
_self	Loads the document into the same frame or window that contains the hypertext link tag	
_parent	In a layout of nested frames, loads the document into the frame that contains the frame with the hyperlink tag	
_top	Loads the document into the full display area, replacing the current frame layout	

All reserved target names begin with the underscore character (_) to distinguish them from other target names. Note that reserved target names are case-sensitive, so you must enter them in lowercase.

Because Debbie wants the contents of tours.htm to display in the links frame, you can use the reserved target name, _self, which overrides the target specified in the <base> tag and instructs the browser to open the page in the same frame that contains the hypertext link.

To use the reserved target name to specify the target for the Tours link:

1. Return to **links.htm** in your text editor.

2. Enter the attribute **target=_self** within the <a> tag for the Tours hypertext link. See Figure 5-24.

Figure 5-24	USING THE _SELF TARGET NAME IN THE LINKS.HTM FILE

```
<html>
<head>
<title>Yale Climbing School Links</title>
<base target="pages">
</head>
<body background="wall2.jpg" text="white" link="white" vlink="white" alink="white">
<font face="Arial, Helvetica, sans-serif" color="white">
<h2>Links</h2>
<font size="2">
<a href="home.htm" target="pages">Home Page</a><br>
<a href="philosph.htm" target="pages">Our Philosophy</a><br>
<a href="lessons.htm" target="pages">Climbing Lessons</a><br>
<a href="tours.htm" target=_self>Tours</a><br>
<a href="staff.htm">Staff</a>
</font>
</body>
</html>
```

page will appear in the frame containing the hypertext link

3. Save your changes to links.htm.

The tours.htm Web page is an expanded table of contents for Web pages containing information about specific tours. Debbie wants each of these pages to display in the "pages" frame. To do this, you specify the "pages" frame as the default hyperlink target in tours.htm. The tours.htm file also contains a hyperlink that takes the user back to links.htm. You should specify _self as the target for this hyperlink.

To modify tours.htm as you did links.htm:

1. Using your text editor, open **tours.htm** from the tutorial.05/tutorial folder on your Data Disk.

2. Insert the tag **<base target="pages">** directly above the </head> tag. This code displays the individual tour pages in the "pages" frame when a user clicks any of the tour hyperlinks.

3. Enter the attribute **target=_self** within the <a> tag that points to links.htm. The original table of contents, links.htm, displays in the Links frame. See Figure 5-25.

Figure 5-25   **REVISED TOURS.HTM FILE**

```
<html>
<head>
<title>Yale Climbing School Links</title>
<base target="pages">
</head>
<body background="wall3.jpg" text="white" link="white" vlink="white" alink="white">
<font face="Arial, Helvetica, sans-serif" color="white">
<h2>Links</h2>
<font size="2">
<a href="home.htm">Home Page</a><br>
<a href="philosph.htm">Our Philosophy</a><br>
<a href="lessons.htm">Climbing Lessons</a><br>
<a href="links.htm" target=_self>Tours</a><br>
      <a href="grepon.htm">Petit Grepon</a><br>
      <a href="lumpy.htm">Lumpy Ridge</a><br>
      <a href="nface.htm">North Face</a><br>
      <a href="kieners.htm">Kiener's</a><br>
      <a href="diamond.htm">The Diamond</a><br>
      <a href="eldorado.htm">Eldorado</a><br>
<a href="staff.htm">Staff</a>
</font>
</body>
</html>
```

4. Save your changes to tours.htm.

   TROUBLE? If you need to revert back to the original version of tours.htm for any reason, it is saved in the tutorial.05/tutorial folder of your Data Disk as tourstxt.htm

5. Reload **yale.htm** in your Web browser.

6. Verify that the Tours link works as you intended. As you click on the link, the table of contents list should alternately collapse and expand. In addition, click on the individual tour pages links to verify that they display correctly in the "pages" frame. See Figure 5-26.

Figure 5-26   **VIEWING A TOUR PAGE**

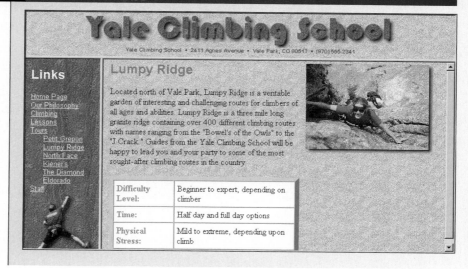

The technique employed here is commonly used for tables of contents that double as hypertext links. Clicking the Tours hypertext link gives the effect that the list is expanding and contracting, but what is actually happening is that one table of contents file is being replaced by another.

The final link you need to create points to a Web page of staff biographies. Debbie asked another employee to produce the contents of this Web page, and the results are shown in Figure 5-27.

Figure 5-27   STAFF WEB PAGE

As you can see, this Web page also uses frames. How can this Web page be displayed within your frame layout? If you specify the "pages" frame as the target, the result will be a series of nested frame images as shown in Figure 5-28.

Figure 5-28   A NESTED FRAME LAYOUT

This is not what Debbie wants. She wants the Staff Web page to load into the full display area, replacing the frame layout with its own layout. To target a link to the full display area, you use the _top reserved target name. The _top target is often used when a framed page is accessed from another. It's also used when you are linking to pages that lie outside your Web site altogether.

For example, a link to the Colorado Tourism Board Web site should not display within a frame on the YCS Web site for two reasons. First, once you go outside your Web site, you lose control of the frame layout, and you could easily end up with nested frame images. The second reason is that such a design could easily confuse users, making it appear as if the Colorado Tourism Board is a component of the Yale Climbing School.

To specify the target for the Staff link:

1. Return to **links.htm** in your text editor.

2. Enter the attribute **target=_top** within the <a> tag for the Staff link. See Figure 5-29.

| Figure 5-29 | REVISED LINKS.HTM PAGE USING THE _TOP RESERVED TARGET NAME |

```
<html>
<head>
<title>Yale Climbing School Links</title>
<base target="pages">
</head>
<body background="wall2.jpg" text="white" link="white" vlink="white" alink="white">
<font face="Arial, Helvetica, sans-serif" color="white">
<h2>Links</h2>
<font size="2">
<a href="home.htm" target="pages">Home Page</a><br>
<a href="philosph.htm" target="pages">Our Philosophy</a><br>
<a href="lessons.htm" target="pages">Climbing Lessons</a><br>
<a href="tours.htm" target=_self>Tours</a><br>
<a href="staff.htm" target=_top>Staff</a>
</font>
</body>
</html>
```

3. Save your changes to links.htm.

Because tours.htm also acts as a detailed table of contents, you should edit the hypertext link to the Staff page in that file. This way, a user can click the Staff hypertext link from both the table of contents with the expanded list of tours and the original table of contents.

To edit tours.htm:

1. Return to **tours.htm** in your text editor.

2. Enter the attribute **target=_top** within the <a> tag for the Staff link.

3. Save your changes to tours.htm.

4. Using your Web browser, reload **yale.htm**. Verify that the Staff link now opens the Staff page and replaces the existing frame layout with its own. Be sure to test the Staff link from both the original table of contents and the table of contents with the expanded list of tours.

TROUBLE? If the Staff link does not work properly, verify that you used lowercase letters for the reserved target name.

Debbie has viewed all the hypertext links on the YCS Web site and is quite satisfied with the results. However, she wonders what would happen if a user with an older browser encountered the page. Is there some way to accommodate browsers that don't support frames? Yes, by using the <noframes> tag.

Using the <noframes> Tag

To allow your Web site to be viewable using browsers that do not support frames, as well as by those that do, you can use the <noframes> tag to create a section of your HTML file containing code for browsers incapable of viewing frames. The general syntax for the <noframes> tag is:

```
<html>
<head>
<title>Page Title</title>
</head>
<frameset>
      Frame Definitions
</frameset>
<noframes>
<body>
      Page Layout
</body>
</noframes>
</html>
```

When a browser that supports frames processes this code, it ignores everything within the <noframes> tags and concentrates solely on the code within the <frameset> tags. When a browser that doesn't support frames processes this HTML code, it doesn't know what to do with the <frameset> and <noframes> tags, so it ignores them. However it does know how to render whatever appears within the <body> tags. This way, both types of browsers are supported within a single HTML file. Note that when you use the <noframes> tag, you must include <body> tags.

REFERENCE WINDOW | **RW**

Supporting Frame-Blind Browsers
- Create a version of your page that does not use frames.
- In the framed version of the page, insert the following tags:
  ```
  <noframes>
  </noframes>
  ```
- Copy the HTML code between the <body> tags, including both the <body> and </body> tags, from the nonframed version of the page.
- Paste the HTML code between the <noframes> and </noframes> tags in the framed version of the page.

The Yale Climbing School has been using the nonframed Web site displayed in Figure 5-30 for several years.

Figure 5-30   **FRAMELESS VERSION OF THE YCS WEB SITE**

If you want this Web page to display for frame-blind browsers but still use your framed version, copy the HTML code, including the <body> tags, from the source code of the non-framed Web page and place it within a pair of <noframes> tags in the framed Web page, yale.htm.

To insert support for frame-blind browsers:

1. Using your text editor, open **yale.htm**.

2. Create a blank line immediately above the </html> tag.

3. Enter the following HTML code:

```
<!-- Noframes version of this page -->
<noframes>
</noframes>
```

4. Save your changes to the file.

Next copy the code from the noframe page into yale.htm.

5. Using your text editor, open **noframes.htm** from the tutorial.05/tutorial folder on your Data Disk.

6. Copy the HTML code between the opening and closing <body> tags. Be sure to include both the opening and closing <body> tags in your copy selection.

7. Return to **yale.htm** in your text editor.

8. Create a blank line immediately below the <noframes> tag.

9. Paste the text you copied from noframes.htm in the blank line you created below the <noframes> tag. Figure 5-31 shows the beginning and end of the revised code.

| Figure 5-31 | INSERTING THE NOFRAMES CODE INTO THE YALE.HTM FILE |

```
<frameset rows="85,*">
    <!-- Company Logo -->
    <frame src="head.htm" scrolling="no" marginheight="0" noresize name="logo">
    <!-- Nested Frames -->
    <frameset cols="140,*">
        <!-- List of YCS Links -->
        <frame src="links.htm" noresize name="links">
        <!-- YCS Home Page -->
        <frame src="home.htm" marginheight="0" marginwidth="10" noresize name="pages">
    </frameset>
</frameset>
<!-- Noframes version of this page -->
<noframes>
<body background="wall.jpg" link="white" vlink="white" alink="white">
<table width="620" cellpadding="5">
<tr>
```

```
        <p>We provide five levels of instruction, ranging from Beginner to
        Advanced, including lessons in aid and ice climbing. Members of our
        experienced staff have led expeditions in Mexico, Nepal and Pakistan.
        All have intimate knowledge of Rocky Mountain National Park and know the
        best places to go to help you experience the wonder and beauty of the
        park.</p>
        <p>So call us today, and start climbing tomorrow!</p>
    </td>
</tr>
</table>

</body>
</noframes>
</html>
```

10. Save your changes to yale.htm.

To test your Web page, use a browser that does not support frames. You can obtain early versions of Netscape Navigator and Internet Explorer from their respective Web sites. Note that the table structure of the frameless page closely matches the frame layout you created. In this case, the first row is a single cell that spans two columns and displays the company logo, and the second row contains the list of links in the first cell and the home page text in the second cell.

Another way of supporting browsers that do not display frames is to create a Web page that contains links to the framed and nonframed versions of your Web site. A user with an older browser can thereby avoid the frames. This technique also provides users with the option of not viewing frames, even though their browsers have the ability to. Some people just don't like frames.

REFERENCE WINDOW   **RW**

Tips for Using Frames

- Create framed and frameless versions of your Web page to accommodate all browsers, and be sure to provide links to both versions.
- Do not turn off vertical or horizontal scrolling unless you are certain that all the content for a frame can be displayed within the frame borders.
- Assign names to all of your frames to make your HTML code easier to read and interpret.
- Simplify your HTML code by using the <base> tag when most of the hyperlinks in your framed page point to the same target.
- Never display pages that lie outside your Web site, such as Web pages created by other businesses or organizations, within a frame.

Working **with Frame Borders**

There are additional attributes you can apply to the <frame> tag that allow you to change border size and appearance. For example, you can remove borders from your frames to free up more space for text and images, or you can change the color of the frame border so that it matches or complements the color scheme for your Web site.

REFERENCE WINDOW   **RW**

Modifying Frame Borders

- To define a color for your frame borders, add the bordercolor attribute to either the <frameset> or <frame> tag:

  ```
  <frameset bordercolor="color">
  ```

  or

  ```
  <frame bordercolor="color">
  ```

  where *color* is either the color name or color value. Enter the bordercolor attribute in the <frameset> tag to change all of the frame border colors in a set of frames. In Internet Explorer, enter the attribute in the <frame> tag to change the color of a single frame border (Note: In Netscape, using the bordercolor attribute in a single <frame> tag applies the color to all of the frames.)
- To change the width of your frame borders, apply the border attribute to the <frameset> tag:

  ```
  <frameset border="value">
  ```

  where *value* is the width of the border in pixels. You cannot change the width of individual frame borders. Note that you can also change border width in Internet Explorer using the framespacing attribute; this attribute is not supported by Netscape Navigator.

Setting the Border Color

To change the color of a frame's border, use the bordercolor attribute. The attribute can be applied either to an entire set of frames, using the <frameset> tag, or to individual frames, using the <frame> tag. The syntax for this attribute is:

```
<frameset bordercolor="color">
```

or

```
<frame bordercolor="color">
```

where *color* is either a color name or a color value. Applying the bordercolor attribute to the <frameset> tag affects all of the frames and nested frames within the set. If you apply the bordercolor attribute to a single <frame> tag, that particular color of the border changes in Internet Explorer, but in Netscape Navigator, all of the frame borders change. It is important to remember that when you apply these types of tags and attributes to your Web page, you should always view the page using different browsers and, if possible, browser versions.

Debbie asks you to test the bordercolor attribute on the YCS Web site by changing the color of the frame borders to brown.

To change the frame border color:

1. Return to **yale.htm** in your text editor.

2. Enter the attribute **bordercolor="brown"** within the initial <frameset> tag.

3. Save your changes to the file, and then reload it in your Web browser. Figure 5-32 shows the frames with a brown border.

Figure 5-32   **WEB SITE WITH BROWN FRAME BORDER**

Setting the Border Width

Another way of modifying frame borders is to change their widths using the border attribute. Unlike the bordercolor attribute, this attribute can be used only in the <frameset> tag, and not in individual <frame> tags. The syntax for the border attribute is:

```
<frameset border="value">
```

where *value* is the width of the frame borders in pixels.

To see how this attribute affects the appearance of your Web page, Debbie asks you to use it to remove the frame borders by setting the width to 0 pixels.

To change the size of the frame borders:

1. Return to **yale.htm** in your text editor.

2. Delete the bordercolor attribute that you entered in the previous set of steps. You don't need this attribute because you're going to remove the frame borders entirely.

3. Enter the **attribute border="0"** within the first <frameset> tag. See Figure 5-33.

Figure 5-33	REMOVING THE FRAME BORDERS

setting the width of the frame border to zero has the effect of removing the border

```
<frameset rows="85,*" border="0">
   <!-- Company Logo -->
   <frame src="head.htm" scrolling="no" marginheight="0" noresize name="logo">
   <!-- Nested Frames -->
   <frameset cols="140,*">
      <!-- List of YCS Links -->
      <frame src="links.htm" noresize name="links">
      <!-- YCS Home Page -->
      <frame src="home.htm" marginheight="0" marginwidth="10" noresize name="pages">
   </frameset>
</frameset>
```

4. Save your changes to yale.htm and then reload it in your Web browser. As shown in Figure 5-34, the frame borders have been removed from the page.

5. Close any YCS files that may still be open.

Figure 5-34   THE YCS WEB SITE WITHOUT FRAME BORDERS

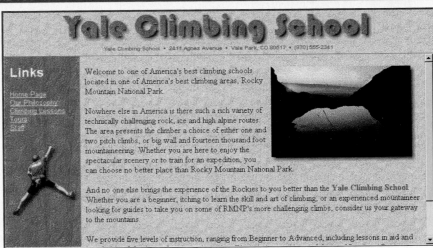

By removing the borders, you've created more space for the text and images in each of the Web pages. You've also created the impression of a "seamless" Web page. Some Web designers prefer not to show frame borders in order to give the illusion of having a single Web page rather than three separate ones, while other Web designers believe that hiding frame borders can confuse users as they navigate the Web site.

You can create a similar effect by using the frameborder attribute. Adding frameborder="no" to a <frameset> tag removes the borders from the frames in your page. Internet Explorer also supports the framespacing attribute, which has the same effect as the border attribute. Note that Netscape does not support this attribute.

Creating **Floating Frames**

Another way of using frames is to create a floating frame. Introduced by Internet Explorer 3.0 and added to the HTML 4.0 specifications, a **floating frame**, or **internal frame**, is displayed as a separate box or window within a Web page. The frame can be placed within a Web page in much the same way as an inline image. The syntax for a floating frame is:

```
<iframe src="URL" frameborder="option">
</iframe>
```

where *URL* is the name and location of the file you want to display in the floating frame and the frameborder attribute determines whether the browser displays a border ("yes") or not ("no") around the frame.

In addition to these attributes, you can use some of the other attributes you used with fixed frames, such as the marginwidth, marginheight, and name attributes. Figure 5-35 describes some of the other attributes associated with the <iframe> tag.

Figure 5-35	ATTRIBUTES OF THE <IFRAME> TAG
ATTRIBUTE	**DESCRIPTION**
align="*alignment*"	How the frame is aligned with the surrounding text (use "left" or "right" to flow text around the inline frame.)
border="*value*"	The size of the border around the frame, in pixels
frameborder="*type*"	Specifies whether to display a border ("yes") or not ("no")
classid="*URL*"	The class identifier of the object
height="*value*" width="*value*"	The height and width of the frame, in pixels
hspace="*value*" vspace="*value*"	The horizontal and vertical space around the frame, in pixels
marginheight="*value*" marginwidth="*value*"	The size of the internal margins of the frame, in pixels
name="*text*"	The name of the frame
scrolling="*type*"	Specifies whether the frame can be scrolled ("yes") or not ("no")
src="*URL*"	The location and filename of the page displayed in the frame

Debbie is interested in floating frames, and she would like you to create a staff page that employs this technique.

To create a floating frame:

1. Using your text editor, open **iftxt.htm** from the tutorial.05/tutorial folder of your Data Disk.

2. Save the file as **iframe.htm**.

3. Immediately following the </center> tag, insert the following HTML code. See Figure 5-36.

```
<iframe width="400" height="250" align="right"
hspace="5" src="bios.htm">
</iframe>
```

Figure 5-36	CREATING A FLOATING FRAME

html code to create a floating frame

```
<html>
<head>
<title>The YCS Staff</title>
</head>
<body background="wall.jpg">

<center><img src="logo.jpg" alt="The Yale Climbing School"><br>
<font face="Arial, Helvetica, sans-serif" size="1" color="green"><b>
 Yale Climbing School  &#149; 
 2411 Agnes Avenue  &#149; 
 Vale Park, CO 80517  &#149; 
 (970) 555-2341
</b></font>
<hr width="100%">
</center>

<iframe width="400" height="250" align="right" hspace="5" src="bios.htm">
</iframe>

<h1><font face="Arial, Helvetica, sans-serif" color="brown">Staff</font></h1>
The staff at the Yale Climbing School is here to help with all of your climbing needs.
All of our instructors are fully qualified with years of climbing and teaching experience.
Scroll through the biographies at the right for more information.
</body>
</html>
```

4. Save your changes to iframe.htm and close the file.

5. Open iframe.htm in your Web browser. Figure 5-37 shows the resulting Web page.

Figure 5-37	VIEWING A FLOATING FRAME

floating frame

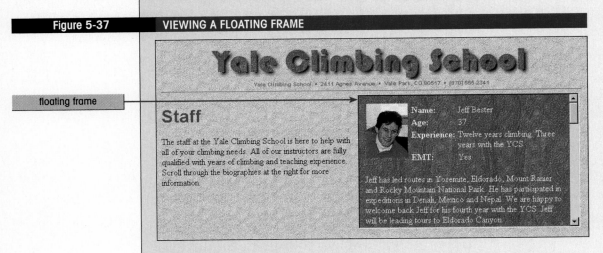

TROUBLE? If you're running Netscape version 4.7 or earlier, you will not see the floating frame displayed in Figure 5-37.

6. Use the scroll bars in the floating frame to view the entire list of staff biographies.

7. Close your Web browser.

If you want to use floating frames in your Web page, you must make sure that your users are running at least Internet Explorer 3.0 or Netscape 6.2. Users of other browsers and browser versions might not be able to view floating frames.

You've completed your work for Debbie and the Yale Climbing School. Using frames, you've created an interesting presentation that is both attractive and easy to navigate. Debbie is pleased and will get back to you if she needs any additional work done.

Session 5.2 QUICK CHECK

1. When you click a hypertext link inside a frame, in what frame will the Web page appear by default?

2. What HTML code would you use to assign the name "Address" to a frame with the document source address.htm?

3. What HTML code would you use to direct a hypertext link to a frame named "News"?

4. What HTML code would you use to point a hypertext link to the document "sales.htm" with the result that the sales.htm file is loaded into the entire display area, overwriting any frames in the process?

5. What HTML code would you use to direct all hypertext links in a document to the "News" target?

6. Describe what you would do to make your Web page readable by browsers that support frames and by those that do not.

7. What HTML tag would you use to set the frame border color of every frame on the page to red?

8. What HTML tag would you use to set the frame border width to 5 pixels?

REVIEW ASSIGNMENTS

Debbie has asked you to revise the layout for the YCS Web site. She would like links for all of the Web pages to display in separate frames so that users can always click a link for a specific page or collection of pages no matter where they are in the Web site. Figure 5-38 shows a preview of the frames you'll create for the Yale Climbing School.

To implement Debbie's suggestions:

Figure 5-38

You'll create the following files for the YCS Web site:

- tlist.htm—contains a list of links to the tour pages
- slist.htm—contains a list of links to staff bios
- tours2.htm—a frame layout displaying YCS tours
- staff2.htm—a frame layout displaying YCS staff bios
- tourlink.htm—a Web page containing a link to tour2.htm
- staflink.htm—a Web page containing a link to staff2.htm
- head2.htm—a Web page containing the company logo and links to three pages
- yale2.htm—a frame layout displaying all of the YCS Web pages

To create the YCS Web site:

1. Using your text editor, open **tlisttxt.htm** from the tutorial.05/review folder of your Data Disk and save it as **tlist.htm**.

2. Define "Tours" as the default target for links in this file.

3. Save your changes to **tlist.htm** and close the file.

4. Using your text editor, open **slisttxt.htm** and save it as **slist.htm**. Set "Bios" as the default target for links on this page. Save your changes and close the file.

5. Using your text editor, open **tourstxt.htm** and save it as **tours2.htm**. In the **tours2.htm** file do the following:

   - Create a frame layout consisting of two columns of frames. The first frame should be 140 pixels wide, the second frame should occupy the remaining space.
   - Make the frame borders 5 pixels wide and brown in color.
   - The source for the first frame should be the **tlist.htm** file.
   - The source for the second frame should be the **grepon.htm** file. Assign the frame the name "Tours".
   - Do not allow users to resize either frame in the frameset.
   - Add comments describing the contents of each frame.

6. Save your changes and close the file.

7. Using your text editor, open **stafftxt.htm** and save it as **staff2.htm**.

   - In staff2.htm create a frame layout containing two columns. Make the first frame 140 pixels wide; the second frame should occupy the remaining space.
   - Make the frame borders 5 pixels wide and brown in color
   - The first frame should have a margin height of 1 pixel and a margin width of 10 pixels. The source for this frame should be the slist.htm file.
   - Display the contents of the bester.htm file in the second frame. Name the frame "Bios". You do not have to specify a margin height or width.
   - Do not allow users to resize either frame.
   - Add comments describing the two frames.

8. Save your changes to staff2.htm and close the file.

9. Using your text editor, open **tltxt.htm** and save it as **tourlink.htm**. Set the target of the hyperlinks in this file to the target name "docs". Save your changes and close the file.

10. Open **sltxt.htm** in your text editor and save it as **staflink.htm**. Set the target of the hyperlinks to the target name "docs". Save your changes and close the file.

11. Open **headtxt.htm** in your text editor and save it as **head2.htm**. Once again, point the target of the hyperlinks to the "docs" target name. Close the file, saving your changes.

12. Open **yale2txt.htm** in your text editor and save the file as **yale2.htm**.

   ■ In yale2.htm create a frame layout containing three rows of frames. The first frame should be 85 pixels high, the third frame should be 30 pixels high, and the middle frame should occupy the remaining space.

   ■ Make the frame borders brown, 5 pixels in width. Do not allow users to resize the frames.

   ■ Display **head2.htm** in the first frame. Set the margin height to 0 pixels.

   ■ Display the contents of the **home.htm** file in the second frame and name the frame "docs". Set the second frame's margin height to 0 pixels and the margin width to 10 pixels.

   ■ Insert a frameset containing three columns into the third frame. The first and third columns of the nested frameset should be 100 pixels wide; the second column should occupy the remaining space. Use **staflink.htm** as the source for the first frame, **footer.htm** as the source for the second frame, and **tourlink.htm** as the source for the third frame. Set the margin width and height of each frame to 5 pixels. Make the frame borders brown and 5 pixels wide. Do not allow users to resize the frames.

13. For browsers that don't support frames, insert the contents of **noframes.htm** into yale2.htm.

14. Save your changes to yale2.htm and close the file.

15. Open **yale2.htm** in your Web browser, and verify that you can view all of the Web pages in the YCS Web site in the appropriate frames.

16. Hand in the files used by this Web site to your instructor.

CASE PROBLEMS

Case 1. Doc-Centric Copiers   Located in Salt Lake City, Doc-Centric is one of the nation's leading manufacturers of personal and business copiers. The annual shareholders' convention in Chicago is approaching, and the general manager, David Edgars, wants you to create an online report for the convention participants. The report will run off a computer located in the convention hall and will be accessible to everyone. David feels that creating a Web presentation to run locally on the computer is the best way of presenting the sales data. Using hyperlinks between various reports will enable Doc-Centric Copiers to make a wealth of information available to shareholders in an easy-to-use format. Most of the Web pages have been created for you. Your job is to display that information using frames. A preview of the layout you'll create is shown in Figure 5-39.

Figure 5-39

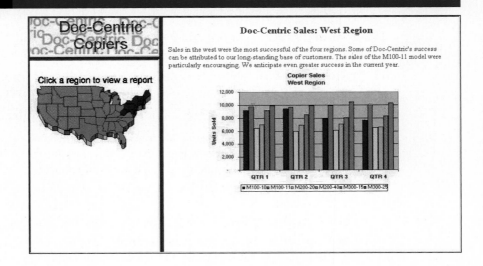

You'll use the following files in the Doc-Centric Web presentation:

- dcc.htm, a frame layout of all of the Doc-Centric Web pages
- dccmw.htm, a page describing sales data for the Midwest region
- dccne.htm, a page describing sales data for the Northeast region
- dccs.htm, a page describing sales data for the South region
- dccw.htm, a page describing sales data for the West region
- head.htm, a page with the company logo
- map.htm, a page with a map of the company's sales regions
- report.htm, a page welcoming shareholders to the convention

To create the Doc-Centric Copiers sales presentation:

1. Using your text editor, open **dcctxt.htm** from the tutorial.05/case1 folder on your Data Disk, and save it as **dcc.htm** in the same folder.

2. Create a frame layout with the following design documents:

   - The layout contains two columns with a blue frame border, 10 pixels in width. The first frame should be 240 pixels wide. The second frame should occupy the remaining space in the design window.
   - Create two rows of nested frames in the first frame. The first row should be 75 pixels high; the second row should fill up the remaining space. Display the contents of the **head.htm** file in the first row. Display the contents of the **map.htm** file in the second row. Name the first frame "logo", the second frame "usmap".
   - In the second frame, display the contents of the report.htm file. Name the frame "reports".
   - Add comments describing the contents of the various frames.

3. Using your text editor, open **maptxt.htm** and save it as **map.htm**.

4. Direct each link in the map.htm file to the reports target, so that the pages will appear in the reports frame. Save your changes and close the file.

5. Using your text editor, open **headtxt.htm** and save it as **head.htm**. Direct the hyperlinks in this file to the reports target. Close the file, saving your changes.

6. Use your Web browser to view dcc.htm. What improvements could be made to the page? What should be removed?

7. Return to **dcc.htm** in your text editor and reduce the margin for the logo frame to 1 pixel. Reduce the margin width for the usmap frame to 1 pixel, and change that frame's margin height to 30 pixels.

8. Remove scroll bars from both the logo and usmap frames.

9. View the Web page again to verify that the problems you identified in Step 6 have been resolved.

10. Return to dcc.htm in your text editor, and lock the size of the frames to prevent users from changing the frame sizes.

Explore ▶ 11. Using your Web browser, reload **dcc.htm** and test the image map in the usmap frame. Verify that each of the four sales reports is correctly displayed in the reports frame. Click the company logo in the upper-left frame and verify that it redisplays the opening page in the reports frame.

12. Print a page displaying one of the sales reports. Print a copy of the dcc.htm and map.htm files.

13. Hand in your files and printouts to your instructor.

Case 2. Browyer Realty   Linda Browyer is the owner of Browyer Realty, a real estate company in Minnesota. She's asked you to help her design a Web page for the listings in her book. Linda envisions a Web page that displays basic information about a listing, including the owner's description. She would like to have several photos of the listing on the page, but rather than cluttering up the layout with several images, she would like users to be able to view different images by clicking a link on the page. Linda wants the images to open within the listing page, not in a separate Web page. Figure 5-40 shows a preview of the page you'll create for Linda.

Figure 5-40

To create this page you'll create a floating frame that displays Web pages containing different photos of the listing. There are 13 pages you'll display in the floating frame, named img01.htm, img02.htm, and so forth.

To create the Browyer Realty listing:

1. Using your text editor, open **listtxt.htm** from the tutorial.05/case2 folder of your Data Disk in your text editor and save it as **listing.htm**.

Explore

2. Directly above the paragraph beginning with the line, "There is much more...," insert a floating frame with the following attributes:

   ■ The source of the frame is the img01.htm file.

   ■ The name of the frame is "images".

   ■ The frame is aligned with the left margin of the page.

   ■ The frame is 300 pixels wide and 240 pixels high.

   ■ The frame's margin width and height are 0 pixels.

   ■ There is no frame border.

3. Insert a comment above the floating frame indicating its purpose in the Web page.

4. Change each of the 13 entries in the list of photos to a hypertext link. Direct the first entry to img01.htm, the second entry to img02.htm, and so forth.

5. Display the 13 hypertext links you created in the previous step in the "images" floating frame.

6. Save your changes to the file.

7. Using your Web browser, open **listing.htm**. Verify that each link displays a different photo and photo caption in the Web page and that the rest of the page remains unchanged.

8. Hand in the files for this Web site to your instructor.

Case 3. SkyWeb Astronomy   Dr. Andrew Weiss of Central Ohio University maintains an astronomy page for his students called SkyWeb. In his Web site he discusses many aspects of astronomy and observing. One of the pages he wants your help with involves the Messier catalog, a list of deep sky objects of particular interest to astronomers and amateur observers.

Dr. Weiss wants his page to contain a slide show of various Messier objects, displaying both a photo of the object and a text box describing the object's history and features. He wants his users to be able to click a forward or backward button to move through the slide show. The rest of the Web page remains unchanged as users view the presentation. Figure 5-41 shows a preview of the page that Dr. Weiss wants to create.

Figure 5-41

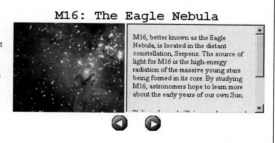

To create a presentation like this, you'll need to insert one floating frame inside of another. Dr. Weiss has created the text you need for the Web site. Your job is to create the frames needed to complete the Web page.

To create the SkyWeb Web page:

1. Using your text editor, open **mxxtxt.htm** from the tutorial.05/case3 folder of your Data Disk and save it as **m01.htm**.

Explore

2. The m01.htm file displays an image of the Messier object M1 and also contains a text box describing this stellar object. Replace the title and heading for the Web page with the text "M1: The Crab Nebula".

3. Replace the inline image mxx.jpg with the image m01.jpg

4. Replace the inline image mxxdesc.jpg with a floating frame of the same dimensions, displaying the contents of the file m01desc.htm

5. Direct the hypertext link for the Previous button located at the bottom of the page to the file **m57.htm**. Note that you'll create this file later.

6. Direct the hypertext link for the Next button to the file m13.htm—another file you'll create shortly.

7. Save your changes to **m01.htm**.

8. With m01.htm as a guide, use your text editor to create similar Web pages for the other eight Messier objects. Save the files as **m13.htm**, **m16.htm**, **m20.htm**, **m27.htm**, **m31.htm**, **m42.htm**, **m51.htm**, and **m57.htm**. The titles and headings for these pages are:

   - M13: Hercules Globular Cluster
   - M16: The Eagle Nebula
   - M20: The Trifid Nebula
   - M27: The Dumbbell Nebula
   - M31: The Andromeda Galaxy
   - M42: The Orion Nebula
   - M51: The Whirlpool Galaxy
   - M57: The Ring Nebula

   The floating frame for each page should point to the file containing descriptive text on the Messier object. For example, the floating frame for the m13.htm file should display the m13desc.htm file and so forth.

   The Previous and Next buttons in each page should point to the previous and next Messier object files. For example, the buttons in m27.htm should point to m20.htm and m31.htm. The Next button for m57.htm should point to m01.htm. Save your changes to all the files, and then close them.

9. Using your text editor, open **messtxt.htm** and save it as **messier.htm**.

10. At the beginning of the third paragraph, insert a floating frame.

    - Make the source of the floating frame m01.htm.
    - Align the frame with the right margin of the page.
    - Make the frame 460 pixels wide by 240 pixels high.
    - Make the margin width and height 0 pixels.
    - Set the horizontal space around the frame to 5 pixels.
    - There should be no border around the frame.

11. Insert a comment before the floating frame describing its purpose.

12. Save your changes to messier.htm and close the file.

13. Open messier.htm in your Web browser. Click the Previous and Next buttons and verify that you can navigate through the list of Messier objects without disturbing the rest of the Web page. Verify that you can use the scroll bars around the description box to view descriptions of each object.

14. Hand in the files for this Web site to your instructor.

Case 4. Warner Peripherals, Inc.   Warner Peripherals, a company located in Tucson, makes high-quality peripherals for computers. The company is an industry leader and has been delivering innovative technical solutions to consumers for more than 20 years. Its most popular products include the SureSave line of tape drives and the SureRite line of disk drives. You've been asked to consolidate several Web pages describing these products into a single Web presentation using frames. The files shown in Figure 5-42 are available for your use.

Figure 5-42

FILE	DESCRIPTION
drive15l.htm	Description of the 15L SureRite hard drive
drive20m.htm	Description of the 20M SureRite hard drive
drive33m.htm	Description of the 33M SureRite hard drive
drive60s.htm	Description of the 60S SureRite hard drive
tape800.htm	Description of the 800 SureSave tape backup drive
tape3200.htm	Description of the 3200 SureSave tape backup drive
tape9600.htm	Description of the 9600 SureSave tape backup drive
wlogo.htm	An Web page containing the Warner Peripherals logo

To create the Warner Peripherals Web presentation:

1. Create a table of contents page that includes hypertext links to the files listed in Figure 5-42. The design of this Web page is up to you. Save this page as **wtoc.htm** in the tutorial.05/case4 folder of your Data Disk.

2. In the same folder, create a file named **warner.htm** that consolidates the logo page, table of contents page, and product description pages into a single page, using frames. Include comment tags in the file describing each element of the page.

3. Test your Web page and verify that each link works properly and appears in the correct frame.

4. Print a copy of the page and the HTML code.

5. Save your work and close your Web browser and text editor.

QUICK CHECK ANSWERS

Session 5.1

1. Frames are windows appearing within the browser's display area, each capable of displaying the contents of a different HTML file.
2. Because there is no page body. Instead, the browser displays the <body> tags from other pages.
3. <frameset rows="2, 50%,*">
4. <frame src="home.htm">
5. <frame src="home.htm" scrolling="no">
6. <frame src="home.htm" marginheight="3">
7. 3 pixels
8. <frame src="home.htm" noresize>

Session 5.2

1. The frame containing the hypertext link
2. <frame src="address.htm" name="Address">
3. <a href="*URL*" target="News">
4. <a href="sales.htm" target=_top>
5. Place the tag <base target="News"> in the <head> section of the HTML file
6. Create a section starting with the <noframes> tag. After the <noframes> tag enter a <body> tag to identify the text and images you want frame-blind browsers to display. Complete this section with a </body> tag followed by a </noframes> tag.
7. <frameset bordercolor="red">
8. <frameset borderwidth="5">

HTML Color Names

The following is a list of HTML color names and their corresponding hexadecimal values. To view these colors, you must have a system capable of displaying at least 256 colors (8-bit). As with other aspects of Web page design, you should test these colors on a variety of browsers before using them. Different browsers may render these colors differently, or not at all. Remember, this is not a list of Web-safe, or browser safe, colors.

Extended Color Names

COLOR NAME	HEXADECIMAL VALUE	COLOR NAME	HEXADECIMAL VALUE
aliceblue	#F0F8FF	darksalmon	#E9967A
antiquewhite	#FAEBD7	darkseagreen	#8FBC8F
aqua	#00FFFF	darkslateblue	#483086
aquamarine	#70DB93	darkslategray	#2F4F4F
azure	#F0FFFF	darkturquoise	#00CED1
beige	#F5F5DC	darkviolet	#9400D3
bisque	#FFE4C4	deeppink	#FF1493
black	#000000	deepskyblue	#00BFFF
blanchedalmond	#FFEBCD	dimgray	#696969
blue	#0000FF	dodgerblue	#1E90FF
blueviolet	#8A2BE2	firebrick	#B22222
brown	#A52A2A	floralwhite	#FFFAF0
burlywood	#DEB887	forestgreen	#228B22
cadetblue	#5F9EA0	fuchsia	#FF00FF
chartreuse	#7FFF00	gainsboro	#DCDCDC
chocolate	#D2691E	ghostwhite	#F8F8FF
coral	#FF7F50	gold	#CD7F32
cornflowerblue	#6495ED	goldenrod	#DAA520
cornsilk	#FFF8DC	gray	#BEBEBE
crimson	#DC143C	green	#008000
cyan	#00FFFF	greenyellow	#ADFF2F
darkblue	#00008B	honeydew	#F0FFF0
darkcyan	#008B8B	hotpink	#FF69B4
darkgoldenrod	#B8860B	indianred	#CD5C5C
darkgray	#A9A9A9	indigo	#4B0082
darkgreen	#006400	ivory	#FFFFF0
darkkhaki	#BDB76B	khaki	#F0D58C
darkmagenta	#8B008B	lavender	#E6E6FA
darkolivegreen	#556B2F	lavenderblush	#FFF0F5
darkorange	#FF8C00	lawngreen	#7CFC00
darkorchid	#9932CC	lemonchiffon	#FFFACD
darkred	#8B0000	lightblue	#ADD8E6

COLOR NAME	HEXADECIMAL VALUE
lightcoral	#F08080
lightcyan	#E0FFFF
lightgoldenrodyellow	#FAFAD2
lightgrey	#03D3D3
lightgreen	#90EE90
lightpink	#FFB6C1
lightsalmon	#FFA07A
lightseagreen	#20B2AA
lightskyblue	#87CEFA
lightslategray	#778899
lightsteelblue	#B0C4DE
lightyellow	#FFFFE0
lime	#00FF00
limegreen	#32CD32
Linen	#FAF0E6
magenta	#FF00FF
maroon	#800000
mediumaquamarine	#66CDAA
mediumblue	#0000CD
mediumorchid	#BA55D3
mediumpurple	#9370DB
mediumseagreen	#3CB371
mediumslateblue	#7B68EE
mediumspringgreen	#00FA9A
mediumturquoise	#48D1CC
mediumvioletred	#C71585
midnightblue	#191970
mintcream	#F5FFFA
mistyrose	#FFE4E1
moccasin	#FFE4B5
navajowhite	#FFDEAD
navy	#000080
oldlace	#FDF5E6
olive	#808000
olivedrab	#6B8E23
orange	#FFA500
orangered	#FF4500
orchid	#DA70D6

COLOR NAME	HEXADECIMAL VALUE
palegoldenrod	#EEE8AA
palegreen	#98FB98
paleturquoise	#AFEEEE
palevioletred	#DB7093
papayawhip	#FFEFD5
peachpuff	#FFDAB9
peru	#CD853F
pink	#FFC0CB
plum	#DDA0DD
powderblue	#B0E0E6
purple	#800080
red	#FF0000
rosybrown	#BC8072
royalblue	#4169E1
saddlebrown	#8B4513
salmon	#FA8072
sandybrown	#F4A460
seagreen	#2E8B57
seashell	#FFF5EE
sienna	#A0522D
silver	#C0C0C0
skyblue	#87CEEB
slateblue	#6A5ACD
slategray	#708090
snow	#FFFAFA
springgreen	#00FF7F
steelblue	#4682B4
tan	#D2B48C
teal	#008080
thistle	#D8BFD8
tomato	#FF6347
turquoise	#40E0D0
violet	#EE82EE
wheat	#F5DEB3
white	#FFFFFF
whitesmoke	#F5F5F5
yellow	#FFFF00
yellowgreen	#9ACD32

HTML Character Entities

The following table lists the extended character set for HTML, also known as the ISO Latin-1 Character set. Characters can be defined by name or by numeric value. For example, to define the registered trademark symbol, ®, you can use either &reg or &#174.

Not all code names are recognized by all browsers. Some older browsers that support only the HTML 2.0 standard do not recognize the code name "&times", for instance. Code names that may not be recognized by older browsers are marked with an asterisk in the following table.

CHARACTER	CODE	CODE NAME	DESCRIPTION
	&#09		Tab
	&#10		Line feed
	&#32		Space
!	&#33		Exclamation mark
"	&#34	&quot	Double quotation mark
#	&#35		Pound sign
$	&#36		Dollar sign
%	&#37		Percent sign
&	&#38	&amp	Ampersand
'	&#39		Apostrophe
(	&#40		Left parenthesis
)	&#41		Right parenthesis
*	&#42		Asterisk
+	&#43		Plus sign
,	&#44		Comma
-	&#45		Hyphen
.	&#46		Period
/	&#47		Forward slash
0 - 9	&#48 - &#57		Numbers 0-9
:	&#58		Colon
;	&#59		Semicolon
<	&#60	&lt	Less than sign
=	&#61		Equal sign
>	&#62	&gt	Greater than sign
?	&#63		Question mark
@	&#64		Commercial at sign
A - Z	&#65 - &#90		Letters A-Z
[	&#91		Left square bracket
\	&#92		Back slash
]	&#93		Right square bracket

CHARACTER	CODE	CODE NAME	DESCRIPTION
^	&#94		Caret
_	&#95		Horizontal bar (underscore)
`	&#96		Grave accent
a - z	&#97 - &#122		Letters a-z
{	&#123		Left curly brace
|	&#124		Vertical bar
}	&#125		Right curly brace
~	&#126		Tilde
,	&#130		Comma
ƒ	&#131		Function sign (florin)
„	&#132		Double quotation mark
…	&#133		Ellipses
†	&#134		Dagger
‡	&#135		Double dagger
ˆ	&#136		Circumflex
‰	&#137		Permil
Š	&#138		Capital S with hacek
‹	&#139		Left single angle
Œ	&#140		Capital OE ligature
	&#141 - &#144		Unused
`	&#145		Single beginning quotation mark
'	&#146		Single ending quotation mark
"	&#147		Double beginning quotation mark
"	&#148		Double ending quotation mark
•	&#149		Bullet
–	&#150		En dash
—	&#151		Em dash
~	&#152		Tilde
™	&#153	&trade*	Trademark symbol
š	&#154		Small s with hacek
›	&#155		Right single angle
œ	&#156		Lowercase oe ligature
Ÿ	&#159		Capital Y with umlaut
		*	Non-breaking space
¡	&#161	&iexcl*	Inverted exclamation mark
¢	&#162	&cent*	Cent sign
£	&#163	&pound*	Pound sterling

CHARACTER	CODE	CODE NAME	DESCRIPTION
¤	&#164	&curren*	General currency symbol
¥	&#165	&yen*	Yen sign
¦	&#166	&brvbar*	Broken vertical bar
§	&#167	&sect*	Section sign
¨	&#168	&uml*	Umlaut
©	&#169	&copy*	Copyright symbol
ª	&#170	&ordf*	Feminine ordinal
«	&#171	&laquo*	Left angle quotation mark
¬	&#172	&not*	Not sign
−	&#173	&shy*	Soft hyphen
®	&#174	&reg*	Registered trademark
¯	&#175	&macr*	Macron
°	&#176	&deg*	Degree sign
±	&#177	&plusmn*	Plus/minus symbol
²	&#178	&sup2*	Superscript 2
³	&#179	&sup3*	Superscript 3
´	&#180	&acute*	Acute accent
µ	&#181	&micro*	Micro sign
¶	&#182	&para*	Paragraph sign
·	&#183	&middot*	Middle dot
ç	&#184	&cedil*	Cedilla
¹	&#185	&sup1*	Superscript 1
º	&#186	&ordm*	Masculine ordinal
»	&#187	&raquo*	Right angle quotation mark
¼	&#188	&frac14*	Fraction one-quarter
½	&#189	&frac12*	Fraction one-half
¾	&#190	&frac34*	Fraction three-quarters
¿	&#191	&iquest*	Inverted question mark
À	&#192	&Agrave	Capital A, grave accent
Á	&#193	&Aacute	Capital A, acute accent
Â	&#194	&Acirc	Capital A, circumflex accent
Ã	&#195	&Atilde	Capital A, tilde
Ä	&#196	&Auml	Capital A, umlaut
Å	&#197	&Aring	Capital A, ring
Æ	&#198	&Aelig	Capital AE ligature
Ç	&#199	&Ccedil	Capital C, cedilla
È	&#200	&Egrave	Capital E, grave accent

CHARACTER	CODE	CODE NAME	DESCRIPTION
É	&#201	&Eacute	Capital E, acute accent
Ê	&#202	&Ecirc	Capital E, circumflex accent
Ë	&#203	&Euml	Capital E, umlaut
Ì	&#204	&Igrave	Capital I, grave accent
Í	&#205	&Iacute	Capital I, acute accent
Î	&#206	&Icirc	Capital I, circumflex accent
Ï	&#207	&Iuml	Capital I, umlaut
Ð	&#208	&ETH*	Capital ETH, Icelandic
Ñ	&#209	&Ntilde	Capital N, tilde
Ò	&#210	&Ograve	Capital O, grave accent
Ó	&#211	&Oacute	Capital O, acute accent
Ô	&#212	&Ocirc	Capital O, circumflex accent
Õ	&#213	&Otilde	Capital O, tilde
Ö	&#214	&Ouml	Capital O, umlaut
×	&#215	&times*	Multiplication sign
Ø	&#216	&Oslash	Capital O slash
Ù	&#217	&Ugrave	Capital U, grave accent
Ú	&#218	&Uacute	Capital U, acute accent
Û	&#219	&Ucirc	Capital U, circumflex accent
Ü	&#220	&Uuml	Capital U, umlaut
Ý	&#221	&Yacute	Capital Y, acute accent
þ	&#222	&THORN	Capital THORN, Icelandic
ß	&#223	&szlig	Small sz ligature
à	&#224	&agrave	Small a, grave accent
á	&#225	&aacute	Small a, acute accent
â	&#226	&acirc	Small a, circumflex accent
ã	&#227	&atilde	Small a, tilde
ä	&#228	&auml	Small a, umlaut
å	&#229	&aring	Small a, ring
æ	&#230	&aelig	Small ae ligature
ç	&#231	&ccedil	Small c, cedilla
è	&#232	&egrave	Small e, grave accent
é	&#233	&eacute	Small e, acute accent
ê	&#234	&ecirc	Small e, circumflex accent
ë	&#235	&euml	Small e, umlaut
ì	&#236	&igrave	Small i, grave accent
í	&#237	&iacute	Small i, acute accent

CHARACTER	CODE	CODE NAME	DESCRIPTION
î	&#238	&icirc	Small i, circumflex accent
ï	&#239	&iuml	Small i, umlaut
ð	&#240	&eth	Small eth, Icelandic
ñ	&#241	&ntilde	Small n, tilde
ò	&#242	&ograve	Small o, grave accent
ó	&#243	&oacute	Small o, acute accent
ô	&#244	&ocirc	Small o, circumflex accent
õ	&#245	&otilde	Small o, tilde
ö	&#246	&ouml	Small o, umlaut
÷	&#247	&divide*	Division sign
ø	&#248	&oslash	Small o slash
ù	&#249	&ugrave	Small u, grave accent
ú	&#250	&uacute	Small u, acute accent
û	&#251	&ucirc	Small u, circumflex accent
ü	&#252	&uuml	Small u, umlaut
ý	&#253	&yacute	Small y, acute accent
þ	&#254	&thorn	Small thorn, Icelandic
ÿ	&#255	&yuml	Small y, umlaut

Putting a Document on the World Wide Web

Once you've completed your work on your HTML file, you're probably ready to place it on the World Wide Web for others to see. To make a file available to the World Wide Web, it must be located on a computer connected to the Web called a **Web server**.

Your **Internet Service Provider (ISP)**—the company or institution through which you have Internet access—usually has a Web server available for your use. Because each Internet Service Provider has a different procedure for storing Web pages, you should contact your ISP to learn its policies and procedures. Generally you should be prepared to do the following:

- Extensively test your files with a variety of browsers and under different display conditions. Eliminate any errors and design problems before you place the page on the Web.
- If your HTML documents have a three-letter "htm" extension, rename those files with the four-letter extension "html." Some Web servers will require the four-letter extension for all Web pages.
- Check the hyperlinks and inline objects in each of your documents to verify that they point to the correct filenames. Verify the filenames with respect to upper and lower cases. Some Web servers distinguish between a file named "Image.gif" and one named "image.gif." To be safe, use only lowercase letters in all your filenames.
- If your hyperlinks use absolute pathnames, change them to relative pathnames.
- Find out from your ISP the name of the folder into which you'll be placing your HTML documents. You may also need a special user name and password to access this folder.
- Use **FTP**, a protocol used on the Internet to transfer files, or e-mail to place your pages in the appropriate folder on your Internet Service Provider's Web server. Some Web browsers, like Internet Explorer and Netscape Navigator, have this capability built in, allowing you to easily transfer your files to the Web server.
- Decide on a name for your site on the World Wide Web (such as "http://www.jackson_electronics.com"). Choose a name that will be easy for customers and interested parties to remember and return to.
- If you select a special name for your Web site, you may have to register it. Registration information can be found at http://www.internic.net. Your ISP may also provide this service for a fee. Registration is necessary to ensure that any name you give to your site is unique and not already in use. Usually you will have to pay a yearly fee to use a special name for your Web site.
- Add your site to the indexes of search pages on the World Wide Web. This is not required, but it will make it easier for people to find your site. Each search facility has different policies regarding adding information about Web sites to its index. Be aware that some will charge a fee for their services.

Once you've completed these steps, your work will be available on the World Wide Web in a form that is easy for users to access.

HTML
TAGS AND
ATTRIBUTES

The following list provides descriptions and browser compatibility information for the major HTML tags and attributes and is organized alphabetically. For example, a value of 4.0 in the Internet Explorer column indicates that the tag is supported by Internet Explorer 4.0 and above. Both opening and closing tags are provided when required, e.g., <table> and </table>; a single tag means that no closing tag is required. Deprecated tags are indicated as such.

You can view additional information about the latest HTML specifications at *http://www.w3.org*. Additional information about browser support for HTML tags is available at *http://www.htmlcompendium.org/*.

The following variables are used throughout this appendix:

- *Character* A single text character
- *Color* An HTML color name or hexadecimal color value
- *CGI Script* The name of a CGI script on the Web server
- *Document* The file name or URL of a file
- *List* A list of items separated by commas, usually enclosed in double quotation marks
- *Mime-Type* A MIME data type, such as "text/css", "audio/wav", or "video/x-msvideo"
- *Options* Limited to a specific set of values that are shown below the attribute
- *Text* A text string
- *URL* The URL for a Web page or file
- *Value* A number (usually an integer)

HTML supports six common attributes that apply to nearly all HTML tags.

COMMON ATTRIBUTES	DESCRIPTION	HTML	IE	NETSCAPE
class="Text"	The class attribute specifies the class or group to which a tag belongs.	4.0	3.0	4.0
dir="Option" (ltr | rtl)	The dir attribute indicates the text direction as related to the lang attribute. The ltr attribute value displays text from left to right; the rtl displays text from right to left.	4.0	5.5	
id="Text"	The id attribute specifies a unique identifier to be associated with each tag. Unlike the class attribute, an id value can be associated with a single tag.	4.0	3.0	4.0
lang="Text"	The lang attribute identifies the language used for the Web page content.	4.0	4.0	
style="Style Declarations"	The style attribute defines an inline style for the tag.	4.0	3.0	4.0
title="Text"	The title attribute provides information about the tag and identifies the tag for scripts.	2.0	4.0	6.0

TAGS AND ATTRIBUTES	DESCRIPTION	HTML	IE	NETSCAPE
<!-- -->	Text within the <!> tag is invisible to visitors using a browser.	2.0	1.0	1.0
<!doctype>	Specifies the Document Type Definition for a document.	2.0	2.0	1.0
<a> ... </a>	Marks the beginning and end of a hypertext link.	2.0	1.0	1.0
accesskey="Character"	Specifies an accelerator key for the element, which can be accessed by pressing the Character key along with the Alt key.	4.0	4.0	
coords="Value 1, Value 2..."	The coordinates (relative to the top left corner of the image) of the hotspot when the <a> tag is applied to an inline image. The coordinates used depend on the shape of the hotspot. Rectangle: coords="x_left, y_upper, x_right, y_lower" Circle: coords="x_center, y_center, radius" Polygon: coords="x1, y1, x2, y2, x3, y3, ..."	4.0		
href="URL"	Indicates the target filename, or URL for a hypertext link.	3.2	1.0	2.0
name="Text"	Specifies a name for the enclosed text, allowing it to be a target of a hypertext link.	2.0	1.0	1.0

TAGS AND ATTRIBUTES	DESCRIPTION	HTML	IE	NETSCAPE
rel="*Text*"	Specifies the relationship between the current page and the link specified by the href attribute.	2.0	2.0	
rev="*Text*"	Specifies a reverse relationship between the current page and the link specified by the href attribute.	2.0	2.0	
shape="*Option*" (rect | circle | polygon)	The shape of the hotspot when the <a> tag is applied to an inline image.	3.2	1.0	2.0
tabindex="*Value*"	Specifies the order for tabs in a form.	4.0	4.0	
target="*Text*"	Specifies the default target window or frame for the hypertext link.	4.0	3.0	1.0
title="*Text*"	Provides a title for the document whose address is provided by the href attribute.	2.0	2.0	
type="*Mime-Type*"	The data type of the linked document.	4.0		
<abbr> ... </abbr>	Indicates text in an abbreviated form (for example, WWW, HTTP, URL).	4.0		6.2
<acronym> ... </acronym>	Indicates a text acronym (for example, wac, radar).	3.0	4.0	6.2
<address> ... </address>	Used for information such as addresses and authorship. The text is typically italicized and indented.	2.0	1.0	1.0
<applet> ... </applet>	Supported by all Java-enabled browsers, allows Java applet in an HTML document. It has been deprecated in favor of the <object> tag in HTML 4.0.	3.2	3.0	2.0
align="*Option*" (absmiddle | | absbottom | absmiddle | baseline | bottom | center | | left | middle | right | texttop | top)	Specifies the alignment of the applet with the surrounding text.	3.2	3.0	2.0
alt="*Text*"	Specifies alternate text to be shown in place of the Java applet.	3.2	3.0	3.0
archive="*URL*"	Specifies the URL of an archive containing classes and other resources to be preloaded for use with the Java applet.	4.0		3.0
codebase="*URL*"	Specifies the base URL for the applet. If not specified, the browser uses the same location as the current document.	3.2	3.0	2.0
code="*Text*"	Specifies the name of the class file that contains the Java applet.	3.2	3.0	2.0

TAGS AND ATTRIBUTES	DESCRIPTION	HTML	IE	NETSCAPE
datafld="*Text*"	Specifies the column from a data source that supplies bound data for use with the applet.		4.0	
datasrc="*Text*"	Specifies the ID of the data source that is to be used with the applet.		4.0	
height="*Value*"	Specifies the height of the applet, in pixels.	3.2	3.0	2.0
hspace="*Value*"	Specifies the horizontal space around the applet, in pixels.	3.2	3.0	2.0
mayscript	Allows access to an applet by programs embedded in the document.	4.0		
name="*Text*"	The name assigned to the Java applet.	3.2	3.0	2.0
object="*Text*"	Specifies a resource containing a serialized representation of an applet's state. It is interpreted relative to the applet's code base. The serialized data contains the applet's class name, but not the implementation. The class name is used to retrie ve the implementation from a class file or archive.	4.0		
vspace="*Value*"	Specifies the vertical space around the applet, in pixels.	3.2	3.0	2.0
width="*Value*"	The width of the applet, in pixels.	3.2	3.0	2.0
\<area\>	Defines the type and coordinates of a hotspot within an image map.	3.2	2.0	1.0
coords="*Value 1, Value2…*"	The hotspot coordinates, which depend on the shape of the hotspot.	3.2	2.0	1.0
	Rectangle: coords="*x_left, y_upper, x_right, y_lower*" Circle: coords="*x_center, y_center, radius*" Polygon: coords= "*x_1, y_1, x_2, y_2, x_3, y_3, …*"			
href="*URL*"	Indicates the target, filename or URL to which the hotspot points.	3.2	2.0	1.0
shape="*Option*" (rect | circle | polygon)	The shape of the hotspot	3.2	2.0	1.0
target="*Text*"	Specifies the default target window or frame for the hotspot.	4.0	3.0	2.0

TAGS AND ATTRIBUTES	DESCRIPTION	HTML	IE	NETSCAPE
`<b> ... </b>`	Displays the enclosed text in bold type.	2.0	2.0	1.0
`<base>`	Allows you to specify a URL for the HTML document. It is used by some browsers to interpret relative hyperlinks.	2.0	2.0	1.0
href="*URL*"	Specifies the URL from which all relative hyperlinks are based.	2.0	2.0	4.0
target="*Text*"	Specifies the default target window or frame for every hypertext link in the document.	4.0	3.0	2.0
`<basefont>`	Specifies the default appearance of text in the document (deprecated).	3.2	2.0	1.0
color="*Color*"	The color name or value of the text.	4.0	1.0	4.0
face="*List*"	The font of the text. Multiple fonts can be specified. The browser attempts to render the text using fonts in the order specified in the list.	4.0	1.0	3.0
size="*Value*"	The size of the font in points.	3.2	2.0	1.1
`<bdo> ... </bdo>`	Overrides the current direction of text. The *dir* attribute is required.	4.0	5.0	6.2
dir="*Option*" (ltr | rtl)	Specifies the text direction, ltr (left to right), or rtl (right to left).	4.0	5.0	6.1
`<bgsound>`	Plays a background sound clip when the page is first opened.		2.0	
balance="*Value*"	Defines how the volume will be divided between two speakers, where "*Value*" is an integer between -10,000 and 10,000.		4.0	
loop="*Value*"	Specifies the number of times the sound clip is played; loop can either be a digit or infinite.		3.0	
src="*URL*"	The sound file used for the sound clip		2.0	
volume="*Value*"	Defines the volume of the background sound, where "*Value*" is an integer between 0 and 10,000.		4.0	
`<big> ... </big>`	Increases the size of the enclosed text. The exact appearance of the text depends on the browser and the default font size (deprecated).	3.2	2.0	2.0
`<blink> ... </blink>`	Instructs the enclosed text to blink on and off.		4.1	1.0
`<blockquote> ... </blockquote>`	Sets off long quotes or citations usually, by indenting the enclosed text from both margins.	2.0	1.1	1.0

TAGS AND ATTRIBUTES	DESCRIPTION	HTML	IE	NETSCAPE
<body> ... </body>	Encloses all text, images, and other elements on the Web page to be visible to the user.	2.0	1.0	1.0
alink="Color"	Color of activated hypertext links which are links the user has pressed with the mouse button, but has not yet released	3.2	4.1	1.1
background="URL"	The image file used for the Web page background	2.0	2.0	1.1
bgcolor="Color"	The color of the Web page background	3.2	2.0	1.1
bgproperties="fixed"	Prevents the background image from scrolling with the Web page.		2.0	
bottommargin="Value"	Specifies the size of the bottom margin, in pixels.		4.0	
leftmargin="Value"	Specifies the size of the left margin, in pixels.		2.0	
link="Color"	Color of all unvisited links (deprecated).	3.2	1.0	1.1
rightmargin="Value"	Specifies the size of the right margin, in pixels.		2.0	
scroll="Option" (no I yes)	Turns the scroll bars on and off (the default value is "yes").		4.0	
text="Color"	Color of all text in the document (deprecated).	3.2	1.0	1.1
topmargin="Value"	Specifies the size of the top margin, in pixels.		2.0	
vlink="Color"	Color of previously visited links.	3.2	1.0	1.1
<button> ... </button>	Buttons created with the <button> tag behave like buttons created with the <input> tag, but they offer more rendering possibilities.	4.0	4.1	6.1
accesskey="Character"	Specifies an accelerator key for the element, which can be accessed by pressing the Character key along with the Alt key.	4.0	4.0	6.2
disabled	Disables the button.	4.0	4.0	6.0
name="Text"	Specifies the button name.	4.0	5.0	6.0
value="Text"	Specifies the initial value of the button.	4.0	5.0	6.0
tabindex="Value"	Specifies the tab order in the form.	4.0	4.2	6.1
type="Option" (submit I reset I button)	Specifies the type of button. Setting the type to button creates a pushbutton for use with client-side scripts.	4.0	4.0	6.0

TAGS AND ATTRIBUTES	DESCRIPTION	HTML	IE	NETSCAPE
<caption> ... </caption>	Encloses the table caption.	3.0	2.0	1.1
align="*Option*" (left | right | center | top | bottom)	Specifies the alignment of the caption with respect to the table (the left, right, and center options are supported only by Internet Explorer 3.0 and above deprecated).	3.0	2.0	1.1
valign="*Option*" (top | bottom)	Specifies the vertical alignment of the caption with respect to the table.		2.0	
<center> ... </center>	Centers the enclosed text or image (deprecated).	3.2	1.0	1.0
<cite> ... </cite>	Used for citations and is usually displayed in italics.	2.0	1.0	1.0
<code> ... </code>	Used to display a sample of code. The text usually appears in a monospace font.	2.0	1.0	1.0
<col> ... </col>	Specifies the settings for a column or group of columns.	4.0	3.0	6.1
align="*Option*" (char | center | justify | left | right)	Specifies the horizontal alignment of text within a column.	4.0	4.0	
bgcolor="*Value*"	Applies a background color to all cells in the column (deprecated).		4.0	
span="*Value*"	Specifies the columns modified by the <col> tag.	4.0	3.0	6.1
valign="*Option*" (top | middle | bottom)	Specifies the vertical alignment of text within a column.	4.0	4.0	
width= "*Value*"	Specifies the width for each column or column group.	4.0	3.0	6.1
<colgroup> ... </colgroup>	Encloses a group of <col> tags, and groups columns together to set their alignment attributes.	4.0	3.1	6.1
align="*Option*" (char | center | justify | left | right)	Specifies the horizontal alignment of text within a column group.	4.0	4.1	
char="*Character*"	Specifies a character with which to align the values in the column (a period usually is used to align monetary values).	4.0		
charoff="*Value*"	Specifies the number of characters to offset the column data from the alignment character specified in the char attribute.	4.0		
span="*Value*"	Specifies the columns within the column group.	4.0	3.1	

TAGS AND ATTRIBUTES	DESCRIPTION	HTML	IE	NETSCAPE
valign="*Option*" (top | middle | bottom)	Specifies the vertical alignment of text within a column group.	4.0	4.1	
width= "*Value*"	Specifies the width of each column for the column group (deprecated).	4.0	4.1	
<dd>	Formats text to be used as definitions in a <dl> list.	2.0	1.0	1.0
<del> ... </del>	Used to indicate that text has been deleted from the document. Deleted text usually appears as strikethrough text.	3.0	4.0	6.1
cite="*URL*"	Specifies the URL for a document that has additional information about the deleted text.	4.0		
datetime="*Date*"	Specifies the date and time of the deletion.	4.0		
tabindex="Value"	Uses a number to identify an object's position in the tab order for keyboard navigation.		5.5	
<dfn> ... </dfn>	Used for the defining instance of a term, which is the first time the term is used. The enclosed text is usually italicized.	3.0	1.0	6.1
<div> ... </div>	Indicates a block of content for a document.	3.0	3.1	2.0
align="*Option*" (left | center | justify | right)	Horizontal alignment text options within the <div> tag.	3.0	3.0	3.0
<dl> ... </dl>	Encloses a definition list in which the <dd> definition term is left-aligned, and the <dt> relative definition is indented.	2.0	1.0	1.0
compact	Reduces the space between list items.	2.0	4.0	1.0
<dt>	Used to format the definition term in a <dl> list.	2.0	1.0	1.0
<em> ... </em>	Used to emphasize text. Typically, the enclosed text is displayed in italics.	2.0	1.0	1.0
<embed> ... </embed>	Specifies an object to be embedded in the document.		3.0	1.0
Accesskey = "*Character*"	Specifies a keyboard navigation accelerator for the element.		5.5	
autostart="*Option*" (true | false)	Specifies whether the embedded object should be started automatically when the page is loaded.		3.0	1.0
align="*Option*" (bottom | left | right | top)	Specifies the alignment of the embedded object with the surrounding text.		1.0	4.0
alt="*Text*"	Text to display if the browser cannot display the embedded object.		1.0	

TAGS AND ATTRIBUTES	DESCRIPTION	HTML	IE	NETSCAPE
border="*Value*"	The size of the border around the embedded object, in pixels.		1.0	
height="*Value*"	The height of the embedded object, in pixels.		1.0	4.0
hidden="*Option*" (true | false)	Specifies whether the embedded object is hidden or not.		4.0	
hspace="*Value*"	The amount of space to the left and right of the image, in pixels (deprecated).		4.0	
type="*Mime-Type*"	Specifies the data type of the embedded object.		4.0	
units="*Option*" (en | pixels)	Specifies the unit of measurement to be used with the embedded object.		4.0	
vspace="*Value*"	The amount of space above and below the embedded object, in pixels (deprecated).		4.0	
width="*Value*"	The width of the embedded object, in pixels.		1.0	4.0
\<fieldset\> ... \</fieldset\>	Allows designers to group form controls and labels, making it easier for users to understand the purpose of the control, and facilitating movement between fields.	4.0	4.2	6.2
accesskey="*Character*"	Specifies a keyboard navigation accelerator for the element.	4.0	5.5	
align="*Option*" (top | bottom | middle | left | right)	Specifies the alignment of the legend with respect to the field set (tag deprecated).	3.2	4.0	
\<font\> ... \</font\>	Controls the appearance of the text it encloses. Deprecated in favor of \<styles\>.	3.0	2.0	1.1
color="*Color*"	The color of the enclosed text.	3.0	2.0	2.0
face="*List*"	The font face of the text. Multiple font faces can be specified, separated by commas. The browser attempts to render the text in the order specified by the list.	3.0	2.0	3.0
point-size="*Value*"	Point size of the text (used with downloadable fonts).			4.0
size="*Value*"	Size of the font in points; it can be absolute or relative. Specifying a size=5 sets the font to 5 points. Specifying a size=+5 sets the font size 5 points larger than the size specified in the \<basefont\> tag.	3.0	2.0	4.0
weight="*Value*"	The weight of the font, ranging from 100 (the lightest) to 900 (the heaviest).			4.0

TAGS AND ATTRIBUTES	DESCRIPTION	HTML	IE	NETSCAPE
<form> … </form>	Marks the beginning and end of a Web page form.	2.0	1.0	1.0
action="*URL*"	Specifies the URL to which the contents of the form are to be sent.	2.0	1.0	1.0
autocomplete="*Option*" (yes | no)	Automatically finish filling in information the user has previously entered into an input field.		5.0	
enctype="*Text*"	Specifies the encoding type used to submit the data to the server.	2.0	1.0	1.0
hidefocus="*Option*" (true | false)	Hides focus on an element's content.		5.5	
method="*Option*" (post | get)	Specifies the method of accessing the URL indicated *in the action attribute.*	2.0	1.0	1.0
target="*Text*"	The frame or window that displays the results of the form.	4.0	3.0	2.0
<frame>	Defines a single frame within a set of frames.	4.0	3.0	2.0
bordercolor="*Color*"	Specifies the color of the frame border		4.0	3.5
frameborder="*Option*" (yes | no)	Specifies whether the frame border is visible.	4.0	3.0	3.5
hidefocus="*Option*" (true | false)	Hides focus on an element's content.		5.5	
longdesc="*URL*"	Specifies the URL of a document that contains a long description of the frame's content (used in conjunction with the title attribute).	4.0		
marginheight="*Value*"	Specifies the amount of space above and below the frame object and the frame borders.	4.0	3.0	2.0
marginwidth="*Value*"	Specifies the amount of space to the left and right of the frame object, in pixels.	4.0	3.0	2.0
name="*Text*"	Label assigned to the frame.	4.0	3.0	2.0
noresize	Prevents users from resizing the frame.	4.0	3.0	2.0
scrolling="*Option*" (yes | no | auto)	Specifies whether scroll bars are visible. ("auto" is the default and displays scroll bars as needed)	4.0	3.0	2.0
src="*URL*"	Specifies the document or URL of the object to be displayed in the frame.	4.0	3.0	2.0

TAGS AND ATTRIBUTES	DESCRIPTION	HTML	IE	NETSCAPE
`<frameset> ... </frameset>`	Marks the beginning and end of a set of frames.	4.0	3.0	2.0
border="*Value*"	The size of the frame borders, in pixels.		3.0	6.0
bordercolor="*Color*"	The color of the frame borders.		4.0	3.5
cols="*List*"	The size of each column in a set of frames. Columns can be specified as pixels, as a percentage of the display area, or with an asterisk (*) indicating that any remaining space be allotted to that column.	4.0	3.0	2.0
frameborder="*Option*" (yes | no)	Specifies whether the frame borders are visible.		3.0	3.5
framespacing="*Value*"	Specifies the amount of space between frames, in pixels.		3.1	
hidefocus="*Option*" (true | false)	Hides focus on the content of an element.		5.5	
rows="*List*"	The size of each row in a set of frames. Rows can be specified as pixels, as a percentage of the display area, or with an asterisk (*) indicating that any remaining space be allotted to that column.		3.0	2.0
`<h1> ... </h1>` `<h2> ... </h2>` `<h3> ... </h3>` `<h4> ... </h4>` `<h5> ... </h5>` `<h6> ... </h6>`	Used to display the six levels of text headings ranging from the largest (`<h1>`), to the smallest (`<h6>`).	2.0	1.0	1.0
align="*Option*" (left | right | center | justify)	The alignment of the heading (deprecated).	3.0	1.0	1.0
`<head> ... </head>`	Encloses code that provides information about the document.	2.0	1.0	1.0
`<hr>`	Creates a horizontal line.	2.0	1.0	1.0
align="*Option*" (left | center | right)	Alignment of the horizontal line (deprecated) (the default is "center")	3.2	1.0	1.1
color="*Color*"	Specifies a color for the line (deprecated).		3.0	
noshade	Removes 3D shading from the line (deprecated).	3.0	1.0	1.1
size="*Value*"	Specifies the thickness of the line, in pixels (deprecated).	3.2	1.0	1.1
width="*Value*"	Specified the width of the line in pixels or as a percentage of the display area (deprecated).	3.2	1.0	1.1

TAGS AND ATTRIBUTES	DESCRIPTION	HTML	IE	NETSCAPE
<html> ... </html>	Indicates the beginning and end of the HTML document.	2.0	1.0	1.0
xmlns = "*Text*"	Declares a namespace for XML-based custom tags in the document.		5.0	
<i> ... </i>	Italicizes the enclosed text.	2.0	1.0	1.0
<iframe> ... </iframe>	Allows a frame to be inserted within a block of text. Inserting an inline frame within a section of text allows you to insert one HTML document in the middle of another.	4.0	3.0	6.0
align="*Option*" (absbottom | absmiddle | baseline justify | left | middle | right | texttop)	Specifies the alignment for a floating frame (deprecated).	4.0	3.0	6.0
frameborder="*Option*" (yes | no)	Specifies whether the frame borders are visible.	4.0	3.0	6.0
height="*Value*"	Specifies the height of the floating frame, in pixels.	4.0	3.0	6.0
hspace="*Value*"	Specifies the horizontal space around the inline frame, in pixels.		3.0	
marginheight="*Value*"	Specifies the amount of space above and below the frame object and the frame borders.	4.0	3.0	6.0
marginwidth="*Value*"	Specifies the amount of space to the left and right of the frame object, in pixels.	4.0	3.0	6.0
name="*Text*"	Label assigned to the frame.	4.0	3.0	6.0
noresize	Prevents users from resizing the frame.		4.0	
scrolling="*Option*" (yes | no | auto)	Specifies whether scroll bars are visible (Auto is the default and displays scroll bars as needed).	4.0	3.0	6.0
src="*URL*"	Specifies the document or URL of the object to be displayed in the frame.	4.0	3.0	6.0
vspace="*Value*"	Specifies the vertical space around the inline frame, in pixels.		3.2	
width="*Value*"	Specifies the width of the floating frame, in pixels.	4.0	3.0	6.0
<ilayer> ... </ilayer>	Used to create an inflow layer with a relative position; it displays where it naturally would in the document.			4.0

TAGS AND ATTRIBUTES	DESCRIPTION	HTML	IE	NETSCAPE
above="*Text*"	Specifies the name of the layer to be displayed above the current layer.			4.0
background="*URL*"	Specifies the URL of the background image.			4.0
below="*Text*"	Specifies the name of the layer to be displayed below the current layer.			4.0
bgcolor="*Color*"	Specifies the background color of the layer.			4.0
clip="*top_x, left_y, bottom_x, right_y*"	Specifies the coordinates of the viewable region of the layer.			4.0
height="*Value*"	The height of the layer in pixels.			4.0
left="*Value*"	Specifies the horizontal offset of the layer, in pixels.			4.0
pagex="*Value*"	Specifies the horizontal position of the layer.			4.0
pagey="*Value*"	Specifies the vertical position of the layer.			4.0
src="*URL*"	Specifies the URL of the document displayed in the layer.			4.0
top="*Value*"	Specifies the vertical offset of the layer, in pixels.			4.0
visibility="*Option*" (hide | inherit | show)	Specifies whether the layer is hidden, shown, or inherits its visibility from the layer that contains it.			4.0
width="*Value*"	The width of the layer, in pixels			4.0
z-index="*Value*"	Specifies the stacking order of the layer relative to the other layers.			4.0
<img>	Used to insert an inline image into the document.	2.0	1.0	1.0
align="*Option*" (left | right | top | texttop | middle | absmiddle | baseline | bottom | absbottom)	Specifies the alignment of the image. Specifying an alignment of left or right aligns the image with the left or right page margin. The other alignment options align the image with surrounding text (deprecated).	2.0	1.0	1.1
alt="*Text*"	Text to display if the browser cannot display the image.	2.0	1.0	1.1
border="*Value*"	The size of the border around the image, in pixels (deprecated).	3.2	1.0	1.1
controls	Displays VCR-like controls under moving images (used in conjunction with the dynsrc attribute).		2.0	

TAGS AND ATTRIBUTES	DESCRIPTION	HTML	IE	NETSCAPE
dynsrc="*URL*"	Specifies the file of a video, AVI clip, or VRML worlds shown inside the page.		2.0	
height="*Value*"	The height of the image, in pixels.	3.0	1.0	1.1
hidefocus="*Option*" (true | false)	Hides focus on the content of an element.		5.5	
hspace="*Value*"	The amount of space to the left and right of the image, in pixels (deprecated).	3.0	1.0	1.1
ismap	Identifies the image as an image map (for use with server-side image maps).	3.0	2.0	2.0
longdesc="*URL*"	The URL of a document that contains a long description of the image (used in conjunction with the alt attribute).	4.0		
loop="*Value*"	Specifies the number of times a moving image should be played (*Value* must be either a digit or "infinite").		2.0	
lowsrc="*URL*"	A low-resolution version of an image that the browser initially displays before loading the high-resolution version.		4.1	1.0
name="*Name*"	Binds the *Name* to the image.	4.0	4.0	3.0
src="*URL*"	The source file of the inline image.	2.0	1.0	1.0
start="*Option*" (fileopen | mouseover)	Tells the browser when to start displaying a moving image file. Fileopen instructs the browser to start when the file is open; mouseover instructs the browser to start when the mouse pointer moves over the image.		2.0	
suppress="*Option*" (true | false)	Suppresses the placeholder icon and any ALT text until the image is located (if suppress="true").			4.0
tabindex="*Value*"	Uses a number to identify the object's position in the tab order for keyboard navigation.		5.5	
usemap="*#Map_Name*"	Identifies the image as an image map and specifies the name of the image map definition to use with the image (for use with client-side image maps).	3.2	1.0	2.0
vspace="*Value*"	The amount of space above and below the image, in pixels (deprecated).	3.2	1.0	1.1
width="*Value*"	The width of the image, in pixels.	3.0	1.0	1.1

TAGS AND ATTRIBUTES	DESCRIPTION	HTML	IE	NETSCAPE
\<input> ... \</input>	Creates an input object for use in a Web page form.	1.0	2.0	1.0
accesskey="*Character*"	Specifies an accelerator key for the element, which can be accessed by pressing the *Character* key along with the Alt key.	4.0	4.0	
align="*Option*" (left | right | top | texttop | middle | absmiddle | baseline | bottom | absbottom)	Specifies the alignment of an input image (similar to the align attribute with the \<img> tag).	2.0	2.0	1.1
alt="*Text*"	Alternate text description of image buttons for browsers that do not support inline images.	4.0	4.0	
checked	Specifies that an input check box or input radio button is selected.	2.0	1.0	1.0
disabled	Disables the control.	4.0	4.0	
maxlength="*Value*"	Specifies the maximum number of characters that can be inserted into an input text box.	2.0	1.0	1.0
name="*Text*"	The label given to the input object.	2.0	1.0	1.0
readonly	Prevents the value of the control from being modified.	4.0	4.0	6.1
size="*Value*"	The visible size, in characters, of an input text box.	2.0	1.0	1.0
src="*URL*"	The source file of the graphic used for an input image object.	2.0	1.0	1.0
tabindex="*Value*"	Specifies the tab order in the form.	4.0	4.0	6.3
type="*Option*" (checkbox | hidden | image | password | radio | reset | buttonsubmit | text | file)	Specifies the type of input object.	2.0	1.0	1.0
usemap="*#Map_Name*"	Identifies the input image as an image map (similar to the usemap attribute used with the \<img> tag).	4.0		2.0
value="*Value*"	Specifies the information that initially appears in the input object.	2.0	2.0	2.0
width="*Value*"	The width of the input image, in pixels		4.1	1.1
\<ins> ... \</ins>	Indicates that the text has been inserted into the document.	3.0	4.0	6.2
cite="*URL*"	Specifies the URL for a document that has additional information about the inserted text.		4.0	

TAGS AND ATTRIBUTES	DESCRIPTION	HTML	IE	NETSCAPE
datetime="*Date*"	Specifies the date and time of the insertion.		4.0	
<isindex>	Identifies the file as a searchable document. Deprecated in favor of <input>.	2.0	1.0	1.0
action="*CGI Script*"	Sends the submitted text to the program identified by *CGI Script*.		1.0	1.0
prompt="*Text*"	The text to be placed before the text-input field.	3.0	1.0	1.1
<label> ... </label>	Used to create labels for form controls.	4.0	4.0	6.2
accesskey="*Character*"	Specifies an accelerator key for the element, which can be accessed by pressing the *Character* key along with the Alt key.	4.0	4.0	6.2
datafld="*Text*"	Specifies the column from a data source that supplies bound data for use with the label.		4.0	6.2
dataformatas="*Option*" (text | html)	Specifies whether the data in the data source column is formatted as plain text or as HTML code.		4.0	6.2
datasrc="*Text*"	Specifies the ID of the data source that is to be used with the label.		4.0	
for="*Text*"	Indicates the name or ID of the element to which the label is applied.	4.0	4.0	6.2
<layer> ... </layer>	Used to create an inflow layer with an absolutely defined position in the document.			4.0
above="*Text*"	Specifies the name of the layer to be displayed above the current layer.			4.0
background="*URL*"	Specifies the URL of the background image			4.0
below="*Text*"	Specifies the name of the layer to be displayed below the current layer.			4.0
bgcolor="*Color*"	Specifies the background color of the layer.			4.0
clip="*top_x, left_y, bottom_x, right_y*"	Specifies the coordinates of the viewable region of the layer.			4.0
height="*Value*"	Specifies the height of the layer, in pixels.			4.0
left="*Value*"	Specifies the horizontal offset of the layer, in pixels.			4.0
pagex="*Value*"	Specifies the horizontal position of the layer.			4.0
pagey="*Value*"	Specifies the vertical position of the layer.			4.0
src="*URL*"	Specifies the URL of the document displayed in the layer.			4.0

TAGS AND ATTRIBUTES	DESCRIPTION	HTML	IE	NETSCAPE
top="*Value*"	Specifies the vertical offset of the layer, in pixels.			4.0
visibility="*Option*" (hide | inherit | show)	Specifies whether the layer is hidden, shown, or inherits its visibility from the layer that contains it.			4.0
width="*Value*"	Specifies the width of the layer, in pixels.			4.0
z-index="*Value*"	Specifies the stacking order of the layer relative to the other layers.		4.0	
<legend> ... </legend>	Allows a caption to be assigned to a fieldset (see the <fieldset> tag above).	4.0	4.0	6.2
accesskey="*Character*"	Specifies an accelerator key for the element, which can be accessed by pressing the *Character* key along with the Alt key.	4.0	4.0	6.2
align="*Option*" (top | bottom | left | right)	Specifies the position of the legend with respect to the field set.	4.0	4.0	6.2
<li>	Identifies list items in a <dir>.	2.0	1.0	1.0
<map> ... </map>	Specifies information about a client-side image map (note that it must enclose <area> tags).	3.2	1.0	1.0
name="*Text*"	The name of the image map.	3.2	1.0	2.0
<marquee> ... </marquee>	Used to create an area containing scrolling text.		2.0	
align="*Option*" (top | middle | bottom)	The alignment of the scrolling text within the marquee.		2.0	
behavior="*Option*" (scroll | slide | alternate)	Controls the behavior of the text in the marquee. scroll causes the text to repeatedly scroll across the page, slide causes the text to slide onto the page and stop at the margin, alternate causes the text to move from margin to margin.		2.0	
bgcolor="*Color*"	The background color of the marquee.		2.0	
datfld="*Text*"	The column name in the data source that is bound to the marquee.		4.0	
dataformatas="*Option*" (text | html)	Indicates the format of the bound data.		4.0	
direction="*Option*" (left | right | down | up)	The direction that the text scrolls on the page.		2.0	
height="*Value*"	The height of the marquee, either in pixels or as a percentage of the display area.		2.0	

TAGS AND ATTRIBUTES	DESCRIPTION	HTML	IE	NETSCAPE
hidefocus="*Option*" (true | false)	Hides focus on the content of an element.		5.5	
hspace="*Value*"	The amount of space to the left and right of the marquee, in pixels.		2.0	
loop="*Value*"	The number of times the marquee is scrolled (the "*Value*" must be either a digit or infinite.		2.0	
scrollamount="*Value*"	The amount of space between successive draws of the text in the marquee.		2.0	
scrolldelay="*Value*"	The amount of time between scrolling actions, in milliseconds.		2.0	
tabindex="*Value*"	Uses a number to identify the object's position In the tabbing order for keyboard navigation.	4.0	5.5	
truespeed="*Value*"	Indicates that the scrolldelay attribute value should be honored for its exact value, otherwise any value less than 60 milliseconds is rounded up.		4.0	
vspace="*Value*"	The amount of space above and below the marquee, in pixels.		2.0	
width="*Value*"	The width of the marquee, in pixels or as a percentage of the display area.		2.0	
<menu> ... </menu>	Encloses an unordered list of items, similar to a <ul> or <dir> list. Deprecated in favor of <ul>.	2.0	1.0	1.0
compact	Reduces the space between menu items.	2.0		
<meta>	Identifies information about the document not defined by other HTML tags and attributes; it can include special instructions for the Web server.	2.0	1.0	1.0
content="*Text*"	Contains information associated with the Name or http-equiv attributes.	2.0	2.0	1.1
http-equiv="*Text*"	Instructs the browser to request the server to perform different http operations.	2.0	2.0	1.1
name="*Text*"	The type of information specified in the content attribute.	2.0	2.0	1.1
<nobr> ... </nobr>	Prevents line breaks for the enclosed text. This tag is not often used.		1.0	1.1
<noembed> ... </noembed>	Used to display alternate content for older browsers that do not support the <embed> tag.		3.0	2.0

TAGS AND ATTRIBUTES	DESCRIPTION	HTML	IE	NETSCAPE
<noframes> … </noframes>	Enables browsers that do not support frames to display a page that uses frames (the tag encloses the <body> tag).	4.0	3.0	2.0
<noscript> … </noscript>	Used to enclose HTML tags for browsers that do not support client-side scripts.	4.0	3.0	3.5
<object> … </object>	Allows designers to control whether data is rendered externally or by a program, specified by the author, that renders the data within the user agent. (Most browsers have built-in mechanisms for rendering common data types such as text, GIF images, colors, fonts, and a handful of graphic elements.)	4.0	3.1	6.1
accesskey="*Character*"	Specifies an accelerator key for the object, which can be accessed by pressing the *Character* key along with the Alt key.		4.0	
archive="*URL*"	Specifies the URL of an archive containing classes and other resources that are preloaded for use with the object.	4.0		6.0
align="*Option*" (top | bottom | middle | left | right)	Specifies the alignment of the embedded object, relative to the surrounding text (deprecated).	4.0	3.0	6.1
border="*Value*"	Specifies the width of the embedded object's border, in pixels.	4.0		6.0
classid="*URL*"	Specifies the URL of the embedded object.	4.0	3.0	6.0
codebase="*URL*"	Specifies the base path used to resolve relative references within the embedded object.	4.0	3.0	6.0
codetype="*Text*"	Specifies the type of data object.	4.0	3.0	6.0
data="*URL*"	Specifies the location of data for the embedded object.	4.0	3.0	6.0
datafld="*Text*"	Specifies the column from a data source that supplies bound data for use with the object.		4.0	
datasrc="*Text*"	Specifies the ID of the data source to be used with the object.		4.0	
declare	Declares the object without installing it in the page.	4.0		
height="*Value*"	Specifies the height of the embedded object, in pixels.	4.0	3.0	6.0
hidefocus ="*Option*" (true | false)	Hides focus on the content of the element.		5.5	

TAGS AND ATTRIBUTES	DESCRIPTION	HTML	IE	NETSCAPE
hspace="*Value*"	Specifies the horizontal space around the embedded object, in pixels (deprecated).	4.0	3.0	6.0
name="*Text*"	Specifies the name of the embedded object.	4.0	3.0	6.0
standby="*Text*"	Specifies a message for the browser to display while rendering the embedded object.	4.0		
tabindex="*Value*"	Specifies the tab order of the object when it is placed in a form.	4.0	4.0	
type="*Mime-Type*"	Specifies the data type of the object.	4.0	3.0	6.0
usemap="*URL*"	The URL of the image map to be used with the object.	4.0		6.1
vspace="*Value*"	Specifies the vertical space around the embedded object, in pixels.	4.0	3.0	6.1
width="*Value*"	Specifies the width of the embedded object, in pixels.	4.0	3.0	6.1
<ol> ... </ol>	Encloses an ordered list of <li> items. Typically, ordered lists are rendered as numbered lists.	2.0	1.0	1.0
compact	Reduces the space between ordered list items.	2.0		
start="*Value*"	The value of the starting number in the ordered list (deprecated).	3.2	2.0	2.0
type="*Option*" (A l a l I l i l 1)	Specifies how ordered items are marked. A=uppercase letters, a=lowercase letters, I=uppercase Roman numerals, i=lowercase Roman numerals, and 1 (default)=digits (deprecated).	3.2	1.0	1.0
<optgroup> ... </optgroup>	Used to create a grouping of items in a selection list, as defined by the <option> tag.	4.0	6.0	6.0
disabled	Disables the group of option items.	4.0		6.0
label="*Text*"	Specifies a label for the option group.	4.0		6.0
<option> ... </option>	Used for each item in a selection list. This tag must be placed within <select> tags.	2.0	1.0	1.0
disabled	Disables the option item.	3.0	4.0	6.0
selected	The default or selected option in the selection list.	2.0	1.0	1.0
value="*Value*"	The value returned to the server when the user selects this option.	2.0	1.0	1.0

TAGS AND ATTRIBUTES	DESCRIPTION	HTML	IE	NETSCAPE
`<p> ... </p>`	Defines the beginning and end of a paragraph of text.	2.0	1.0	1.0
align="*Option*" (left | center | right)	The alignment of the paragraph text (deprecated).	3.0	1.0	1.1
`<param> ... </param>`	Specifies a set of values that may be required by an object at run-time. Any number of param elements may display in the content of an `<object>` or `<applet>` tag, in any order, but they must be located at the start of the content in the enclosing `<object>` or `<applet>` tag.	3.2	3.0	2.0
datafld="*Text*"	Specifies the column name in the data source that is bound to the parameter's value.		4.0	
dataformatas="*Option*" (text | html)	Specifies whether the data in the data source column is formatted as plain text or as HTML code.		4.0	
datasrc="*URL*"	Specifies the URL of the data source from which to draw the data.		4.0	
name="*Text*"	Specifies the name of the parameter.	3.2	3.0	2.0
value="*Text*"	Specifies the value of the parameter.	3.2	3.0	2.0
valuetype="*Option*" (data | ref | object)	Specifies the type of the value attribute.	4.0	6.0	
`<plaintext> ... </plaintext>`	Displays text in a fixed-width (monospace) font. It is supported, although inconsistently, by some early versions of Netscape.	2.0	1.0	1.0
`<pre> ... </pre>`	Retains the preformatted appearance of the text in the HTML file, including any line breaks or spaces, and is usually displayed in a fixed-width (monspace) font.	2.0	2.0	1.0
`<q> ... </q>`	Identifies the enclosed text as a short quotation.	3.0	4.0	6.2
cite="*URL*"	Specifies the URL for a document containing additional information about the quoted text.	4.0		6.2
`<rt>`	Used with the `<ruby>` element to create "ruby text," or annotations or pronunciation guides for words and phrases.		5.0	
`<ruby>...</ruby>`	Used with the `<rt>` element to create annotations or pronunciation guides for words and phrases.	4.0	5.0	

TAGS AND ATTRIBUTES	DESCRIPTION	HTML	IE	NETSCAPE
`<s> ... </s>`	Displays the enclosed text with a horizontal line striking through it. Deprecated in favor of `<del>`.	4.0	2.0	3.0
`<samp> ... </samp>`	Displays text in a fixed-width font.	2.0	1.0	1.0
`<script> ... </script>`	Places a client-side script withina document. This element may be displayed any number of times in the head or body of an HTML document.	3.2	3.0	3.0
defer	Instructs the browser to defer executing the script.	4.0	4.0	
event="*Text*"	Specifies an event in response to which, a script should be run (this attribute must be used in conjunction with the for attribute).	4.0	4.0	
for="*Text*"	Indicates the name or ID of the element to which an event, defined by the event attribute, is applied.	4.0	4.0	
language="*Text*"	Specifies the language of the client-side script (see JavaScript for JavaScript commands).	4.0	3.0	3.0
src="*URL*"	Specifies the source of the external script file.	4.0	3.0	3.0
type="*Mime-Type*"	Specifies the data type of the scripting language (use text/javascript for JavaScript commands).	4.0	4.0	
`<select> ... </select>`	Encloses a set of `<option>` tags for use in creating selection lists.	2.0	2.0	2.0
accesskey="*Character*"	Specifies an accelerator key for the element, which can be accessed by pressing the *Character* key along with the Alt key.	4.0	4.0	
align="*Option*" (left | right | top | texttop | middle | absmiddle | baseline | bottom | absbottom)	Specifies the alignment of an input image (similar to the align option with the `<img>` tag)	2.0	2.0	1.1
disabled	Disables the selection list.	4.0	4.0	
hidefocus="*Option*" (true | false)	Hides focus on the content of an element.		5.5	
multiple	Allows the user to select multiple options from a selection list.	2.0	2.0	2.0
name="*Text*"	The name assigned to the selection list.	2.0	2.0	2.0
size="*Value*"	The number of visible items in the selection list.	2.0	2.0	2.0
tabindex="*Value*"	Specifies the tab order in the form.	4.0	4.0	

TAGS AND ATTRIBUTES	DESCRIPTION	HTML	IE	NETSCAPE
`<small> ... </small>`	Decreases the size of the enclosed text. The exact appearance of the text depends on the browser and the default font size (deprecated).	3.0	3.0	2.0
`<span> ... </span>`	Acts as a container for inline content.	4.0	3.0	4.0
datafld=*"Text"*	Specifies the column of a data source that supplies bound data for use with the spanned text.		4.0	
dataformatas=*"Option"* (text | html)	Specifies whether the data in the data source column is formatted as plain text or HTML code.		4.0	
datasrc=*"Text"*	Specifies the ID of the data source that is to be used with the spanned text.		4.0	
`<strike> ... </strike>`	Displays the enclosed text with a horizontal line striking through it. Deprecated in favor of `<del>`.	3.2	2.0	3.0
`<strong> ... </strong>`	Used to place emphasis on the enclosed text, usually with a bold font.	2.0	1.0	1.0
`<style> ... </style>`	Encloses style declarations for the document.	4.0	3.0	4.0
disabled	Disables the style declarations.		4.0	
media=*"Option"* (all | aural | Braille | print | projection | screen)	Specifies the destination medium for the style information.	4.0	4.0	
type=*"Text"*	Defines the type of stylesheet.	3.2	3.0	4.0
`<sub> ... </sub>`	Displays the enclosed text as a subscript.	2.0	3.0	2.0
`<sup> ... </sup>`	Displays the enclosed text as a superscript.	2.0	3.0	2.0
`<table> ... </table>`	The `<table>` tag is used to identify the beginning and end of a table.	2.0	1.0	1.1
align=*"Option"* (char | left | center | right)	Specifies the horizontal alignment of the table on the page (deprecated).	3.0	3.0	2.0
background= *"URL"*	Specifies a background image for the table.	3.0	4.0	
bgcolor=*"Color"*	Specifies a background color for the table (deprecated).	4.0	2.0	3.0
border=*"Value"*	Specifies the width of the table border, in pixels.	3.0	2.0	2.0
bordercolor=*"Color"*	Specifies the color of the table border.		4.0	
bordercolordark=*"Color"*	Specifies the color of the shaded edge of the table border.		2.0	
bordercolorlight=*"Color"*	Specifies the color of the unshaded edge of the table border.		2.0	

TAGS AND ATTRIBUTES	DESCRIPTION	HTML	IE	NETSCAPE
cellpadding="*Value*"	Specifies the space between table cells, in pixels.	3.2	2.0	1.1
cellspacing="*Value*"	Specifies the space between cell text and the cell border, in pixels.	3.2	2.0	1.1
cols="*Value*"	Specifies the number of columns in the table.	3.0	3.1	4.2
rows="*Value*"	Specifies the number of rows that can be displayed in the table when data binding is used.	4.0	4.0	
datasrc="*URL*"	Specifies the URL of the table's data source.	4.0	3.0	6.0
frame="*Option*" (above | below | box | hsides | lhs | rhs | void | vsides)	Specifies the display of table borders: above = top border only, below = bottom border only, box = borders on all four sides, hsides = top and bottom borders, lhs = left side border, rhs = right side border, void = no borders, vsides =left and right side borders.	4.0	3.1	6.0
height="*Value*"	The height of the table, in pixels or as a percentage of the display area.		2.0	1.1
hspace="*Value*"	Specifies the horizontal space, in pixels, between the table and surrounding text.			2.0
rules="*Option*" (all | cols | none | rows)	Specifies the display of internal table borders: all = borders between every row and column, cols = borders between every column, none = no internal table borders, rows = borders between every row.	4.0	3.0	
vspace="*Value*"	Specifies the vertical space, in pixels, between the table and surrounding text.			2.0
width="*Value*"	The width of the table, in pixels or as a percentage of the display area.	3.0	2.0	1.0
<tbody> ... </tbody>	Identifies text displayed in the table body, as opposed to text in the table header, <thead> tag, or in the table footer, <tbody> tag.	4.0	4.0	6.0
align="*Option*" (char | left | center | right)	The horizontal alignment of text in the cells of the table body.	4.0	4.0	6.1
bgcolor="*Color*"	Specifies a background color for the table body.		4.0	6.1
char="*Character*"	Specifies a character with which to align the values in the column.	4.0		
charoff="*Value*"	Specifies the number of characters to offset the column data from the alignment character specified in the char attribute.	4.0		

TAGS AND ATTRIBUTES	DESCRIPTION	HTML	IE	NETSCAPE
valign="*Option*" (top │ middle │ bottom)	The vertical alignment of text in the cells in the table body.	4.0	4.0	6.1
<td> ... </td>	Encloses the text to display in a table cell.	2.0	2.0	1.1
abbr="*Text*"	Specifies an abbreviated name for the header cell.	4.0		
align="*Option*" (left │ center │ right)	Specifies the horizontal alignment of cell text.	2.0	2.0	2.0
axis="*Text*"	Specifies a name for a group of related table headers.	4.0		
background="*URL*"	Specifies a background image for the cell.	4.0	4.0	
bgcolor="*Color*"	Specifies a background color for the cell.	4.0	2.0	3.0
bordercolor="*Color*"	Specifies the color of the cell border.		2.0	
bordercolordark="*Color*"	Specifies the color of the shaded edge of the cell border.		2.0	
bordercolorlight="*Color*"	Specifies the color of the unshaded edge of the cell border.		2.0	
colspan="*Value*"	Specifies the number of columns to span the cell.	3.2	2.0	2.0
height="*Value*"	The height of the cell, in pixels or as a percentage of the display area.	3.2	2.0	2.0
nowrap	Prohibits the browser from wrapping text in the cell (deprecated).	3.0	2.0	1.1
rowspan="*Value*"	Specifies the number of rows to span the cell.	3.2	2.0	1.1
scope="*Option*" (col │ colgroup │ row │ rowgroup)	Specifies the table cells for which the current cell provides header information. A scope value of col indicates that the cell is a header for the rest of the column, colgroup indicates that the cell is a header for the current column group, row indicates that the cell is a header for the current row, and rowgroup indicates that the cell is a he ader for the current row group.	4.0		
valign="*Option*" (top │ middle │ bottom)	Specifies the vertical alignment of cell text.	3.0	2.0	1.1
width= "*Value*"	The width of the cell, in pixels or as a percentage of the width of the table (deprecated).	3.2	2.0	1.1
<textarea> ... </textarea>	Creates a text box.	2.0	2.0	1.0
accesskey="*Character*"	Specifies an accelerator key for the element, which can be accessed by pressing the *Character* key along with the Alt key.	4.0	4.0	6.2

TAGS AND ATTRIBUTES	DESCRIPTION	HTML	IE	NETSCAPE
cols="*Value*"	Specifies the height of the text box, in characters.	2.0	2.0	2.0
disabled	Disables the text area.	4.0	4.0	
name="*Text*"	Specifies the name assigned to the text box.	2.0	2.0	1.0
readonly	Prevents the text area's value from being modified.	4.0	4.0	6.1
rows="*Value*"	Specifies the width of the text box, in characters.	2.0	2.0	2.0
tabindex="*Value*"	Specifies the tab order in the form.	4.0	4.0	6.3
wrap="*Option*" (off | virtual | physical)	Specifies how text is wrapped within the text box: off turns off text wrapping, virtual wraps the text but sends the text to the server as a single line, physical wraps the text and sends the text to the server as it appears in the text box.		4.0	2.0
<tfoot> ... </tfoot>	Encloses footer information that is displayed in the table footer when the table prints on multiple pages.	4.0	3.0	6.1
align="*Option*" (char | center | left | right)	The horizontal alignment of the table footer.	4.0	4.0	6.1
bgcolor="*Color*"	Specifies a background color for the table footer.		4.0	6.1
char="*Character*"	Specifies a character with which to align the values in the column.	4.0	4.1	6.1
charoff="*Value*"	Specifies the number of characters to offset the column data from the alignment character specified in the char attribute.	4.0		
valign="*Option*" (top | middle | bottom)	The vertical alignment of the table footer.	4.0	4.0	6.1
<th> ... </th>	Encloses the text that displays in an individual table header cell.	3.0	2.0	1.1
abbr="*Text*"	Specifies an abbreviated name for the header cell.	4.0		
align="*Option*" (center | char | left | right)	Specifies the horizontal alignment of header cell text.	3.0	2.0	1.1
background="*URL*"	Specifies a background image for the header cell.		3.1	4.3
bgcolor="*Color*"	Specifies a background color for the header cell.	4.0	2.0	3.0

TAGS AND ATTRIBUTES	DESCRIPTION	HTML	IE	NETSCAPE
bordercolor="*Color*"	Specifies the color of the header cell border.		2.0	
bordercolordark="*Color*"	Specifies the color of the shaded edge of the header cell border.		3.0	
bordercolorlight="*Color*"	Specifies the color of the unshaded edge of the header cell border.		2.0	
char="*Character*"	Specifies a character with which to align the values in the column.	4.0		
charoff="*Value*"	Specifies the number of characters to offset the column data from the alignment character specified in the char attribute.	4.0		
colspan="*Value*"	Specifies the number of columns to span the header cell.	3.0	2.0	1.1
headers="*List*"	Specifies a list of ID values that correspond to the header cells related to this cell.	4.0		
height="*Value*"	The height of the header cell, in pixels or as a percentage of the display area.	3.2	2.0	1.1
nowrap	Prohibits the browser from wrapping text in the header cell.	3.0	2.0	1.1
rowspan="*Value*"	Specifies the number of rows to span the header cell.	3.0	2.0	1.1
scope="*Option*" (col | colgroup | row | rowgroup)	Specifies the table cells for which the current cell provides header information. A scope value of col indicates that the cell is a header for the rest of the column, colgroup indicates that the cell is a header for the current column group, row indicates that the cell is a header for the current row, and rowgroup indicates that the cell is a header for the current row group.	4.0		
valign="*Option*" (top | middle | bottom)	Specifies the vertical alignment of header cell text.	3.0	2.0	1.1
width= "*Value*"	The width of the header cell in pixels or as a percentage of the width of the table.	3.2	2.0	1.1
<thead> ... </thead>	Encloses header information that is displayed in the table header when the table is printed on multiple pages.	3.0	3.0	
align="*Option*" (left | center | right)	The horizontal alignment of the table header.	4.0	4.1	6.1
bgcolor="*Color*"	Specifies a background color for the table cells within the <thead> tags.		4.0	

TAGS AND ATTRIBUTES	DESCRIPTION	HTML	IE	NETSCAPE
char="*Character*"	Specifies a character with which to align the values in the table header columns.	4.0		
charoff="*Value*"	Specifies the number of characters to offset the column data from the alignment character as specified in the char attribute.	4.0		
valign="*Option*" (top | middle | bottom)	The vertical alignment of the table header.	4.0	4.1	6.1
<title> ... </title>	Specifies the text that displays in the title bar.	2.0	1.0	1.1
<tr> ... </tr>	Encloses table cells within a single row.	3.0	2.0	1.1
align="*Option*" (left | center | right)	Specifies the horizontal alignment of text in a row.	3.0	2.0	1.1
bgcolor="*Color*"	Specifies a background color for the header cell.	4.0	2.0	3.0
bordercolor="*Color*"	Specifies the color of the header cell border.		2.0	
bordercolordark="*Color*"	Specifies the color of the shaded edge of the header cell border.		2.0	
bordercolorlight="*Color*"	Specifies the color of the unshaded edge of the header cell border.		2.0	
char="*Character*"	Specifies a character with which to align the Values in the table row.	4.0		
charoff="*Value*"	Specifies the number of characters to offset the column data from the alignment character as specified in the char attribute.	4.0		
valign="*Option*"	The vertical alignment of the text in the table row	3.0	2.0	2.0
<tt> ... </tt>	Displays text in a fixed-width, or monospace, font.	2.0	1.0	1.0
<u> ... </u>	Underlines the enclosed text. The <u> tag should be avoided because it can be confused with hypertext links, which are often underlined. Deprecated in favor of <styles>.	3.0	1.0	3.5
<ul> ... </ul>	Encloses an unordered list of <li> items. Typically, unordered lists are rendered as bulleted lists.	2.0	1.0	1.0
compact	Reduces the space between unordered list items.	2.0		
Type="*Option*" (circle | disk | square)	Specifies the type of bullet used for displaying each <li> item in the <ul> list.	3.2	4.0	1.0
<var> ... </var>	Used for text that represents a variable and is typically displayed in italics.	2.0	1.0	1.0

TAGS AND ATTRIBUTES	DESCRIPTION	HTML	IE	NETSCAPE
<wbr> ... </wbr>	Used in conjunction with the <nobr> tag, this tag overrides tags that may preclude the use of line breaks and instructsthe browser to insert a line break if necessary. This tag is not often used.		1.0	1.0
<xmp> ... </xmp>	Displays blocks of text in a fixed-width, or monospace, font. This tag is obsolete and should not be used. Deprecated in favor of the <pre> tag.	2.0	1.0	1.0

WORKING WITH XHTML

Introducing XHTML

XHTML (Extensible Hypertext Markup Language) represents the next phase in the development of markup languages for the World Wide Web. In order to understand what XHTML is and why it was created, we first have to look back at the development of the Web itself.

SGML

XHTML has its roots in the Standard Generalized Markup Language (SGML). Introduced in the 1980s, SGML was a vehicle used to create the general structure of markup languages. SGML is device-independent and system-independent, which means that it can be used with almost any type of document stored in almost any format. SGML has been widely used to create documents in businesses and government organizations of all sizes. For example, think of the daunting task of documenting all of the parts used in manufacturing the space shuttle while at the same time, creating a structure that shuttle engineers can use to quickly retrieve and edit that information. SGML provides tools to manage documentation projects of this magnitude.

But there is a price to pay to support such complex document; thus, SGML is limited to those organizations that can afford the cost and overhead of maintaining large SGML environments. SGML is most useful for creating applications, based on the SGML architecture, that apply to specific types of documents. The most famous of these applications is Hypertext Markup Language, or HTML, the language of the World Wide Web.

HTML

The success of the World Wide Web is due in no small part to HTML. HTML allows Web authors to easily create documents that can be displayed across different operating systems. Creating Web sites with HTML is a straight forward process that does not require a programming background. This ease of use has made it popular with many different types of users. Millions of Web sites have been created with HTML, and there is every indication that HTML will continue to be an important language of the Web for a long time to come.

Despite its popularity, HTML is not without limitations and flaws that continue to frustrate Web designers. The major problem is that people are interested in Web pages not only for their appearance, but also for their *content*, and HTML was not designed with data content in mind. The wide variety of HTML tags can help a Web designer describe how the page should display, but it is more difficult to use those same tags to describe what the page *is*.

In response to this limitation, developers have added features to HTML, such as the CLASS attribute, that allow Web designers to attach descriptive information to each tag. Web designers can also make use of the <meta> tag to record information about the contents of a document. These additional HTML features are helpful, but they don't entirely solve the problem of effectively describing and cataloging data in an HTML document.

A second problem of HTML is that it is not extensible and therefore can't be modified to meet specific needs. As a result of the demands of the market and competition, the various Web browsers have developed their own unique flavors of HTML. Netscape Communicator saw a need for frames, so it introduced a version of HTML that included the <frameset> and <frame> tags, both of which were not part of standard HTML. Internet Explorer saw a need for internal frames and introduced the <iframe> tag, and that innovation also represented a departure from standard HTML.

The result was a confusing mix of competing HTML standards, one for each browser and indeed, each browser version. The innovations offered by Netscape, Internet Explorer, and others certainly increased the scope and power of HTML, but they did so at the expense of clarity. Web designers could not easily create Web sites without taking into account the cross-browser compatibility of the code in the Web pages.

Finally, HTML can be inconsistently applied. Some browsers require all tag attributes to be enclosed within quotes; some don't. Some browsers require all paragraphs to include an ending </p> tag; others do not. The lack of standards can make it easier to write HTML code, but it also means that code that is read by one browser may be rejected by another. This also has an impact on the design of Web browsers. Knowing that HTML would be inconsistently applied, browser developers must increase the size and complexity of their software in order to accommodate all possible contingencies. That's a headache for the developers, but it's also a problem for consumers. In recent years the Web has branched out, leaving behind desktop computers and workstations and moving toward smaller, handheld devices. Those smaller devices limit the size of the software that can be run on them. If HTML could be made "cleaner," it would be easier for a handheld device to access the Web.

Due partly to the reasons just outlined, the Web was in need of a language that could more effectively handle data content, be easily customized by developers, but at the same time be consistent and rigid enough for developers to easily develop applications for. In response to these needs, XML was created.

XML

Like HTML, the specifications for **XML (Extensible Markup Language)** are developed by the W3C. The consortium established 10 design goals for the language that promised, among other things, that XML would be easy to develop and use, accessible to nonprogrammers, and compatible with SGML. While XML is sometimes referred to as a markup language, it is actually more of a meta-markup language because it is a markup language that is used to create other markup languages. Unlike HTML, which is an SGML application, XML should be considered a subset of SGML—without SGML's complexity and overhead. XML has been used to create a variety of markup languages, including MathML used for mathematical documents and CML for documenting chemical structures.

One of the major differences between HTML and XML is that XML documents must fulfill requirements for both syntax and content. XML documents fall into two categories: well-formed and valid. A **well-formed** XML document is one that fulfills the basic syntax of XML. A **valid** XML document is a well-formed document that, in addition, fulfills criteria defined by the user for both content and structure. For example, an XML author can control the type of data entered into an XML document and define how it is entered. This is done by attaching a **document type definition (DTD)** to the document that defines how data is stored in the document. In order to confirm that an XML document is either well-formed or valid, it must be processed with an **XML parser**. A document that is neither well-formed nor valid is rejected by the parser. XML thereby avoids the irregularity that plagues HTML, but allows XML authors some flexibility in designing their own DTDs for special needs.

XHTML

This takes us back to XHTML, which combines the features of HTML and XML. An XHTML document is actually an XML document, but the structure and content conform to what we think of as HTML. This means that an XHTML document has to be well-formed, obeying the syntax rules of XML, and valid, obeying the rules for content and structure defined by any DTD attached to the document.

There are three types of DTDs you can use with an XHTML document: the strict DTD, the transitional DTD, and the frameset DTD. The **strict DTD** is used for completely "clean" HTML documents that contain no browser-specific extensions, or deprecated elements, and which use only Cascading Style Sheets to format the Web page. The **transitional DTD** is used for documents that are designed for older browsers that may not support Cascading Style Sheets. It allows for the use of deprecated elements and formatting done directly in the HTML tags, such as using the bgcolor or text attributes within the <body> tag. The **frameset DTD** is used for files containing frames. By using one of these three DTD types, along with an XML parser, a Web designer can ensure that the file fulfills the requirements of XHTML for both syntax and content.

Working with the Syntax of XHTML

XHTML code is very similar to HTML code, although there are some important differences worth noting. Some of these differences are because XHTML demands strict adherence to its syntax. Because of this, you should be aware that code that has been accepted by your Web browser may not be accepted in XHTML.

XHTML Syntax

Figure E-1 lists some syntax rules enforced by XHTML.

Figure E-1	XHTML SYNTAX RULES	
RULE	**INCORRECT**	**CORRECT**
Elements must be properly nested	<p>This text is bold</p>	<p>This text is bold</p>
Tag names must be lowercase	<P>This is a paragraph.</P>	<p>This is a paragraph.</p>
Two-sided elements must be closed	<p>First paragraph <p>Second paragraph	<p>First paragraph</p> <p>Second paragraph</p>
Empty elements must be closed	This is a line break. 	This is a line break.
Attribute names must be in lowercase	<td ALIGN="right">	<td align="right">
Attribute values must be within quotation marks	<table width=620>	<table width="620">
Attributes must include attribute values	<option selected>	<option selected="selected">

Note that XHTML uses a different form for empty tags. Empty elements must end with </>. Thus, the following empty tags:

```
<hr>
<br>
<img src="logo.gif">
```

are written in XHTML as:

```
<hr />
<br />
<img src="logo.gif" />
```

XHTML also allows Web designers to write these elements as two-sided tags containing no content, i.e.:

```
<hr></hr>
<br></br>
<img src="logo.gif"></img>
```

In reality, many browsers do not support this second form.

Another area where XHTML departs from HTML is in **attribute minimization**, in which attribute values are not required. XHTML does not allow attribute minimization. Figure E-2 lists the minimized attributes in HTML and how they should be written in XHTML.

| Figure E-2 | MINIMIZED ATTRIBUTES IN HTML AND XHTML |

HTML	XHTML
compact	compact="compact"
checked	checked="checked"
declare	declare="declare"
readonly	readonly="readonly"
disabled	disabled="disabled"
selected	selected="selected"
defer	defer="defer"
ismap	ismap="ismap"
nohref	nohref="nohref"
noshade	noshade="noshade"
nowrap	nowrap="nowrap"
multiple	multiple="multiple"
noresize	noresize="noresize"

For example the following HTML tag:

```
<input type="radio" checked>
```

must be written in XHTML as:

```
<input type="radio" checked="checked">
```

In addition, there are other rules that involve the way elements can be nested within the same or different elements. For example, XHTML prohibits the following nested conditions:

- The <a> tag cannot contain other <a> tags.
- The <pre> tag cannot contain the following tags: <img>, <object>, <big>, <small>, <sub>, and <sup>.
- The <button> tag cannot contain the following tags: <input>, <select>, <textarea>, <label>, <button>, <form>, <fieldset>, <iframe>, and <isindex>.
- The <label> tag cannot contain other <label> tags.
- The <form> tag cannot contain other <form> tags.
- An inline element may not contain a block-level element.

Beyond these rules, there are differences in how HTML and XHTML implement certain attributes.

Using the Name and ID Attributes

HTML uses the name attribute to identify elements within an HTML document. XHTML does not support the name attribute and, instead, uses the id attribute. Thus, the following HTML tags:

```
<a name="top">
<form name="order">
<img name="logo">
<map name="parkmap">
<frame name="document">
```

are written in XHTML as:

```
<a id="top">
<form id="order">
<img id="logo">
<map id="parkmap">
<frame id="document">
```

This can create problems with older browsers that do not support replacing the name attribute with the id attribute. If you are designing Web pages to be read by older browsers, you can include both the name and id attribute, as follows:

```
<a name="top" id="top">
```

Currently, the name attribute is deprecated in XHTML 1.0, and future versions of XHTML plan to remove support for this attribute entirely.

Working with Embedded Style Sheets and Scripts

Embedded style sheets and scripts contain code that a Web browser can process, but which are not part of the XHTML specifications. If an XML parser encounters these code elements, it rejects the document for not being well-formed. XML, and therefore XHTML, allows you to create **CDATA** sections containing text that the XML parser does not process, but can be read by a Web browser. The syntax for creating an embedded style sheet or script is:

```
<style>
   <![CDATA[
      embedded style declarations
   ]]>
</style>


<script>
   <![CDATA[
      JavaScript commands and functions
   ]]>
</script>
```

Currently, many browsers do not support the method of embedded style or script commands. If you want to use XHTML, you must place your style and script commands in an external file.

The Structure of an XHTML Document

An XHTML document consists of three parts: the DOCTYPE, the Head, and the Body. The DOCTYPE section indicates which of the three XHTML DTD types (Strict, Transitional, or Frameset) is being applied to the document, the Head section includes information on the document, and the Body section includes the main content of the document. A valid XHTML document must conform to the following general structure:

```
<!DOCTYPE DTD_declaration>
<html>
<head>
<title> ... </title>
</head>
<body>
   ...
</body>
</html>
```

where *DTD_declaration* is the document type. If this structure is not conformed to, the file is rejected by the XML parser. To specify the Strict DTD, enter the following DOCTYPE declaration:

```
<!DOCTYPE html PUBLIC "-//W3C//DTD XHTML 1.0 Strict//EN"
"http://www.w3.org/TR/xhtml1/DTD/xhtml1-strict.dtd">
```

The DOCTYPE declaration for the Transition DTD is:

```
<!DOCTYPE html PUBLIC "-
//W3C//DTD XHTML 1.0 Transitional//EN"
"http://www.w3.org/TR/xhtml1/DTD/xhtml1-transitional.dtd">
```

The Frameset DTD declaration is:

```
<!DOCTYPE html PUBLIC "-//W3C//DTD XHTML 1.0 Frameset//EN"
"http://www.w3.org/TR/xhtml1/DTD/xhtml1-frameset.dtd">
```

Case distinctions are important in XHTML, so you should duplicate these DOCTYPE declarations, including the distinction between upper- and lowercase letters.

Note that you only need to include a <!DOCTYPE> declaration if you want your XHTML to be valid. The document can still be well-formed (fulfilling the basic syntax of XHTML) without it. However, in most cases, Web designers want their documents to be both well-formed and valid. Figure E-3 indicates the tags supported by the three DTDs: Strict (S), Transitional (T), and Frameset (F).

Figure E-3   **TAGS ASSOCIATED WITH XHTML DTDS**

TAG	DTD	TAG	DTD	TAG	DTD	TAG	DTD
<!-->	S,T,F	<colgroup>	S,T,F	<ins>	S,T,F	<script>	S,T,F
<!DOCTYPE>	S,T,F	<dd>	S,T,F	<isindex>	T,F	<select>	S,T,F
<a>	S,T,F	<del>	S,T,F	<kbd>	S,T,F	<small>	S,T,F
<abbr>	S,T,F	<dfn>	S,T,F	<label>	S,T,F	<span>	S,T,F
<acronym>	S,T,F	<dir>	T,F	<legend>	S,T,F	<strike>	T,F
<address>	S,T,F	<div>	S,T,F	<li>	S,T,F	<strong>	S,T,F
<applet>	T,F	<dl>	S,T,F	<link>	S,T,F	<style>	S,T,F
<area />	S,T,F	<dt>	S,T,F	<map>	S,T,F	<sub>	S,T,F
<b>	S,T,F	<em>	S,T,F	<menu>	T,F	<sup>	S,T,F
<base />	S,T,F	<fieldset>	S,T,F	<meta>	S,T,F	<table>	S,T,F
<basefont />	T,F	<font>	T,F	<noframes>	T,F	<tbody>	S,T,F
<bdo>	S,T,F	<form>	S,T,F	<noscript>	S,T,F	<td>	S,T,F
<big>	S,T,F	<frame>	F	<object>	S,T,F	<textarea>	S,T,F
<blockquote>	S,T,F	<frameset>	F	<ol>	S,T,F	<tfoot>	S,T,F
<body>	S,T,F	<h1> to <h6>	S,T,F	<optgroup>	S,T,F	<th>	S,T,F
 	S,T,F	<head>	S,T,F	<option>	S,T,F	<thead>	S,T,F
<button>	S,T,F	<hr />	S,T,F	<p>	S,T,F	<title>	S,T,F
<caption>	S,T,F	<html>	S,T,F	<param>	S,T,F	<tr>	S,T,F
<center>	T,F	<i>	S,T,F	<pre>	S,T,F	<tt>	S,T,F
<cite>	S,T,F	<iframe>	T,F	<q>	S,T,F	<u>	T,F
<code>	S,T,F	<img />	S,T,F	<s>	T,F	<ul>	S,T,F
<col>	S,T,F	<input>	S,T,F	<samp>	S,T,F	<var>	S,T,F

As XHTML evolves, support for **modularization,** where XHTML elements are broken down into smaller modules, will increase. Modularization allows alternative platforms, such as handheld devices, to load only those XHTML elements they need and makes it easier for developers to create more efficient and flexible platforms for viewing XHTML documents.

Converting From HTML To XHTML

At first glance, it may seem that converting to XHTML is hardly worth the effort of adhering to a strict syntax and set of supported elements. The benefits are mostly for developers because it results in a more mature standard and provides more precise control over the development of Web documents.

Fortunately, there are many tools available to make the transition from HTML to XHTML. Users can access **HTML Tidy**, a freeware utility that "cleans up" HTML files, removing coding errors, and makes them conform to XHTML standards. You can learn more about HTML Tidy at *http://tidy.sourceforge.net/*.

The W3C also supports tools to test whether your files conform to XHTML or HTML 4.01 standards. You can access their validation service at *http://validator.w3.org/*. You can use the validation service by either specifying the URL of your Web page or by uploading your HTML file to the site.

Special Characters
& (ampersand), HTML 1.31–32,
HTML B.01
' (apostrophe), HTML B.01
* (asterisk), HTML 5.08,
HTML B.01
@ (at sign), HTML B.01
\ (backslash), HTML B.01
^ (caret), HTML B.02
: (colon), HTML 2.27, HTML B.01
, (comma), HTML B.01, B.02
© (copyright symbol),
HTML 1.31–32, HTML B.03
{} (curly braces), HTML B.02
$ (dollar sign), HTML B.01
• (dot symbol), HTML 1.44,
HTML 2.03
" (double quotes), HTML B.01,
HTML B.02
... (ellipsis), HTML 1.41,
HTML B.02
= (equal sign), HTML B.01
! (exclamation point), HTML B.01
/ (forward slash), HTML 1.11,
HTML 2.23, HTML 2.24,
HTML 2.27, HTML B.01
> (greater-than symbol),
HTML 1.32, HTML B.01
- (hyphen), HTML B.01
< (less-than symbol), HTML 1.32,
HTML B.01
() (parentheses), HTML B.01
% (percent sign), HTML B.01
. (period), HTML 2.25,
HTML B.01
(pound sign), HTML 1.31–32,
HTML 2.08, HTML 2.20,
HTML B.01, HTML 3.09
? (question mark), HTML B.01
® (registered trademark) symbol,
HTML 1.32, HTML B.03
; (semicolon), HTML 1.31–32,
HTML B.01
[] (square brackets), HTML B.01
™ (trademark symbol),
HTML 1.32, HTML B.02
~ (tilde), HTML B.02
_ (underscore), HTML 5.24,
HTML B.02
| (vertical bar), HTML 2.24,
HTML B.03

A

<a> tag, HTML 2.04–10,
HTML 2.15–19, HTML 2.24–25,
HTML 5.20–22, HTML 5.25,
HTML D.02
<abbr> tag, HTML D.03

absbottom attribute, HTML 3.28
absmiddle attribute, HTML 3.28
Absolute Backgrounds Textures
Archive Web site, HTML 3.17
absolute pathnames,
HTML 2.23–24, HTML 2.27
aclogo1.gif, HTML 3.22–23
aclogo2.gif, HTML 3.32
aclogo.gif, HTML 3.48
<acronymn> tag, HTML D.03
address box, HTML 1.14
address.htm, HTML 4.41–42
<address> tag, HTML D.03
Adobe Photoshop, HTML 3.32
Adventure Bound River Expeditions
Web site, HTML 2.35
align attribute, HTML 1.11,
HTML 1.16, HTML 1.30,
HTML 3.27–29, HTML 4.23–26,
HTML 5.35
aligning. *See also* align attribute
captions, HTML 4.12
cells, HTML 4.24–26
columns, HTML 4.04–05
graphics, HTML 1.30,
HTML 3.27–29
headings, HTML 1.11, HTML 1.16
horizontal lines, HTML 1.33
paragraphs, HTML 1.30
tables, HTML 4.22–26
text, HTML 1.11, HTML 1.16,
HTML 1.30, HTML 2.03,
HTML 4.22–26, HTML 4.29
alt attribute, HTML 3.32–33
alt.surfing newsgroup, HTML 2.28
AltaVista directory, HTML 2.13
ampersand (&), HTML 1.31–32,
HTML B.01
anchors. *See also* links
case sensitivity of, HTML 2.22
creating, HTML 2.04–07,
HTML 2.10, HTML 2.20
creating links to, HTML 2.07–10,
HTML 2.20–22,
HTML 2.24–25
described, HTML 2.04
displaying documents in a new
window and, HTML 2.25
headings and, HTML 2.04–07,
HTML 2.10
URLs and, HTML 2.24–25
AniMagic, HTML 3.23
animated GIFs, HTML 3.20,
HTML 3.23–24, HTML 3.51–53.
See also GIF (Graphics
Interchange Format)
Animated GIFs Web site,
HTML 3.24

Animation Express Web site,
HTML 3.24
Animation Factory Web site,
HTML 3.24
Animation Library Web site,
HTML 3.24
apartmnt.htm, HTML 3.54
apostrophe ('), HTML B.01
<applet> tag, HTML D.03–04
arac2.htm, HTML 3.48
Arcadium Amusement Park Web
site, HTML 3.03–47
arcadium.htm, HTML 3.13–33,
HTML 3.38–46
arcatxt2.htm, HTML 3.48
arcatxt.htm, HTML 3.09
Arches National Park Web site,
HTML 2.35
<area> tag, HTML 3.41–42,
HTML D.04
artcltxt.htm, HTML 4.44
articles.htm, HTML 4.44–49,
HTML 4.51–52
asterisk (*), HTML B.01
at sign (@), HTML B.01
attribute(s). *See also* attributes
(listed by name)
case-sensitivity of, HTML 2.08
described, HTML 1.11
minimization, HTML E.04–05
six common, HTML D.01–02
XHTML and, HTML E.04–05
augmented linear structure,
HTML 2.12

B

<b> tag, HTML 1.28–29,
HTML 1.44, HTML 4.12,
HTML 4.46, HTML D.05.
See also boldface font
background attribute, HTML 1.42,
HTML 2.35, HTML 3.15–16,
HTML 4.32–33
background graphics. *See also*
background attribute
color of, HTML 3.09,
HTML 4.29–33
designing, HTML 3.16–17
for tables, HTML 4.29–33,
HTML 4.43–44
for Web pages, HTML 3.15–18
backslash (\), HTML B.01
<base> tag, HTML 5.21–22
<basefont> tag, HTML D.05
baseline attribute, HTML 3.28
<bdo> tag, HTML D.05
Berners–Lee, Timothy, HTML 1.05

bgcolor attribute, HTML 3.09, HTML 4.29–33
bgproperties attribute, HTML 3.19
<bgsound> tag, HTML D.05
<big> tag, HTML 1.27–28
blank. *See also* **spaces**
    lines, HTML 1.20–21
    spaces, HTML 1.20
_blank keyword, HTML 2.25
<blink> tag, HTML D.05
<blockquote> tag, HTML D.05
<body> tag, HTML 1.12–13, HTML 3.08–09, HTML 3.15, HTML 3.19, HTML D.06
boldface font, HTML 1.11, HTML 1.26–29, HTML 1.44. *See also* **<b> tag**
    captions and, HTML 4.12
    tables and, HTML 4.46
boldness attribute, HTML 3.19
border(s)
    3D effects for, HTML 4.31–32
    color of, HTML 4.31–32, HTML 5.31
    for frames, HTML 4.18–20, HTML 5.13, HTML 5.31–34
    for graphics, HTML 3.44–46
    removing, HTML 5.33–34
    sizing, HTML 5.31, HTML 5.33
    for tables, HTML 4.14–16, HTML 4.18, HTML 4.31–32
border attribute, HTML 3.44–46, HTML 4.14–16, HTML 5.32, HTML 5.35
bordercolor attribute, HTML 4.31, HTML 5.32
bordercolordark attribute, HTML 4.31–32
bordercolorlight attribute, HTML 4.31–32
bottom attribute, HTML 3.28
bottommargin attribute, HTML 3.19
**
 tag, HTML 3.37–38**
Braille, HTML 1.08
breakfst.htm, HTML 3.50–51
breakfst.jpg, HTML 3.50–51
breaktxt.htm, HTML 3.50–51
browser(s). *See also* **previewing; Internet Explorer browser (Microsoft); Netscape Navigator browser**
    captions and, HTML 4.12
    character tags and, HTML 1.28–29
    color and, HTML 3.05–06, HTML 3.09–10
    compatibility across, HTML 1.08–09
    described, HTML 1.06–07
    display area, size of, HTML 4.20

    extensions, HTML 1.08–09
    fonts and, HTML 3.12–14
    frames and, HTML 5.02–03, HTML 5.28–31
    graphics and, HTML 3.25, HTML 3.37
    headings and, HTML 1.11–12
    horizontal lines and, HTML 1.33
    HTML character entities and, HTML B.01
    images and, HTML 1.30–31
    interpretation of tags by, HTML 1.07
    mailto: URLs and, HTML 2.31
    printing Web pages with, HTML 1.34, HTML 2.34
    refresh action for, HTML 1.16, HTML 1.18
    -safe colors, HTML 3.34–35, HTML A.01–02
    tables and, HTML 4.12, HTML 4.19–20, HTML 4.23, HTML 4.31–33
    testing links with, HTML 2.09
    text–based versus graphical, HTML 1.07
    types of, HTML 1.07
    uploading Web pages with, HTML C.01
    viewing documents with, HTML 1.07
    windows, displaying documents in new, HTML 2.25–27
Browyer Realty Web site, HTML 5.41–42
bulleted lists, HTML 1.40. *See also* **lists**
business.htm, HTML 3.54
button.jpg, HTML 2.10
<button> tag, HTML D.06

C

cable connections, HTML 1.04
Canyonlands National Park Web site, HTML 2.35
Capitol Reef National Park Web site, HTML 2.35
<caption> tag, HTML 4.12–13, HTML D.07
captions
    aligning, HTML 4.12
    for tables, HTML 4.12–13
caret (^), HTML B.02
case sensitivity, HTML 1.11–12, HTML 2.08, HTML 2.22, HTML C.01, HTML E.06
CDATA sections, HTML E.05–06
cell(s)
    adding text to, HTML 4.09–10

    aligning, HTML 4.24–26
    backgrounds, HTML 4.29–30, HTML 4.32–33
    formatting, HTML 4.07–08
    inserting graphics in, HTML 4.39
    inserting links in, HTML 4.39–41
    inserting text in, HTML 4.41–42, HTML 4.45–46
    padding, HTML 4.17–18
    row-spanning, HTML 4.26–29
    sizing, HTML 4.22
    spacing, HTML 4.16–17
cellspacing attribute, HTML 4.16–17
center attribute, HTML 1.16, HTML 2.03
<center> tag, HTML D.07
CERN (European Center for Particle Physics), HTML 1.05
Chamberlain Civic Center Web site, HTML 4.58–59
character tags. *See also* **characters, special; symbols**
    applying, HTML 1.28–29
    creating, HTML 1.26–29
    logical, HTML 1.26–27
characters, special. *See also* **character tags; symbols**
    adding, HTML 1.31–32
    codes for, comprehensive list of, HTML B.01–05
    described, HTML 1.31
    for foreign languages, HTML 1.31–32, HTML B.02–05
checked attribute, HTML E.04
chem2.htm, HTML 1.38, HTML 2.33, HTML 2.34
chem2txt.htm, HTML 2.33
chem.htm, HTML 1.12, HTML 1.14–36, HTML 2.03–09, HTML 2.15–21, HTML 2.23–27
chemtxt.htm, HTML 2.03
child.htm, HTML 1.40
ChildLink Web site, HTML 1.39–45
<cite> tag, HTML 1.26–27, HTML D.07
City of Green River Web site, HTML 2.35
CLASS attribute, HTML D.02, HTML E.02
classes.htm, HTML 2.38–39
classid attribute, HTML 5.35
classtxt.htm, HTML 2.38
client-side image maps, HTML 3.37–40. *See also* **image maps**
clouds.jpg, HTML 3.17–18, HTML 3.25

club.htm, HTML 2.38–39
clubtxt.htm, HTML 2.38
Coastal University Web site, HTML 1.41–42
<code> tag, HTML 1.26–27, HTML D.07
<col> tag, HTML 4.33–35, HTML D.07
<colgroup> tag, HTML 4.34–35, HTML D.07–08
College Board Web site, HTML 2.24–27
colon (:), HTML 2.27, HTML B.01
color
    background, HTML 3.09, HTML 4.29–33
    of borders, HTML 4.31–32, HTML 5.31
    browser-safe, HTML 3.34–35, HTML A.01–02
    design tips for, HTML 3.33–35
    of fonts, HTML 3.12, HTML 3.14–15
    hexadecimal values for, HTML 4.29, HTML A.01–02
    of horizontal lines, HTML 1.33
    managing, HTML 3.34–35
    names, HTML 3.05–07, HTML D.01, HTML A.01–02
    palettes, HTML 3.34–35
    RGB (red-green-blue), HTML 3.06–07
    schemes, HTML 3.08–10, HTML 4.29–33
    for tables, HTML 4.29–33
    transparent, HTML 3.22–23
    values, HTML 3.06–07
    working with, HTML 3.04–08
color attribute, HTML 1.33
cols attribute, HTML 5.07–08
colspan attribute, HTML 4.26–29
column(s)
    aligning, HTML 4.04–05
    background color for, HTML 4.29–33
    formatting, HTML 4.33–35
    frame layout with, HTML 5.07–08, HTML 5.11–13
    groups, HTML 4.33–35
    sizing, HTML 4.22, HTML 4.36, HTML 5.07–08
    spanning, HTML 4.26–29
    width, HTML 4.22, HTML 4.36, HTML 5.07–08
comma (,), HTML B.01, B.02
comments
    creating, HTML 4.37–39, HTML 4.44–45, HTML 4.53
    described, HTML 4.37

compact attribute, HTML E.04
compatibility, with browsers, checking for, HTML 1.13. *See also* browsers; previewing
CompuServe, HTML 3.24–25
cont2txt.htm, HTML 2.34
Contact page, HTML 2.10–20, HTML 2.30–31, HTML 2.34
contact2.htm, HTML 2.34
contact.htm, HTML 2.15–20, HTML 2.30–31
conttxt.htm, HTML 2.15
converters, HTML 1.09
copying, Web page contents, HTML 4.45–46, 4.51–52
copyright symbol (©), HTML 1.31–32, HTML B.03
Course Technology Web site, HTML 2.27
curly braces ({}), HTML B.02

D

dc100.htm, HTML 3.53
dc100.jpg, HTML 3.53
dc100txt.htm, HTML 3.53
dc250.htm, HTML 3.53
dc250txt.htm, HTML 3.53
dc500.htm, HTML 3.53
dcc.htm, HTML 5.40
dccmw.htm, HTML 5.40
dccne.htm, HTML 5.40
dccs.htm, HTML 5.40
dcctxt.htm, HTML 5.40
dccw.htm, HTML 5.40
dclist1.gif, HTML 3.52–53
dclist2.gif, HTML 3.53
dclist3.gif, HTML 3.53
dclist4.gif, HTML 3.53
<dd> tag, HTML 1.24, HTML D.08
declare attribute, HTML E.04
defer attribute, HTML E.04
definition lists
    creating, HTML 1.24–25
    described, HTML 1.24
<del> tag, HTML D.08
destinations. *See also* links
    creating anchors that serve as, HTML 2.04–07
    creating links to, HTML 2.07–10
    described, HTML 2.02
<df> tag, HTML D.08
<dfn> tag, HTML D.08
dHome Web site, HTML 4.57–58
dhome.htm, HTML 4.58
dhometxt.htm, HTML 4.58
Diamond Health Club Web site, HTML 2.37–38
dinner.htm, HTML 3.51
dinner.jpg, HTML 3.51

dir attribute, HTML D.02
directory path. *See also* directory pathnames
    described, HTML 1.30, HTML 2.23
    URLs and, HTML 2.27
directory pathnames. *See also* directory path
    absolute, HTML 2.23–24, HTML 2.27
    relative, HTML 2.25, HTML 2.27
disabled attribute, HTML E.04
dithering, HTML 3.34
<div> tag, HTML D.08
<dl> tag, HTML 1.24, HTML D.08
dlogo.jpg, HTML 4.62
Doc-Centric Copiers Web site, HTML 5.39–40
DOCTYPE section, HTML E.06–07
<!doctype> tag, HTML D.02, HTML E.07
document type definitions. *See* DTDs (document type definitions)
dollar sign ($), HTML B.01
dot symbol (•), HTML 1.44, HTML 2.03
double quotes ("), HTML B.01, HTML B.02
downloading graphics, HTML 3.33–34
drive letters, in path names, HTML 2.24
DTDs (document type definitions)
    basic description of, HTML E.02–03
    Frameset, HTML E.06–07
    Strict, HTML E.06–07
    tags associated with, HTML E.07
    Transitional, HTML E.06–07
    types of, HTML E.06–07
dube.jpg, HTML 1.30, HTML 2.33
Dunston Retreat Center Web site, HTML 4.60–61
dunston.htm, HTML 4.62
dunsttxt.htm, HTML 4.62

E

ellipsis (...), HTML 1.41, HTML B.02
<em> tag, HTML 1.26, HTML 1.28, HTML D.08
e-mail
    addresses, HTML 2.29–31
    links, HTML 2.29–31, HTML 2.38–39
<embed> tag, HTML D.08–09

Emery County Web site,
    HTML 2.35
equal sign (=), HTML B.01
euler.htm, HTML 1.42
euler.jpg, HTML 1.42
eulertxt.htm, HTML 1.42
exclamation point (!), HTML B.01
<!> tag, HTML D.02
extended character set,
    HTML B.01–05. *See also*
    characters, special; symbols
Extensible HyperText Markup
    Language. *See* XHTML
    (Extensible HyperText Markup
    Language)
Extensible Markup Language.
    See XML (Extensible Markup
    Language)
extensions, described,
    HTML 1.08–09
external images, HTML 1.29–30.
    See also images

F

family.htm, HTML 3.54
features.htm, HTML 4.49
febtxt.htm, HTML 4.60
fiber-optic cable, HTML 1.04
<fieldset> tag, HTML D.09
File Transfer Protocol (FTP).
    See FTP (File Transfer Protocol)
file(s)
    extensions, HTML, 1.12–13,
        HTML C.01
    location path information for,
        HTML 1.30, HTML 2.23–24
    renaming, HTML 2.15
fixed-width (monospace) fonts,
    HTML 4.04–05, HTML 4.06
flakes.jpg. HTML 1.43–44
floating (internal) frames,
    HTML 5.34–36. *See also* frames
Fly Fishing the Green River Web
    site, HTML 2.35
folders. *See also* directory path
    links to documents in other,
        HTML 2.22–24
    links to documents within the
        same, HTML, 2.15–22
font(s). *See also* text
    basic description of,
        HTML 3.10–15
    boldface, HTML 1.11,
        HTML 1.26–29, HTML 1.44,
        HTML 4.12, HTML 4.46
    captions and, HTML 4.12
    character tags and, HTML 1.26–29
    color, HTML 3.12,
        HTML 3.14–15

face, changing, HTML 3.12–14
fixed-width, HTML 4.04–05,
    HTML 4.06
headings and, HTML 1.11,
    HTML 1.15–16
italic, HTML 1.26–29,
    HTML 4.12
proportional, HTML 4.04
size, HTML 3.11–12,
    HTML 3.19, HTML 4.04–05,
    HTML 4.46–47
style sheets and, HTML 1.08
tables and, HTML 4.04–05,
    HTML 4.46–47
types of, HTML 4.04
<font> tag, HTML 3.10–15,
    HTML 3.19,
    HTML 4.46–47, HTML D.09
footers, in tables, HTML 4.11–12
foreign languages, special
    characters for, HTML 1.31–32,
    HTML B.02–05
<form> tag, HTML D.10
formulas, formatting,
    HTML 1.36–38, HTML 1.42
forward slash (/), HTML 1.11,
    HTML 2.23, HTML 2.24,
    HTML 2.27, HTML B.01
frame(s)
    assigning names to,
        HTML 5.19–20
    controlling the appearance of,
        HTML 5.13–17
    creating, HTML 4.18–20, HTML 5.34–36
    floating (internal), HTML 5.34–36
    introduction to, HTML 5.02–17
    layout, creating, HTML 5.06–07
    orientation of, HTML 5.07–08
    planning, HTML 5.05–06
    retrieving pages in specific,
        HTML 5.19
    scroll bars for, HTML 5.13–16
    size of, HTML 5.07–08,
        HTML 5.17
    source, specifying, HTML 5.09–11
    tips for using, HTML 5.31
frame attribute, HTML 4.18–20
<frame> tag, HTML 5.09–11,
    HTML 5.19, HTML 5.31–34,
    HTML D.10, HTML E.02
frameborder attribute,
    HTML 5.34, HTML 5.35
<frameset> tag, HTML 5.06,
    HTML 5.07–08,
    HTML 5.10–12, D.11,
    HTML E.02
Free Backgrounds Web site,
    HTML 3.17
frosttxt.htm. HTML 1.44
FTP (File Transfer Protocol)

servers, links to, HTML 2.27–29
uploading Web pages with,
    HTML C.01

G

GIF (Graphics Interchange
    Format) files, HTML 1.30,
    HTML 3.20–25
    animated, HTML 3.20,
        HTML 3.23–24,
        HTML 3.51–53
    compression of, HTML 3.24–25
    dithering and, HTML 3.34
    GIF87 format, HTML 3.20–22
    GIF89a format, HTML 3.20,
        HTML 3.22–23
    interlacing, HTML 3.20–22
    noninterlacing, HTML 3.20–22
    spacer, HTML 3.23,
        HTML 3.52–53
    transparent, HTML 3.20,
        HTML 3.22–23
GIF Construction Set, HTML 3.23
GIFMation, HTML 3.23
graphical tables. *See also* tables
    described, HTML 4.02–03
    structure of, defining,
        HTML 4.07–4.13
    <td> tag and, HTML 4.07–10
    <tr> tag and, HTML 4.07–10
graphic(s). *See also* background
    graphics; *specific formats*
    aligning, HTML 1.30,
        HTML 3.27–29
    alternate text for, HTML 3.32–33
    borders for, HTML 3.44–46
    creating links to, HTML 2.05
    designating, as links, HTML 2.08
    design tips for, HTML 3.33–35
    downloading, HTML 3.33–34
    external, HTML 1.29–30
    frames and, HTML 5.10–11
    inline, HTML 1.29–30,
        HTML 1.40–44, HTML 2.05,
        HTML 2.08
    inserting, HTML 1.29–31,
        HTML 1.40–44
    location path information for,
        HTML 1.30
    logos, HTML 3.22–24,
        HTML 3.51–53, HTML
        4.35–36, HTML 4.39,
        HTML 5.10–11
    one-sided tags and, HTML 1.11
    placement of, HTML 3.27–32
    reusing, HTML 3.34–35
    size of, HTML 3.27–34
    space around/between,
        HTML 3.23, HTML 3.29–30,
        HTML 3.52–53

tiling, HTML 3.16
transparent, HTML 3.20,
    HTML 3.22–23
**grback.jpg, HTML 2.34,
    HTML 2.35**
**greater-than symbol (>),
    HTML 1.32, HTML B.01**
**Green River State Park Web site,
    HTML 2.35**
grepon.htm, HTML 5.38
**grrock.jpg, HTML 2.34,
    HTML 2.35**

H

**<h1...h6> tag, HTML 1.11,
    HTML 1.15–16, HTML 1.27–28,
    HTML 1.40, HTML 2.04–07,
    HTML 2.10.** *See also* **headings**
**Hamlet Web site, HTML 2.12,
    HTML 2.14**
**<head> tag, HTML 1.12–13,
    HTML D.11**
**head2.htm, HTML 5.38,
    HTML 5.39**
**head.htm, HTML 5.40,
    HTML 5.41**
headings
    adding anchors to,
        HTML 2.04–07, HTML 2.10
    aligning, HTML 1.11, HTML 1.16
    changing, HTML 2.02
    creating, HTML 1.14–17,
        HTML 1.40, HTML 4.10–4.11
    creating links to, HTML 2.07–10
    described, HTML 1.10–11
    fonts for, HTML 1.11,
        HTML 1.15–16
    identifying, HTML 4.11–12
    removing, HTML 2.02
    for tables, HTML 4.10–4.12
headtxt.htm, HTML 5.41
**height attribute, HTML 3.31–32,
    HTML 4.20–21, HTML 5.35**
**hexadecimal values, for color,
    HTML 3.07, HTML A.01–02**
**hierarchical structure, of Web
    pages, HTML 2.12–13**
highway.htm, HTML 4.47–48
**home pages, creating your own,
    HTML 2.39–40.** *See also* **Web
    pages; Web sites**
**home.htm, HTML 5.11,
    HTML 5.39**
horizontal lines
    aligning, HTML 1.33
    described, HTML 1.10–11
    inserting, HTML 1.32–36
hotspots, HTML 3.36–39
house.jpg, HTML 3.54

**<hr> tag, HTML 1.32–36,
    HTML D.11–12.** *See also*
    horizontal lines
**href attribute, HTML 2.07–08,
    HTML 2.15, HTML 2.25**
**hspace attribute, HTML 3.29–30,
    HTML 5.35**
**HTML (HyperText Markup
    Language).**
    See also **HTML documents**
    basic description of, HTML 1.07–09
    converting to/from, HTML 1.09,
        HTML E.08
    editors, definition of, HTML 1.09
    future of, HTML 1.08–09
    versions of, HTML 1.08
    XHTML and, HTML 1.08–09,
        HTML E.01–08
    XML and, HTML 1.08–09
**HTML Compendium Web site,
    HTML D.01–29**
HTML documents. *See also* **HTML
    (HyperText Markup Language)**
    basic tags for, HTML 1.12–13
    content, use of the term,
        HTML 1.11
    creating, overview of,
        HTML 1.10–14,
        HTML 2.02–04
    creating links between,
        HTML 2.15–22
    displaying, in new windows,
        HTML 2.25–27
    linking to sections of,
        HTML 2.20–22
    in other folders, links to,
        HTML 2.22–24
HTML Tidy utility, HTML E.08
**HTTP (HyperText Transfer
    Protocol), HTML 2.27**
hyperlink(s)
    creating, HTML 2.03,
        HTML 2.07–10, HTML
        2.10–22
    described, HTML 1.05,
        HTML 2.02
    to documents on your computer,
        HTML 2.16
    to documents within other folders,
        HTML 2.22–24
    e-mail, HTML 2.29–31,
        HTML 2.38–39
    external, HTML 2.25
    frames and, HTML 5.03–05,
        HTML 5.18–22
    graphical, HTML 3.44–46
    hierarchical structure and,
        HTML 2.12–13
    linear structures and,
        HTML 2.12, 2.13

to locations on the Internet,
        HTML 2.10–22,
        HTML 2.24–27,
        HTML 2.34–36
    mixed structures and, HTML 2.14
    to newsgroups, HTML 2.27–29
    previewing, HTML 2.09,
        HTML 2.17, HTML 2.21
    to specific locations within a page,
        HTML 2.02–10,
        HTML 2.20–22
    tags, HTML 2.08–09
    targets, specifying,
        HTML 5.20–21
    testing, HTML 2.09, HTML 2.20
    text, HTML 2.03–04
    Web page structure and,
        HTML 2.11–15
hypertext, described, HTML 1.05.
    See also **hyperlinks**
hyphen (-), HTML B.01

I

**<i> tag, HTML 1.27–29,
    HTML 4.12, HTML D.12**
**id attribute, HTML D.02,
    HTML E.05**
<iframe> tag, HTML D.12
iftxt.htm, HTML 5.35–36
<ilayer> tag, HTML D.12–13
image(s). *See also* **background
    graphics;** *specific formats*
    aligning, HTML 1.30,
        HTML 3.27–29
    alternate text for, HTML 3.32–33
    borders for, HTML 3.44–46
    creating links to, HTML 2.05
    designating, as links, HTML 2.08
    design tips for, HTML 3.33–35
    downloading, HTML 3.33–34
    external, HTML 1.29–30
    frames and, HTML 5.10–11
    inline, HTML 1.29–30,
        HTML 1.40–44, HTML 2.05,
        HTML 2.08
    inserting, HTML 1.29–31,
        HTML 1.40–44
    location path information for,
        HTML 1.30
    logos, HTML 3.22–24,
        HTML 3.51–53,
        HTML 4.35–36, HTML 4.39,
        HTML 5.10–11
    maps, HTML 3.35–44
    one-sided tags and, HTML 1.11
    placement of, HTML 3.27–32
    reusing, HTML 3.34–35
    size of, HTML 3.27–34

space around/between,
HTML 3.23, HTML 3.29–30,
HTML 3.52–53
tiling, HTML 3.16
transparent, HTML 3.20,
HTML 3.22–23
ImageMagik, HTML 3.23
<img> tag, HTML 1.30,
HTML 1.31, HTML 3.27–33,
HTML D.13–14
index.htm, HTML 2.23,
HTML 2.24, HTML 2.27
index.html, HTML 2.27
inline images. *See also* **images**
described, HTML 1.29–30
inserting, HTML 1.30,
HTML 1.40–44
used as anchors, HTML 2.05
used as links, HTML 2.08
<input> tag, HTML D.15
<ins> tag, HTML D.15–16
interlacing
GIFs, HTML 3.20–22
JPEGs, HTML 3.26
Internet
described, HTML 1.04
downloading graphics from,
HTML 3.33–34
history of, HTML 1.04
links to locations on, HTML 2.22,
HTML 2.24–27,
HTML 2.34–36
objects, linking to other,
HTML 2.27–31
Service Providers (ISPs),
HTML 2.31, HTML C.01
Internet Explorer browser. *See also*
browsers
captions and, HTML 4.12
described, HTML 1.07
frames and, HTML 5.30
headings and, HTML 1.11–12
mailto: URLs and, HTML 2.31
previewing Web pages with,
HTML 1.13–14
tables and, HTML 4.12,
HTML 4.19–20,
HTML 4.31–32
uploading Web pages with,
HTML C.01
intro.gif, HTML 3.52
intro.htm, HTML 3.52,
HTML 3.53, HTML 4.57–58
introtxt.htm, HTML 3.52,
HTML 4.57–58
<isindex> tag, HTML D.16
ismap attribute, HTML E.04
ISO Latin-1 Character set,
HTML B.01–B.05. *See also*
special characters

ISPs (Internet Service Providers),
HTML 2.31, HTML C.01
italic font, HTML 1.26–29,
HTML 4.12

J

JPEG (Joint Photographic Experts
Group) format, HTML 1.30–31,
HTML 1.42–44. *See also* **images**
basic description of,
HTML 3.25–27
compression of, HTML 3.25–26
dithering and, HTML 3.34
progressive/interlacing,
HTML 3.26

K

karts.htm, HTML 3.48
<kbd> tag, HTML 1.26–27
Kelsey's Diner Web site,
HTML 3.50–51
king.htm, HTML 3.49–50
kingtext.htm, HTML 3.49
kirk.jpg, HTML 1.45

L

<label> tag, HTML D.16
lang attribute, HTML D.02
languages, foreign, special
characters for, HTML 1.31–32,
HTML B.02–05
LANs (local area networks),
HTML 1.04
<layer> tag, HTML D.16–17
left attribute, HTML 3.28
left.jpg, HTML 2.37
leftmargin attribute, HTML 3.19
<legend> tag, HTML D.17
Lempel-Ziv-Welch (LZW)
compression, HTML 3.24–25
less-than symbol (<), HTML 1.32,
HTML B.01
<li> tag, HTML 1.22–25,
HTML 1.38, HTML D.17
line(s)
blank, HTML 1.20–21
horizontal, HTML 1.10–11,
HTML 1.32–36
line.gif, HTML 3.50
linear structure, of Web pages,
HTML 2.12, HTML, 2.13
link(s)
creating, HTML 2.03,
HTML 2.07–10,
HTML 2.10–22
described, HTML 1.05,
HTML 2.02

to documents on your computer,
HTML 2.16
to documents within other folders,
HTML 2.22–24
e-mail, HTML 2.29–31,
HTML 2.38–39
external, HTML 2.25
frames and, HTML 5.03–05,
HTML 5.18–22
graphical, HTML 3.44–46
hierarchical structure and,
HTML 2.12–13
linear structures and,
HTML 2.12, 2.13
to locations on the Internet,
HTML 2.10–22,
HTML 2.24–27,
HTML 2.34–36
mixed structures and, HTML 2.14
to newsgroups, HTML 2.27–29
previewing, HTML 2.09,
HTML 2.17, HTML 2.21
to specific locations within a page,
HTML 2.02–10,
HTML 2.20–22
tags, HTML 2.08–09
targets, specifying,
HTML 5.20–21
testing, HTML 2.09, HTML 2.20
text, HTML 2.03–04
Web page structure and,
HTML 2.11–15
link2txt.htm, HTML 2.34
Links page, HTML 2.10–21,
HTML 2.23, HTML 2.34
links2.htm, HTML 2.34
links.htm, HTML 2.15–20,
HTML 2.23, HTML 4.39–40,
HTML 5.05, HTML 5.20–22,
HTML 5.24, HTML 5.27
links.jpg, HTML 4.58
linktxt.htm, HTML 2.15
listing.htm, HTML 5.42–43
listings.gif, HTML 3.54
lists
bulleted, HTML 1.40
definition, HTML 1.24–25
creating, HTML 1.10–11,
HTML 1.14, HTML 1.22–26
nesting, HTML 1.23–24
ordered, 1.22–24, HTML 1.40
unordered, HTML 1.23–26,
HTML 2.36
listtxt.htm, HTML 5.42
logos, HTML 3.22–24,
HTML 3.51–53.
See also **graphics**
frames and, HTML 5.10–11
tables and, HTML 4.35–36,
HTML 4.39

lunch.htm, HTML 3.51
lunch.jpg, HTML 3.51
lunchtxt.htm, HTML 3.51
Lynx browser, HTML 1.07,
   HTML 4.03. *See also* browsers

M

m01.htm, HTML 5.43–44
m57.htm, HTML 5.44
mailto: links, HTML 2.29–31,
   HTML 2.38–39
mansions.htm, HTML 3.54
map.htm, HTML 5.40,
   HTML 5.41
<map> tag, HTML 3.39–41,
   HTML 3.43, HTML D.17
maptxt.htm, HTML 5.41
marginheight attribute,
   HTML 5.14–15, HTML 5.35
margins, for frames, HTML 5.13,
   HTML 5.15–16
markup languages, described,
   HTML 1.07. *See also* markup
   tags (listed by name); *specific
   languages*
<marquee> tag, HTML D.17–18
mathematical symbols. *See* special
   characters
members.htm, HTML 2.38–39
membtxt.htm, HTML 2.38
<menu> tag, HTML D.18
messier.htm, HTML 5.44–45
messtxt.htm, HTML 5.44
<meta> tag, HTML D.18,
   HTML E.02
Microsoft FTP server, HTML 2.28
Microsoft Outlook,
   HTML 2.28–30
Microsoft Word, HTML 1.09,
   HTML 1.13
Microsoft WordPad,
   HTML 1.12–13
middle attribute, HTML 3.28
middle dot symbol (•),
   HTML 1.44, HTML 2.03
Midwest University Center for
   Diversity Web site,
   HTML 3.48–50
MIME (Multipurpose Internet
   Mail Extensions), HTML D.01
mixed structures, of Web pages,
   HTML 2.14
mlk.gif, HTML 3.49
modularization, HTML E.07
monitors
   display area, sizing tables for,
     HTML 4.20
   resolution of, HTML 4.20
move1a.htm, HTML 2.36–37

move1.htm, HTML 2.36–37
move2a.htm, HTML 2.36–37
move2.htm, HTML 2.36–37
move3a.htm, HTML 2.36–37
move3.htm, HTML 2.36–37
move4a.htm, HTML 2.36–37
move4.htm, HTML 2.36–37
multiple attribute, HTML E.04
Multipurpose Internet Mail
   Extensions). *See* MIME
   (Multipurpose Internet Mail
   Extensions)
mxxtxt.htm, HTML 5.43
myresume.htm, HTML 1.45
myweb.htm, HTML 2.39–40

N

name attribute, HTML 5.19–20,
   HTML 5.35, HTML E.05
nested
   lists, HTML 1.23–24
   tags, HTML 1.30,
     HTML 5.11–13, HTML E.05
Netscape Navigator browser. *See
   also* browsers
   captions and, HTML 4.12
   described, HTML 1.07
   extensions, HTML 1.08–09
   frames and, HTML 5.30
   headings and, HTML 1.11–12
   mailto: URLs and, HTML 2.31
   previewing Web pages with,
     HTML 1.13–14
   tables and, HTML 4.12,
     HTML 4.19–20,
     HTML 4.31–32
   uploading Web pages with,
     HTML C.01
   warning messages, HTML 1.13–14
network(s). *See also* Internet
   described, HTML 1.04
   local area (LANs), HTML 1.04
   socket connections, HTML 1.13
   wide area (WANs), HTML 1.04
newhome.htm, HTML 3.54
newsgroup(s)
   described, HTML 2.28
   links to, HTML 2.27–29
newsreaders, HTML 2.28–29
<nl> tag, HTML 1.38
<nobr> tag, HTML D.18
<noembed> tag, HTML D.18
noframes.htm, HTML 5.29–30,
   HTML 5.39
<noframes> tag, HTML 5.28–31,
   HTML D.19
nohref attribute, HTML E.04
nonbreaking space, HTML 1.32,
   HTML 2.03, HTML B.02

noninterlacing GIFs,
   HTML 3.20–22
noresize attribute, HTML E.04
<noscript> tag, HTML D.19
noshade attribute, HTML 1.33,
   HTML E.04
Notepad, HTML 1.18,
   HTML 1.09, HTML 1.12–13.
   See also text editors
nowrap attribute, HTML E.04

O

<object> tag, HTML D.19–20
<ol> tag, HTML 1.22–25,
   HTML 1.40, HTML D.20
operating systems, previewing
   Web pages with different,
   HTML 1.08
<optgroup> tag, HTML D.20
<option> tag, HTML D.20
ordered lists
   creating, HTML 1.22–24,
     HTML–1.40
   described, HTML 1.22
   nesting, HTML 1.23–24
Outlook (Microsoft),
   HTML 2.28–30

P

<p> tag, HTML 1.17–22,
   HTML D.21
page layout
   diagramming, 4.53
   fonts and, HTML 4.46–47
   with tables, HTML 4.35–54
page1.htm, HTML 4.38,
   HTML 4.41–42,
   HTML 4.51–52
page1txt.htm, HTML 4.38
paragraphs. *See also* text
   adding space between, HTML 1.12
   aligning, HTML 1.30
   creating, HTML 1.14,
     HTML 1.17–22
   entering text for, HTML 1.17–22
   previewing, HTML 1.18,
     HTML 1.20
<param> tag, HTML D.21
parch3.jpg, HTML 4.43
parentheses, HTML B.01
Park City Gazette Web site,
   HTML 4.01–64
parks.htm, HTML 2.23,
   HTML 2.24
parsers, HTML E.02–03,
   HTML E.05–06, HTML E.07
patents, HTML 3.25

path. *See also* **pathnames**
described, HTML 1.30,
HTML 2.23
URLs and, HTML 2.27
pathnames. *See also* **path**
absolute, HTML 2.23–24,
HTML 2.27
relative, HTML 2.25, HTML 2.27
pback.jpg, HTML 3.52
pclogo.jpg, HTML 4.39
PDAs (personal data assistants),
HTML 1.07, HTML 1.08
percent sign (%), HTML B.01
period (.), HTML 2.25, B.01
photo.jpg, HTML 2.10
Photoshop (Adobe), HTML 3.32
pi.jpg, HTML 1.42
Pixal Digital Products Web site,
HTML 3.51–53
pixal.htm, HTML 3.53
pixaltxt.htm, HTML 3.52
pixels
described, HTML 1.33
sizing horizontal lines in,
HTML 1.33
<plaintext> tag, HTML D.21
plogo.jpg, HTML 3.52,
HTML 3.53
pmap2.jpg, HTML 3.48
PNG (portable network graphics),
HTML 3.25
portability, HTML 1.07,
HTML 1.08, HTML 2.24
pound sign (#), HTML 1.31–32,
HTML 2.08, HTML 2.20,
HTML B.01
<pre> tag, HTML 4.05–07,
HTML D.21
previewing
anchors, HTML 2.06
described, HTML 1.08,
HTML 1.13–14
at different access speeds,
HTML 1.08
heading tags, HTML 1.16–17
links, HTML 2.09, HTML 2.17,
HTML 2.21
paragraph text, HTML 1.18,
HTML 1.20
printing
text files, HTML 1.34–35
Web pages, HTML 1.34–35,
HTML 2.34
protocols
appearance of, in URLs,
HTML 2.27
FTP (File Transfer Protocol),
2.27–29, HTML C.01
HTTP (HyperText Transfer
Protocol), HTML 2.27

Q

<q> tag, HTML D.21
question mark (?), HTML B.01

R

Race Results Web site,
HTML 4.03–20, HTML 4.45–47
race2.htm, HTML 4.03–07,
HTML 4.11–13, HTML 4.15–18,
HTML 4.21–32, HTML 4.45–46
racetxt1.htm, HTML 4.03
racetxt3.htm, HTML 4.07
readonly attribute, HTML E.04
red.jpg, HTML 3.53
Refresh command, HTML 1.16
registered trademark (®) symbol,
HTML 1.32, HTML B.03
relative pathnames, HTML 2.25,
HTML 2.27
Reload command, HTML 1.16
report.htm, HTML 5.40
resumes, HTML 1.45
RGB triplets, HTML 3.06–07
ride.jpg, HTML 3.26–27,
HTML 3.30–31
rides.htm, HTML 3.48
right attribute, HTML 3.28
right.jpg, HTML 2.37
rightmargin attribute, HTML 3.19
Rock Hotel Web site,
HTML 2.34–36
rock.htm, HTML 2.23,
HTML 2.24, HTML 2.25
row(s)
background color for,
HTML 4.29–33
creating, HTML 4.07–08
groups, HTML 4.11–12
frame layout with, HTML 5.07–08,
HTML 5.11–13
height, HTML 5.07–08
spanning, HTML 4.26–29
rows attribute, HTML 5.07–08
rowspan attribute, HTML 4.26–29
<rt> tag, HTML D.21
<ruby> tag, HTML D.21
rule attribute, HTML 4.18–20
runner.jpg. HTML 1.43,
HTML 1.45

S

<s> tag, HTML D.22
Safety Palette, HTML 3.34–35
<samp> tag, HTML D.22
satellite connections, HTML 1.04
scr attribute, HTML 5.35

screens. *See* **monitors; splash**
screens
<script> tag, HTML D.21
scripts, HTML E.05–06
scroll bars
for frames, HTML 5.13–16
removing, HTML 5.14–15
scrolling attribute, HTML 5.14,
HTML 5.35
search pages, HTML C.01
<select> tag, HTML D.22
selected attribute, HTML E.04
semicolon (;), HTML 1.31–32,
HTML B.01
server(s)
described, HTML 1.06–07,
HTML C.01
HTML formatting and,
HTML 1.07
links to, HTML 2.27–29
mailto: URLs and, HTML 2.31
moving Web pages to new,
HTML 2.24
relative pathnames and, HTML 2.24
-side image maps, HTML 3.36–37
uploading Web page to,
HTML C.01
SGML (Standard Generalized
Markup Language)
HTML and, HTML 1.07,
HTML 1.13
XHTML and, HTML E.01
size attribute, HTML 1.33,
HTML 3.19, HTML 4.14
SkyWeb Astronomy Web site,
HTML 5.43–44
slist.htm, HTML 5.38
slisttxt.htm, HTML 5.38
sltxt.htm, HTML 5.39
<small> tag, HTML 1.27–28,
HTML 2.34, HTML D.23
spaces
around/between graphics,
HTML 3.23, HTML 3.29–30,
HTML 3.52–53
between paragraphs, HTML 1.12
blank, HTML 1.20, HTML 3.23,
HTML 3.52–53
nonbreaking, HTML 1.32,
HTML 2.03, HTML B.02
using spacer GIFs to create,
HTML 3.23, HTML 3.52–53
span attribute, HTML 4.34
<span> tag, HTML D.23
special character symbols. *See also*
character tags; symbols
adding, HTML 1.31–32
codes for, comprehensive list of,
HTML B.01–05
described, HTML 1.31

for foreign languages,
HTML 1.31–32,
HTML B.02–05
specifications, HTML 1.08
**speech recognition software,
HTML 1.08**
splash screens, HTML 3.51–53
square brackets ([]), HTML B.01
**src attribute, HTML 1.30,
HTML 1.31**
staff2.htm, HTML 5.38
staff.htm, HTML 5.05
**staflink.htm, HTML 5.38,
HTML 5.39**
**Standard Generalized Markup
Language (SGML).** *See* **SGML
(Standard Generalized Markup
Language)**
standards, HTML 1.08
**Stephen Dubé's Chemistry Web
site, HTML 1.03,
HTML 1.10–38, HTML 2.02–34**
storyboarding, HTML 2.11–13
<strike> tag, HTML D.23
**<strong> tag, HTML 1.26–27,
HTML D.23**
style attribute, HTML D.02
**style sheets, HTML 1.08,
HTML E.05–06**
<style> tag, HTML D.23
**<sub> tag, HTML 1.27–28,
HTML 1.36–38, HTML D.23**
subject catalogs, HTML 2.13
**subscript numbers,
HTML 1.27–28,
HTML 1.36–38**
**<sup> tag, HTML 1.27–28,
HTML D.23**
symbols. *See also* **special characters**
& (ampersand), HTML 1.31–32,
HTML B.01
' (apostrophe), HTML B.01
* (asterisk), HTML 5.08,
HTML B.01
@ (at sign), HTML B.01
\ (backslash), HTML B.01
^ (caret), HTML B.02
: (colon), HTML 2.27,
HTML B.01
, (comma), HTML B.01, B.02
© (copyright symbol),
HTML 1.31–32, HTML B.03
{} (curly braces), HTML B.02
$ (dollar sign), HTML B.01
• (dot symbol), HTML 1.44,
HTML 2.03
" (double quotes), HTML B.01,
HTML B.02
... (ellipsis), HTML 1.41,
HTML B.02

= (equal sign), HTML B.01
! (exclamation point), HTML B.01
/ (forward slash), HTML 1.11,
HTML 2.23, HTML 2.24,
HTML 2.27, HTML B.01
> (greater-than symbol),
HTML 1.32, HTML B.01
- (hyphen), HTML B.01
< (less-than symbol), HTML 1.32,
HTML B.01
() (parentheses), HTML B.01
% (percent sign), HTML B.01
. (period), HTML 2.25, B.01
(pound sign), HTML 1.31–32,
HTML 2.08, HTML 2.20,
HTML B.01, HTML 3.09
? (question mark), HTML B.01
® (registered trademark) symbol,
HTML 1.32, HTML B.03
; (semicolon), HTML 1.31–32,
HTML B.01
[] (square brackets), HTML B.01
™ (trademark symbol),
HTML 1.32, HTML B.02
~ (tilde), HTML B.02
_ (underscore), HTML 5.24,
HTML B.02
| (vertical bar), HTML 2.24,
HTML B.03
**syntax, use of the term,
HTML 1.08**

T

**tab character, HTML 1.20,
HTML B.01**
table(s). *See also* **cells;
columns; rows**
aligning, HTML 4.22–26
backgrounds, HTML 4.32–33
basic description of,
HTML 4.02–03
borders for, HTML 4.14–16,
HTML 4.18–20,
HTML 4.31–32
captions, HTML 4.12–13
color schemes for, HTML 4.29–33
combining, HTML 4.51–54
creating, HTML 4.02–4.14
customizing, HTML 4.14–20
fonts and, HTML 4.46–47
footers, HTML 4.11–12
gridlines, HTML 4.19
headings, HTML 4.10–4.12
inserting graphics in, HTML 4.39
inserting links in, HTML 4.39–41
inserting text in, HTML 4.41–42,
HTML 4.45–46
modifying the appearance of,
HTML 4.14–20

outer, HTML 4.37–42,
HTML 4.51–54
page layout with, HTML 4.35–54
sizing, HTML 4.20–22,
HTML 4.36, HTML 4.46
structure of, defining,
HTML 4.07–13
**<table> tag, HTML 4.07–08,
HTML 4.14–16, HTML 4.20–21,
HTML D.23–24**
tags
associated with XHTML DTDs,
HTML E.07
browser compatibility information
for, HTML D.01–29
comprehensive list of,
HTML D.01–29
creating basic, HTML 1.12–13
deprecated, HTML 3.19
described, HTML 1.07,
HTML 1.11
empty, HTML E.03–04
nesting, HTML 1.30,
HTML 5.11–13, HTML E.05
one-sided, HTML 1.11
opening/closing, HTML 1.11
two-sided, HTML 1.11
tan.jpg, HTML 3.50
target(s)
names, reserved, HTML 5.22–28
specifying, HTML 5.20–21
**target attribute, HTML 2.25,
HTML 5.20–21**
**<tbody> tag, HTML 4.11–12,
HTML D.24–25**
**<td> tag, HTML 4.07–10,
HTML 4.22, HTML 4.26–29,
HTML 4.30, HTML D.25**
teletype machines, HTML 1.08
text. *See also* **fonts; paragraphs**
aligning, HTML 1.11,
HTML 1.16, HTML 1.30,
HTML 2.03, HTML 4.22–26,
HTML 4.29
style sheets for, HTML 1.08
word wrap feature for, HTML 1.18
text editors
creating anchors with, HTML 2.06
creating tags with, HTML 1.12–13
definition of, HTML 1.09
Notepad, HTML 1.18,
HTML 1.09, HTML 1.12–13
printing HTML with, HTML 1.35
text tables
aligning columns in,
HTML 4.04–05
creating, HTML 4.03–07
defined, HTML 4.02

fonts for, HTML 4.04–05, HTML 4.06
<pre> tag and, HTML 4.05–07
<textarea> tag, HTML D.25–26
textop attribute, HTML 3.28
Texture Station Web site, HTML 3.17
<tfoot> tag, HTML 4.11–12, HTML D.26
<th> tag, HTML 4.10–4.11, HTML 4.22, HTML 4.26–29, D.26–27
<thead> tag, HTML 4.11–12, HTML D.27–28
thumbnails, HTML 3.34
tilde (~), HTML B.02
tiling graphics, HTML 3.16
title attribute, HTML D.02
<title> tag, HTML 1.12–13, HTML 1.14, HTML 2.35, D.28
tlist.htm, HTML 5.38
tlisttxt.htm, HTML 5.38
tltxt.htm, HTML 5.39
toddler.htm, HTML 3.48
toddtxt.htm, HTML 3.48
top attribute, HTML 3.28
topmargin attribute, HTML 3.19
tourlink.htm, HTML 5.38, HTML 5.39
tours2.htm, HTML 5.38
tours.htm, HTML 5.22–28
tourstxt.htm, HTML 5.38
<tr> tag, HTML 4.07–10, HTML 4.30, HTML D.28
trademark symbol (™), HTML 1.32, HTML B.02
transparent GIFs, HTML 3.20, HTML 3.22–23
TravelWeb E-ZineMagazine Web site, HTML 4.62–63
Tri-State Realty Web site, HTML 3.53–54
tristate.gif, HTML 3.54
tristate.htm, HTML 3.54
tsback.gif, HTML 3.54
<tt> tag, HTML 1.27–28, HTML D.28
tw.html, HTML 4.63
Two4U's Color Page, HTML 3.08
type attribute, HTML 1.22, HTML 1.23

U

<u> tag, HTML 1.27–28
<ul> tag, HTML 1.23–25, HTML 1.40, HTML D.28
underscore (_), HTML B.02
Unisys Corporation, HTML 3.25
UNIX, HTML 1.07, HTML 4.03

unordered lists
described, HTML 1.23
creating, HTML 1.23–26, HTML 2.36
nesting, HTML 1.23–24
URLs (Uniform Resource Locators). *See also* **links**
described, HTML 2.24–25
for FTP servers, HTML 2.27–29
links to, HTML 2.24–31, HTML 2.34–36
mailto:, HTML 2.29–31, HTML 2.38–39
protocols in, HTML 2.27
Usenet newsgroups, HTML 2.27–29
<uu> tag, HTML D.28

V

validation, HTML E.08
valign attribute, HTML 4.24–26
<var> tag, HTML 1.26–27, HTML D.28
vertical bar (|), HTML 2.24, HTML B.03
video clips, HTML 1.11
vspace attribute, HTML 3.29–30, HTML 5.35

W

W3C (World Wide Web Consortium)
described, HTML 1.08, HTML D.01–29
extensions and, HTML 1.08–09
tag extensions supported by, HTML 3.19
XHTML and, HTML E.02–03, HTML E.08
XML and, HTML E.02
wall.jpg, HTML 3.48
WANs (wide area networks), HTML 1.04. *See also* networks
Warner Peripherals Web site, HTML 5.45–46
warner.htm, HTML 5.45
water.htm, HTML 3.48
Way Out West Tours Web site, HTML 2.35
<wbr> tag, HTML D.29
Web Animation Library Web site, HTML 3.24
Web page(s)
anchors on, HTML 2.04–10, HTML 2.20–22, HTML 2.24–25
backgrounds, HTML 1.42, HTML 2.35

blank lines on, HTML 1.20–21
creating your own, HTML 2.39–40
described, HTML 1.05–06
e-mail links on, HTML 2.29–31, HTML 2.38–39
horizontal lines on, HTML 1.10–11, HTML 1.32–36
links to other, HTML 2.10–22
links to specific locations within, HTML 2.02–10, HTML 2.20–22
lists on, HTML 1.10–11, HTML 1.14, HTML 1.22–26
naming, HTML C.01
networks and, HTML 1.04, HTML 1.13
printing, HTML 1.34, HTML 2.34
registering, HTML C.01
storage of, in folders, HTML 2.15–24
storyboarding, HTML 2.11–13
structure of, HTML 2.11–15
Web servers
described, HTML 1.06–07, HTML C.01
HTML formatting and, HTML 1.07
links to, HTML 2.27–29
mailto: URLs and, HTML 2.31
moving Web pages to new, HTML 2.24
relative pathnames and, HTML 2.24
-side image maps, HTML 3.36–37
uploading Web page to, HTML C.01
Web sites (listed by name). *See also* **Web pages**
Absolute Backgrounds Textures Archive Web site, HTML 3.17
Adventure Bound River Expeditions Web site, HTML 2.35
Animated GIFs Web site, HTML 3.24
Animation Express Web site, HTML 3.24
Animation Factory Web site, HTML 3.24
Animation Library Web site, HTML 3.24
Arcadium Amusement Park Web site, HTML 3.03–47
Arches National Park Web site, HTML 2.35
Browyer Realty Web site, HTML 5.41–42

Canyonlands National Park Web site, HTML 2.35

Capitol Reef National Park Web site, HTML 2.35

Chamberlain Civic Center Web site, HTML 4.58–59

ChildLink Web site, HTML 1.39–45

City of Green River Web site, HTML 2.35

Coastal University Web site, HTML 1.41–42

College Board Web site, HTML 2.24–27

Course Technology Web site, HTML 2.27

dHome Web site, HTML 4.57–58

Diamond Health Club Web site, HTML 2.37–38

Doc-Centric Copiers Web site, HTML 5.39–40

Dunston Retreat Center Web site, HTML 4.60–61

Emery County Web site, HTML 2.35

Fly Fishing the Green River Web site, HTML 2.35

Free Backgrounds Web site, HTML 3.17

Green River State Park Web site, HTML 2.35

Hamlet Web site, HTML 2.12, HTML 2.14

HTML Compendium Web site, HTML D.01–29

Kelsey's Diner Web site, HTML 3.50–51

Midwest University Center for Diversity Web site, HTML 3.48–50

Park City Gazette Web site, HTML 4.01–64

Pixal Digital Products Web site, HTML 3.51–53

Race Results Web site, HTML 4.03–20, HTML 4.45–47

Rock Hotel Web site, HTML 2.34–36

SkyWeb Astronomy Web site, HTML 5.43–44

Stephen Dubé's Chemistry Web site, HTML 1.03, HTML 1.10–38, HTML 2.02–34

Texture Station Web site, HTML 3.17

TravelWeb E-ZineMagazine Web site, HTML 4.62–63

Tri-State Realty Web site, HTML 3.53–54

Warner Peripherals Web site, HTML 5.45–46

Way Out West Tours Web site, HTML 2.35

Web Animation Library Web site, HTML 3.24

WebGround Web site, HTML 3.17

Western College for the Arts Web site, HTML 2.36–37

Yale Climbing School (YCS) Web site, HTML 5.01–5.39

WebGround Web site, HTML 3.17

Web-safe colors, HTML 3.34–35, HTML A.01–02

welcome.htm, HTML 4.61

welctext.htm, HTML 4.61

Western College for the Arts Web site, HTML 2.36–37

wide area networks (WANs). *See* **WANs (wide area networks)**

width attribute, HTML 1.33, HTML 3.31–32, HTML 4.20–21, HTML 4.22, HTML 5.35

Word (Microsoft), HTML 1.09, HTML 1.13

WordPad (Microsoft), HTML 1.12–13

World Wide Web. *See also* **Internet; Web pages; Web sites (listed by name)**
development of, HTML 1.04–06

diversity of resources offered by, HTML 2.27

introduction to, HTML 1.04–09

structure of, HTML 1.04–09

uploading Web pages to, HTML C.01

World Wide Web Consortium (W3C). *See* **W3C (World Wide Web Consortium)**

wtoc.htm, HTML 5.45

X

Xara, HTML 3.23

XBM files, HTML 3.25

XHTML (Extensible HyperText Markup Language), HTML 1.09, HTML E.01–08
converting from HTML to, HTML E.08

documents, structure of, HTML E.06–07

syntax, HTML E.03–04

XML (Extensible Markup Language)
basic description of, HTML 1.08–09, HTML E.02–03

documents, valid, HTML E.02–03, HTML E.07

documents, well-formed, HTML E.02–03

parsers, HTML E.02–03, HTML E.05–06, HTML E.07

XHTML and, HTML E.02–03

<xmp> tag, HTML D.29

XPM files, HTML 3.25

Y

Yale Climbing School (YCS) Web site, HTML 5.01–39

yale2.htm, HTML 5.38, HTML 5.39

yale2txt.htm, HTML 5.39

yale.htm, HTML 5.09, HTML 5.15–21, HTML 5.29–30, HTML 5.32–33

yaletxt.htm, HTML 5.09

Z

ZSPC Super Color Chart, HTML 3.08

File Finder

Tutorial	Location in Tutorial	Name and Location of Data Files	Student Saves File As...	Student Creates New File
Tutorial 1	Session 1.1			
Tutorial 1	Session 1.2			chem.htm
Tutorial 1	Session 1.3	tutorial.01/tutorial/**chem.htm** (saved from last session) tutorial.01/tutorial/dube.jpg	chem.htm	
Tutorial 1	Review Assignment	tutorial.01/tutorial/chem.htm (saved from the Tutorial) tutorial.01/Review/**dube.jpg**	chem2.htm (saved in the Review folder)	
Tutorial 1	Case Problem 1	tutorial.01/case1/newborn.jpg		child.htm
Tutorial 1	Case Problem 2	tutorial.01/case2/eulertxt.htm tutorial.01/case2/euler.jpg tutorial.01/case2/pi.jpg	euler.htm	
Tutorial 1	Case Problem 3	tutorial.01/case3/frosttxt.htm tutorial.01/case3/flakes.jpg tutorial.01/case3/runner.jpg	frostrun.htm	
Tutorial 1	Case Problem 4	tutorial.01/case4/kirk.jpg		myresume.htm
Tutorial 2	Session 2.1	tutorial.02/tutorial/chemtxt.htm tutorial.02/tutorial/dube.jpg	chem.htm	
Tutorial 2	Session 2.2	tutorial.02/tutorial/conttxt.htm tutorial.02/tutorial/linktxt.htm	contact.htm links.htm	
Tutorial 2	Session 2.3	tutorial.01/tutorial/chem.htm (saved from last session) tutorial.02/tutorial/contact.htm (saved from last session) tutorial.02/tutorial/links.htm (saved from last session)	chem.htm contact.htm links.htm	
Tutorial 2	Review Assignment	tutorial.02/Review/chem2txt.htm tutorial.02/Review/cont2txt.htm tutorial.02/Review/link2txt.htm tutorial.02/Review/dube.jpg	chem2.htm contact2.htm links2.htm	
Tutorial 2	Case Problem 1	tutorial.02/case1/grback.jpg tutorial.02/case1/grrock.jpg		rock.htm
Tutorial 2	Case Problem 2	tutorial.02/case2/move1a.htm tutorial.02/case2/move2a.htm tutorial.02/case2/move3a.htm tutorial.02/case2/move4a.htm tutorial.02/case2/left.jpg tutorial.02/case2/right.jpg tutorial.02/case2/lvb1.jpg tutorial.02/case2/lvb2.jpg tutorial.02/case2/lvb3.jpg tutorial.02/case2/lvb4.jpg	move1.htm move2.htm move3.htm move4.htm	
Tutorial 2	Case Problem 3	tutorial.02/case3/clubtxt.htm tutorial.02/case3/classtxt.htm tutorial.02/case3/membtxt.htm tutorial.02/case3/aerobic.gif tutorial.02/case3/pushup.gif tutorial.02/case3/diamonds.jpg	club.htm classes.htm members.htm	
Tutorial 2	Case Problem 4			myweb.htm
Tutorial 3	Session 3.1	tutorial.03/tutorial/arcatxt.htm tutorial.03/tutorial/clouds.jpg	arcadium.htm	
Tutorial 3	Session 3.2	tutorial.03/tutorial/aradium.htm (saved from last session) tutorial.03/tutorial/aclogo2.gif tutorial.03/tutorial/ride.jpg	arcadium.htm	

Tutorial	Location in Tutorial	Name and Location of Data Files	Student Saves File As...	Student Creates New File
		File Finder		
Tutorial 3	Session 3.3	tutorial.03/tutorial/aradium.htm (saved from last session) tutorial.03/tutorial/parkmap.gif tutorial.03/tutorial/water.htm tutorial.03/tutorial/karts.htm tutorial.03/tutorial/rides.htm	arcadium.htm	
Tutorial 3	Review Assignment	tutorial.03/review/arcatxt2.htm tutorial.03/review/toddtxt.htm tutorial.03/review/water.htm tutorial.03/review/karts.htm tutorial.03/review/rides.htm tutorial.03/review/pmap2.gif tutorial.03/review/wall.jpg tutorial.03/review/toddler.jpg	arca2.htm toddler.htm	
Tutorial 3	Case Problem 1	tutorial.03/case1/kingtxt.htm tutorial.03/case1/mlk.gif tutorial.03/case1/i.gif tutorial.03/case1/line.gif	king.htm	
Tutorial 3	Case Problem 2	tutorial.03/case2/breaktxt.htm tutorial.03/case2/lunchtxt.htm tutorial.03/case2/dinnrtxt.htm tutorial.03/case2/breakfst.jpg tutorial.03/case2/lunch.jpg tutorial.03/case2/dinner.jpg tutorial.03/case2/tan.jpg	breakfast.htm lunch.htm dinner.htm	
Tutorial 3	Case Problem 3	tutorial.03/case3/introtxt.htm tutorial.03/case3/pixaltxt.htm tutorial.03/case3/dc100txt.htm tutorial.03/case3/dc250txt.htm tutorial.03/case3/dc500txt.htm tutorial.03/case3/spacer.gif tutorial.03/case3/intro.gif tutorial.03/case3/pback.jpg tutorial.03/case3/dclist1.gif tutorial.03/case3/dclist2.gif tutorial.03/case3/dclist3.gif tutorial.03/case3/dclist4.gif tutorial.03/case3/dc100.jpg tutorial.03/case3/dc250.jpg tutorial.03/case3/dc500.jpg tutorial.03/case3/pclogo.jpg	intro.htm pixal.htm dc100.htm dc250.htm dc500.htm	
Tutorial 3	Case Problem 4	tutorial.03/case4/apartmnt.htm tutorial.03/case4/business.htm tutorial.03/case4/family.htm tutorial.03/case4/mansions.htm tutorial.03/case4/newhome.htm tutorial.03/case4/house.jpg tutorial.03/case4/listings.gif tutorial.03/case4/tristate.gif tutorial.03/case4/tsback.gif		tristate.htm
Tutorial 4	Session 4.1	tutorial.04/tutorial/racetxt1.htm tutorial.04/tutorial/racetxt2.htm tutorial.04/tutorial/blake.jpg tutorial.04/tutorial/parch.jpg	race1.htm race2.htm	
Tutorial 4	Session 4.2	tutorial.04/tutorial/race1.htm (saved from last session) tutorial.04/tutorial/blake.jpg tutorial.04/tutorial/parch.jpg	race1.htm	

File Finder

Tutorial	Location in Tutorial	Name and Location of Data Files	Student Saves File As...	Student Creates New File
Tutorial 4	Session 4.3	tutorial.04/tutorial/page1txt.htm tutorial.04/tutorial/artcltxt.htm tutorial.04/tutorial/race2.htm (saved from last session) tutorial.04/tutorial/address.htm tutorial.04/tutorial/features.htm tutorial.04/tutorial/highway.htm tutorial.04/tutorial/links.htm tutorial.04/tutorial/brline.gif tutorial.04/tutorial/blake.jpg tutorial.04/tutorial/parch.jpg tutorial.04/tutorial/parch2.jpg tutorial.04/tutorial/parch3.jpg tutorial.04/tutorial/pclogo.jpg	page1.htm articles.htm	
Tutorial 4	Review Assignment	tutorial.04/review/sighttxt.htm tutorial.04/review/arttxt.htm tutorial.04/review/page2txt.htm tutorial.04/review/tips.htm tutorial.04/review/brline.gif tutorial.04/review/cougar.jpg tutorial.04/review/parch.jpg tutorial.04/review/parch2.jpg tutorial.04/review/parch3.jpg tutorial.04/review/pclogo.jpg	sighting.htm article2.htm page2.htm	
Tutorial 4	Case Problem 1	tutorial.04/case1/introtxt.htm tutorial.04/case1/dhometxt.htm tutorial.04/case1/address.htm tutorial.04/case1/footer.htm tutorial.04/case1/textbox.htm tutorial.04/case1/uses.htm tutorial.04/case1/back.jpg tutorial.04/case1/back2.jpg tutorial.04/case1/back3.jpg tutorial.04/case1/back4.jpg tutorial.04/case1/back5.jpg tutorial.04/case1/dhome.jpg tutorial.04/case1/links.jpg	intro.htm dhome.htm	
Tutorial 4	Case Problem 2	tutorial.04/case2/febtxt.htm tutorial.04/case2/ccc.gif tutorial.04/case2/back.jpg	feb.htm	
Tutorial 4	Case Problem 3	tutorial.04/case3/dunsttxt.htm tutorial.04/case3/welctxt.htm tutorial.04/case3/address.htm tutorial.04/case3/events.htm tutorial.04/case3/letter.htm tutorial.04/case3/next.htm tutorial.04/case3/adams.jpg tutorial.04/case3/back.jpg tutorial.04/case3/dlogo.jpg tutorial.04/case3/dunston.jpg	dunston.htm welcome.htm	
Tutorial 4	Case Problem 4	tutorial.04/case4/twlinks.htm tutorial.04/case4/twlinks2.htm tutorial.04/case4/luxair.txt tutorial.04/case4/photo.txt tutorial.04/case4/toronto.txt tutorial.04/case4/yosemite.txt tutorial.04/case4/ppoint.jpg tutorial.04/case4/ppoint2.jpg tutorial.04/case4/twlogo.jpg tutorial.04/case4/yosemite.jpg		tw.htm